Early praise for *Agile Web Development with Rails 5.1*

The best book to get started in the Rails world. A comprehensive, coherent, and concise overview of the Ruby on Rails framework. It treats learning in a gradual way, creating an application from scratch using the latest technologies.

➤ **Luis Miguel Cabezas Granado**
Ruby on Rails and PHP developer at Junta de Extremadura (Spain) and PHP book writer at Anaya Multimedia,

I liked how the book guided me through each step of the tasks. This book gives a thorough introduction to Rails, and I'd suggest it to anyone who wants to start development with Rails.

➤ **Gábor László Hajba**
Software Developer, EBCONT Enterprise Technologies

The book was really pleasant to read; I liked how it creates a foundational understanding of Rails with a realistic scenario and then builds upon it for the more advanced topics.

➤ **Alessandro Bahgat**
Software Engineer, Google

Agile Web Development with Rails 5.1

Sam Ruby
David Bryant Copeland
with Dave Thomas

The Pragmatic Bookshelf

Raleigh, North Carolina

Many of the designations used by manufacturers and sellers to distinguish their products are claimed as trademarks. Where those designations appear in this book, and The Pragmatic Programmers, LLC was aware of a trademark claim, the designations have been printed in initial capital letters or in all capitals. The Pragmatic Starter Kit, The Pragmatic Programmer, Pragmatic Programming, Pragmatic Bookshelf, PragProg and the linking *g* device are trademarks of The Pragmatic Programmers, LLC.

Every precaution was taken in the preparation of this book. However, the publisher assumes no responsibility for errors or omissions, or for damages that may result from the use of information (including program listings) contained herein.

Our Pragmatic books, screencasts, and audio books can help you and your team create better software and have more fun. Visit us at *https://pragprog.com.*

The team that produced this book includes:

Publisher: Andy Hunt
VP of Operations: Janet Furlow
Development Editor: Susannah Davidson Pfalzer
Indexing: Potomac Indexing, LLC
Copy Editor: Molly McBeath
Layout: Gilson Graphics

For sales, volume licensing, and support, please contact *support@pragprog.com.*

For international rights, please contact *rights@pragprog.com.*

Printed in the United States of America.
ISBN-13: 978-1-68050-251-0
Printed on acid-free paper.
Book version: P1.0—November 2017

Contents

Part II — Building an Application

Part III — Rails in Depth

Foreword to the Rails 5 Edition

You've made a great decision to learn Ruby on Rails. The language, framework, and community have never been in better shape, and the community has never been easier to join than it is today. The early days of the frontier are gone, and while some of the cowboy excitement went with it, what we have instead is a sophisticated, modern, and functional state.

The spoils of such progress will hopefully become apparent as you work your way through this book. Ruby on Rails takes care of an inordinate amount of what most developers need most of the time. In the world of web development, that's an awful lot! An overwhelming lot at times.

But don't be intimidated. You don't need to understand every fine point and every minutia before you can begin to make progress. Ruby on Rails has been designed to flatten the learning curve as much as possible while at the same time encouraging you to level up over time.

Becoming an expert in full-stack web development won't happen overnight. Even Ruby on Rails can't replace the inherent depth of knowledge required to understand every facet, from HTTP to databases to JavaScript to object-oriented best practices to testing methodologies. One day you'll be able to converse fluently about all that, but don't worry or expect that to be "twenty-one days from now" (or whatever snake-oil sales speak some publishers might try to push on you).

The journey from here to there is half the fun. You've arrived in a community that cares an extraordinary amount about the craft of writing great software for the web. This might seem a little strange at first: is it really possible to care that much whether an if-statement is at the beginning of a conditional or if it's an unless-statement at the end? Yes, yes it is. Helping more programmers develop an eye for such details is a big part of our mission here.

Because Ruby on Rails isn't just about getting stuff done quickly. That's part of it, but it's the lesser one. The greater appeal is in making software for the web fun, rewarding, and inspiring. To make learning all the nooks and crannies of our crazy craft an adventure.

Every new version of Rails expands the scope of what we try to tackle together. This is unapologetically not a minimalist framework. And Rails 5 is no different. With this major new version we've opened the door to a major new domain: the real-time web. You're in for a real treat here as well.

But let's not get ahead of ourselves. You have much to learn, and I can't wait to see what you do with it. I've been programming in Ruby and working on Rails for the past thirteen years. It never ceases to inspire and motivate me to see new developers discover our wonderful language and framework for the first time. In some ways, I'm even jealous.

Welcome to Ruby on Rails!

David Heinemeier Hansson

Preface to the Rails 5.1 Edition

Rails 1.0 was released in December 2005. In the years since, it has gone from a relatively unknown leading-edge tool to a successful and stable foundation with a large set of associated libraries that others benchmark themselves against.

The book you're about to read was there from the start, and it has evolved with Rails. It began as a full reference to a small framework when online documentation was scarce and inconsistent. It's now an introduction to the entire Rails ecosystem—one that leaves you with many pointers to more information that you can explore based on your needs and desires.

This book didn't just evolve along with Rails: Rails evolved with it. The content in this book has been developed in consultation with the Rails core team. Not only is the code you'll see in this book tested against each release of Rails, but the converse is also true: Rails itself is tested against the code in this book and won't be released until those tests pass.

So read this book with confidence that the scenarios not only work but also describe how the Rails developers themselves feel about how best to use Rails. We hope you get as much pleasure out of reading this book as we had in developing it.

This book covers Rails 5.1.1. While some of the commands you'll be using are new, the underlying development model remains the same. Even when new major features are added, such as direct support for Webpack, the changes are evolutionary, not revolutionary.

Rails 5.1 introduced two major new features and a lot of small improvements. Before Rails 5.1, using modern JavaScript and front-end tools like Webpack, PostCSS, or React was difficult. These tools were designed very differently from the way Rails manages front-end assets. Rails 5.1 brings *Webpacker*, a preset configuration for *Webpack*, which allows simple integration between Rails and the entire JavaScript ecosystem. This was no small feat, yet for you as a developer it's nothing more than a few new command-line invocations away.

Rails 5.1 also provides direct support for something every Rails developer has been doing for years: executing system tests in a real live web browser. When you use a lot of JavaScript, it's hard to test your app without running it in a browser, and Rails now provides a definitive way to do that, fully integrated with the rest of Rails' awesome testing support.

We've also added some coverage of Active Job, Rails' built-in background job queueing library, as well as an update on how you can change or extend Rails. Here you'll learn how to use RSpec as an alternative to Rails' testing library and Slim as an alternative to ERB for writing HTML templates. You'll also learn how to use cssnext for translating CSS that's not supported by browsers to CSS that is. Rails is accurately described as "opinionated software," but it's much more malleable to differing opinions than it might seem. As Rails' creator David Heinemeier Hansson says, Rails should "push up a big tent."[1]

---

1.   http://rubyonrails.org/doctrine/#big-tent

Acknowledgments

Rails is constantly evolving and, as it has, so has this book. Parts of the Depot application were rewritten several times, and all of the text and code was updated. The avoidance of features as they become deprecated has repeatedly changed the structure of the book, as what was once hot became just lukewarm.

So, this book would not exist without a massive amount of assistance from the Ruby and Rails communities. We had many helpful reviewers of drafts of this edition:

Alessandro Bahgat	Nigel Lowry	Nick Watts
Jacob Chae	Peter Perlepes	Luis Miguel Cabezas Granado
Gábor László Hajba	Craig Russell	

Of course, none of this would exist without the developers contributing to Ruby on Rails every day. In particular, the Rails core team has been incredibly helpful, answering questions, checking out code fragments, and fixing bugs—even to the point where part of the release process includes verifying that new releases of Rails don't break the examples provided in this book.

Sam Ruby and David Bryant Copeland

Introduction

Ruby on Rails is a framework that makes it easier to develop, deploy, and maintain web applications. During the 12+ years since its initial release, Rails went from being an unknown toy to a worldwide phenomenon. More importantly, it has become the framework of choice for the implementation of a wide range of applications.

Why is that?

Rails Simply Feels Right

A large number of developers were frustrated with the technologies they were using to create web applications. It didn't seem to matter whether they used Java, PHP, or .NET—there was a growing sense that their jobs were just too damn hard. And then, suddenly, along came Rails, and Rails was easier.

But easy on its own doesn't cut it. We're talking about professional developers writing real-world websites. They wanted to feel that the applications they were developing would stand the test of time—that they were designed and implemented using modern, professional techniques. So, these developers dug into Rails and discovered it wasn't just a tool for hacking out sites.

For example, *all* Rails applications are implemented using the Model-View-Controller (MVC) architecture. MVC is not a new concept for web development —the earliest Java-based web frameworks (like Struts) base their design on it. But Rails takes MVC further: when you develop in Rails, you start with a working application, each piece of code has its place, and all the pieces of your application interact in a standard way.

Professional programmers write tests. And again, Rails delivers. All Rails applications have testing support baked right in. As you add functionality to the code, Rails automatically creates test stubs for that functionality. The framework makes it easy to test applications, and, as a result, Rails applications tend to get tested.

Rails applications are written in Ruby, a modern, object-oriented language. Ruby is concise without being unintelligibly terse. You can express ideas naturally and cleanly in Ruby code. This leads to programs that are easy to write and (just as important) easy to read months later.

Rails takes Ruby to the limit, extending it in novel ways that make our programming lives easier. Using Rails makes our programs shorter and more readable. It also allows us to perform tasks that would normally be done in external configuration files inside the codebase instead. This makes it far easier to see what's happening. The following code defines the model class for a project. Don't worry about the details for now. Instead, think about how much information is being expressed in a few lines of code:

```
class Project < ApplicationRecord
  belongs_to :portfolio

  has_one     :project_manager
  has_many    :milestones
  has_many    :deliverables, through: milestones

  validates   :name, :description, presence: true
  validates   :non_disclosure_agreement, acceptance: true
  validates   :short_name, uniqueness: true
end
```

A major philosophical underpinning of Rails that keeps code short and readable is the DRY principle, which stands for *Don't Repeat Yourself* (see *The Pragmatic Programmer [HT99]*). Every piece of knowledge in a system should be expressed in one place. Rails uses the power of Ruby to bring that to life. You'll find little duplication in a Rails application; you say what you need to say in one place—a place often suggested by the conventions of the MVC architecture—and then move on. For programmers used to other web frameworks, where a simple change to the database schema could involve a dozen or more code changes, this was a revelation—and it still is.

From that principle, Rails is founded on the *Rails Doctrine*,[1] which is a set of nine pillars that explain why Rails works the way it does and how you can be most successful in using it. Not every pillar is relevant when just starting out with Rails, but one pillar in particular is most important: convention over configuration.

Convention over configuration means that Rails has sensible defaults for just about every aspect of knitting together your application. Follow the conventions, and you can write a Rails application using less code than a typical

---

1. http://rubyonrails.org/doctrine/

JavaScript application uses in JSON configuration. If you need to override the conventions, Rails makes that easy, too.

Developers coming to Rails find something else, too. Rails doesn't merely play catch-up with the de facto web standards: it helps define them. And Rails makes it easy for developers to integrate features such as Ajax, modern JavaScript frameworks, RESTful interfaces, and WebSockets into their code because support is built in. (And if you're not familiar with any of these terms, never fear—you'll learn what they mean as you proceed through the book).

Rails was extracted from a real-world, commercial application. It turns out that the best way to create a framework is to find the central themes in a specific application and then package them in a generic foundation of code. When you're developing your Rails application, you're starting with half of a really good application already in place.

But there's something else to Rails—something that's hard to describe. Somehow, it feels right. Of course, you'll have to take our word for that until you write some Rails applications for yourself (which should be in the next forty-five minutes or so...). That's what this book is all about.

Rails Is Agile

The title of this book is *Agile Web Development with Rails 5.1*. You may be surprised to discover that we don't have explicit sections on applying agile practices *X*, *Y*, and *Z* to Rails coding. In fact, you won't find mention of many agile practices, such as Scrum or Extreme Programming, at all.

Over the years since Rails was introduced, the term *agile* has gone from being relatively unknown, to being overhyped, to being treated as a formal set of practices, to receiving a well-deserved amount of pushback against formal practices that were never meant to be treated as gospel, to a return back to the original principles.

But it's more than that. The reason is both simple and subtle. Agility is part of the fabric of Rails.

Let's look at the values expressed in the Agile Manifesto (Dave Thomas was one of the seventeen authors of this document) as a set of four preferences:[2]

- Individuals and interactions over processes and tools
- Working software over comprehensive documentation

---

2. http://agilemanifesto.org/

- Customer collaboration over contract negotiation
- Responding to change over following a plan

Rails is all about individuals and interactions. It involves no heavy toolsets, no complex configurations, and no elaborate processes, just small groups of developers, their favorite editors, and chunks of Ruby code. This leads to transparency; what the developers do is reflected immediately in what the customer sees. It's an intrinsically interactive process.

The Rails development process isn't driven by documents. You won't find 500-page specifications at the heart of a Rails project. Instead, you'll find a group of users and developers jointly exploring their need and the possible ways of answering that need. You'll find solutions that change as both the developers and the users become more experienced with the problems they're trying to solve. You'll find a framework that delivers working software early in the development cycle. This software might be rough around the edges, but it lets the users start to get a glimpse of what you'll be delivering.

In this way, Rails encourages customer collaboration. When customers see how quickly a Rails project can respond to change, they start to trust that the team can deliver what's required, not just what's been requested. Confrontations are replaced by "What if?" sessions.

The agile way of working that Rails encourages is tied to the idea of being able to respond to change. The strong, almost obsessive, way that Rails honors the DRY principle means that changes to Rails applications impact a lot less code than the same changes would in other frameworks. And since Rails applications are written in Ruby, where concepts can be expressed accurately and concisely, changes tend to be localized and easy to write. The deep emphasis on both unit and system testing, along with support for test fixtures and stubs during testing, gives developers the safety net they need when making those changes. With a good set of tests in place, changes are less nerve-racking.

Rather than constantly trying to link Rails processes to agile principles, we've decided to let the framework speak for itself. As you read through the tutorial chapters, try to imagine yourself developing web applications this way, working alongside your customers and jointly determining priorities and solutions to problems. Then, as you read the more advanced concepts that follow in Part III, see how the underlying structure of Rails can enable you to meet your customers' needs faster and with less ceremony.

One last point about agility and Rails—although it's probably unprofessional to mention this—think how much fun the coding will be!

Who This Book Is For

This book is for programmers looking to build and deploy web-based applications. This includes application programmers who are new to Rails (and perhaps even new to Ruby) as well as those who are familiar with the basics but want a more in-depth understanding of Rails.

We presume some familiarity with HTML, Cascading Style Sheets (CSS), and JavaScript—in other words, the ability to view source on web pages. You needn't be an expert on these subjects; the most you'll be expected to do is copy and paste material from the book, all of which can be downloaded.

The focus of this book is on the features and choices made by the Rails core team. More specifically, this book is for *users* of the Rails framework—people who tend to be more concerned about what Rails does, as opposed to how it does it or how to change Rails to suit their needs. Examples of topics not covered in this book include the following:

- Introduced in Rails 4, Turbolinks is a way to load pages more quickly by just loading markup.[3] If you want to know more about how Rails makes your pages load faster, follow that link. But should you instead be content with the knowledge that Rails makes pages load fast and not need to know more, that's OK too.

- Rails itself is highly hackable and extensible, but this book doesn't cover the concept of how to create your own Rails engine.[4] If that topic is of interest to you, we highly recommend *Crafting Rails 4 Applications [Val13]* as a follow-on to this book.

- The Rails team has chosen *not* to include plenty of features—such as user authentication—in the Rails framework itself. That doesn't mean that these features aren't important, but it generally does mean that no single solution is the obvious default for Rails users.

How to Read This Book

The first part of this book makes sure you're ready. By the time you're done with it, you'll have been introduced to Ruby (the language), you'll have been exposed to an overview of Rails, you'll have Ruby and Rails installed, and you'll have verified the installation with a simple example.

---

3. https://github.com/turbolinks/turbolinks/blob/master/README.md
4. http://guides.rubyonrails.org/engines.html

The next part takes you through the concepts behind Rails via an extended example: we build a simple online store. It doesn't take you one by one through each component of Rails (such as "here's a chapter on models, here's a chapter on views," and so forth). These components are designed to work together, and each chapter in this section tackles a specific set of related tasks that involve a number of these components working together.

Most folks seem to enjoy building the application along with the book. If you don't want to do all that typing, you can cheat and download the source code (a compressed tar archive or a zip file).[5]

Be careful if you ever choose to copy files directly from the download into your application: if the timestamps on the files are old, the server won't know that it needs to pick up these changes. You can update the timestamps using the touch command on either Mac OS X or Linux, or you can edit the file and save it. Alternatively, you can restart your Rails server.

Part III, *Rails in Depth*, on page 305, surveys the entire Rails ecosystem. This starts with the functions and facilities of Rails that you'll now be familiar with. It then covers a number of key dependencies that the Rails framework makes use of that contribute directly to the overall functionality that the Rails framework delivers. Finally, we survey a number of popular plugins that augment the Rails framework and make Rails an open ecosystem rather than merely a framework.

Along the way, you'll see various conventions we've adopted:

Live code

Most of the code snippets we show come from full-length, running examples that you can download.

To help you find your way, if a code listing can be found in the download, you'll see a bar before the snippet (like the one here):

```
rails51/demo1/app/controllers/say_controller.rb
class SayController < ApplicationController
➤   def hello
➤   end

    def goodbye
    end
end
```

---

5.   http://pragprog.com/titles/rails51/source_code

The bar contains the path to the code within the download. If you're reading the ebook version of this book and your ebook viewer supports hyperlinks, you can click the bar and the code should appear in a browser window. Some browsers may mistakenly try to interpret some of the HTML templates as HTML. If this happens, view the source of the page to see the real source code.

And in some cases involving the modification of an existing file where the lines to be changed may not be immediately obvious, you'll also see some helpful little triangles to the left of the lines that you'll need to change. Two such lines are indicated in the previous code.

David says

Every now and then you'll come across a "David says" sidebar. Here's where David Heinemeier Hansson gives you the real scoop on some particular aspect of Rails—rationales, tricks, recommendations, and more. Because he's the fellow who invented Rails, these are the sections to read if you want to become a Rails pro.

Joe asks

Joe, the mythical developer, sometimes pops up to ask questions about stuff we talk about in the text. We answer these questions as we go along.

This book isn't meant to be a reference manual for Rails. Our experience is that reference manuals aren't the way most people learn. Instead, we show most of the modules and many of their methods, either by example or narratively in the text, in the context of how these components are used and how they fit together.

Nor do we have hundreds of pages of API listings. There's a good reason for this: you get that documentation whenever you install Rails, and it's guaranteed to be more up-to-date than the material in this book. If you install Rails using RubyGems (which we recommend), start the gem documentation server (using the gem server command), and you can access all the Rails APIs by pointing your browser at http://localhost:8808.

In addition, you'll see that Rails helps you by producing responses that clearly identify any error found, as well as traces that tell you not only the point at which the error was found but also how you got there. You'll see an example on page 139. If you need additional information, peek ahead to *Iteration E2: Handling Errors*, on page 138, to see how to insert logging statements.

If you get really stuck, plenty of online resources can help. In addition to the code listings mentioned, you can find more resources on the Pragmatic Bookshelf site page for this book, including links to the book forum and errata.[6] The resources listed on these pages are shared resources. Feel free to post not only questions and problems to the forum but also any suggestions and answers you may have to questions that others have posted.

Let's get started! The first steps are to install Ruby and Rails and to verify the installation with a simple demonstration.

Part I

Getting Started

In this chapter, you'll see:
• Installing Ruby, RubyGems, SQLite 3, and Rails
• Development environments and tools

CHAPTER 1

Installing Rails

In Part I of this book, we'll introduce you to both the Ruby language and the Rails framework. But we can't get anywhere until you've installed both and verified that they're operating correctly.

To get Rails running on your system, you need the following:

• A Ruby interpreter. Rails is written in Ruby, and you'll be writing your applications in Ruby too. Rails 5.1 recommends Ruby version 2.4 but will run on Ruby version 2.3 and 2.2. It won't work on prior versions of Ruby.

• Ruby on Rails. This book was written using Rails version 5.1 (specifically, Rails 5.1.3).

• A JavaScript interpreter. Both Microsoft Windows and Mac OS X have JavaScript interpreters built in, and Rails will use the version already on your system. On other operating systems, you may need to install a JavaScript interpreter separately.

• Some libraries, depending on the operating system.

• A database. We're using both SQLite 3 and MySQL 5.5 in this book.

To be able to run and debug some of the more advanced JavaScript portions of this book, you will need two additional things: Yarn, which is a package manager for JavaScript, and ChromeDriver, which is a tool for automated testing of web applications.

For a development machine, that's about all you'll need (apart from an editor, and we'll talk about editors separately). However, if you're going to deploy your application, you'll also need to install a production web server (as a minimum) along with some support code to let Rails run efficiently. We devote a whole chapter to this, starting in Chapter 17, *Task L: Deployment and Production*, on page 279, so we won't talk about it more here.

These aren't the only choices available to you. You can place your development environment in a virtual machine or have it hosted in the cloud. The cloud is an excellent choice if you're impatient and have a high-speed Internet connection, as you'll be up and running in minutes. A virtual machine takes more disk space but is excellent for learning purposes, as nothing you'll do will affect the other uses you have for your desktop or laptop machine and vice versa.

So how do you get all this installed? It depends on your choice of development environment.

Installing on Cloud9

Cloud9 provides you with a free development environment with everything you need preinstalled.[1] To sign up, all you need is an email address or a GitHub account (see the following screenshot).

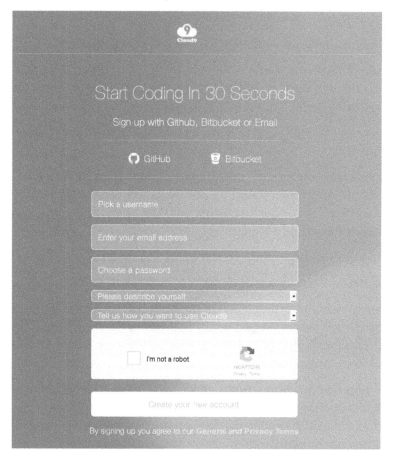

Next, you need to create a workspace. Be sure to click the Ruby template, as shown in the following screenshot.

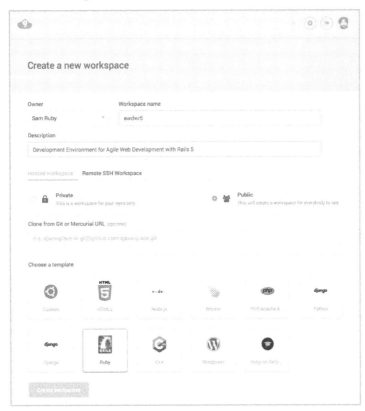

Cloud9 helpfully creates an initial Rails project for you. On the left is a list of files and folders. If you click a file, you see its contents in the pane at the top right. At the bottom is a window where you can enter commands.

Once you familiarize yourself with the IDE, start over by removing these files, because we'll be taking you through the steps to create a project. Do this by entering the command rm -rf *, as shown in the screenshot on page 6. Don't be afraid as you are entering this command in the web browser window. This will only delete files in the cloud; nothing on your machine will be touched.

Next, you need to install the version of Rails that we'll use to develop our application:

```
$ sudo gem install rails --version=5.1.3 --no-ri --no-rdoc
```

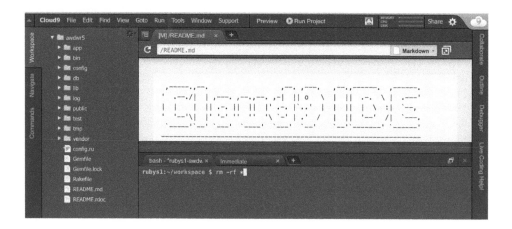

Finally, install Yarn and ChromeDriver, and ensure that ChromeDriver is in your path:

```
$ sudo apt install yarn chromium-chromedriver
$ sudo ln -s /usr/lib/chromium-browser/chromedriver /usr/local/bin
```

More information on how to run Rails on Cloud9 can be found on the community.c9.io website.[2] Follow that link to check for any recent updates. At the time of this writing, you need to be aware of only two things.

First, the command to start the Rails server needs two additional parameters. So if at any point in the book you're told to run bin/rails server, run bin/rails server -b $IP -p $PORT instead.

Second, should you want to use MySQL (as we do in *Using MySQL for the Database*, on page 285), you'll need to specify the username, password and host to be used to connect to the database server.

For many people, these two small accommodations are well worth the benefits of writing software in the cloud.

At this point, you're ready to go. Skip to *Choosing a Rails Version*, on page 16, to ensure that the version of Rails you have installed matches the version described in this edition. See you there.

---

2.   https://community.c9.io/t/running-a-rails-app/1615

Installing on a Virtual Machine

The Rails team helpfully provides a virtual machine definition for Ruby on Rails development.[3] If you have both Git and Vagrant installed, you can be up and running with the three commands listed on that page (and repeated below).

```
$ git clone https://github.com/rails/rails-dev-box.git
$ cd rails-dev-box
$ vagrant up
```

If you don't have Git installed, you can download rails-dev-box as a zip file by clicking the link at the top right of the page.

Fedora users may need to install libvirt.[4]

The important thing to note is that the rails-dev-box directory will be shared with the virtual machine, where it'll be mounted as /vagrant. Run the following commands to see this in action:

```
$ vagrant ssh
vagrant@rails-dev-box:~$ ls /vagrant
bootstrap.sh  MIT-LICENSE  README.md  Vagrantfile
```

Edit files using your favorite text editor and see them change on the virtual machine. Once you're comfortable with this, you have one last step before you're ready to go—installing Rails itself:

```
$ sudo gem install rails --version=5.1.3 --no-ri --no-rdoc
```

Finally, install Yarn and ChromeDriver, and ensure that ChromeDriver is in your path:

```
$ sudo apt install yarn chromedriver
$ sudo ln -s /usr/lib/chromium-browser/chromedriver /usr/local/bin
```

You're ready to go! Skip to *Choosing a Rails Version*, on page 16, to ensure that the version of Rails you have installed matches the version described in this edition. See you there.

---

3. https://github.com/rails/rails-dev-box#requirements
4. https://developer.fedoraproject.org/tools/vagrant/vagrant-libvirt.html

Vagrant on Windows

If you're not familiar with command windows and text editors, skip ahead to the next section. Once you complete that section, you can either continue with the version of Ruby on your machine or with the Rails Dev Box.

Although Vagrant will normally download and install Oracle's VirtualBox for you, this process might not work, and you'll need to download it separately.[a]

Next, Windows might not recognize Oracle's signature as valid. If you downloaded VirtualBox from the virtualbox.org site, you can proceed anyway by clicking View Downloads, right-clicking the name of the download, and selecting "Run anyway." If Windows stops this from proceeding, click "More info" and click "Run anyway" once again. These steps are generally not recommended for downloading from disreputable sites, so be sure that you're downloading from virtualbox.org.

Once the installation wizard starts, read and accept the license terms and default options and proceed (see the following screenshot).

---

a. https://www.virtualbox.org/wiki/Downloads

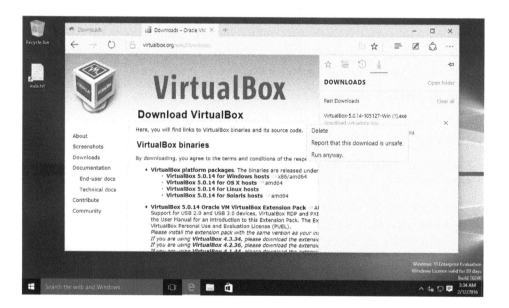

Installing on Windows

First, you need to install Ruby using the RubyInstaller for Windows package.[5] At the time of this writing, the latest version of Ruby available via RubyInstaller is Ruby 2.3.3. While Rails recommends Ruby version 2.4, this version will work with Rails 5.

Installing Ruby takes a few steps: first you need to install the base language and then the development kit.

Base installation is a snap. After you click Save/Download, click Run and then click OK. Select "I accept the License" (after reading it carefully, of course) and then click Next. Select "Add Ruby executables to your PATH," click Install (see the following screenshot), and then click Finish.

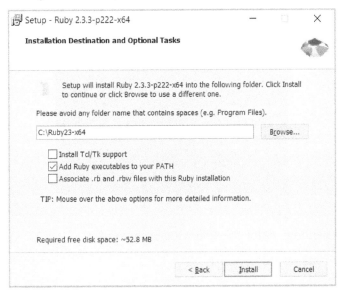

Download and extract the development kit for Ruby 2.0 and higher. Override the extraction destination with C:\ruby\devkit, as in the following screenshot.

---

5.   http://rubyinstaller.org/downloads

Once that completes, find Start Command Prompt with Ruby in your Start menu (see the following screenshot), and launch this program.

Within that window, enter the following commands:

```
> cd \ruby\devkit
> ruby dk.rb init
> ruby dk.rb install
```

Next, install Node.js.[6] The LTS version is recommended for most users. After you click Save/Download, click Run and then click Next. Again, read and then accept the terms in the license agreement, click Next three more times, and then click Install. If you're prompted to do so, click Yes to allow the program to be installed on your computer. Finally, click Finish.

This next step is optional but highly recommended: install Git.[7] Git is widely used in the Ruby and Rails ecosystem, and the more familiar you are with it,

---

6.   http://nodejs.org/download/
7.   http://git-scm.com/download

the easier it will be interact with some of the more advanced tools and techniques. It's also a really great version control system! After you click Save/Download, click Run. If you're prompted to do so, click Yes to allow the program to be installed on your computer. Click Next, read the license agreement, click Next four more times, select Use Git from the Windows Command Prompt (see the following screenshot), and then click Next five more times. Click Finish, and then review and close the Release Notes window.

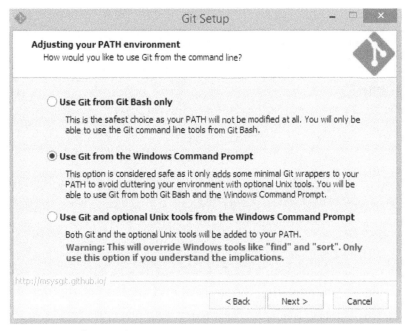

Next, install Yarn.[8] The Installer version is recommended for most users. After you click Save/Download, click Run and then click Next. Again, read and then accept the terms in the license agreement, click Next two more times, and then click Install. If you're prompted to do so, click Yes to allow the program to be installed on your computer. Finally, click Finish.

Lastly, install ChromeDriver.[9] To do that, click on the latest release (currently ChromeDriver 2.29) and then click on the win32.zip version of the file. After it finishes downloading, click Open and then right-click on "chromedriver" and select Copy. Next double-click "This PC" in the leftmost column of the window, double-click C:\, double-click Windows, and then anywhere within this window right-click and select Paste. Click Continue.

---

8.   https://yarnpkg.com/en/docs/install#windows-tab

9.   https://sites.google.com/a/chromium.org/chromedriver/downloads

Finally, open a command window by returning to your Windows Start screen, typing the word command, and selecting Command Prompt. From here, first enter these commands, as shown in the following screenshot, to verify that Ruby, Node, and Git were installed correctly:

```
> ruby -v
> node -v
> git --version
```

Next, configure Git, adjusting the user.name and user.email as appropriate:

```
> git config --global user.name "John Doe"
> git config --global user.email johndoe@example.com
```

Finally, install Rails itself with the following command:

```
> gem install rails --version=5.1.3 --no-ri --no-rdoc
```

This will take a while. Once it completes, skip to *Choosing a Rails Version*, on page 16, to ensure that the version of Rails you have installed matches the version described in this edition. See you there.

Installing on Mac OS X

Since Mac OS X ships with Ruby 2.0.0, you need to download a newer version of Ruby that works with Rails 5. The easiest way to do this is to use Homebrew.

Before you start, go to your Utilities folder and drag the Terminal application onto your dock. You'll be using this during the installation and then frequently as a Rails developer. Open the terminal and run the following command:

[handwritten: ~ space between \ + HTTPS:]

```
> ruby -e "$(curl -fsSL \
    https://raw.githubusercontent.com/Homebrew/install/master/install)"
```

When it asks you to install the Xcode command line tools, say yes.

Next, you have a choice. You can let Homebrew update your version of Ruby to the latest (currently Ruby 2.4.1). Or you can install rbenv and install a parallel version of Ruby alongside the system version of Ruby.

Upgrading your version of Ruby is the most straightforward path and can be done with a single command:

```
$ brew install ruby
```

Alternatively, you can install rbenv and use it to install Ruby 2.4.1:

```
$ brew install rbenv ruby-build
$ echo 'eval "$(rbenv init -)"' >> ~/.bash_profile
$ source ~/.bash_profile

$ rbenv install 2.4.1          *[handwritten: 2.7.2]*
$ rbenv global 2.4.1
```

If you had previously installed ruby-build and it can't find the definition for Ruby 2.4.1, you might need to reinstall ruby-build and try again:

```
$ brew reinstall --HEAD ruby-build
$ rbenv install 2.4.1
$ rbenv global 2.4.1
```

These are the two most popular routes for Mac developers. RVM and chruby are two other alternatives.[10,11]

Whichever path you take, run the following command to see which version of Ruby you're working with:

```
$ ruby -v
```

You should see the following type of result:

```
ruby 2.4.1p111 (2017-03-22 revision 58053) [x86_64-darwin16]
```

Next, run this command to update Rails to the version used by this book:

```
$ gem install rails --version=5.1.3 --no-ri --no-rdoc
```

Finally, install Yarn and ChromeDriver:

```
$ brew install yarn
$ brew install chromedriver
```

---

10. https://rvm.io/rvm/install

11. https://github.com/postmodern/chruby#readme

OK, you OS X users are done. You can skip forward to join the Cloud, Vagrant, and Windows users in *Choosing a Rails Version*, on page 16. See you there.

Installing on Linux

Start with your platform's native package-management system, be it apt, dpkg, portage, rpm, rug, synaptic, up2date, or yum.

The first step is to install the necessary dependencies. The following instructions are for Ubuntu 16.04 (Xenial Xerus); if you're on a different operating system, you may need to adjust both the command and the package names.

Run this command:

```
$ sudo apt install apache2 curl git libmysqlclient-dev mysql-server
```

Note that you may need to run sudo apt-get update to refresh your list of available packages. Next, you'll need to install Node, which requires a couple of steps:

```
$ curl -sL https://deb.nodesource.com/setup_8.x | sudo -E bash -
$ sudo apt-get install -y nodejs
```

You'll be prompted for a root password for your MySQL server. If you leave it blank, you'll be prompted multiple times. If you specify a password, you need to use that password when you create a database in Iteration K1 on page 286.

Next, you need to install both Ruby and Rails:

```
$ sudo apt install ruby2.3 ruby2.3-dev
$ sudo gem install rails --version=5.1.3 --no-ri --no-rdoc
```

If this works for you, you're done with the necessary installation steps and can proceed to *Choosing a Rails Version*, on page 16.

Many people prefer instead to have a separate installation of Ruby on their machine dedicated to support their application, and therefore they choose to download and build Ruby. The easiest way we've found to do this is to use RVM. Installing RVM is described on the RVM site.[12] An overview of the steps is included here.

First, install RVM:

```
$ curl -L https://get.rvm.io | bash -s stable
```

---

12. https://rvm.io/rvm/install

Next, select the "Run command as login shell" check box in the Gnome Terminal Profile Preference. Refer to the Integrating RVM with gnome-terminal page for instructions.[13]

Exit your command window or Terminal application and open a new one. This causes your .bash_login to be reloaded.

Execute the following command, which installs the prerequisites for your specific operating system:

```
$ rvm requirements --autolibs=enable
```

Once this is complete, you can proceed to install the Ruby interpreter:

```
$ rvm install 2.4.1
```

This step will take a while as it downloads, configures, and compiles the necessary executables. Once it completes, use that environment and install rails:

```
$ rvm use 2.4.1
$ gem install rails --version=5.1.3 --no-ri --no-rdoc
```

With the exception of the rvm use statement, each of the previous instructions needs to be done only once. The rvm use statement must be repeated each time you open a shell window. The use keyword is optional, so you can abbreviate this to rvm 2.4.1. You can also choose to make it the default Ruby interpreter for new Terminal sessions with the following command:

```
$ rvm --default 2.4.1
```

You can verify successful installation by using the following command:

```
$ rails -v
```

Finally, install Yarn and ChromeDriver,[14,15] and ensure that ChromeDriver is in your path:

```
$ curl -sS https://dl.yarnpkg.com/debian/pubkey.gpg | \
  sudo apt-key add -
$ echo "deb https://dl.yarnpkg.com/debian/ stable main" | \
  sudo tee /etc/apt/sources.list.d/yarn.list
$ sudo apt update
$ sudo apt install yarn chromium-chromedriver
$ sudo ln -s /usr/lib/chromium-browser/chromedriver /usr/local/bin
```

---

13. https://rvm.io/integration/gnome-terminal/
14. https://yarnpkg.com/lang/en/docs/install/#linux-tab
15. https://sites.google.com/a/chromium.org/chromedriver/

If you have trouble, try the suggestions listed under the Troubleshooting Your Install heading on the RVM site.[16]

At this point, we've covered Windows, Mac OS X, and Linux. Instructions after this point are common to all three operating systems.

Choosing a Rails Version

The previous instructions helped you install the version of Rails used by the examples in this book. But occasionally you might not want to run that version. For example, a newer version with some fixes or new features might become available. Or perhaps you're developing on one machine but intending to deploy on another machine that contains a version of Rails that you don't have any control over.

If either of these situations applies to you, you need to be aware of a few things. For starters, you can use the gem command to find out all the versions of Rails you have installed:

```
$ gem list --local rails
```

You can also verify which version of Rails you're running as the default by using the rails --version command. It should return 5.1.3.

If it doesn't, insert the version of Rails surrounded by underscores before the first parameter of any rails command. Here's an example:

```
$ rails _5.1.3_ --version
```

This is particularly handy when you create a new application, because once you create an application with a specific version of Rails, it'll continue to use that version of Rails—even if newer versions are installed on the system—until *you* decide it's time to upgrade. To upgrade, simply update the version number in the Gemfile that's in the root directory of your application and run bundle install.

Setting Up Your Development Environment

The day-to-day business of writing Rails programs is pretty straightforward. Everyone works differently; here's how we work.

The Command Line

We do a lot of work at the command line. Although an increasing number of GUI tools help generate and manage a Rails application, we find the command

---

line is still the most powerful place to be. It's worth spending a little while getting familiar with the command line on your operating system. Find out how to use it to edit commands that you're typing, how to search for and edit previous commands, and how to complete the names of files and commands as you type.

So-called tab completion is standard on Unix shells such as Bash and Zsh. It allows you to type the first few characters of a filename, hit Tab, and have the shell look for and complete the name based on matching files.

Version Control

We keep all our work in a version control system (currently Git). We make a point of checking a new Rails project into Git when we create it and committing changes once we've passed the tests. We normally commit to the repository many times an hour.

If you're not familiar with Git, don't worry, because this book will introduce you to the few commands that you'll need to follow along with the application being developed. If you ever need it, extensive documentation is available online.[17]

If you're working on a Rails project with other people, consider setting up a continuous integration (CI) system. When anyone checks in changes, the CI system will check out a fresh copy of the application and run all the tests. It's a common way to ensure that accidental breakages get immediate attention. You can also set up your CI system so that your customers can use it to play with the bleeding-edge version of your application. This kind of transparency is a great way to ensure that your project isn't going off the tracks.

Editors

We write our Rails programs using a programmer's editor. We've found over the years that different editors work best with different languages and environments. For example, Dave originally wrote this chapter using Emacs because he thinks that its Filladapt mode is unsurpassed when it comes to neatly formatting XML as he types. Sam updated the chapter using Vim. But many think that neither Emacs nor Vim is ideal for Rails development. Although the choice of editor is a personal one, here are some suggestions for features to look for in a Rails editor:

---

17. https://git-scm.com/book/en/v2

- Support for syntax highlighting of Ruby and HTML—ideally, support for .erb files (a Rails file format that embeds Ruby snippets within HTML).

- Support for automatic indentation and reindentation of Ruby source. This is more than an aesthetic feature: having an editor indent your program as you type is the best way to spot bad nesting in your code. Being able to reindent is important when you refactor your code and move stuff. (TextMate's ability to reindent when it pastes code from the clipboard is convenient.)

- Support for insertion of common Ruby and Rails constructs. You'll be writing lots of short methods, and if the IDE creates method skeletons with a keystroke or two, you can concentrate on the interesting stuff inside.

- Good file navigation. As you'll see, Rails applications are spread across many files; for example, a newly created Rails application enters the world containing forty-six files spread across thirty-four directories. That's before you've written a thing.

  You need an environment that helps you navigate quickly among these. You'll add a line to a controller to load a value, switch to the view to add a line to display it, and then switch to the test to verify you did it all right. Something like Notepad, where you traverse a File Open dialog box to select each file to edit, won't cut it. We prefer a combination of a tree view of files in a sidebar, a small set of keystrokes that help us find a file (or files) in a directory tree by name, and some built-in smarts that know how to navigate (say) between a controller action and the corresponding view.

- Name completion. Names in Rails tend to be long. A nice editor will let you type the first few characters and then suggest possible completions to you at the touch of a key.

We hesitate to recommend specific editors, because we've used only a few in earnest and we'll undoubtedly leave someone's favorite editor off the list. Nevertheless, to help you get started with something other than Notepad, here are some suggestions:

- Atom is a modern, full-featured, highly customizable cross-platform text editor.[18]

- TextMate is the favorite of many programmers who prefer to do their development on Mac OS X, including David Heinemeier Hansson.[19]

---

18. https://atom.io
19. http://macromates.com/

- Sublime Text is a cross-platform alternative that some see as the de facto successor to TextMate.[20]

- jEdit is a fully featured editor with support for Ruby.[21] It has extensive plugin support.

- Komodo is ActiveState's IDE for dynamic languages, including Ruby.[22]

- RubyMine is a commercial IDE for Ruby and is available for free to qualified educational and open source projects.[23] It runs on Windows, Mac OS X, and Linux.

- NetBeans Ruby and Rails plugin is an open source plugin for the popular NetBeans IDE.[24]

Where's My IDE?

If you're coming to Ruby and Rails from languages such as C# and Java, you may be wondering about IDEs. After all, we all know that it's impossible to code modern applications without at least 100 MB of IDE supporting our every keystroke. For you enlightened ones, here's the point in the book where we recommend you sit down—ideally, propped up on each side by a pile of framework references and 1,000-page Made Easy books.

It may surprise you to know that most Rails developers don't use fully fledged IDEs for Ruby or Rails (although some of the environments come close). Indeed, many Rails developers use plain old editors. And it turns out that this isn't as much of a problem as you might think. With other, less expressive languages, programmers rely on IDEs to do much of the grunt work for them, because IDEs do code generation, assist with navigation, and compile incrementally to give early warning of errors.

With Ruby, however, much of this support isn't necessary. Editors such as TextMate and BBEdit give you 90 percent of what you'd get from an IDE but are far lighter weight. About the only useful IDE facility that's missing is refactoring support.

Ask experienced developers who use your kind of operating system which editor they use. Spend a week or so trying alternatives before settling in.

---

20. http://www.sublimetext.com/
21. http://www.jedit.org/
22. http://www.activestate.com/komodo-ide
23. http://www.jetbrains.com/ruby/features/index.html
24. http://plugins.netbeans.org/plugin/38549

The Desktop

We're not going to tell you how to organize your desktop while working with Rails, but we will describe what we do.

Most of the time, we're writing code, running tests, and poking at an application in a browser. So, our main development desktop has an editor window and a browser window permanently open. We also want to keep an eye on the logging that's generated by the application, so we keep a terminal window open. In it, we use tail -f to scroll the contents of the log file as it's updated. We normally run this window with a small font so it takes up less space. If we see something interesting flash by, we increase the font size to investigate.

We also need access to the Rails API documentation, which we view in a browser. In the Introduction, we talked about using the gem server command to run a local web server containing the Rails documentation. This is convenient, but it unfortunately splits the Rails documentation across a number of separate documentation trees. If you're online, you can see a consolidated view of all the Rails documentation in one place.[25]

Rails and Databases

The examples in this book were written using SQLite 3 (version 3.7.4 or thereabouts). If you want to follow along with our code, it's probably simplest if you use SQLite 3 as well. If you decide to use something else, it won't be a major problem. You may have to make minor adjustments to any explicit SQL in our code, but Rails pretty much eliminates database-specific SQL from applications.

If you want to connect to a database other than SQLite 3, Rails also works with DB2, MySQL, Oracle Database, Postgres, Firebird, and SQL Server. For all but SQLite 3, you'll need to install a database driver—a library that Rails can use to connect to and use with your database engine. This section contains links to instructions to get that done.

The database drivers are all written in C and are primarily distributed in source form. If you don't want to bother building a driver from source, take a careful look at the driver's website. Many times you'll find that the author also distributes binary versions.

If you can't find a binary version or if you'd rather build from source anyway, you need a development environment on your machine to build the library.

---

25. http://api.rubyonrails.org/

For Windows, you need a copy of Visual C++. For Linux, you need gcc and friends (but these will likely already be installed).

On OS X, you need to install the developer tools (they come with the operating system but aren't installed by default). You also need to install your database driver into the correct version of Ruby. If you installed your own copy of Ruby, bypassing the built-in one, it's important to have this version of Ruby first in your path when building and installing the database driver. You can use the which ruby command to make sure you're *not* running Ruby from /usr/bin.

The following are the available database adapters and the links to their respective home pages:

DB2	https://rubygems.org/gems/ibm_db/
Firebird	https://rubygems.org/gems/fireruby
MySQL	https://rubygems.org/gems/mysql2
Oracle Database	https://rubygems.org/gems/activerecord-oracle_enhanced-adapter
Postgres	https://rubygems.org/gems/pg
SQL Server	https://github.com/rails-sqlserver
SQLite	https://github.com/luislavena/sqlite3-ruby

MySQL and SQLite adapters are also available for download as RubyGems (mysql2 and sqlite3, respectively).

What We Just Did

- We installed (or upgraded) the Ruby language.

- We installed (or upgraded) the Rails framework.

- We installed a JavaScript package manager named Yarn.

- We installed a tool that provides support for automated testing of web applications named ChromeDriver.

- We selected an editor.

- We installed (or upgraded) the SQLite 3 database.

Now that we have Rails installed, let's use it. It's time to move on to the next chapter, where you'll create your first application.

In this chapter, you'll see:
- Creating a new application
- Starting the server
- Accessing the server from a browser
- Producing dynamic content
- Adding hypertext links
- Passing data from the controller to the view
- Basic error recovery and debugging

CHAPTER 2

Instant Gratification

Let's write a simple application to verify that we have Rails snugly installed on our machines. Along the way, you'll get a peek at the way Rails applications work.

Creating a New Application

When you install the Rails framework, you also get a new command-line tool, rails, that's used to construct each new Rails application you write.

Why do we need a tool to do this? Why can't we just hack away in our favorite editor and create the source for our application from scratch? Well, we could just hack. After all, a Rails application is just Ruby source code. But Rails also does a lot of magic behind the curtain to get our applications to work with a minimum of explicit configuration. To get this magic to work, Rails needs to find all the various components of your application. As you'll see later (in *Where Things Go*, on page 307), this means we need to create a specific directory structure, slotting the code we write into the appropriate places. The rails command creates this directory structure for us and populates it with some standard Rails code.

To create your first Rails application, pop open a shell window, and navigate to a place in your filesystem where you want to create your application's directory structure. In our example, we'll be creating our projects in a directory called work. In that directory, use the rails command to create an application called demo. Be slightly careful here—if you have an existing directory called demo, you'll be asked if you want to overwrite any existing files. (Note: if you want to specify which Rails version to use, as described in *Choosing a Rails Version*, on page 16, now is the time to do so.)

```
rubys> cd work
work> rails new demo
create
create  README.md
create  Rakefile
create  config.ru
  :      :       :
remove  config/initializers/cors.rb
remove  config/initializers/new_framework_defaults_5_1.rb
   run  bundle install
Fetching gem metadata from https://rubygems.org/...........
  :      :       :
Bundle complete! 16 Gemfile dependencies, 70 gems now installed.
Use `bundle show [gemname]` to see where a bundled gem is installed.
       run  bundle exec spring binstub --all
* bin/rake: spring inserted
* bin/rails: spring inserted
work>
```

The command has created a directory named demo. Pop down into that directory and list its contents (using ls on a Unix box or using dir on Windows). You should see a bunch of files and subdirectories:

```
work> cd demo
demo> ls -p
Gemfile         app/         db/            public/
Gemfile.lock    bin/         lib/           test/
README.md       config/      log/           tmp/
Rakefile        config.ru    package.json   vendor/
```

All these directories (and the files they contain) can be intimidating to start with, but you can ignore most of them for now. In this chapter, we'll only use two of them directly: the bin directory, where we'll find the Rails executables; and the app directory, where we'll write our application.

Examine your installation using the following command:

```
demo> bin/rails about
```

Windows users need to prefix the command with ruby and use a backslash:

```
demo> ruby bin\rails about
```

If you get a Rails version other than 5.1.3, reread *Choosing a Rails Version*, on page 16.

This command also detects common installation errors. For example, if it can't find a JavaScript runtime, it provides you with a link to available runtimes.

As you can see from the bin/ prefix, this is running the rails command from the bin directory. This command is a wrapper, or *binstub*, for the Rails executable. It serves two purposes: it ensures that you're running with the correct version of every dependency, and it speeds up the startup times of Rails commands by preloading your application.

If you see a bunch of messages concerning already initialized constants or a possible conflict with an extension, consider deleting the demo directory, creating a separate RVM gemset,[1] and starting over. If that doesn't work, use bundle exec[2] to run rails commands:

```
demo> bundle exec rails about
```

Once you get bin/rails about working, you have everything you need to start a stand-alone web server that can run our newly created Rails application. So, without further ado, let's start our demo application:

```
demo> bin/rails server
=> Booting Puma
=> Rails 5.1.3 application starting in development on http://localhost:3000
=> Run `rails server -h` for more startup options
Puma starting in single mode...
* Version 3.9.1 (ruby 2.4.1-p111), codename: Private Caller
* Min threads: 5, max threads: 5
* Environment: development
* Listening on tcp://localhost:3000
Use Ctrl-C to stop
```

As the second line of the startup tracing indicates, we started a web server on port 3000. The localhost part of the address means that the Puma web server will only accept requests that originate from your machine. We can access the application by pointing a browser at the URL http://localhost:3000. The result is shown in the screenshot on page 26.

If you look at the window where you started the server, you can see tracing showing that you started the application. We're going to leave the server running in this console window. Later, as we write application code and run it via our browser, we'll be able to use this console window to trace the incoming requests. When the time comes to shut down your application, you can press Ctrl-C in this window to stop the server. (Don't do that yet—we'll be using this particular application in a minute.)

---

1. https://rvm.io/gemsets/basics/
2. http://gembundler.com/v1.3/bundle_exec.html

Yay! You're on Rails!

Rails version: 5.1.3
Ruby version: 2.4.1 (x86_64-darwin16)

If you want to enable this server to be accessed by other machines on your network, you can specify 0.0.0.0 as the host to bind to:

```
demo> bin/rails server -b 0.0.0.0
```

At this point, we have a new application running, but it has none of our code in it. Let's rectify this situation.

Hello, Rails!

We can't help it—we just have to write a Hello, World! program to try a new system. Let's start by creating a simple application that sends our cheery greeting to a browser. After we get that working, we'll embellish it with the current time and links.

As you'll explore further in Chapter 3, *The Architecture of Rails Applications*, on page 39, Rails is a Model-View-Controller (MVC) framework. Rails accepts incoming requests from a browser, decodes the request to find a controller, and calls an action method in that controller. The controller then invokes a particular view to display the results to the user. The good news is that Rails takes care of most of the internal plumbing that links all these actions. To write our Hello, World! application, we need code for a controller and a view, and we need a route to connect the two. We don't need code for a model, because we're not dealing with any data. Let's start with the controller.

In the same way that we used the rails command to create a new Rails application, we can also use a generator script to create a new controller for our project. This command is rails generate. So, to create a controller called say, we make sure we're in the demo directory and run the command, passing in the name of the controller we want to create and the names of the actions we intend for this controller to support:

```
demo> bin/rails generate controller Say hello goodbye
create  app/controllers/say_controller.rb
 route  get 'say/goodbye'
 route  get 'say/hello'
invoke  erb
create    app/views/say
create    app/views/say/hello.html.erb
create    app/views/say/goodbye.html.erb
invoke  test_unit
create    test/controllers/say_controller_test.rb
invoke  helper
create    app/helpers/say_helper.rb
invoke    test_unit
invoke  assets
invoke    coffee
create      app/assets/javascripts/say.coffee
invoke    scss
create      app/assets/stylesheets/say.scss
```

The rails generate command logs the files and directories it examines, noting when it adds new Ruby scripts or directories to our application. For now, we're interested in one of these scripts and (in a minute) the .html.erb files.

The first source file we'll be looking at is the controller. You can find it in the app/controllers/say_controller.rb file. Let's take a look at it:

rails51/demo1/app/controllers/say_controller.rb
```
class SayController < ApplicationController
  def hello
  end

  def goodbye
  end
end
```

Pretty minimal, eh? SayController is a class that inherits from ApplicationController, so it automatically gets all the default controller behavior. What does this code have to do? For now, it does nothing—we simply have empty action methods named hello() and goodbye(). To understand why these methods are named this way, you need to look at the way Rails handles requests.

Rails and Request URLs

Like any other web application, a Rails application appears to its users to be associated with a URL. When you point your browser at that URL, you're talking to the application code, which generates a response to you.

Let's try it now. Navigate to the URL http://localhost:3000/say/hello in a browser. You'll see something that looks like the following screenshot.

Say#hello

Find me in app/views/say/hello.html.erb

Our First Action

At this point, we can see not only that we've connected the URL to our controller but also that Rails is pointing the way to our next step—namely, to tell Rails what to display. That's where views come in. Remember when we ran the script to create the new controller? That command added several files and a new directory to our application. That directory contains the template files for the controller's views. In our case, we created a controller named say, so the views will be in the app/views/say directory.

By default, Rails looks for templates in a file with the same name as the action it's handling. In our case, that means we need to replace a file called hello.html.erb in the app/views/say directory. (Why .html.erb? We'll explain in a minute.) For now, let's put some basic HTML in there:

```
rails51/demo1/app/views/say/hello.html.erb
<h1>Hello from Rails!</h1>
```

Save the hello.html.erb file, and refresh your browser window. You should see it display our friendly greeting, as in the following screenshot.

Hello from Rails!

In total, we've looked at two files in our Rails application tree. We looked at the controller, and we modified a template to display a page in the browser.

These files live in standard locations in the Rails hierarchy: controllers go into app/controllers, and views go into subdirectories of app/views. You can see this structure in the following diagram.

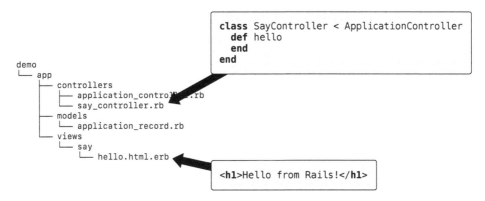

Making It Dynamic

So far, our Rails application is pretty boring—it just displays a static page. To make it more dynamic, let's have it show the current time each time it displays the page.

To do this, we need to change the template file in the view—it now needs to include the time as a string. That raises two questions. First, how do we add dynamic content to a template? Second, where do we get the time from?

Dynamic Content

You can create dynamic templates in Rails in many ways. The most common way, which we'll use here, is to embed Ruby code in the template. That's the template file is named hello.html.erb; the .html.erb suffix tells Rails to expand the content in the file using a system called ERB.

ERB is a filter, installed as part of the Rails installation, that takes an .erb file and outputs a transformed version. The output file is often HTML in Rails, but it can be anything. Normal content is passed through without being changed. However, content between <%= and %> is interpreted as Ruby code and executed. The result of that execution is converted into a string, and that value is substituted in the file in place of the <%=...%> sequence. For example, change hello.html.erb to display the current time:

```
rails51/demo2/app/views/say/hello.html.erb
<h1>Hello from Rails!</h1>
<p>
  It is now <%= Time.now %>
</p>
```

When we refresh our browser window, we see the time displayed using Ruby's standard format, as shown in the following screenshot.

Hello from Rails!

It is now 2017-08-13 11:58:13 -0400

Notice that the time displayed updates each time the browser window is refreshed. It looks as if we're really generating dynamic content.

Making Development Easier

You might have noticed something about the development we've been doing so far. As we've been adding code to our application, we haven't had to restart the running application. It's been happily chugging away in the background. And yet each change we make is available whenever we access the application through a browser. What gives?

It turns out that the Rails dispatcher is pretty clever. In development mode (as opposed to testing or production), it automatically reloads application source files when a new request comes along. That way, when we edit our application, the dispatcher makes sure it's running the most recent changes. This is great for development.

However, this flexibility comes at a cost: it causes a short pause after you enter a URL before the application responds. That's caused by the dispatcher reloading stuff. For development it's a price worth paying, but in production it would be unacceptable. For this reason, this feature is disabled for production deployment. See Chapter 17, *Task L: Deployment and Production*, on page 279.

Adding the Time

Our original problem was to display the time to users of our application. We now know how to make our application display dynamic data. The second issue we have to address is working out where to get the time from.

We've shown that the approach of embedding a call to Ruby's Time.now() method in our hello.html.erb template works. Each time they access this page, users will see the current time substituted into the body of the response. And for our trivial application, that might be good enough. In general, though, we probably want to do something slightly different. We'll move the determination of the time to be displayed into the controller and leave the view with the job of displaying it. We'll change our action method in the controller to set the time value into an instance variable called @time:

```
rails51/demo3/app/controllers/say_controller.rb
class SayController < ApplicationController
  def hello
➤    @time = Time.now
  end

  def goodbye
  end
end
```

In the .html.erb template, we'll use this instance variable to substitute the time into the output:

```
rails51/demo3/app/views/say/hello.html.erb
<h1>Hello from Rails!</h1>
<p>
➤    It is now <%= @time %>
</p>
```

When we refresh our browser window, we again see the current time, showing that the communication between the controller and the view was successful.

Why did we go to the extra trouble of setting the time to be displayed in the controller and then using it in the view? Good question. In this application, it doesn't make much difference, but by putting the logic in the controller instead, we buy ourselves some benefits. For example, we may want to extend our application in the future to support users in many countries. In that case, we'd want to localize the display of the time, choosing a time appropriate to the user's time zone. That would require a fair amount of application-level code, and it would probably not be appropriate to embed it at the view level. By setting the time to display in the controller, we make our application more flexible: we can change the time zone in the controller without having to update any view that uses that time object. The time is *data*, and it should be supplied to the view by the controller. We'll see a lot more of this when we introduce models into the equation.

The Story So Far

Let's briefly review how our current application works.

1. The user navigates to our application. In our case, we do that using a local URL such as http://localhost:3000/say/hello.

2. Rails then matches the route pattern, which it previously split into two parts and analyzed. The say part is taken to be the name of a controller,

so Rails creates a new instance of the Ruby SayController class (which it finds in app/controllers/say_controller.rb).

3. The next part of the pattern, hello, identifies an action. Rails invokes a method of that name in the controller. This action method creates a new Time object holding the current time and tucks it away in the @time instance variable.

4. Rails looks for a template to display the result. It searches the app/views directory for a subdirectory with the same name as the controller (say) and in that subdirectory for a file named after the action (hello.html.erb).

5. Rails processes this file through the ERB templating system, executing any embedded Ruby and substituting in values set up by the controller.

6. The result is returned to the browser, and Rails finishes processing this request.

This isn't the whole story. Rails gives you lots of opportunities to override this basic workflow (and we'll be taking advantage of them shortly). As it stands, our story illustrates convention over configuration, one of the fundamental parts of the philosophy of Rails. Rails applications are typically written using little or no external configuration. That's because Rails provides convenient defaults, and because you apply certain conventions to how a URL is constructed, which file a controller definition is placed in, or which class name and method names are used. Things knit themselves together in a natural way.

Linking Pages Together

It's a rare web application that has just one page. Let's see how we can add another stunning example of web design to our Hello, World! application.

Normally, each page in our application will correspond to a separate view. While we'll also use a new action method to handle the new page, we'll use the same controller for both actions. This needn't be the case, but we have no compelling reason to use a new controller right now.

We already defined a goodbye action for this controller, so all that remains is to update the scaffolding that was generated in the app/views/say directory. This time the file we'll be updating is called goodbye.html.erb, because by default templates are named after their associated actions:

```
rails51/demo4/app/views/say/goodbye.html.erb
<h1>Goodbye!</h1>
<p>
  It was nice having you here.
</p>
```

Fire up your trusty browser again, but this time point to our new view using the URL http://localhost:3000/say/goodbye. You should see something like this screenshot.

Goodbye!

It was nice having you here.

Now we need to link the two screens. We'll put a link on the hello screen that takes us to the goodbye screen, and vice versa. In a real application, we might want to make these proper buttons, but for now we'll use hyperlinks.

We already know that Rails uses a convention to parse the URL into a target controller and an action within that controller. So, a simple approach would be to adopt this URL convention for our links.

The hello.html.erb file would contain the following:

```
...
<p>
  Say <a href="/say/goodbye">Goodbye</a>!
</p>
...
```

And the goodbye.html.erb file would point the other way:

```
...
<p>
  Say <a href="/say/hello">Hello</a>!
</p>
...
```

This approach would certainly work, but it's a bit fragile. If we were to move our application to a different place on the web server, the URLs would no longer be valid. It also encodes assumptions about the Rails URL format into our code; it's possible a future version of Rails could change that format.

Fortunately, these aren't risks we have to take. Rails comes with a bunch of *helper methods* that can be used in view templates. Here, we'll use the link_to() helper method, which creates a hyperlink to an action. (The link_to() method can do a lot more than this, but let's take it gently for now.) Using link_to(), hello.html.erb becomes the following:

rails51/demo5/app/views/say/hello.html.erb
```
<h1>Hello from Rails!</h1>
<p>
  It is now <%= @time %>
</p>
➤ <p>
➤   Time to say
➤   <%= link_to "Goodbye", say_goodbye_path %>!
➤ </p>
```

There's a link_to() call within an ERB <%=...%> sequence. This creates a link to a URL that will invoke the goodbye() action. The first parameter in the call to link_to() is the text to be displayed in the hyperlink, and the next parameter tells Rails to generate the link to the goodbye() action.

Let's stop for a minute to consider how we generated the link. We wrote this:

```
link_to "Goodbye", say_goodbye_path
```

First, link_to() is a method call. (In Rails, we call methods that make it easier to write templates *helpers*.) If you come from a language such as Java, you might be surprised that Ruby doesn't insist on parentheses around method parameters. You can always add them if you like.

say_goodbye_path is a precomputed value that Rails makes available to application views. It evaluates to the /say/goodbye path. Over time, you'll see that Rails provides the ability to name all the routes that you use in your application.

Let's get back to the application. If we point our browser at our hello page, it now contains the link to the goodbye page, as shown in the following screenshot.

Hello from Rails!

It is now 2017-08-13 11:58:24 -0400

Time to say Goodbye!

We can make the corresponding change in goodbye.html.erb, linking it back to the initial hello page:

rails51/demo5/app/views/say/goodbye.html.erb
```
<h1>Goodbye!</h1>
<p>
  It was nice having you here.
</p>
➤ <p>
➤   Say <%= link_to "Hello", say_hello_path %> again.
➤ </p>
```

So far, we've just done things that should work, and—unsurprisingly—they've worked. But the true test of the developer friendliness of a framework is how it responds when things go wrong. As we've not invested much time into this code yet, now is a perfect time to try to break things.

When Things Go Wrong

Let's start by introducing a typo in the source code—one that perhaps is introduced by a misfiring autocorrect function in your favorite editor:

rails51/demo5/app/controllers/say_controller.rb
```
class SayController < ApplicationController
  def hello
    @time = Time.know
  end

  def goodbye
  end
end
```

Refresh the following page in your browser: http://localhost:3000/say/hello. You should see something like the following screenshot.

For security reasons, the web console is configured to only be shown when accessed from the same machine as the web server is running on. If you are running on a different machine (as you would be should you be running on c9), you will need to adjust the configuration to see this. For example, to enable the web console to be seen by all, add the following to config/environments/development.rb and restart your server:

```
config.web_console.whitelisted_ips = %w( 0.0.0.0/0 ::/0 )
```

What you see is that Ruby tells you about the error ("undefined method 'know'"), and Rails shows you the extracted source where the code can be found (Rails.root), the stack traceback, and request parameters (at the moment, None). It also provides the ability to toggle the display of session and environment dumps.

If you're running Ruby 2.3.0 or later, you'll even see a suggestion: "Did you mean? now." What a nice touch.

At the bottom of the window you see an area consisting of white text on a black background, looking much like a command-line prompt. This is the Rails *web console*. You can use it to try out suggestions and evaluate expressions. Let's try it out, as shown in the following screenshot.

```
>> Time.now                                                        x
=> 2017-04-22 22:49:05 -0400
>> █
```

All in all, helpful stuff.

We've broken the code. Now, let's break the other thing we've used so far: the URL. Visit the following page in your browser: http://localhost:3000/say/hullo. You should see something like the screenshot on page 37.

This is similar to what we saw before, but in place of source code we see a list of possible routes, how they can be accessed, and the controller action they're associated with. We'll explain this later in detail, but for now look at the Path Match input field. If you enter a partial URL in there, you can see a list of routes that match. That's not needed right now, as we have only two routes, but can be helpful later when we have many.

At this point, we've completed our toy application and in the process verified that our installation of Rails is functioning properly and provides helpful information when things go wrong. After a brief recap, it's now time to move on to building a real application.

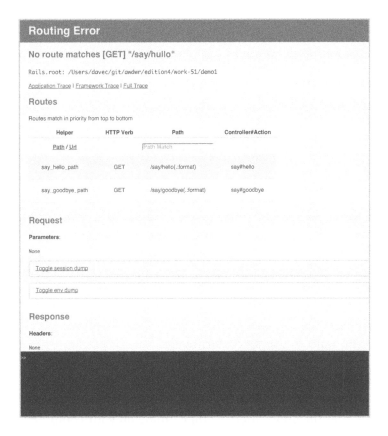

What We Just Did

We constructed a toy application that showed you the following:

- How to create a new Rails application and how to create a new controller in that application

- How to create dynamic content in the controller and display it via the view template

- How to link pages together

- How to debug problems in the code or the URL

This is a great foundation, and it didn't take much time or effort. This experience will continue as we move on to the next chapter and build a much bigger application.

Playtime

Here's some stuff to try on your own:

- Experiment with the following expressions:
  - Addition: <%= 1+2 %>
  - Concatenation: <%= "cow" + "boy" %>
  - Time in one hour: <%= 1.hour.from_now.localtime %>
- A call to the following Ruby method returns a list of all the files in the current directory:

```
@files = Dir.glob('*')
```

Use it to set an instance variable in a controller action, and then write the corresponding template that displays the filenames in a list on the browser.

Hint: you can iterate over a collection using something like this:

```
<% @files.each do |file| %>
  file name is: <%= file %>
<% end %>
```

You might want to use a <ul> for the list.

Cleaning Up

Maybe you've been following along and writing the code in this chapter. If so, chances are that the application is still running on your computer. When we start coding our next application in Chapter 6, *Task A: Creating the Application*, on page 71, we'll get a conflict the first time we run it because it'll also try to use the computer's port 3000 to talk with the browser. Now is a good time to stop the current application by pressing Ctrl-C in the window you used to start it. Microsoft Windows users may need to press Ctrl-Pause/Break instead.

Now let's move on to an overview of Rails.

CHAPTER 3

The Architecture of Rails Applications

One of the interesting features of Rails is that it imposes some fairly serious constraints on how you structure your web applications. Surprisingly, these constraints make it easier to create applications—a lot easier. Let's see why.

Models, Views, and Controllers

Back in 1979, Trygve Reenskaug came up with a new architecture for developing interactive applications. In his design, applications were broken into three types of components: models, views, and controllers.

The *model* is responsible for maintaining the state of the application. Sometimes this state is transient, lasting for just a couple of interactions with the user. Sometimes the state is permanent and is stored outside the application, often in a database.

A model is more than data; it enforces all the business rules that apply to that data. For example, if a discount shouldn't be applied to orders of less than $20, the model enforces the constraint. This makes sense; by putting the implementation of these business rules in the model, we make sure that nothing else in the application can make our data invalid. The model acts as both a gatekeeper and a data store.

The *view* is responsible for generating a user interface, normally based on data in the model. For example, an online store has a list of products to be displayed on a catalog screen. This list is accessible via the model, but it's a view that formats the list for the end user. Although the view might present the user with various ways of inputting data, the view itself never handles incoming data. The view's work is done once the data is displayed. There may well be many views that access the same model data, often for different purposes. The online store has a view that displays product information on a catalog page, and another set of views used by administrators to add and edit products.

Controllers orchestrate the application. Controllers receive events from the outside world (normally, user input), interact with the model, and display an appropriate view to the user.

This triumvirate—the model, view, and controller—together form an architecture known as MVC. To learn how the three concepts fit together, see the following figure.

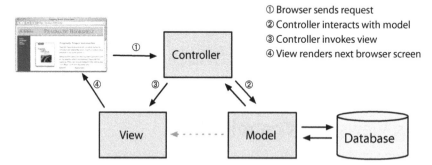

① Browser sends request
② Controller interacts with model
③ Controller invokes view
④ View renders next browser screen

The MVC architecture was originally intended for conventional GUI applications, where developers found that the separation of concerns led to far less coupling, which in turn made the code easier to write and maintain. Each concept or action was expressed in a single, well-known place. Using MVC was like constructing a skyscraper with the girders already in place—it was a lot easier to hang the rest of the pieces with a structure already there. During the development of our application, we'll make heavy use of Rails's ability to generate *scaffolding* for our application.

Ruby on Rails is an MVC framework, too. Rails enforces a structure for your application: you develop models, views, and controllers as separate chunks of functionality, and it knits them together as your program executes. One of the joys of Rails is that this knitting process is based on the use of intelligent defaults so that you typically don't need to write any external configuration metadata to make it all work. This is an example of the Rails philosophy of favoring convention over configuration.

In a Rails application, an incoming request is first sent to a router, which works out where in the application the request should be sent and how the request should be parsed. Ultimately, this phase identifies a particular method (called an *action* in Rails parlance) somewhere in the controller code. The action might look at data in the request, it might interact with the model, and it might cause other actions to be invoked. Eventually the action prepares information for the view, which renders something to the user.

Rails handles an incoming request as shown in the following figure. In this example, the application has previously displayed a product catalog page, and the user has just clicked the Add to Cart button next to one of the products. This button posts to http://localhost:3000/line_items?product_id=2, where line_items is a resource in the application and 2 is the internal ID for the selected product.

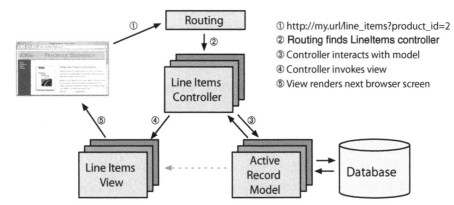

① http://my.url/line_items?product_id=2
② Routing finds LineItems controller
③ Controller interacts with model
④ Controller invokes view
⑤ View renders next browser screen

The routing component receives the incoming request and immediately picks it apart. The request contains a path (/line_items?product_id=2) and a method (this button does a POST operation; other common methods are GET, PUT, PATCH, and DELETE). In this simple case, Rails takes the first part of the path, line_items, as the name of the controller and the product_id as the ID of a product. By convention, POST methods are associated with create() actions. As a result of all this analysis, the router knows it has to invoke the create() method in the LineItemsController controller class (we'll talk about naming conventions in *Naming Conventions*, on page 315).

The create() method handles user requests. In this case, it finds the current user's shopping cart (which is an object managed by the model). It also asks the model to find the information for product 2. It then tells the shopping cart to add that product to itself. (See how the model is being used to keep track of all the business data? The controller tells it *what* to do, and the model knows *how* to do it.)

Now that the cart includes the new product, we can show it to the user. The controller invokes the view code, but before it does, it arranges things so that the view has access to the cart object from the model. In Rails, this invocation is often implicit; again, conventions help link a particular view with a given action.

That's all there is to an MVC web application. By following a set of conventions and partitioning your functionality appropriately, you'll discover that your code becomes easier to work with and your application becomes easier to extend and maintain. That seems like a good trade.

If MVC is simply a question of partitioning your code a particular way, you might be wondering why you need a framework such as Ruby on Rails. The answer is straightforward: Rails handles all of the low-level housekeeping for you—all those messy details that take so long to handle by yourself—and lets you concentrate on your application's core functionality. Let's see how.

Rails Model Support

In general, we want our web applications to keep their information in a relational database. Order-entry systems will store orders, line items, and customer details in database tables. Even applications that normally use unstructured text, such as weblogs and news sites, often use databases as their back-end data store.

Although it might not be immediately apparent from the database queries you've seen so far, relational databases are designed around mathematical set theory. This is good from a conceptual point of view, but it makes it difficult to combine relational databases with object-oriented (OO) programming languages. Objects are all about data and operations, and databases are all about sets of values. Operations that are easy to express in relational terms are sometimes difficult to code in an OO system. The reverse is also true.

Over time, folks have worked out ways of reconciling the relational and OO views of their corporate data. Let's look at the way that Rails chooses to map relational data onto objects.

Object-Relational Mapping

Object-relational mapping (ORM) libraries map database tables to classes. If a database has a table called orders, our program will have a class named Order. Rows in this table correspond to objects of the class—a particular order is represented as an object of the Order class. Within that object, attributes are used to get and set the individual columns. Our Order object has methods to get and set the amount, the sales tax, and so on.

In addition, the Rails classes that wrap our database tables provide a set of class-level methods that perform table-level operations. For example, we might need to find the order with a particular ID. This is implemented as a class method that returns the corresponding Order object. In Ruby code, that might look like this:

```
order = Order.find(1)
puts "Customer #{order.customer_id}, amount=$#{order.amount}"
```

Sometimes these class-level methods return collections of objects:

```
Order.where(name: 'dave').each do |order|
  puts order.amount
end
```

Finally, the objects corresponding to individual rows in a table have methods that operate on that row. Probably the most widely used is save(), the operation that saves the row to the database:

```
Order.where(name: 'dave').each do |order|
  order.pay_type = "Purchase order"
  order.save
end
```

So, an ORM layer maps tables to classes, rows to objects, and columns to attributes of those objects. Class methods are used to perform table-level operations, and instance methods perform operations on the individual rows.

In a typical ORM library, you supply configuration data to specify the mappings between entities in the database and entities in the program. Programmers using these ORM tools often find themselves creating and maintaining a boatload of XML configuration files.

Active Record

Active Record is the ORM layer supplied with Rails. It closely follows the standard ORM model: tables map to classes, rows to objects, and columns to object attributes. It differs from most other ORM libraries in the way it's configured. By relying on convention and starting with sensible defaults, Active Record minimizes the amount of configuration that developers perform.

To show this, here's a program that uses Active Record to wrap our orders table:

```
require 'active_record'

class Order < ApplicationRecord
end

order = Order.find(1)
order.pay_type = "Purchase order"
order.save
```

This code uses the new Order class to fetch the order with an id of 1 and modify the pay_type. (For now, we've omitted the code that creates a database connection.) Active Record relieves us of the hassles of dealing with the underlying database, leaving us free to work on business logic.

But Active Record does more than that. As you'll see when we develop our shopping cart application, starting in Chapter 5, *The Depot Application*, on page 65, Active Record integrates seamlessly with the rest of the Rails framework. If a web form sends the application data related to a business object, Active Record can extract it into our model. Active Record supports sophisticated validation of model data, and if the form data fails validations, the Rails views can extract and format errors.

Active Record is the solid model foundation of the Rails MVC architecture.

Action Pack: The View and Controller

When you think about it, the view and controller parts of MVC are pretty intimate. The controller supplies data to the view, and the controller receives events from the pages generated by the views. Because of these interactions, support for views and controllers in Rails is bundled into a single component, *Action Pack*.

Don't be fooled into thinking that your application's view code and controller code will be jumbled up because Action Pack is a single component. Quite the contrary; Rails gives you the separation you need to write web applications with clearly demarcated code for control and presentation logic.

View Support

In Rails, the view is responsible for creating all or part of a response to be displayed in a browser, to be processed by an application, or to be sent as an email. At its simplest, a view is a chunk of HTML code that displays some fixed text. More typically, you'll want to include dynamic content created by the action method in the controller.

In Rails, dynamic content is generated by templates, which come in three flavors. The most common templating scheme, called Embedded Ruby (ERB), embeds snippets of Ruby code within a view document, in many ways similar to the way it's done in other web frameworks, such as PHP or JavaServer Pages (JSP). Although this approach is flexible, some are concerned that it violates the spirit of MVC. By embedding code in the view, we risk adding logic that should be in the model or the controller. As with everything, while judicious use in moderation is healthy, overuse can become a problem. Maintaining a clean separation of concerns is part of the developer's job.

You can also use ERB to construct JavaScript fragments on the server that are then executed on the browser. This is great for creating dynamic Ajax interfaces. We talk about these starting in *Iteration F2: Creating an Ajax-Based Cart*, on page 159.

Rails also provides libraries to construct XML or JSON documents using Ruby code. The structure of the generated XML or JSON automatically follows the structure of the code.

And the Controller!

The Rails controller is the logical center of your application. It coordinates the interaction among the user, the views, and the model. However, Rails handles most of this interaction behind the scenes; the code you write concentrates on application-level functionality. This makes Rails controller code remarkably easy to develop and maintain.

The controller is also home to a number of important ancillary services:

- It's responsible for routing external requests to internal actions. It handles people-friendly URLs extremely well.

- It manages caching, which can give applications orders-of-magnitude performance boosts.

- It manages helper modules, which extend the capabilities of the view templates without bulking up their code.

- It manages sessions, giving users the impression of ongoing interaction with our applications.

We've already seen and modified a controller in *Hello, Rails!*, on page 26 and we will be seeing and modifying a number of controllers in the development of a sample application, starting with the products controller in *Iteration C1: Creating the Catalog Listing*, on page 103.

There's a lot to Rails. But before going any further, let's have a brief refresher —and for some of you, a brief introduction—to the Ruby language.

In this chapter, you'll see:
- Objects: names and methods
- Data: strings, arrays, hashes, and regular expressions
- Control: if, while, blocks, iterators, and exceptions
- Building blocks: classes and modules
- YAML and marshaling
- Common idioms that you'll see used in this book

CHAPTER 4

Introduction to Ruby

Many people who are new to Rails are also new to Ruby. If you're familiar with a language such as Java, JavaScript, PHP, Perl, or Python, you'll find Ruby pretty easy to pick up.

This chapter isn't a complete introduction to Ruby. It doesn't cover topics such as precedence rules (as in most other programming languages, 1+2*3==7 in Ruby). It's only meant to explain enough Ruby that the examples in the book make sense.

This chapter draws heavily from material in *Programming Ruby [FH13]*. If you think you need more background on the Ruby language (and at the risk of being grossly self-serving), we'd like to suggest that the best way to learn Ruby and the best reference for Ruby's classes, modules, and libraries is *Programming Ruby [FH13]* (also known as the PickAxe book). Welcome to the Ruby community!

Ruby Is an Object-Oriented Language

Everything you manipulate in Ruby is an object, and the results of those manipulations are themselves objects.

When you write object-oriented code, you're normally looking to model concepts from the real world. Typically, during this modeling process you discover categories of things that need to be represented. In an online store, the concept of a line item could be such a category. In Ruby, you'd define a *class* to represent each of these categories. You then use this class as a kind of factory that generates *objects*—instances of that class. An object is a combination of state (for example, the quantity and the product ID) and methods that use that state (perhaps a method to calculate the line item's total cost). We'll show how to create classes in *Classes*, on page 56.

You create objects by calling a *constructor*, a special method associated with a class. The standard constructor is called new(). Given a class called LineItem, you could create line item objects as follows:

```
line_item_one = LineItem.new
line_item_one.quantity = 1
line_item_one.sku       = "AUTO_B_00"
```

You invoke methods by sending a message to an object. The message contains the method's name, along with any parameters the method may need. When an object receives a message, it looks into its own class for a corresponding method. Let's look at some method calls:

```
"dave".length
line_item_one.quantity()
cart.add_line_item(next_purchase)
submit_tag "Add to Cart"
```

Parentheses are generally optional in method calls. In Rails applications, you'll find that most method calls involved in larger expressions have parentheses, while those that look more like commands or declarations tend not to have them.

Methods have names, as do many other constructs in Ruby. Names in Ruby have special rules—rules that you may not have seen if you come to Ruby from another language.

Ruby Names

Local variables, method parameters, and method names should all start with a lowercase letter or with an underscore: order, line_item, and xr2000 are all valid. Instance variables begin with an at (@) sign—for example, @quantity and @product_id. The Ruby convention is to use underscores to separate words in a multiword method or variable name (so line_item is preferable to lineItem).

Class names, module names, and constants must start with an uppercase letter. By convention they use capitalization, rather than underscores, to distinguish the start of words within the name. Class names look like Object, PurchaseOrder, and LineItem.

Rails uses *symbols* to identify things. In particular, it uses them as keys when naming method parameters and looking things up in hashes. Here's an example:

```
redirect_to :action => "edit", :id => params[:id]
```

As you can see, a symbol looks like a variable name, but it's prefixed with a colon. Examples of symbols include :action, :line_items, and :id. You can think of symbols as string literals magically made into constants. Alternatively, you can consider the colon to mean *thing named*, so :id is the thing named id.

Now that we've used a few methods, let's move on to how they're defined.

Methods

Let's write a method that returns a cheery, personalized greeting. We'll invoke that method a couple of times:

```
def say_goodnight(name)
  result = 'Good night, ' + name
  return result
end

# Time for bed...
puts say_goodnight('Mary-Ellen') # => 'Goodnight, Mary-Ellen'
puts say_goodnight('John-Boy')   # => 'Goodnight, John-Boy'
```

Having defined the method, we call it twice. In both cases, we pass the result to the puts() method, which outputs to the console its argument followed by a newline (moving on to the next line of output).

You don't need a semicolon at the end of a statement as long as you put each statement on a separate line. Ruby comments start with a # character and run to the end of the line. Indentation isn't significant (but two-character indentation is the de facto Ruby standard).

Ruby doesn't use braces to delimit the bodies of compound statements and definitions (such as methods and classes). Instead, you simply finish the body with the end keyword. The return keyword is optional, and if it's not present, the results of the last expression evaluated are returned.

Data Types

While everything in Ruby is an object, some of the data types in Ruby have special syntax support, in particular for defining literal values. In the preceding examples, we used some simple strings and even string concatenation.

Strings

The previous example also showed some Ruby string objects. One way to create a string object is to use *string literals*, which are sequences of characters between single or double quotation marks. The difference between the two forms is the amount of processing Ruby does on the string while constructing the literal. In the single-quoted case, Ruby does very little. With only a few exceptions, what you type into the single-quoted string literal becomes the string's value.

With double-quotes, Ruby does more work. It looks for *substitutions*—sequences that start with a backslash character—and replaces them with a binary value. The most common of these is \n, which is replaced with a newline character. When you write a string containing a newline to the console, the \n forces a line break.

Then, Ruby performs *expression interpolation* in double-quoted strings. In the string, the sequence #{expression} is replaced by the value of expression. We could use this to rewrite our previous method:

```ruby
def say_goodnight(name)
  "Good night, #{name.capitalize}"
end
puts say_goodnight('pa')
```

When Ruby constructs this string object, it looks at the current value of name and substitutes it into the string. Arbitrarily complex expressions are allowed in the #{...} construct. Here we invoked the capitalize() method, defined for all strings, to output our parameter with a leading uppercase letter.

Strings are a fairly primitive data type that contain an ordered collection of bytes or characters. Ruby also provides means for defining collections of arbitrary objects via *arrays* and *hashes*.

Arrays and Hashes

Ruby's arrays and hashes are indexed collections. Both store collections of objects, accessible using a key. With arrays, the key is an integer, whereas hashes support any object as a key. Both arrays and hashes grow as needed to hold new elements. It's more efficient to access array elements, but hashes provide more flexibility. Any particular array or hash can hold objects of differing types; you can have an array containing an integer, a string, and a floating-point number, for example.

You can create and initialize a new array object by using an *array literal*—a set of elements between square brackets. Given an array object, you can access individual elements by supplying an index between square brackets, as the next example shows. Ruby array indices start at zero:

```ruby
a = [ 1, 'cat', 3.14 ]   # array with three elements
a[0]                      # access the first element (1)
a[2] = nil                # set the third element
                          # array now [ 1, 'cat', nil ]
```

You may have noticed that we used the special value nil in this example. In many languages, the concept of *nil* (or *null*) means *no object*. In Ruby, that's not the case; nil is an object, like any other, that happens to represent nothing.

The <<() method is often used with arrays. It appends a single value to its receiver:

```
ages = []
for person in @people
  ages << person.age
end
```

Ruby has a shortcut for creating an array of words:

```
a = [ 'ant', 'bee', 'cat', 'dog', 'elk' ]
# this is the same:
a = %w{ ant bee cat dog elk }
```

Ruby hashes are similar to arrays. A hash literal uses braces rather than square brackets. The literal must supply two objects for every entry: one for the key, the other for the value. For example, you may want to map musical instruments to their orchestral sections:

```
inst_section = {
  :cello    => 'string',
  :clarinet => 'woodwind',
  :drum     => 'percussion',
  :oboe     => 'woodwind',
  :trumpet  => 'brass',
  :violin   => 'string'
}
```

The thing to the left of the => is the key, and that on the right is the corresponding value. Keys in a particular hash must be unique; if you have two entries for :drum, the last one will *win*. The keys and values in a hash can be arbitrary objects: you can have hashes in which the values are arrays, other hashes, and so on. In Rails, hashes typically use symbols as keys. Many Rails hashes have been subtly modified so that you can use either a string or a symbol interchangeably as a key when inserting and looking up values.

The use of symbols as hash keys is so commonplace that Ruby has a special syntax for it, saving both keystrokes and eyestrain:

```
inst_section = {
  cello:    'string',
  clarinet: 'woodwind',
  drum:     'percussion',
  oboe:     'woodwind',
  trumpet:  'brass',
  violin:   'string'
}
```

Doesn't that look much better?

Feel free to use whichever syntax you like. You can even intermix usages in a single expression. Obviously, you'll need to use the arrow syntax whenever the key is *not* a symbol. One other thing to watch out for: if the *value* is a symbol, you'll need to have at least one space between the colons or else you'll get a syntax error:

```
inst_section = {
  cello:    :string,
  clarinet: :woodwind,
  drum:     :percussion,
  oboe:     :woodwind,
  trumpet:  :brass,
  violin:   :string
}
```

Hashes are indexed using the same square bracket notation as arrays:

```
inst_section[:oboe]    #=> 'woodwind'
inst_section[:cello]   #=> 'string'
inst_section[:bassoon] #=> nil
```

As the preceding example shows, a hash returns nil when indexed by a key it doesn't contain. Normally this is convenient, because nil means false when used in conditional expressions.

You can pass hashes as parameters on method calls. Ruby allows you to omit the braces, but only if the hash is the last parameter of the call. Rails makes extensive use of this feature. The following code fragment shows a two-element hash being passed to the redirect_to() method. Note that this is the same syntax that Ruby 2.0.0 and above use for keyword arguments, but it works with Ruby 1.9.3:

```
redirect_to action: 'show', id: product.id
```

One more data type is worth mentioning: the regular expression.

Regular Expressions

A regular expression lets you specify a *pattern* of characters to be matched in a string. In Ruby, you typically create a regular expression by writing /pattern/ or %r{pattern}.

For example, we can use the regular expression /Perl|Python/ to write a pattern that matches a string containing the text *Perl* or the text *Python.*

The forward slashes delimit the pattern, which consists of the two things we're matching, separated by a vertical bar (|). The bar character means either the thing on the left or the thing on the right—in this case, either *Perl* or

Python. You can use parentheses within patterns, just as you can in arithmetic expressions, so we could also write this pattern as /P(erl|ython)/. Programs typically use the =~ match operator to test strings against regular expressions:

```
if line =~ /P(erl|ython)/
  puts "There seems to be another scripting language here"
end
```

You can specify *repetition* within patterns. /ab+c/ matches a string containing an *a* followed by one or more *b*s, followed by a *c*. Change the plus to an asterisk, and /ab*c/ creates a regular expression that matches one *a*, zero or more *b*s, and one *c*.

Backward slashes start special sequences; most notably, \d matches any digit, \s matches any whitespace character, and \w matches any alphanumeric (*word*) character, \A matches the start of the string and \Z matches the end of the string. A backslash before a wildcard character, for example \., causes the character to be matched as is.

Ruby's regular expressions are a deep and complex subject; this section barely skims the surface. See the PickAxe book for a full discussion.

This book will make only light use of regular expressions.

With that brief introduction to data, let's move on to logic.

Logic

Method calls are statements. Ruby also provides a number of ways to make decisions that affect the repetition and order in which methods are invoked.

Control Structures

Ruby has all the usual control structures, such as if statements and while loops. Java, C, and Perl programmers may well get caught by the lack of braces around the bodies of these statements. Instead, Ruby uses the end keyword to signify the end of a body:

```
if count > 10
  puts "Try again"
elsif tries == 3
  puts "You lose"
else
  puts "Enter a number"
end
```

Similarly, while statements are terminated with end:

```
while weight < 100 and num_pallets <= 30
  pallet = next_pallet()
  weight += pallet.weight
  num_pallets += 1
end
```

Ruby also contains variants of these statements. unless is like if, except that it checks for the condition to *not* be true. Similarly, until is like while, except that the loop continues until the condition evaluates to be true.

Ruby *statement modifiers* are a useful shortcut if the body of an if, unless, while, or until statement is a single expression. Simply write the expression, followed by the modifier keyword and the condition:

```
puts "Danger, Will Robinson" if radiation > 3000
distance = distance * 1.2 while distance < 100
```

Although if statements are fairly common in Ruby applications, newcomers to the Ruby language are often surprised to find that looping constructs are rarely used. *Blocks* and *iterators* often take their place.

Blocks and Iterators

Code blocks are chunks of code between braces or between do...end. A common convention is that people use braces for single-line blocks and do/end for multiline blocks:

```
{ puts "Hello" }        # this is a block

do                      ###
  club.enroll(person)   # and so is this
  person.socialize      #
end                     ###
```

To pass a block to a method, place the block after the parameters (if any) to the method. In other words, put the start of the block at the end of the source line containing the method call. For example, in the following code, the block containing puts "Hi" is associated with the call to the greet() method:

```
greet  { puts "Hi" }
```

If a method call has parameters, they appear before the block:

```
verbose_greet("Dave", "loyal customer")  { puts "Hi" }
```

A method can invoke an associated block one or more times by using the Ruby yield statement. You can think of yield as being something like a method call that calls out to the block associated with the method containing the yield.

You can pass values to the block by giving parameters to yield. Within the block, you list the names of the arguments to receive these parameters between vertical bars (|).

Code blocks appear throughout Ruby applications. Often they're used in conjunction with iterators—methods that return successive elements from some kind of collection, such as an array:

```
animals = %w( ant bee cat dog elk )    # create an array
animals.each {|animal| puts animal }   # iterate over the contents
```

Each integer *N* implements a times() method, which invokes an associated block *N* times:

```
3.times { print "Ho! " }     #=>  Ho! Ho! Ho!
```

The & prefix operator allows a method to capture a passed block as a named parameter:

```
def wrap &b
  print "Santa says: "
  3.times(&b)
  print "\n"
end
wrap { print "Ho! " }
```

Within a block, or a method, control is sequential except when an exception occurs.

Exceptions

Exceptions are objects of the Exception class or its subclasses. The raise method causes an exception to be raised. This interrupts the normal flow through the code. Instead, Ruby searches back through the call stack for code that says it can handle this exception.

Both methods and blocks of code wrapped between begin and end keywords intercept certain classes of exceptions using rescue clauses:

```
begin
  content = load_blog_data(file_name)
rescue BlogDataNotFound
  STDERR.puts "File #{file_name} not found"
rescue BlogDataFormatError
  STDERR.puts "Invalid blog data in #{file_name}"
rescue Exception => exc
  STDERR.puts "General error loading #{file_name}: #{exc.message}"
end
```

rescue clauses can be directly placed on the outermost level of a method definition without needing to enclose the contents in a begin/end block.

That concludes our brief introduction to control flow, and at this point you have the basic building blocks for creating larger structures.

Organizing Structures

Ruby has two basic concepts for organizing methods: classes and modules. We cover each in turn.

Classes

Here's a Ruby class definition:

```
Line 1  class Order < ApplicationRecord
          has_many :line_items
          def self.find_all_unpaid
            self.where('paid = 0')
    5     end
          def total
            sum = 0
            line_items.each {|li| sum += li.total}
            sum
   10     end
        end
```

Class definitions start with the class keyword, followed by the class name (which must start with an uppercase letter). This Order class is defined to be a subclass of the ApplicationRecord class.

Rails makes heavy use of class-level declarations. Here, has_many is a method that's defined by Active Record. It's called as the Order class is being defined. Normally these kinds of methods make assertions about the class, so in this book we call them *declarations*.

Within a class body, you can define class methods and instance methods. Prefixing a method name with self. (as we do on line 3) makes it a class method; it can be called on the class generally. In this case, we can make the following call anywhere in our application:

```
to_collect = Order.find_all_unpaid
```

Objects of a class hold their state in *instance variables*. These variables, whose names all start with @, are available to all the instance methods of a class. Each object gets its own set of instance variables.

Instance variables aren't directly accessible outside the class. To make them available, write methods that return their values:

```ruby
class Greeter
  def initialize(name)
    @name = name
  end

  def name
    @name
  end

  def name=(new_name)
    @name = new_name
  end
end

g = Greeter.new("Barney")
g.name    # => Barney
g.name = "Betty"
g.name    # => Betty
```

Ruby provides convenience methods that write these accessor methods for you (which is great news for folks tired of writing all those getters and setters):

```ruby
class Greeter
  attr_accessor  :name       # create reader and writer methods
  attr_reader    :greeting   # create reader only
  attr_writer    :age        # create writer only
end
```

A class's instance methods are public by default; anyone can call them. You'll probably want to override this for methods that are intended to be used only by other instance methods:

```ruby
class MyClass
  def m1      # this method is public
  end
  protected
  def m2      # this method is protected
  end
  private
  def m3      # this method is private
  end
end
```

The private directive is the strictest; private methods can be called only from within the same instance. Protected methods can be called both in the same instance and by other instances of the same class and its subclasses.

Classes aren't the only organizing structure in Ruby. The other organizing structure is a *module*.

Modules

Modules are similar to classes in that they hold a collection of methods, constants, and other module and class definitions. Unlike with classes, you can't create objects based on modules.

Modules serve two purposes. First, they act as a namespace, letting you define methods whose names won't clash with those defined elsewhere. Second, they allow you to share functionality among classes. If a class *mixes in* a module, that module's methods become available as if they had been defined in the class. Multiple classes can mix in the same module, sharing the module's functionality without using inheritance. You can also mix multiple modules into a single class.

Helper methods are an example of where Rails uses modules. Rails automatically mixes these helper modules into the appropriate view templates. For example, if you wanted to write a helper method that's callable from views invoked by the store controller, you could define the following module in the store_helper.rb file in the app/helpers directory:

```ruby
module StoreHelper
  def capitalize_words(string)
    string.split(' ').map {|word| word.capitalize}.join(' ')
  end
end
```

One module that's part of the standard library of Ruby deserves special mention, given its usage in Rails: YAML.

YAML

YAML[1] is a recursive acronym that stands for YAML Ain't Markup Language. In the context of Rails, YAML is used as a convenient way to define the configuration of things such as databases, test data, and translations. Here's an example:

```yaml
development:
  adapter: sqlite3
  database: db/development.sqlite3
  pool: 5
  timeout: 5000
```

In YAML, indentation is important, so this defines development as having a set of four key-value pairs, separated by colons. While YAML is one way to represent data, particularly when interacting with humans, Ruby provides a more general way for representing data for use by applications.

---

1. http://www.yaml.org/

Marshaling Objects

Ruby can take an object and convert it into a stream of bytes that can be stored outside the application. This process is called *marshaling*. This saved object can later be read by another instance of the application (or by a totally separate application), and a copy of the originally saved object can be reconstituted.

Two potential issues arise when you use marshaling. First, some objects can't be dumped. If the objects to be dumped include bindings, procedure or method objects, instances of the IO class, or singleton objects—or if you try to dump anonymous classes or modules—a TypeError will be raised.

Second, when you load a marshaled object, Ruby needs to know the definition of the class of that object (and of all the objects it contains).

Rails uses marshaling to store session data. If you rely on Rails to dynamically load classes, it's possible that a particular class may not have been defined at the point it reconstitutes session data. For that reason, use the model declaration in your controller to list all models that are marshaled. This preemptively loads the necessary classes to make marshaling work.

Now that you have the Ruby basics down, let's give what we learned a whirl with a slightly larger, annotated example that pulls together a number of concepts. We'll follow that with a walk-through of special features that will help you with your Rails coding.

Pulling It All Together

Let's look at an example of how Rails applies a number of Ruby features together to make the code you need to maintain more declarative. You'll see this example again in *Generating the Scaffold*, on page 72. For now, we'll focus on the Ruby-language aspects of the example:

```ruby
class CreateProducts < ActiveRecord::Migration[5.1]
  def change
    create_table :products do |t|
      t.string :title
      t.text :description
      t.string :image_url
➤     t.decimal :price, precision: 8, scale: 2

      t.timestamps
    end
  end
end
```

Even if you didn't know any Ruby, you'd probably be able to decipher that this code creates a table named products. The fields defined when this table is created include title, description, image_url, and price, as well as a few timestamps (we'll describe these in Chapter 23, *Migrations*, on page 411).

Now let's look at the same example from a Ruby perspective. We define a class named CreateProducts, which inherits from the versioned[2] Migration class from the ActiveRecord module, specifying that compatibility with Rails 5.1 is desired. We define one method, named change(). This method calls the create_table() method (defined in ActiveRecord::Migration), passing it the name of the table in the form of a symbol.

The call to create_table() also passes a block that is to be evaluated before the table is created. This block, when called, is passed an object named t, which is used to accumulate a list of fields. Rails defines a number of methods on this object—methods named after common data types. These methods, when called, simply add a field definition to the ever-accumulating set of names.

The definition of decimal also accepts a number of optional parameters, expressed as a hash.

To someone new to Ruby, this is a lot of heavy machinery thrown at solving such a simple problem. To someone familiar with Ruby, none of this machinery is particularly heavy. In any case, Rails makes extensive use of the facilities provided by Ruby to make defining operations (for example, migration tasks) as simple and as declarative as possible. Even small features of the language, such as optional parentheses and braces, contribute to the overall readability and ease of authoring.

Finally, a number of small features—or, rather, idiomatic combinations of features—are often not immediately obvious to people new to the Ruby language. We close this chapter with them.

Ruby Idioms

A number of individual Ruby features can be combined in interesting ways, and the meaning of such idiomatic usage is often not immediately obvious to people new to the language. We use these common Ruby idioms in this book:

---

2. http://blog.bigbinary.com/2016/03/01/migrations-are-versioned-in-rails-5.html

Methods such as empty! and empty?

Ruby method names can end with an exclamation mark (a *bang* method) or a question mark (a *predicate method*). Bang methods normally do something destructive to the receiver. Predicate methods return true or false, depending on some condition.

a || b

The expression a || b evaluates a. If it isn't false or nil, then evaluation stops, and the expression returns a. Otherwise, the statement returns b. This is a common way of returning a default value if the first value hasn't been set.

a ||= b

The assignment statement supports a set of shortcuts: a op= b is the same as a = a op b. This works for most operators:

```
count += 1          # same as count = count + 1
price *= discount   #          price = price * discount
count ||= 0         #          count = count || 0
```

So, count ||= 0 gives count the value 0 if count is nil or false.

obj = self.new

Sometimes a class method needs to create an instance of that class:

```
class Person < ApplicationRecord
  def self.for_dave
    Person.new(name: 'Dave')
  end
end
```

This works fine, returning a new Person object. But later, someone might subclass our class:

```
class Employee < Person
  # ..
end

dave = Employee.for_dave  # returns a Person
```

The for_dave() method was hardwired to return a Person object, so that's what's returned by Employee.for_dave. Using self.new instead returns a new object of the receiver's class, Employee.

lambda

> The lambda operator converts a block into an object of type Proc. An alternative syntax, introduced in Ruby 1.9, is ->. As a matter of style, the Rails team prefers the latter syntax. You can see example usages of this operator in *Scopes*, on page 336:

require File.expand_path('../../config/environment', __FILE__)

> Ruby's require method loads an external source file into our application. This is used to include library code and classes that our application relies on. In normal use, Ruby finds these files by searching in a list of directories, the LOAD_PATH.

> Sometimes we need to be specific about which file to include. We can do that by giving require a full filesystem path. The problem is, we don't know what that path will be—our users could install our code anywhere.

> Wherever our application ends up getting installed, the relative path between the file doing the requiring and the target file will be the same. Knowing this, we can construct the absolute path to the target by using the File.expand_path() method, passing in the relative path to the target file, as well as the absolute path to the file doing the requiring (available in the special __FILE__ variable).

In addition, the web has many good resources that show Ruby idioms and Ruby gotchas. Here are a few of them:

- http://www.ruby-lang.org/en/documentation/ruby-from-other-languages/
- http://en.wikipedia.org/wiki/Ruby_programming_language
- http://www.zenspider.com/Languages/Ruby/QuickRef.html

By this point, you have a firm foundation to build on. You've installed Rails, verified that you have things working with a simple application, read a brief description of what Rails is, and reviewed (or for some of you, learned for the first time) the basics of the Ruby language. Now it's time to put this knowledge in place to build a larger application.

Part II

Building an Application

In this chapter, you'll see:
- Incremental development
- Use cases, page flow, and data
- Priorities

CHAPTER 5

The Depot Application

We could mess around all day hacking together simple test applications, but that won't help us pay the bills. So, let's sink our teeth into something meatier. Let's create a web-based shopping cart application called Depot.

Does the world need another shopping cart application? Nope, but that hasn't stopped hundreds of developers from writing one. Why should we be different?

More seriously, it turns out that our shopping cart will illustrate many of the features of Rails development. You'll see how to create maintenance pages, link database tables, handle sessions, create forms, and wrangle modern JavaScript. Over the next twelve chapters, we'll also touch on peripheral topics such as unit and system testing, security, and page layout.

Incremental Development

We'll be developing this application incrementally. We won't attempt to specify everything before we start coding. Instead, we'll work out enough of a specification to let us start and then immediately create some functionality. We'll try ideas, gather feedback, and continue with another cycle of minidesign and development.

This style of coding isn't always applicable. It requires close cooperation with the application's users, because we want to gather feedback as we go along. We might make mistakes, or the client might ask for one thing at first and later want something different. It doesn't matter what the reason is. The earlier we discover we've made a mistake, the less expensive it'll be to fix that mistake. All in all, with this style of development, there's a lot of change as we go along.

Because of this, we need to use a toolset that doesn't penalize us for changing our minds. If we decide we need to add a new column to a database table or change the navigation among pages, we need to be able to get in there and do it without a bunch of coding or configuration hassle. As you'll see, Ruby on Rails shines when it comes to dealing with change. It's an ideal agile programming environment.

Along the way, we'll be building and maintaining a corpus of tests. These tests will ensure that the application is always doing what we intend to do. Not only does Rails enable the creation of such tests, but it even provides you with an initial set of tests each time you define a new controller.

On with the application.

What Depot Does

Let's start by jotting down an outline specification for the Depot application. We'll look at the high-level use cases and sketch out the flow through the web pages. We'll also try working out what data the application needs (acknowledging that our initial guesses will likely be wrong).

Use Cases

A *use case* is simply a statement about how some entity uses a system. Consultants invent these kinds of phrases to label things we've known all along. (It's a perversion of business life that fancy words always cost more than plain ones, even though the plain ones are more valuable.)

Depot's use cases are simple (some would say tragically so). We start off by identifying two different roles or actors: the *buyer* and the *seller*.

The buyer uses Depot to browse the products we have to sell, select some to purchase, and supply the information needed to create an order.

The seller uses Depot to maintain a list of products to sell, to determine the orders that are awaiting shipment, and to mark orders as shipped. (The seller also uses Depot to make scads of money and retire to a tropical island, but that's the subject of another book.)

For now, that's all the detail we need. We *could* go into excruciating detail about what it means to maintain products and what constitutes an order ready to ship, but why bother? If some details aren't obvious, we'll discover them soon enough as we reveal successive iterations of our work to the customer.

Speaking of getting feedback, let's get some right now. Let's make sure our initial (admittedly sketchy) use cases are on the mark by asking our users. Assuming the use cases pass muster, let's work out how the application will work from the perspectives of its various users.

Page Flow

We always like to have an idea of the main pages in our applications and to understand roughly how users navigate among them. This early in the development, these page flows are likely to be incomplete, but they still help us focus on what needs doing and know how actions are sequenced.

Some folks like to use Photoshop, Word, or (shudder) HTML to mock up web application page flows. We like using a pencil and paper. It's quicker, and the customer gets to play too, grabbing the pencil and scribbling alterations right on the paper.

The first sketch of the buyer flow is shown in the following figure.

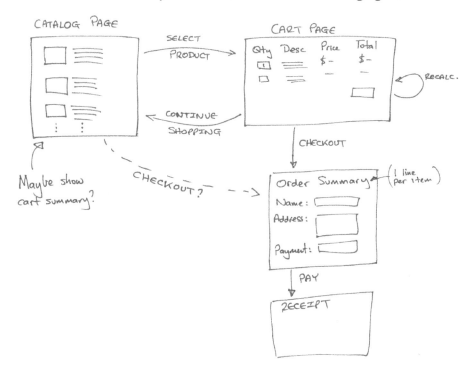

It's pretty traditional. The buyer sees a catalog page, from which he selects one product at a time. Each product selected gets added to the cart, and the cart is displayed after each selection. The buyer can continue shopping using the catalog pages or check out and buy the contents of the cart. During checkout, we capture contact and payment details and then display a receipt page. We don't yet know how we're going to handle payment, so those details are fairly vague in the flow.

The seller flow, shown in the next figure, is also fairly basic. After logging in, the seller sees a menu letting her create or view a product or ship existing orders. When viewing a product, the seller can optionally edit the product information or delete the product entirely.

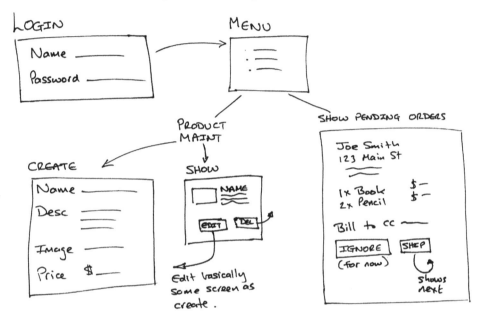

The shipping option is simplistic. It displays each order that hasn't yet been shipped, one order per page. The seller can choose to skip to the next or can ship the order, using the information from the page as appropriate.

The shipping function is clearly not going to survive long in the real world, but shipping is also one of those areas where reality is often stranger than you might think. Overspecify it up front, and we're likely to get it wrong. For now, let's leave it as it is, confident that we can change it as the user gains experience using our application.

Data

Finally, we need to think about the data we're going to be working with.

Notice that we're not using words such as *schema* or *classes* here. We're also not talking about databases, tables, keys, and the like. We're talking about data. At this stage in the development, we don't know if we'll even be using a database.

Based on the use cases and the flows, it seems likely that we'll be working with the data shown in the figure on page 69. Again, using pencil and paper seems a whole lot easier than some fancy tool, but use whatever works for you.

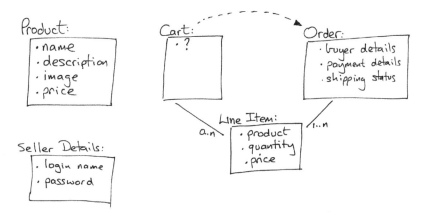

Working on the data diagram raised a couple of questions. As the user buys items, we'll need somewhere to keep the list of products they bought, so we added a cart. But apart from its use as a transient place to keep this product list, the cart seems to be something of a ghost—we couldn't find anything meaningful to store in it. To reflect this uncertainty, we put a question mark inside the cart's box in the diagram. We're assuming this uncertainty will get resolved as we implement Depot.

Coming up with the high-level data also raised the question of what information should go into an order. Again, we chose to leave this fairly open for now. We'll refine this further as we start showing our early iterations to the customer.

General Recovery Advice

Everything in this book has been tested. If you follow along with this scenario precisely, using the recommended version of Rails and SQLite 3 on Linux, Mac OS X, or Windows, everything should work as described. However, deviations from this path can occur. Typos happen to the best of us, and not only are side explorations possible, but they're positively encouraged. Be aware that this might lead you to strange places. Don't be afraid: specific recovery actions for common problems appear in the specific sections where such problems often occur. A few additional general suggestions are included here.

You should only ever need to restart the server in the few places where doing so is noted in the book. But if you ever get truly stumped, restarting the server might be worth trying.

A "magic" command worth knowing, explained in detail in Part III, is bin/rails db:migrate:redo. It'll undo and reapply the last migration.

If your server won't accept some input on a form, refresh the form on your browser and resubmit it.

Finally, you might have noticed that we've duplicated the product's price in the line item data. Here we're breaking the "initially, keep it simple" rule slightly, but it's a transgression based on experience. If the price of a product changes, that price change shouldn't be reflected in the line item price of currently open orders, so each line item needs to reflect the price of the product at the time the order was made.

Again, at this point we'll double-check with the customer that we're still on the right track. (The customer was most likely sitting in the room with us while we drew these three diagrams.)

Let's Code

So, after sitting down with the customer and doing some preliminary analysis, we're ready to start using a computer for development! We'll be working from our original three diagrams, but the chances are pretty good that we'll be throwing them away fairly quickly—they'll become outdated as we gather feedback. Interestingly, that's why we didn't spend too long on them; it's easier to throw something away if you didn't spend a long time creating it.

In the chapters that follow, we'll start developing the application based on our current understanding. However, before we turn that page, we have to answer one more question: what should we do first?

We like to work with the customer so we can jointly agree on priorities. In this case, we'd point out to her that it's hard to develop anything else until we have some basic products defined in the system, so we suggest spending a couple of hours getting the initial version of the product maintenance functionality up and running. And, of course, the client would agree.

In this chapter, you'll see:
- Creating a new application
- Configuring the database
- Creating models and controllers
- Adding a stylesheet
- Updating a layout and a view

CHAPTER 6

Task A: Creating the Application

Our first development task is to create the web interface that lets us maintain our product information—create new products, edit existing products, delete unwanted ones, and so on. We'll develop this application in small iterations, where "small" means measured in minutes. Typically, our iterations involve multiple steps, as in iteration C, which has steps C1, C2, C3, and so on. In this case, the iteration has two steps. Let's get started.

Iteration A1: Creating the Product Maintenance Application

At the heart of the Depot application is a database. Getting this installed and configured and tested before proceeding will prevent a lot of headaches. If you aren't sure what you want, take the defaults, and it'll go easily. If you know what you want, Rails makes it easy for you to describe your configuration.

Creating a Rails Application

In *Creating a New Application*, on page 23, you saw how to create a new Rails application. We'll do the same thing here. Go to a command prompt and type rails new followed by the name of our project. Here, our project is called depot, so make sure you're not inside an existing application directory, and type this:

```
work> rails new depot
```

We see a bunch of output scroll by. When it has finished, we find that a new directory, depot, has been created. That's where we'll be doing our work:

```
work> cd depot
depot> ls -p
Gemfile         Rakefile    config/     lib/            public/     vendor/
Gemfile.lock    app/        config.ru   log/            test/
README.md       bin/        db/         package.json    tmp/
```

Of course, Windows users need to use dir /w instead of ls -p.

Creating the Database

For this application, we'll use the open source SQLite database (which you'll need if you're following along with the code). We're using SQLite version 3 here.

SQLite 3 is the default database for Rails development and was installed along with Rails in Chapter 1, *Installing Rails*, on page 3. With SQLite 3, no steps are required to create a database, and we have no special user accounts or passwords to deal with. So, now you get to experience one of the benefits of going with the flow (or, convention over configuration, as the Rails folks say...ad nauseam).

If it's important to you to use a database server other than SQLite 3, the commands to create the database and grant permissions will be different. You can find some helpful hints in the database configuration section of Configuring Rails Applications in the Ruby on Rails Guides.[1]

Generating the Scaffold

Back in our initial guess at application data on page 69, we sketched out the basic content of the products table. Now let's turn that into reality. We need to create a database table and a Rails *model* that lets our application use that table, a number of *views* to make up the user interface, and a *controller* to orchestrate the application.

So, let's create the model, views, controller, and migration for our products table. With Rails, you can do all that with one command by asking Rails to generate a *scaffold* for a given model. Note that on the command line that follows, we use the singular form, Product. In Rails, a model is automatically mapped to a database table whose name is the plural form of the model's class. In our case, we ask for a model called Product, so Rails associates it with the table called products. (And how will it find that table? The development entry in config/database.yml tells Rails where to look for it. For SQLite 3 users, this'll be a file in the db directory.)

Note that that command is too wide to fit comfortably on the page. To enter a command on multiple lines, put a backslash as the last character on all but the last line, and you'll be prompted for more input. Windows users need to substitute a caret (^) for the backslash at the end of the first line and a backslash for the forward slash in bin/rails:

---

1. http://guides.rubyonrails.org/configuring.html#configuring-a-database

```
depot> bin/rails generate scaffold Product \
        title:string description:text image_url:string price:decimal
  invoke  active_record
  create    db/migrate/20170425000001_create_products.rb
  create    app/models/product.rb
  invoke    test_unit
  create      test/models/product_test.rb
  create      test/fixtures/products.yml
  invoke  resource_route
   route    resources :products
  invoke  scaffold_controller
  create    app/controllers/products_controller.rb
  invoke    erb
  create      app/views/products
  create      app/views/products/index.html.erb
  create      app/views/products/edit.html.erb
  create      app/views/products/show.html.erb
  create      app/views/products/new.html.erb
  create      app/views/products/_form.html.erb
  invoke    test_unit
  create      test/controllers/products_controller_test.rb
  invoke    helper
  create      app/helpers/products_helper.rb
  invoke      test_unit
  invoke    jbuilder
  create      app/views/products/index.json.jbuilder
  create      app/views/products/show.json.jbuilder
  create      app/views/products/_product.json.jbuilder
  create  test_unit
  create    test/system/products_test.rb
  invoke  assets
  invoke    coffee
  create      app/assets/javascripts/products.coffee
  invoke    scss
  create      app/assets/stylesheets/products.scss
  invoke  scss
  create    app/assets/stylesheets/scaffolds.scss
```

The generator creates a bunch of files. The one we're interested in first is the *migration* one, namely, 20170425000001_create_products.rb.

A migration represents a change we either want to make to a database as a whole or to the data contained within the database, and it's expressed in a source file in database-independent terms. These changes can update both the database schema and the data in the database tables. We apply these migrations to update our database, and we can unapply them to roll our database back. We have a whole section on migrations starting in Chapter 23, *Migrations*, on page 411. For now, we'll just use them without too much more comment.

The migration has a UTC-based timestamp prefix (20170425000001), a name (create_products), and a file extension (.rb, because it's Ruby code).

The timestamp prefix that you see will be different. In fact, the timestamps used in this book are clearly fictitious. Typically, your timestamps won't be consecutive; instead, they'll reflect the time the migration was created.

Applying the Migration

Although we've already told Rails about the basic data types of each property, let's refine the definition of the price to have eight digits of significance and two digits after the decimal point:

```
rails51/depot_a/db/migrate/20170425000001_create_products.rb
class CreateProducts < ActiveRecord::Migration[5.1]
  def change
    create_table :products do |t|
      t.string :title
      t.text :description
      t.string :image_url
      t.decimal :price, precision: 8, scale: 2

      t.timestamps
    end
  end
end
```

Now that we're done with our changes, we need to get Rails to apply this migration to our development database. We do this by using the bin/rails db:migrate command:

```
depot> bin/rails db:migrate
==  20170425000001 CreateProducts: migrating ====================================
-- create_table(:products)
   -> 0.0027s
==  CreateProducts: migrated (0.0023s) ==========================================
```

And that's it. Rails looks for all the migrations not yet applied to the database and applies them. In our case, the products table is added to the database defined by the development section of the database.yml file.

OK, all the groundwork has been done. We set up our Depot application as a Rails project. We created the development database and configured our application to be able to connect to it. We created a products controller and a Product model and used a migration to create the corresponding products table. And a number of views have been created for us. It's time to see all this in action.

Seeing the List of Products

With three commands, we've created an application and a database (or a table inside an existing database, if you chose something besides SQLite 3). Before we worry too much about what happened behind the scenes here, let's try our shiny new application.

First, we start a local server, supplied with Rails:

```
depot> bin/rails server
=> Booting Puma
=> Rails 5.1.3 application starting in development on http://localhost:3000
=> Run `rails server -h` for more startup options
Puma starting in single mode...
* Version 3.9.1 (ruby 2.4.1-p111), codename: Private Caller
* Min threads: 5, max threads: 5
* Environment: development
* Listening on tcp://localhost:3000
Use Ctrl-C to stop
```

As it did with our demo application on page 23, this command starts a web server on our local host, port 3000. If you get an error saying Address already in use when you try to run the server, that means you already have a Rails server running on your machine. If you've been following along with the examples in the book, that might well be the Hello, World! application from Chapter 4. Find its console and kill the server using Ctrl-C. If you're running on Windows, you might see the prompt Terminate batch job (Y/N)?. If so, respond with y.

Let's connect to our application. Remember, the URL we give to our browser is http://localhost:3000/products, which has both the port number (3000) and the name of the controller in lowercase (products). The application looks like the following screenshot.

Products

Title Description Image url Price

New Product

That's pretty boring. It's showing us an empty list of products. Let's add some. Click the New Product link. A form should appear, as shown in the following screenshot.

New Product

Title

Description

Image url

Price

Create Product

Back

These forms are simply HTML templates, like the ones you created in *Hello, Rails!*, on page 26. In fact, we can modify them. Let's change the number of rows and columns in the Description field:

rails51/depot_a/app/views/products/_form.html.erb

```erb
<%= form_with(model: product, local: true) do |form| %>
  <% if product.errors.any? %>
    <div id="error_explanation">
      <h2><%= pluralize(product.errors.count, "error") %>
      prohibited this product from being saved:</h2>

      <ul>
      <% product.errors.full_messages.each do |message| %>
        <li><%= message %></li>
      <% end %>
      </ul>
    </div>
  <% end %>

  <div class="field">
    <%= form.label :title %>
    <%= form.text_field :title, id: :product_title %>
  </div>
```

```
<div class="field">
  <%= form.label :description %>
  <%= form.text_area :description, id: :product_description, rows: 10, cols: 60 %>
</div>

<div class="field">
  <%= form.label :image_url %>
  <%= form.text_field :image_url, id: :product_image_url %>
</div>

<div class="field">
  <%= form.label :price %>
  <%= form.text_field :price, id: :product_price %>
</div>

<div class="actions">
  <%= form.submit %>
</div>
<% end %>
```

We'll explore this more in Chapter 8, *Task C: Catalog Display*, on page 103. But for now, we've adjusted one field to taste, so let's fill it in, as shown in the following screenshot (note the use of HTML tags in the description—this is intentional and will make more sense later).

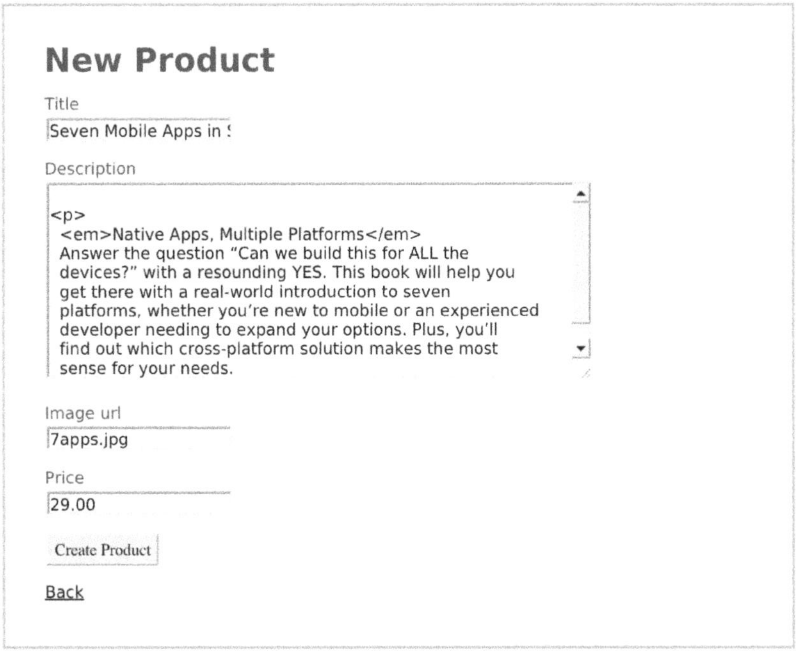

Click the Create button, and you should see that the new product was successfully created. If you now click the Back link, you should see the new product in the list, as shown in the screenshot on page 78.

Perhaps it isn't the prettiest interface, but it works, and we can show it to our client for approval. She can play with the other links (showing details, editing existing products, and so on). We explain to her that this is only a first step—we know it's rough, but we wanted to get her feedback early. (And four commands probably count as early in anyone's book.)

At this point, we've accomplished a lot with only four commands. Before we move on, let's try one more command:

```
bin/rails test
```

Included in the output should be a line that says 0 failures, 0 errors. This is for the model and controller tests that Rails generates along with the scaffolding. They're minimal at this point, but simply knowing that they're there and that they pass should give you confidence. As you proceed through these chapters in Part II, you're encouraged to run this command frequently, because it'll help you spot and track down errors. We'll cover this more in *Iteration B2: Unit Testing of Models*, on page 91.

Note that if you've used a database other than SQLite 3, this step may have failed. Check your database.yml file.

Iteration A2: Making Prettier Listings

Our customer has one more request. (Customers always seem to have one more request, don't they?) The listing of all the products is ugly. Can we pretty it up a bit? And, while we're in there, can we also display the product image along with the image URL?

We're faced with a dilemma here. As developers, we're trained to respond to these kinds of requests with a sharp intake of breath, a knowing shake of the head, and a murmured, "You want what?" At the same time, we also like to show off a bit. In the end, the fact that it's fun to make these kinds of changes using Rails wins out, and we fire up our trusty editor.

Before we get too far, though, it would be nice if we had a consistent set of test data to work with. We *could* use our scaffold-generated interface and type data in from the browser. However, if we did this, future developers working on our codebase would have to do the same. And if we were working as part of a team on this project, each member of the team would have to enter his or her own data. It would be nice if we could load the data into our table in a more controlled way. It turns out that we can. Rails has the ability to import seed data.

To start, we simply modify the file in the db directory named seeds.rb.

We then add the code to populate the products table. This uses the create!() method of the Product model. The following is an extract from that file. Rather than type the file by hand, you might want to download the file from the sample code available online.[2]

While you're there, copy the images into the app/assets/images directory in your application.[3] Be warned: this seeds.rb script removes existing data from the products table before loading the new data. You might not want to run it if you've just spent several hours typing your own data into your application!

```
rails51/depot_a/db/seeds.rb
Product.delete_all
# . . .
Product.create!(title: 'Seven Mobile Apps in Seven Weeks',
  description:
    %{<p>
      <em>Native Apps, Multiple Platforms</em>
      Answer the question "Can we build this for ALL the devices?" with a
      resounding YES. This book will help you get there with a real-world
      introduction to seven platforms, whether you're new to mobile or an
      experienced developer needing to expand your options. Plus, you'll find
      out which cross-platform solution makes the most sense for your needs.
      </p>},
  image_url: '7apps.jpg',
  price: 26.00)
# . . .
```

(Note that this code uses %{...}. This is an alternative syntax for double-quoted string literals, convenient for use with long strings. Note also that because it uses the Rails create!() method, it'll raise an exception if records can't be inserted because of validation errors.)

---

2.   https://media.pragprog.com/titles/rails51/code/rails51/depot_a/db/seeds.rb

3.   https://media.pragprog.com/titles/rails51/code/rails51/depot_a/app/assets/images/

To populate your products table with test data, run the following command:

```
depot> bin/rails db:seed
```

Now let's get the product listing tidied up. This has three pieces: defining a set of style rules, connecting these rules to the page by defining an HTML class attribute on the page, and changing the HTML to make styling the page easier.

We need somewhere to put our style definitions. Rails has a convention for this, and the generate scaffold command that we previously issued has already laid all of the necessary groundwork. As such, we can proceed to fill in the currently empty products.scss stylesheet in the app/assets/stylesheets directory:

```scss
rails51/depot_a/app/assets/stylesheets/products.scss
// Place all the styles related to the Products controller here.
// They will automatically be included in application.css.
// You can use Sass (SCSS) here: http://sass-lang.com/
.products {
  margin: 0;
  padding: 0.5em;
  a {
    padding: 0.354em 0.5em;
    border-radius: 0.354em;
  }
  table {
    border-collapse: collapse;
  }
  td {
    padding: 0.5em;
    margin: 0;
  }

  tr.list_line_odd {
    background-color: #effeef;
  }

  td.image {
    // Hide this on mobile devices
    display: none;

    // Assume anything bigger than 30em
    // is a non-mobile device and can
    // fit the image.
    @media (min-width: 30em) {
      display: block;
      img {
        height: 11.3em;
      }
    }
  }
}
```

```
      td.description {
        h1 {
          font-size: 1.4em;
        }
      }

      td.actions {
        ul {
          padding: 0;
          list-style: none;
          li {
            padding: 0.5em 0.5em;
          }
        }
      }

      tfoot {
        td {
          padding: 0.5em 0;
        }
      }
    }
```

If you choose to download this file, make sure that the timestamp on the file is updated. If the timestamp isn't updated, Rails won't pick up the changes until the server is restarted. You can update the timestamp by going into your favorite editor and saving the file. On Mac OS X and Linux, you can use the touch command.

Look closely at this stylesheet and you'll see that CSS rules are nested, in that the rule for li is defined *inside* the rule for ul, which is itself *inside* the rule for td.actions. This tends to make rules less repetitive and therefore easier to read, write, understand, and maintain.

At this point you're familiar with files ending with .erb being preprocessed for embedded Ruby expressions and statements. If you note that this file ends with .scss, you might guess that the file is preprocessed as *Sassy CSS* before being served as CSS.[4] And you'd be right!

Again, like ERB, SCSS doesn't interfere with writing correct CSS. What SCSS does is provide additional syntax that makes your stylesheets easier to author and easier to maintain. All of this is converted for you by SCSS to standard CSS that your browser understands. You can find out more about SCSS in *Pragmatic Guide to Sass 3 [CC16]*.

---

4. http://sass-lang.com/

Finally, we need to define the products class used by this stylesheet. If you look at the .html.erb files we've created so far, you won't find any reference to stylesheets. You won't even find the HTML <head> section where such references would normally live. Instead, Rails keeps a separate file that's used to create a standard page environment for the entire application. This file, called application.html.erb, is a Rails layout and lives in the layouts directory:

```
rails51/depot_a/app/views/layouts/application.html.erb
<!DOCTYPE html>
<html>
  <head>
    <title>Depot</title>
    <%= csrf_meta_tags %>

    <%= stylesheet_link_tag    'application', media: 'all',
    'data-turbolinks-track': 'reload' %>
    <%= javascript_include_tag 'application', 'data-turbolinks-track': 'reload' %>
  </head>

  <body>
➤    <main class='<%= controller.controller_name %>'>
➤      <%= yield %>
➤    </main>

  </body>
</html>
```

You'll note we've wrapped the content in a <main> tag that has a CSS class of the current controller. This means that when we are rendering a product listing, it will have the CSS class products, and when we render an order, it'll have the class orders. This allows us to target our CSS, because Rails includes all CSS in app/assets/stylesheets on every page, no matter what. If we want to apply a style to, say, a table header only on order pages, we can write .orders th { «css» } and—even though that CSS will be included on *non*-orders pages —it won't apply, because the top-level element won't have the class orders.

Now that we have all the stylesheets in place, we'll use a table-based template, editing the index.html.erb file in app/views/products and replacing the scaffold-generated view:

```
rails51/depot_a/app/views/products/index.html.erb
<% if notice %>
  <aside id="notice"><%= notice %></aside>
<% end %>

<h1>Products</h1>

<table>
  <tfoot>
    <tr>
```

```
    <td colspan="3">
      <%= link_to 'New product', new_product_path %>
    </td>
  </tr>
</tfoot>
<tbody>
  <% @products.each do |product| %>
    <tr class="<%= cycle('list_line_odd', 'list_line_even') %>">
      <td class="image">
        <%= image_tag(product.image_url, class: 'list_image') %>
      </td>
      <td class="description">
        <h1><%= product.title %></h1>
        <p>
          <%= truncate(strip_tags(product.description),
                       length: 80) %>
        </p>
      </td>
      <td class="actions">
        <ul>
          <li><%= link_to 'Show', product %></li>
          <li><%= link_to 'Edit', edit_product_path(product) %></li>
          <li>
            <%= link_to 'Destroy',
                        product,
                        method: :delete,
                        data: { confirm: 'Are you sure?' } %>
          </li>
        </ul>
      </td>
    </tr>
  <% end %>
</tbody>
</table>
```

This template uses a number of built-in Rails features:

- The rows in the listing have alternating background colors. The Rails helper method called does this by setting the CSS class of each row to either list_line_even or list_line_odd, automatically toggling between the two style names on successive lines.

- The truncate() helper is used to display the first eighty characters of the description. But before we call truncate(), we call strip_tags() to remove the HTML tags from the description.

- Look at the link_to 'Destroy' line. See how it has the parameter data: { confirm: 'Are you sure?' }. If you click this link, Rails arranges for your browser to pop up a dialog box asking for confirmation before following the link and deleting the product. (Also, see the sidebar on page 85 for an inside scoop on this action.)

We loaded some test data into the database, we rewrote the index.html.erb file that displays the listing of products, we filled in the products.scss stylesheet, and that stylesheet was loaded into our page by the application.html.erb layout file. Now let's bring up a browser and point to http://localhost:3000/products. The resulting product listing might look something like the following screenshot.

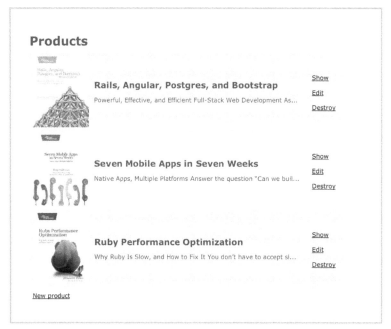

So we proudly show our customer her new product listing and she's pleased. Now it's time to create the storefront.

What We Just Did

In this chapter, we laid the groundwork for our store application:

- We created a development database.

- We used a migration to create and modify the schema in our development database.

- We created the products table and used the scaffold generator to write an application to maintain it.

- We updated an application-wide layout as well as a controller-specific view to show a list of products.

What we've done didn't require much effort, and it got us up and running quickly. Databases are vital to this application but need not be scary. In fact, in many cases we can defer the selection of the database and get started using the default that Rails provides.

Getting the model right is more important at this stage. As you'll see, selection of data types doesn't always fully capture the *essence* of all the properties of the model, even in this small application, so that's what we'll tackle next.

What's with method: :delete?

You may have noticed that the scaffold-generated Destroy link includes the method: :delete parameter. This parameter determines which method is called in the ProductsController class and also affects which HTTP method is used.

Browsers use HTTP to talk with servers. HTTP defines a set of verbs that browsers can employ and defines when each can be used. A regular hyperlink, for example, uses an HTTP GET request. A GET request is defined by HTTP as a means of retrieving data and therefore isn't supposed to have any side effects. Using the method parameter in this way indicates that an HTTP DELETE method should be used for this hyperlink. Rails uses this information to determine which action in the controller to route this request to.

Note that when used within a browser, Rails substitutes the HTTP POST method for PUT, PATCH, and DELETE methods and in the process tacks on an additional parameter so that the router can determine the original intent. Either way, the request isn't cached or triggered by web crawlers.

Playtime

Here's some stuff to try on your own:

- We created tables in our database using a migration. Try examining the tables directly by running bin/rails dbconsole. This will put you directly into the SQLite database that the app uses. Type .help and hit Return to see the commands you can run to examine the database. If you know SQL, you can execute SQL in here as well.

- If you're feeling frisky, you can experiment with rolling back the migration. Type the following:

```
depot> bin/rails db:rollback
```

Your schema will be transported back in time, and the products table will be gone. Calling bin/rails db:migrate again will re-create it. You'll also want to reload the seed data. More information can be found in Chapter 23, *Migrations*, on page 411.

- We mentioned version control in *Version Control*, on page 17, and now would be a great point at which to save your work. Should you happen to choose Git (highly recommended, by the way), you need to do a tiny bit of configuration first; basically, all you need to do is provide your name and email address:

```
depot> git config --global --add user.name "Sam Ruby"
depot> git config --global --add user.email rubys@intertwingly.net
```

You can verify the configuration with the following command:

```
depot> git config --global --list
```

Rails also provides a file named .gitignore, which tells Git which files are not to be version-controlled:

```
rails51/depot_a/.gitignore
# Ignore bundler config.
/.bundle

# Ignore the default SQLite database.
/db/*.sqlite3
/db/*.sqlite3-journal

# Ignore all logfiles and tempfiles.
/log/*
/tmp/*
!/log/.keep
!/tmp/.keep

/node_modules
/yarn-error.log

.byebug_history
```

Note that because this filename begins with a dot, Unix-based operating systems won't show it by default in directory listings. Use ls -a to see it.

At this point, you're fully configured. The only tasks that remain are to add all the files and commit them with a commit message (note that Rails has initialized our repository with git init already):

```
depot> git add .
depot> git commit -m "Depot Scaffold"
```

Being fully configured may not seem very exciting, but it does mean you're free to experiment. If you overwrite or delete a file that you didn't mean to, you can always get back to this point by issuing a single command:

```
depot> git checkout .
```

In this chapter, you'll see:
• Performing validation and error reporting
• Unit testing

CHAPTER 7

Task B: Validation and Unit Testing

At this point, we have an initial model for a product, as well as a complete maintenance application for this data provided for us by Rails scaffolding. In this chapter, we're going to focus on making the model more bulletproof—as in, making sure that errors in the data provided never get committed to the database—before we proceed to other aspects of the Depot application in subsequent chapters.

Iteration B1: Validating!

While playing with the results of iteration A1, our client noticed something. If she entered an invalid price or forgot to set up a product description, the application happily accepted the form and added a line to the database. A missing description is embarrassing, and a price of $0.00 costs her actual money, so she asked that we add validation to the application. No product should be allowed in the database if it has an empty title or description field, an invalid URL for the image, or an invalid price.

So, where do we put the validation? The model layer is the gatekeeper between the world of code and the database. Nothing to do with our application comes out of the database or gets stored into the database that doesn't first go through the model. This makes models an ideal place to put validations; it doesn't matter whether the data comes from a form or from some programmatic manipulation in our application. If a model checks it before writing to the database, the database will be protected from bad data.

Let's look at the source code of the model class (in app/models/product.rb):

```
class Product < ApplicationRecord
end
```

Adding our validation should be fairly clean. Let's start by validating that the text fields all contain something before a row is written to the database. We do this by adding some code to the existing model:

```
validates :title, :description, :image_url, presence: true
```

The validates() method is the standard Rails validator. It checks one or more model fields against one or more conditions.

presence: true tells the validator to check that each of the named fields is present and that its contents aren't empty. The following screenshot shows what happens if we try to submit a new product with none of the fields filled in. Try it by visiting http://localhost:3000/products/new and submitting the form without entering any data. It's pretty impressive: the fields with errors are highlighted, and the errors are summarized in a nice list at the top of the form. That's not bad for one line of code. You might also have noticed that after editing and saving the product.rb file, you didn't have to restart the application to test your changes. The same reloading that caused Rails to notice the earlier change to our schema also means it'll always use the latest version of our code.

We'd also like to validate that the price is a valid, positive number. We'll use the delightfully named numericality() option to verify that the price is a valid number. We also pass the rather verbosely named :greater_than_or_equal_to option a value of 0.01:

```
validates :price, numericality: { greater_than_or_equal_to: 0.01 }
```

Now, if we add a product with an invalid price, the appropriate message will appear, as shown in the following screenshot.

Why test against one cent, rather than zero? Well, it's possible to enter a number such as 0.001 into this field. Because the database stores just two digits after the decimal point, this would end up being zero in the database, even though it would pass the validation if we compared against zero. Checking that the number is at least one cent ensures that only correct values end up being stored.

We have two more items to validate. First, we want to make sure that each product has a unique title. One more line in the Product model will do this. The uniqueness validation will perform a check to ensure that no other row in the products table has the same title as the row we're about to save:

```
validates :title, uniqueness: true
```

Lastly, we need to validate that the URL entered for the image is valid. We'll do this by using the format option, which matches a field against a regular expression. For now, let's just check that the URL ends with one of .gif, .jpg, or .png:

```
validates :image_url, allow_blank: true, format: {
  with:    %r{\.(gif|jpg|png)\Z}i,
  message: 'must be a URL for GIF, JPG or PNG image.'
}
```

The regular expression matches the string against a literal dot, followed by one of three choices, followed by the end of the string. Be sure to use vertical bars to separate options, and backslashes before the dot and the uppercase Z. If you need a refresher on regular expression syntax, see *Regular Expressions*, on page 52.

Note that we use the allow_blank option to avoid getting multiple error messages when the field is blank.

Later, we'd probably want to change this form to let the user select from a list of available images, but we'd still want to keep the validation to prevent malicious folks from submitting bad data directly.

So, in a couple of minutes we've added validations that check the following:

- The title, description, and image URL fields aren't empty.
- The price is a valid number not less than $0.01.
- The title is unique among all products.
- The image URL looks reasonable.

Your updated Product model should look like this:

```
rails51/depot_b/app/models/product.rb
class Product < ApplicationRecord
  validates :title, :description, :image_url, presence: true
  validates :title, uniqueness: true
  validates :image_url, allow_blank: true, format: {
    with:    %r{\.(gif|jpg|png)\Z}i,
    message: 'must be a URL for GIF, JPG or PNG image.'
  }
  validates :price, numericality: { greater_than_or_equal_to: 0.01 }
end
```

Nearing the end of this cycle, we ask our customer to play with the application, and she's a lot happier. It took only a few minutes, but the simple act of adding validation has made the product maintenance pages seem a lot more solid.

Iteration B2: Unit Testing of Models

One of the joys of the Rails framework is that it has support for testing baked right in from the start of every project. As you've seen, from the moment you create a new application using the rails command, Rails starts generating a test infrastructure for you. Let's take a peek inside the models subdirectory to see what's already there:

```
depot> ls test/models
product_test.rb
```

product_test.rb is the file that Rails created to hold the unit tests for the model we created earlier with the generate script. This is a good start, but Rails can help us only so much. Let's see what kind of test goodies Rails generated inside test/models/product_test.rb when we generated that model:

```
rails51/depot_a/test/models/product_test.rb
require 'test_helper'

class ProductTest < ActiveSupport::TestCase
  # test "the truth" do
  #   assert true
  # end
end
```

The generated ProductTest is a subclass of ActiveSupport::TestCase[1]. The fact that ActiveSupport::TestCase is a subclass of the MiniTest::Test class tells us that Rails generates tests based on the MiniTest[2] framework that comes preinstalled with Ruby. This is good news, because it means if we've already been testing our Ruby programs with MiniTest tests (and why wouldn't we be?), we can build on that knowledge to test Rails applications. If you're new to MiniTest, don't worry. We'll take it slow.

Inside this test case, Rails generated a single commented-out test called "the truth". The test...do syntax may seem surprising at first, but here ActiveSupport::TestCase is combining a class method, optional parentheses, and a block to make defining a test method the tiniest bit simpler for you. Sometimes it's the little things that make all the difference.

The assert line in this method is a test. It isn't much of one, though—all it does is test that true is true. Clearly, this is a placeholder, one that's intended to be replaced by your actual tests.

---

1. http://api.rubyonrails.org/classes/ActiveSupport/TestCase.html
2. http://docs.seattlerb.org/minitest/

A Real Unit Test

Let's get on to the business of testing validation. First, if we create a product with no attributes set, we'll expect it to be invalid and for an error to be associated with each field. We can use the model's errors() and invalid?() methods to see if it validates, and we can use the any?() method of the error list to see if an error is associated with a particular attribute.

Now that we know *what* to test, we need to know *how* to tell the test framework whether our code passes or fails. We do that using *assertions*. An assertion is a method call that tells the framework what we expect to be true. The simplest assertion is the assert() method, which expects its argument to be true. If it is, nothing special happens. However, if the argument to assert() is false, the assertion fails. The framework will output a message and will stop executing the test method containing the failure. In our case, we expect that an empty Product model won't pass validation, so we can express that expectation by asserting that it isn't valid:

```
assert product.invalid?
```

Replace the test the truth with the following code:

```ruby
rails51/depot_b/test/models/product_test.rb
test "product attributes must not be empty" do
  product = Product.new
  assert product.invalid?
  assert product.errors[:title].any?
  assert product.errors[:description].any?
  assert product.errors[:price].any?
  assert product.errors[:image_url].any?
end
```

We can rerun just the unit tests by issuing the rails test:models command. When we do so, we now see the test execute successfully:

```
depot> bin/rails test:models
Run options: --seed 63304

# Running:

.

Finished in 0.021068s, 47.4654 runs/s, 237.3268 assertions/s.
1 runs, 5 assertions, 0 failures, 0 errors, 0 skips
```

Sure enough, the validation kicked in, and all our assertions passed.

Clearly, at this point we can dig deeper and exercise individual validations. Let's look at three of the many possible tests.

First, we'll check that the validation of the price works the way we expect:

rails51/depot_c/test/models/product_test.rb
```
test "product price must be positive" do
  product = Product.new(title:       "My Book Title",
                        description: "yyy",
                        image_url:   "zzz.jpg")
  product.price = -1
  assert product.invalid?
  assert_equal ["must be greater than or equal to 0.01"],
    product.errors[:price]

  product.price = 0
  assert product.invalid?
  assert_equal ["must be greater than or equal to 0.01"],
    product.errors[:price]

  product.price = 1
  assert product.valid?
end
```

In this code, we create a new product and then try setting its price to -1, 0, and +1, validating the product each time. If our model is working, the first two should be invalid, and we verify that the error message associated with the price attribute is what we expect.

The last price is acceptable, so we assert that the model is now valid. (Some folks would put these three tests into three separate test methods—that's perfectly reasonable.)

Next, we test that we're validating that the image URL ends with one of .gif, .jpg, or .png:

rails51/depot_c/test/models/product_test.rb
```
def new_product(image_url)
  Product.new(title:       "My Book Title",
              description: "yyy",
              price:       1,
              image_url:   image_url)
end

test "image url" do
  ok = %w{ fred.gif fred.jpg fred.png FRED.JPG FRED.Jpg
           http://a.b.c/x/y/z/fred.gif }
  bad = %w{ fred.doc fred.gif/more fred.gif.more }

  ok.each do |image_url|
    assert new_product(image_url).valid?,
           "#{image_url} shouldn't be invalid"
  end
```

```
  bad.each do |image_url|
    assert new_product(image_url).invalid?,
           "#{image_url} shouldn't be valid"
  end
end
```

Here we've mixed things up a bit. Rather than write the nine separate tests, we've used a couple of loops—one to check the cases we expect to pass validation and the second to try cases we expect to fail. At the same time, we factored out the common code between the two loops.

You'll notice that we also added an extra parameter to our assert method calls. All of the testing assertions accept an optional trailing parameter containing a string. This will be written along with the error message if the assertion fails and can be useful for diagnosing what went wrong.

Finally, our model contains a validation that checks that all the product titles in the database are unique. To test this one, we need to store product data in the database.

One way to do this would be to have a test create a product, save it, then create another product with the same title and try to save it too. This would clearly work. But a much simpler way is to use Rails *fixtures*.

Test Fixtures

In the world of testing, a *fixture* is an environment in which you can run a test. If you're testing a circuit board, for example, you might mount it in a test fixture that provides it with the power and inputs needed to drive the function to be tested.

In the world of Rails, a test fixture is a specification of the initial contents of a model (or models) under test. If, for example, we want to ensure that our products table starts off with known data at the start of every unit test, we can specify those contents in a fixture, and Rails takes care of the rest.

You specify fixture data in files in the test/fixtures directory. These files contain test data in YAML format. Each fixture file contains the data for a single model. The name of the fixture file is significant: the base name of the file must match the name of a database table. Because we need some data for a Product model, which is stored in the products table, we'll add it to the file called products.yml.

Rails already created this fixture file when we first created the model:

```
rails51/depot_a/test/fixtures/products.yml
# Read about fixtures at
# http://api.rubyonrails.org/classes/ActiveRecord/FixtureSet.html
one:
  title: MyString
  description: MyText
  image_url: MyString
  price: 9.99
two:
  title: MyString
  description: MyText
  image_url: MyString
  price: 9.99
```

The fixture file contains an entry for each row that we want to insert into the database. Each row is given a name. In the case of the Rails-generated fixture, the rows are named one and two. This name has no significance as far as the database is concerned—it isn't inserted into the row data. Instead, as you'll see shortly, the name gives us a convenient way to reference test data inside our test code. They also are the names used in the generated integration tests, so for now, we'll leave them alone.

David says:
Picking Good Fixture Names

As with the names of variables in general, you want to keep the names of fixtures as self-explanatory as possible. This increases the readability of the tests when you're asserting that product(:valid_order_for_fred) is indeed Fred's valid order. It also makes it a lot easier to remember which fixture you're supposed to test against, without having to look up p1 or order4. The more fixtures you get, the more important it is to pick good fixture names. So, starting early keeps you happy later.

But what do we do with fixtures that can't easily get a self-explanatory name like valid_order_for_fred? Pick natural names that you have an easier time associating to a role. For example, instead of using order1, use christmas_order. Instead of customer1, use fred. Once you get into the habit of natural names, you'll soon be weaving a nice little story about how fred is paying for his christmas_order with his invalid_credit_card first, then paying with his valid_credit_card, and finally choosing to ship it all off to aunt_mary.

Association-based stories are key to remembering large worlds of fixtures with ease.

Inside each entry you can see an indented list of name-value pairs. As in your config/database.yml, you must use spaces, not tabs, at the start of each of the data lines, and all the lines for a row must have the same indentation. Be careful as you make changes, because you need to make sure the names of the columns are correct in each entry; a mismatch with the database column names can cause a hard-to-track-down exception.

This data is used in tests. In fact, if you rerun bin/rails test now you will see a number of errors, including the following error:

```
Error:
ProductsControllerTest#test_should_get_index:
ActionView::Template::Error: The asset "MyString" is not present in
the asset pipeline.
```

The reason for the failure is that we recently added an image_tag to the product index page and Rails can't find an image by the name MyString (remember that image_tag() is a Rails helper method that produces an HTML <img> element). Let's correct that error and while we are here add some more data to the fixture file with something we can use to test our Product model:

```
rails51/depot_c/test/fixtures/products.yml
# Read about fixtures at
# http://api.rubyonrails.org/classes/ActiveRecord/FixtureSet.html

one:
  title: MyString
  description: MyText
➤ image_url: lorem.jpg
  price: 9.99

two:
  title: MyString
  description: MyText
➤ image_url: lorem.jpg
  price: 9.99

➤ ruby:
➤   title:          Programming Ruby 1.9
➤   description:
➤     Ruby is the fastest growing and most exciting dynamic
➤     language out there.  If you need to get working programs
➤     delivered fast, you should add Ruby to your toolbox.
➤   price:          49.50
➤   image_url:      ruby.jpg
```

Note that the images referenced in image_url do need to exist for the tests to succeed. It doesn't matter what they are as long as they are in app/assets/images when the tests run. You can either create some yourself, or use the ones provided in the downloadable code.

Now that we have a fixture file, we want Rails to load the test data into the products table when we run the unit test. And, in fact, Rails is already doing this (convention over configuration for the win!), but you can control which fixtures to load by specifying the following line in test/models/product_test.rb:

```
class ProductTest < ActiveSupport::TestCase
➤   fixtures :products
    #...
end
```

The fixtures() directive loads the fixture data corresponding to the given model name into the corresponding database table before each test method in the test case is run. The name of the fixture file determines the table that's loaded, so using :products will cause the products.yml fixture file to be used.

Let's say that again another way. In the case of our ProductTest class, adding the fixtures directive means that the products table will be emptied out and then populated with the three rows defined in the fixture before each test method is run.

Note that most of the scaffolding that Rails generates doesn't contain calls to the fixtures method. That's because the default for tests is to load *all* fixtures before running the test. Because that default is generally the one you want, there usually isn't any need to change it. Once again, conventions are used to eliminate the need for unnecessary configuration.

So far, we've been doing all our work in the development database. Now that we're running tests, though, Rails needs to use a test database. If you look in the database.yml file in the config directory, you'll notice Rails actually created a configuration for three separate databases.

- db/development.sqlite3 will be our development database. All of our programming work will be done here.

- db/test.sqlite3 is a test database.

- db/production.sqlite3 is the production database. Our application will use this when we put it online.

Each test method gets a freshly initialized table in the test database, loaded from the fixtures we provide. This is automatically done by the bin/rails test command but can be done separately via bin/rails db:test:prepare.

Using Fixture Data

Now that you know how to get fixture data into the database, we need to find ways of using it in our tests.

Clearly, one way would be to use the finder methods in the model to read the data. However, Rails makes it easier than that. For each fixture it loads into a test, Rails defines a method with the same name as the fixture. You can use this method to access preloaded model objects containing the fixture data: simply pass it the name of the row as defined in the YAML fixture file, and it'll return a model object containing that row's data.

In the case of our product data, calling products(:ruby) returns a Product model containing the data we defined in the fixture. Let's use that to test the validation of unique product titles:

```
rails51/depot_c/test/models/product_test.rb
test "product is not valid without a unique title" do
  product = Product.new(title:       products(:ruby).title,
                        description: "yyy",
                        price:       1,
                        image_url:   "fred.gif")

  assert product.invalid?
  assert_equal ["has already been taken"], product.errors[:title]
end
```

The test assumes that the database already includes a row for the Ruby book. It gets the title of that existing row using this:

```
products(:ruby).title
```

It then creates a new Product model, setting its title to that existing title. It asserts that attempting to save this model fails and that the title attribute has the correct error associated with it.

If you want to avoid using a hardcoded string for the Active Record error, you can compare the response against its built-in error message table:

```
rails51/depot_c/test/models/product_test.rb
test "product is not valid without a unique title - i18n" do
  product = Product.new(title:       products(:ruby).title,
                        description: "yyy",
                        price:       1,
                        image_url:   "fred.gif")

  assert product.invalid?
  assert_equal [I18n.translate('errors.messages.taken')],
               product.errors[:title]
end
```

We'll cover the I18n functions in Chapter 16, *Task K: Internationalization*, on page 253.

Before we move on, we once again try our tests:

```
$ bin/rails test
```

This time we see two remaining failures, both in test/controllers/products_con-trollertest.rb: one in should create product and the other in should update product. Clearly, something we did caused something to do with the creation and update of products to fail. Since we just added validations on how products are created or updated, it's likely this is the source of the problem, and our test is out-of-date.

The specifics of the problem might not be obvious from the test failure message, but the failure for "should create product" gives us a clue: "Product.count didn't change by 1." Since we just added validations, it seems likely that our attempts to create a product in the test are creating an invalid product, which we can't save to the database.

Let's verify this assumption by adding a call to puts() in the controller's create() method:

```
def create
  @product = Product.new(product_params)

  respond_to do |format|
    if @product.save
      format.html { redirect_to @product,
        notice: 'Product was successfully created.' }
      format.json { render :show, status: :created,
        location: @product }
    else
      puts @product.errors.full_messages
      format.html { render :new }
      format.json { render json: @product.errors,
        status: :unprocessable_entity }
    end
  end
end
```

If we rerun just the test for creating a new product, we will see the problem:

```
> bin/rails test test/controllers/products_controller_test.rb:19
# Running:

Title has already been taken
F

Failure:
ProductsControllerTest#test_should_create_product [«path to test»]
"Product.count" didn't change by 1.
Expected: 3
  Actual: 2

bin/rails test test/controllers/products_controller_test.rb:18

Finished in 0.427810s, 2.3375 runs/s, 2.3375 assertions/s.
1 runs, 1 assertions, 1 failures, 0 errors, 0 skips
```

Our puts() is printing the validation error, which in this case is "Title has already been taken." In other words, we're trying to create a product whose title already exists. Instead, let's create a random book title and use that instead of the value coming out of the test fixture. First, we'll create a random title in the setup() block:

```
rails51/depot_b/test/controllers/products_controller_test.rb
require 'test_helper'

class ProductsControllerTest < ActionDispatch::IntegrationTest
  setup do
    @product = products(:one)
    @title = "The Great Book #{rand(1000)}"
  end
```

Next, we'll use that instead of the default @product.title that the Rails generator put into the test. The actual change is highlighted (the use of @title), but the code had to be reformatted to fit the space, so this will look a bit different for you:

```
rails51/depot_b/test/controllers/products_controller_test.rb
test "should create product" do
  assert_difference('Product.count') do

    post products_url, params: {
        product: {
          description: @product.description,
          image_url: @product.image_url,
          price: @product.price,
          title: @title,
        }
      }

  end

  assert_redirected_to product_url(Product.last)
end
```

```
rails51/depot_b/test/controllers/products_controller_test.rb
test "should update product" do

  patch product_url(@product), params: {
      product: {
        description: @product.description,
        image_url: @product.image_url,
        price: @product.price,
        title: @title,
      }
    }

  assert_redirected_to product_url(@product)
end
```

After making these changes, we rerun the tests, and they report that all is well.

Now we can feel confident that our validation code not only works but will continue to work. Our product now has a model, a set of views, a controller, and a set of unit tests. It'll serve as a good foundation on which to build the rest of the application.

What We Just Did

In about a dozen lines of code, we augmented the generated code with validation:

- We ensured that required fields are present.
- We ensured that price fields are numeric and at least one cent.
- We ensured that titles are unique.
- We ensured that images match a given format.
- We updated the unit tests that Rails provided, both to conform to the constraints we've imposed on the model and to verify the new code we added.

We show this to our customer, and although she agrees that this is something an administrator could use, she says that it certainly isn't anything that she would feel comfortable turning loose on her customers. Clearly, in the next iteration we're going to have to focus a bit on the user interface.

Playtime

Here's some stuff to try on your own:

- If you're using Git, now is a good time to commit your work. You can first see which files we changed by using the git status command:

```
depot> git status
# On branch master
# Changes not staged for commit:
#   (use "git add <file>..." to update what will be committed)
#   (use "git checkout -- <file>..." to discard changes in working directory)
#
# modified:   app/models/product.rb
# modified:   test/fixtures/products.yml
# modified:   test/controllers/products_controller_test.rb
# modified:   test/models/product_test.rb
# no changes added to commit (use "git add" and/or "git commit -a")
```

Since we modified only some existing files and didn't add any new ones, you can combine the git add and git commit commands and simply issue a single git commit command with the -a option:

```
depot> git commit -a -m 'Validation!'
```

With this done, you can play with abandon, secure in the knowledge that you can return to this state at any time by using a single `git checkout .` command.

- The `:length` validation option checks the length of a model attribute. Add validation to the `Product` model to check that the title is at least ten characters.

- Change the error message associated with one of your validations.

In this chapter, you'll see:
- Writing our own views
- Using layouts to decorate pages
- Integrating CSS
- Using helpers
- Writing functional tests

## CHAPTER 8

Task C: Catalog Display

All in all, it's been a successful set of iterations. We gathered the initial requirements from our customer, documented a basic flow, worked out a first pass at the data we'll need, and put together the management page for the Depot application's products. It hasn't even taken many lines of code. We even have a small but growing test suite.

Thus emboldened, it's on to our next task. We chatted about priorities with our customer, and she said she'd like to start seeing what the application looks like from the buyer's point of view. Our next task is to create a catalog display.

This also makes a lot of sense from our point of view. Once we have the products safely tucked into the database, it should be fairly straightforward to display them. It also gives us a basis from which to develop the shopping cart portion of the code later.

We should also be able to draw on the work we just did in the product management task. The catalog display is really just a glorified product listing.

Finally, we'll also need to complement our unit tests for the model with some functional tests for the controller.

Iteration C1: Creating the Catalog Listing

We've already created the products controller, used by the seller to administer the Depot application. Now it's time to create a second controller, one that interacts with the paying customers. Let's call it Store:

```
depot> bin/rails generate controller Store index
      create  app/controllers/store_controller.rb
       route  get 'store/index'
      invoke  erb
      create    app/views/store
      create    app/views/store/index.html.erb
      invoke  test_unit
      create    test/controllers/store_controller_test.rb
      invoke  helper
      create    app/helpers/store_helper.rb
      invoke    test_unit
      invoke  assets
      invoke    coffee
      create      app/assets/javascripts/store.coffee
      invoke    scss
      create      app/assets/stylesheets/store.scss
```

As in the previous chapter, where we used the generate utility to create a controller and associated scaffolding to administer the products, here we've asked it to create a controller (the StoreController class in the store_controller.rb file) containing a single action method, index().

While everything is already set up for this action to be accessed via http://localhost:3000/store/index (feel free to try it!), we can do better. Let's simplify things and make this the root URL for the website. We do this by editing config/routes.rb:

rails51/depot_d/config/routes.rb
```
Rails.application.routes.draw do
  root 'store#index', as: 'store_index'

  resources :products
  # For details on the DSL available within this file, see
  # http://guides.rubyonrails.org/routing.html
end
```

We've replaced the get 'store/index' line with a call to define a root path, and in the process we added an as: 'store_index' option. The latter tells Rails to create store_index_path and store_index_url accessor methods, enabling existing code—and tests!—to continue to work correctly. Let's try it. Point a browser at http://localhost:3000/, and up pops our web page. See the following screenshot.

Store#index

Find me in app/views/store/index.html.erb

It might not make us rich, but at least we know everything is wired together correctly. It even tells us where to find the template file that draws this page.

Let's start by displaying a list of all the products in our database. We know that eventually we'll have to be more sophisticated, breaking them into categories, but this'll get us going.

We need to get the list of products out of the database and make it available to the code in the view that'll display the table. This means we have to change the index() method in store_controller.rb. We want to program at a decent level of abstraction, so let's assume we can ask the model for a list of the products:

rails51/depot_d/app/controllers/store_controller.rb
```ruby
class StoreController < ApplicationController
  def index
➤     @products = Product.order(:title)
  end
end
```

We asked our customer if she had a preference regarding the order things should be listed in, and we jointly decided to see what happens if we display the products in alphabetical order. We do this by adding an order(:title) call to the Product model.

Now we need to write our view template. To do this, edit the index.html.erb file in app/views/store. (Remember that the path name to the view is built from the name of the controller [store] and the name of the action [index]. The .html.erb part signifies an ERB template that produces an HTML result.)

rails51/depot_d/app/views/store/index.html.erb
```erb
<% if notice %>
  <aside id="notice"><%= notice %></aside>
<% end %>

<h1>Your Pragmatic Catalog</h1>

<ul class="catalog">
  <% @products.each do |product| %>
    <li>
      <%= image_tag(product.image_url) %>
      <h2><%= product.title %></h2>
      <p>
        <%= sanitize(product.description) %>
      </p>
      <div class="price">
        <%= product.price %>
      </div>
    </li>
  <% end %>
</ul>
```

Note the use of the sanitize() method for the description. This allows us to safely[1] add HTML stylings to make the descriptions more interesting for our customers.

We also used the image_tag() helper method. This generates an HTML <img> tag using its argument as the image source.

Next we add a stylesheet, making use of the fact that in Iteration A2 on page 82 we set things up so that pages created by the StoreController will define an HTML class by the name of store:

rails51/depot_d/app/assets/stylesheets/store.scss
```scss
// Place all the styles related to the Store controller here.
// They will automatically be included in application.css.
// You can use Sass (SCSS) here: http://sass-lang.com/

.store {
  max-width: 80em;
  ul.catalog {
    border-top: solid 0.250em;
    list-style: none;
    padding: 0;
    margin: 0;
    li {
      padding: 1em;
      margin: 0;
      border-bottom: solid thin #ddd;

      // This makes sure our <li> has enough height
      // to hold the entire image, since it's floated
      &::after {
        clear: both;
        content: " ";
        display: block;
      }
      img {
        float: left;
        padding: 1em;
        margin-right: 1em;
        margin-bottom: 1em;
        box-shadow: 0.176em 0.176em 0.354em 0px rgba(0,0,0,0.75);
      }
      .price {
        font-size: 1.414em;
      }
    }
  }
}
```

---

1.   http://www.owasp.org/index.php/Cross-site_Scripting_%28XSS%29

A page refresh brings up the display shown in the following screenshot. It's still pretty basic, and it seems to be missing something. The customer happens to be walking by as we ponder this, and she points out that she'd also like to see a decent-looking banner and sidebar on public-facing pages.

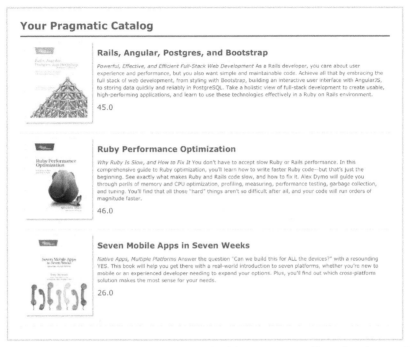

At this point in the real world, we'd probably want to call in the design folks. But, Pragmatic Web Designer is off getting inspiration on a beach somewhere and won't be back until later in the year, so let's put a placeholder in for now. It's time for another iteration.

Iteration C2: Adding a Page Layout

The pages in a typical website often share a similar layout; the designer will have created a standard template that's used when content is placed. Our job is to modify this page to add decoration to each of the store pages.

So far, we've made only minimal changes to application.html.erb—namely, to add a class attribute in Iteration A2 on page 82. As this file is the layout used for all views for all controllers that don't otherwise provide a layout, we can change the look and feel of the entire site by editing one file. This makes us feel better about putting a placeholder page layout in for now; we can update it when the designer eventually returns from the islands.

Let's update this file to define a banner and a sidebar:

rails51/depot_e/app/views/layouts/application.html.erb

```
<!DOCTYPE html>
<html>
  <head>
➤    <title>Pragprog Books Online Store</title>
    <%= csrf_meta_tags %>

    <%= stylesheet_link_tag 'application', media: 'all',
                            'data-turbolinks-track': 'reload' %>
    <%= javascript_include_tag 'application',
                               'data-turbolinks-track': 'reload' %>
  </head>

  <body>
➤    <header class="main">
➤      <%= image_tag 'logo.svg', alt: 'The Pragmatic Bookshelf' %>
➤      <h1><%= @page_title %></h1>
➤    </header>
➤    <section class="content">
➤      <nav class="side_nav">
➤        <ul>
➤          <li><a href="/">Home</a></li>
➤          <li><a href="/questions">Questions</a></li>
➤          <li><a href="/news">News</a></li>
➤          <li><a href="/contact">Contact</a></li>
➤        </ul>
➤      </nav>
                        <main class='<%= controller.controller_name %>'>
          <%= yield %>
        </main>
➤    </section>
  </body>
</html>
```

Apart from the usual HTML gubbins, this layout has three Rails-specific items. The Rails stylesheet_link_tag() helper method generates a <link> tag to our application's stylesheet and specifies an option to enable Turbolinks,[2] which transparently works behind the scenes to speed up page changes within an application. Similarly, the javascript_include_tag() method generates a <script> to load our application's scripts.

Finally, the csrf_meta_tags() method sets up all the behind-the-scenes data needed to prevent cross-site request forgery attacks, which will be important once we add forms in Chapter 12, *Task G: Check Out!*, on page 175.

---

2.   https://github.com/rails/turbolinks

Inside the body, we set the page heading to the value in the @page_title instance variable. By default, this is blank, meaning there won't be an H1 rendered, but any controller that sets the variable @page_title can override this. The real magic, however, takes place when we invoke yield. This causes Rails to substitute in the page-specific content—the stuff generated by the view invoked by this request. Here, this'll be the catalog page generated by index.html.erb.

To make this all work, first rename the application.css file to application.scss. If you didn't opt to try Git as was suggested in *Playtime*, on page 85, now is a good time to do so. The command to rename a file using Git is git mv. Once you've renamed this file, either through Git or by using the underlying operating system commands, add the following lines:

rails51/depot_e/app/assets/stylesheets/application.scss

```scss
/*
 * This is a manifest file that'll be compiled into application.css, which will
 * include all the files listed below.
 *
 * Any CSS and SCSS file within this directory, lib/assets/stylesheets, or any
 * plugin's vendor/assets/stylesheets directory can be referenced here using a
 * relative path.
 *
 * You're free to add application-wide styles to this file and they'll appear
 * at the bottom of the compiled file so the styles you add here take
 * precedence over styles defined in any other CSS/SCSS files in this
 * directory. Styles in this file should be added after the last require_*
 * statement. It is generally better to create a new file per style scope.
 *
 *= require_tree .
 *= require_self
 */
body {
  margin: 0;
  padding: 0;
}
header.main {
  text-align: center; // center on mobile
  @media (min-width: 30em) {
    text-align: left; // left align on desktop
  }
  background: #282;
  margin: 0;
  h1 {
    display: none;
  }
}
```

```
.content {
  margin: 0;
  padding: 0;

  display: flex;
  display: -webkit-flex;
  flex-direction: column; // mobile is horizontally laid out
  -webkit-box-orient: vertical;
  -webkit-box-direction: normal;

  @media (min-width: 30em) {
    flex-direction: row;  // desktop is vertically laid out
    -webkit-box-orient: horizontal;
  }

  nav {
    padding-bottom: 1em;
    background: #141;
    text-align: center;  // mobile has centered nav
    @media (min-width: 30em) {
      text-align: left; // desktop nav is left-aligned
      padding: 1em;     // and needs more padding
    }
    ul {
      list-style: none;
      margin: 0;
      padding: 0;
      @media (min-width: 30em) {
        padding-right: 1em; // give desktop some extra space
      }
      li {
        margin: 0;
        padding: 0.5em;
        text-transform: uppercase;
        letter-spacing: 0.354em;
        a {
          color: #bfb;
          text-decoration: none;
        }
        a:hover {
          background: none;
          color: white;
        }
      }
    }
  }
  main {
    padding: 0.5em;
  }
}
```

As is explained in the comments, this manifest file will automatically include all stylesheets available in this directory and in any subdirectory. This is accomplished via the require_tree directive.

We could instead list the names of individual stylesheets that we want to be linked in the stylesheet_link_tag(), but because we're in the layout for the entire application and because this layout is already set up to load all stylesheets, let's leave it alone for now.

The page design is fairly minimal, though we've added a lot of padding, margins, and other specing directives to ensure a decent layout for the side nav and main content. Some of the sizes we've used might seem strange (e.g., 0.354em), but everything should work out. Anytime we need padding, margin, or any other size, we'll use one of a few hand-picked sizes that ensure our layout is always decent.

We're also making heavy use of Sass, which is what the file rename enabled us to do. Sass allows us to nest CSS rules, to constrain where they apply. For example, we've specified that the ul inside a nav that's inside content with the CSS class content has list-style of none. Without Sass, we'd have to write this:

```
.content nav ul {
  list-style: none;
}
```

For any reasonable amount of CSS, this can become hard to maintain and understand. Sass allows nesting like so:

```
.content {
  nav {
    ul {
      list-style: none;
    }
  }
}
```

Sass also allows *media queries*,[3] which we're using to account for differences we'd like to see between mobile devices and desktop computers.

Refresh the page, and the browser window looks something like the screenshot on page 112. It won't win any design awards, but it'll show our customer roughly what the final page will look like.

---

3. https://developer.mozilla.org/en-US/docs/Web/CSS/Media_Queries/Using_media_queries

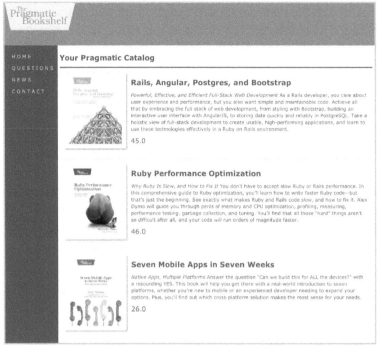

The stylesheet is designed using a *mobile-first* method, where the default styles are designed to look great on a mobile device. Try shrinking your browser window's width (or enter its responsive design mode) to see the mobile design. We've used *media queries* to tweak the layout for larger-than-mobile devices.[4] This might feel backward, but it's likely more and more people will use our site from a mobile device than from a desktop computer. And, most mobile designs work great on desktops, too!

Looking at this page, we spot a minor problem with how prices are displayed. The database stores the price as a number, but we'd like to show it as dollars and cents. A price of 12.34 should be shown as $12.34, and 13 should display as $13.00. We'll tackle that next.

Iteration C3: Using a Helper to Format the Price

Ruby provides a sprintf() function that can be used to format prices. We could place logic that makes use of this function directly in the view. For example, we could say this:

```
<%= sprintf("$%0.02f", product.price) %>
```

---

4.   https://developer.mozilla.org/en-US/docs/Web/CSS/Media_Queries/Using_media_queries

This would work, but it embeds knowledge of currency formatting into the view. If we display prices of products in several places and want to internationalize the application later, this would be a maintenance problem.

Instead, let's use a helper method to format the price as a currency. Rails has an appropriate one built in, called number_to_currency().

Using our helper in the view is just a matter of invoking them as regular methods; in the index template, we change this:

```
<%= product.price %>
```

to the following:

```
rails51/depot_e/app/views/store/index.html.erb
<div class="price">
  <%= number_to_currency(product.price) %>
</div>
```

When we refresh, we see a nicely formatted price, as in the following screenshot.

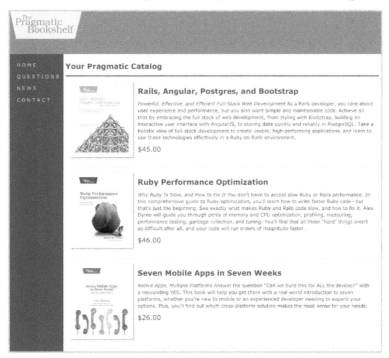

Although it looks nice enough, we're starting to get a nagging feeling that we really should be running and writing tests for all this new functionality, particularly after our experience of adding logic to our model.

Iteration C4: Functional Testing of Controllers

Now for the moment of truth. Before we focus on writing new tests, we need to determine if we've broken anything. Remembering our experience after we added validation logic to our model, with some trepidation we run our tests again:

depot> **bin/rails test**

This time, all is well. We added a lot, but we didn't break anything. That's a relief, but our work isn't done yet; we still need tests for what we just added.

The unit testing of models that we did previously seemed straightforward enough. We called a method and compared what it returned against what we expected it to return. But now we're dealing with a server that processes requests and a user viewing responses in a browser. What we need is *functional* tests that verify that the model, view, and controller work well together. Never fear: Rails has you covered.

First, let's take a look at what Rails generated for us:

```
rails51/depot_d/test/controllers/store_controller_test.rb
require 'test_helper'

class StoreControllerTest < ActionDispatch::IntegrationTest
  test "should get index" do
    get store_index_url
    assert_response :success
  end

end
```

The should get index test gets the index and asserts that a successful response is expected. That certainly seems straightforward enough. That's a reasonable beginning, but we also want to verify that the response contains our layout, our product information, and our number formatting. Let's see what that looks like in code:

```
rails51/depot_e/test/controllers/store_controller_test.rb
require 'test_helper'

class StoreControllerTest < ActionDispatch::IntegrationTest
  test "should get index" do
    get store_index_url
    assert_response :success
➤   assert_select 'nav.side_nav a', minimum: 4
➤   assert_select 'main ul.catalog li', 3
➤   assert_select 'h2', 'Programming Ruby 1.9'
➤   assert_select '.price', /\$[,\d]+\.\d\d/
  end

end
```

The four lines we added take a look *into* the HTML that's returned, using CSS selector notation. As a refresher, selectors that start with a number sign (#) match on id attributes; selectors that start with a dot (.) match on class attributes; and selectors that contain no prefix match on element names.

So the first select test looks for an element named a that's contained in a nav element that has the class side_nav. This test verifies that a minimum of four such elements are present. Pretty powerful stuff, assert_select(), eh?

The next three lines verify that all of our products are displayed. The first verifies that there are three li elements inside a ul with the class catalog, which is itself inside the main element. The next line verifies that there's an h2 element with the title of the Ruby book that we'd entered previously. The fourth line verifies that the price is formatted correctly. These assertions are based on the test data that we put inside our fixtures:

```
rails51/depot_e/test/fixtures/products.yml
# Read about fixtures at
# http://api.rubyonrails.org/classes/ActiveRecord/FixtureSet.html

one:
  title: MyString
  description: MyText
  image_url: lorem.jpg
  price: 9.99

two:
  title: MyString
  description: MyText
  image_url: lorem.jpg
  price: 9.99

ruby:
  title:          Programming Ruby 1.9
  description:
    Ruby is the fastest growing and most exciting dynamic
    language out there.  If you need to get working programs
    delivered fast, you should add Ruby to your toolbox.
  price:          49.50
  image_url:      ruby.jpg
```

Maybe you noticed that the type of test that assert_select() performs varies based on the type of the second parameter. If it's a number, it's treated as a quantity. If it's a string, it's treated as an expected result. Another useful type of test is a regular expression, which is what we use in our final assertion. We verify that there's a price that has a value that contains a dollar sign followed by any number (but at least one), commas, or digits; followed by a decimal point; followed by two digits.

One final point before we move on: both validation and functional tests will test the behavior of controllers only; they won't retroactively affect any objects that already exist in the database or in fixtures. In the previous example, two products contain the same title. Such data will cause no problems and will go undetected up to the point when such records are modified and saved.

We've touched on only a few things that assert_select() can do. More information can be found in the online documentation.[5]

That's a lot of verification in a few lines of code. We can see that it works by rerunning just the functional tests (after all, that's all we changed):

```
depot> bin/rails test:controllers
```

Now not only do we have something recognizable as a storefront, but we also have tests that ensure that all of the pieces—the model, view, and controller —are all working together to produce the desired result. Although this sounds like a lot, with Rails it wasn't much at all. In fact, it was mostly HTML and CSS and not much in the way of code or tests. Before moving on, let's make sure that it'll stand up to the onslaught of customers we're expecting.

Iteration C5: Caching of Partial Results

If everything goes as planned, this page will definitely be a high-traffic area for the site. To respond to requests for this page, we'd need to fetch every product from the database and render each one. We can do better than that. After all, the catalog doesn't change that often, so there's no need to start from scratch on each request.

So we can see what we're doing, we're first going to modify the configuration for the development environment to turn on caching. To make this easy, Rails provides a handy command to toggle caching on and off in the development environment:

```
depot> bin/rails dev:cache
```

Note that this command will cause your server to automatically restart.

Next we need to plan our attack. Thinking about it, we only need to rerender things if a product changed, and even then we need to render only the products that actually changed. So we need to make two small changes to our template.

---

5.   https://github.com/rails/rails-dom-testing

First, we mark the sections of our template that we need to update if any product changes, and then inside that section we mark the subsection that we need in order to update any specific product that changed:

```
rails51/depot_e/app/views/store/index.html.erb
<% if notice %>
  <aside id="notice"><%= notice %></aside>
<% end %>

<h1>Your Pragmatic Catalog</h1>

<ul class="catalog">
  <% cache @products do %>
    <% @products.each do |product| %>
      <% cache product do %>
        <li>
          <%= image_tag(product.image_url) %>
          <h2><%= product.title %></h2>
          <p>
            <%= sanitize(product.description) %>
          </p>
          <div class="price">
            <%= number_to_currency(product.price) %>
          </div>
        </li>
      <% end %>
    <% end %>
  <% end %>
</ul>
```

In addition to bracketing the sections, we identify the data to associate with each: the complete set of products for the overall store and the individual product we're rendering with the entry. Whenever the specified data changes, the section will be rerendered.

Bracketed sections can be nested to arbitrary depth, which is why those in the Rails community have come to refer to this as "Russian doll" caching.[6]

With this, we're done! Rails takes care of all of the rest, including managing the storage and deciding when to invalidate old entries. If you're interested, you can turn all sorts of knobs and make choices as to which backing store to use for the cache. It's nothing you need to worry about now, but it might be worth bookmarking the overview page of Caching with Rails in the Ruby on Rails Guides.[7]

---

6.   http://37signals.com/svn/posts/3113-how-key-based-cache-expiration-works
7.   http://guides.rubyonrails.org/caching_with_rails.html

As far as verifying that this works is concerned, you're going to get some insight into the work the server is doing behind the scenes. Go back to your server window and watch what happens when you refresh the page. The first time you load the page, you should see some SQL that is loading the products like Product Load (0.2ms) SELECT "products".* FROM "products" ORDER BY "products"."title" ASC. When you refresh the page again, it will still work, but you *won't* see that SQL run. You *should* see some SQL that Rails runs to check if its cache is outdated, like so: SELECT COUNT(*) AS "size", MAX("products"."updated_at") AS timestamp FROM "products".

If you still aren't convinced, you can add a configuration option to config/environments/development.rb called enable_fragment_cache_logging, like so:

```
# Enable/disable caching. By default caching is disabled.
if Rails.root.join('tmp/caching-dev.txt').exist?
  config.action_controller.enable_fragment_cache_logging = true
  config.action_controller.perform_caching = true

  config.cache_store = :memory_store
```

You'll need to restart your server for this to take effect, but after doing that, you should see log messages that look like this:

```
Read fragment views/products/1-20170611205537670088/cb43383298…
Write fragment views/products/1-20170611205537670088/cb4338329…
Read fragment views/products/3-20170611204944061952/cb43383298…
Write fragment views/products/3-20170611204944061952/cb4338329…
Read fragment views/products/2-20170611204944059695/cb43383298…
```

Once you're satisfied that caching is working, turn caching off in development so that further changes to the template will always be visible immediately:

```
depot> bin/rails dev:cache
```

Once again, wait for the server to restart, and verify that changes to the template show up as quickly as you save them.

What We Just Did

We've put together the basis of the store's catalog display. The steps were as follows:

1. Create a new controller to handle customer-centric interactions.

2. Implement the default index() action.

3. Add a call to the order() method within the Store controller to control the order in which the items on the website are listed.

4. Implement a view (a .html.erb file) and a layout to contain it (another .html.erb file).

5. Use a helper to format prices the way we want.

6. Make use of a CSS stylesheet.

7. Write functional tests for our controller.

8. Implement fragment caching for portions of the page.

It's time to check it all in and move on to the next task—namely, making a shopping cart!

Playtime

Here's some stuff to try on your own:

- Add a date and time to the sidebar. It doesn't have to update; just show the value at the time the page was displayed.

- Experiment with setting various number_to_currency helper method options, and see the effect on your catalog listing.

- Write some functional tests for the product management application using assert_select. The tests will need to be placed into the test/controllers/products_controller_test.rb file.

- A reminder: the end of an iteration is a good time to save your work using Git. If you've been following along, you have the basics you need at this point. You'll explore more Git functionality in *Prepping Your Deployment Server*, on page 288.

In this chapter, you'll see:
  • Sessions and session management
  • Adding relationships among models
  • Adding a button to add a product to a cart

## CHAPTER 9

Task D: Cart Creation

Now that we have the ability to display a catalog containing all our wonderful products, it would be nice to be able to sell them. Our customer agrees, so we've jointly decided to implement the shopping cart functionality next. This is going to involve a number of new concepts, including sessions, relationships among models, and adding a button to the view—so let's get started.

Iteration D1: Finding a Cart

As users browse our online catalog, they will (we hope) select products to buy. The convention is that each item selected will be added to a virtual shopping cart, held in our store. At some point, our buyers will have everything they need and will proceed to our site's checkout, where they'll pay for the stuff in their carts.

This means that our application will need to keep track of all the items added to the cart by the buyer. To do that, we'll keep a cart in the database and store its unique identifier, cart.id, in the session. Every time a request comes in, we can recover that identifier from the session and use it to find the cart in the database.

Let's go ahead and create a cart:

```
depot> bin/rails generate scaffold Cart
  ...
depot> bin/rails db:migrate
== CreateCarts: migrating =========================================================
-- create_table(:carts)
   -> 0.0012s
== CreateCarts: migrated (0.0014s) ================================================
```

Rails makes the current session look like a hash to the controller, so we'll store the ID of the cart in the session by indexing it with the :cart_id symbol:

rails51/depot_f/app/controllers/concerns/current_cart.rb
```ruby
module CurrentCart

  private

    def set_cart
      @cart = Cart.find(session[:cart_id])
    rescue ActiveRecord::RecordNotFound
      @cart = Cart.create
      session[:cart_id] = @cart.id
    end

end
```

The set_cart() method starts by getting the :cart_id from the session object and then attempts to find a cart corresponding to this ID. If such a cart record isn't found (which will happen if the ID is nil or invalid for any reason), this method will proceed to create a new Cart and then store the ID of the created cart into the session.

Note that we place the set_cart() method in a CurrentCart module and place that module in a new file in the app/controllers/concerns directory.[1] This treatment allows us to share common code (even as little as a single method!) among controllers.

Additionally, we mark the method as private, which prevents Rails from ever making it available as an action on the controller.

Iteration D2: Connecting Products to Carts

We're looking at sessions because we need somewhere to keep our shopping cart. We'll cover sessions in more depth in *Rails Sessions*, on page 375, but for now let's move on to implement the cart.

Let's keep things simple. A cart contains a set of products. Based on the Initial guess at application data diagram on page 69, combined with a brief chat with our customer, we can now generate the Rails models and populate the migrations to create the corresponding tables:

```
depot> bin/rails generate scaffold LineItem product:references cart:belongs_to
 ...
depot> bin/rails db:migrate
==  CreateLineItems: migrating ================================================
-- create_table(:line_items)
   -> 0.0013s
==  CreateLineItems: migrated (0.0014s) =======================================
```

---

1. https://signalvnoise.com/posts/3372-put-chubby-models-on-a-diet-with-concerns

The database now has a place to store the references among line items, carts, and products. If you look at the generated definition of the LineItem class, you can see the definitions of these relationships:

rails51/depot_f/app/models/line_item.rb
```
class LineItem < ApplicationRecord
  belongs_to :product
  belongs_to :cart
end
```

The belongs_to() method defines an accessor method—in this case, carts() and products()—but more importantly it tells Rails that rows in line_items are the children of rows in carts and products. No line item can exist unless the corresponding cart and product rows exist. A great rule of thumb for where to put belongs_to declarations is this: if a table has any columns whose values consist of ID values for another table (this concept is known by database designers as *foreign keys*), the corresponding model should have a belongs_to for each.

What do these various declarations do? Basically, they add navigation capabilities to the model objects. Because Rails added the belongs_to declaration to LineItem, we can now retrieve its Product and display the book's title:

```
li = LineItem.find(...)
puts "This line item is for #{li.product.title}"
```

To be able to traverse these relationships in both directions, we need to add some declarations to our model files that specify their inverse relations.

Open the cart.rb file in app/models, and add a call to has_many():

rails51/depot_f/app/models/cart.rb
```
class Cart < ApplicationRecord
  has_many :line_items, dependent: :destroy
end
```

That has_many :line_items part of the directive is fairly self-explanatory: a cart (potentially) has many associated line items. These are linked to the cart because each line item contains a reference to its cart's ID. The dependent: :destroy part indicates that the existence of line items is dependent on the existence of the cart. If we destroy a cart, deleting it from the database, we want Rails also to destroy any line items that are associated with that cart.

Now that the Cart is declared to have many line items, we can reference them (as a collection) from a cart object:

```
cart = Cart.find(...)
puts "This cart has #{cart.line_items.count} line items"
```

Now, for completeness, we should add a has_many directive to our Product model. After all, if we have lots of carts, each product might have many line items referencing it. This time, we make use of validation code to prevent the removal of products that are referenced by line items:

rails51/depot_f/app/models/product.rb
```ruby
class Product < ApplicationRecord
➤   has_many :line_items

➤   before_destroy :ensure_not_referenced_by_any_line_item

    #...

➤   private

➤       # ensure that there are no line items referencing this product
➤       def ensure_not_referenced_by_any_line_item
➤           unless line_items.empty?
➤               errors.add(:base, 'Line Items present')
➤               throw :abort
➤           end
➤       end
end
```

Here we declare that a product has many line items and define a *hook* method named ensure_not_referenced_by_any_line_item(). A hook method is a method that Rails calls automatically at a given point in an object's life. In this case, the method will be called before Rails attempts to destroy a row in the database. If the hook method throws :abort, the row isn't destroyed.

Note that we have direct access to the errors object. This is the same place that the validates() method stores error messages. Errors can be associated with individual attributes, but in this case we associate the error with the base object.

Before moving on, add a test to ensure that a product in a cart can't be deleted:

rails51/depot_f/test/controllers/products_controller_test.rb
```ruby
➤   test "can't delete product in cart" do
➤       assert_difference('Product.count', 0) do
➤           delete product_url(products(:two))
➤       end
➤
➤       assert_redirected_to products_url
➤   end

    test "should destroy product" do
        assert_difference('Product.count', -1) do
            delete product_url(@product)
        end

        assert_redirected_to products_url
    end
```

And change the fixture to make sure that product two is in both carts:

```
rails51/depot_f/test/fixtures/line_items.yml
# Read about fixtures at
# http://api.rubyonrails.org/classes/ActiveRecord/FixtureSet.html

one:
➤   product: two
    cart: one

two:
    product: two
    cart: two
```

We'll have more to say about intermodel relationships starting in *Specifying Relationships in Models*, on page 326.

Iteration D3: Adding a Button

Now that that's done, it's time to add an Add to Cart button for each product.

We don't need to create a new controller or even a new action. Taking a look at the actions provided by the scaffold generator, we find index(), show(), new(), edit(), create(), update(), and destroy(). The one that matches this operation is create(). (new() may sound similar, but its use is to get a form that's used to solicit input for a subsequent create() action.)

Once this decision is made, the rest follows. What are we creating? Certainly not a Cart or even a Product. What we're creating is a LineItem. Looking at the comment associated with the create() method in app/controllers/line_items_controller.rb, you see that this choice also determines the URL to use (/line_items) and the HTTP method (POST).

This choice even suggests the proper UI control to use. When we added links before, we used link_to(), but links default to using HTTP GET. We want to use POST, so we'll add a button this time; this means we'll be using the button_to() method.

We could connect the button to the line item by specifying the URL, but again we can let Rails take care of this for us by simply appending _path to the controller's name. In this case, we'll use line_items_path.

However, there's a problem with this: how will the line_items_path method know *which* product to add to our cart? We'll need to pass it the ID of the product corresponding to the button. All we need to do is add the :product_id option to the line_items_path() call. We can even pass in the product instance itself—Rails knows to extract the ID from the record in circumstances such as these.

In all, the *one* line that we need to add to our index.html.erb looks like this:

rails51/depot_f/app/views/store/index.html.erb

```erb
<% if notice %>
  <aside id="notice"><%= notice %></aside>
<% end %>

<h1>Your Pragmatic Catalog</h1>

<ul class="catalog">
  <% cache @products do %>
    <% @products.each do |product| %>
      <% cache product do %>
        <li>
          <%= image_tag(product.image_url) %>
          <h2><%= product.title %></h2>
          <p>
            <%= sanitize(product.description) %>
          </p>
          <div class="price">
            <%= number_to_currency(product.price) %>
            <%= button_to 'Add to Cart', line_items_path(product_id: product) %>
          </div>
        </li>
      <% end %>
    <% end %>
  <% end %>
</ul>
```

We also need to deal with two formatting issues. button_to creates an HTML
<form>, and that form contains an HTML <div>. Both of these are normally
block elements that appear on the next line. We'd like to place them next to
the price. While we're fixing this we'd also like the button to look a bit nicer
and bigger—there's nothing like a big juicy button to entice users to click it!
We'll handle both with some CSS in store.scss:

rails51/depot_f/app/assets/stylesheets/store.scss

```scss
  .price {
    font-size: 1.414em;
  }
  form, div {
    display: inline;
  }
  input[type="submit"] {
    background-color: #282;
    border-radius: 0.354em;
    border: solid thin #141;
    color: white;
    font-size: 1em;
    padding: 0.354em 1em;
```

```
➤      }
➤      input[type="submit"]:hover {
➤        background-color: #141;
➤      }
     }
```

Now our index page looks like the following screenshot. But before we push
the button, we need to modify the create() method in the line items controller
to expect a product ID as a form parameter. Here's where we start to see how
important the id field is in our models. Rails identifies model objects (and the
corresponding database rows) by their id fields. If we pass an ID to create(),
we're uniquely identifying the product to add.

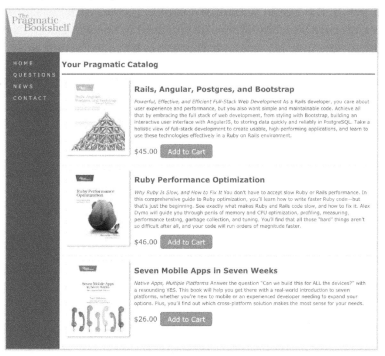

Why the create() method? The default HTTP method for a link is a GET, and for
a button is a POST. Rails uses these conventions to determine which method
to call. Refer to the comments inside the app/controllers/line_items_controller.rb file
to see other conventions. We'll be making extensive use of these conventions
inside the Depot application.

Now let's modify the LineItemsController to find the shopping cart for the current
session (creating one if one isn't there already), add the selected product to
that cart, and display the cart contents.

We use the CurrentCart concern we implemented in Iteration D1 on page 122 to find (or create) a cart in the session:

```
rails51/depot_f/app/controllers/line_items_controller.rb
class LineItemsController < ApplicationController
➤   include CurrentCart
➤   before_action :set_cart, only: [:create]
    before_action :set_line_item, only: [:show, :edit, :update, :destroy]

    # GET /line_items
    #...
end
```

We include the CurrentCart module and declare that the set_cart() method is to be involved before the create() action. We explore action callbacks in depth in *Callbacks*, on page 381, but for now all you need to know is that Rails provides the ability to wire together methods that are to be called before, after, or even around controller actions.

In fact, as you can see, the generated controller already uses this facility to set the value of the @line_item instance variable before the show(), edit(), update(), or destroy() actions are called.

Now that we know that the value of @cart is set to the value of the current cart, all we need to modify is a few lines of code in the create() method in app/controllers/line_items_controller.rb. to build the line item itself:

```
rails51/depot_f/app/controllers/line_items_controller.rb
  def create
➤     product = Product.find(params[:product_id])
➤     @line_item = @cart.line_items.build(product: product)

      respond_to do |format|
        if @line_item.save
➤         format.html { redirect_to @line_item.cart,
            notice: 'Line item was successfully created.' }
          format.json { render :show,
            status: :created, location: @line_item }
        else
          format.html { render :new }
          format.json { render json: @line_item.errors,
            status: :unprocessable_entity }
        end
      end
  end
```

We use the params object to get the :product_id parameter from the request. The params object is important inside Rails applications. It holds all of the parameters passed in a browser request. We store the result in a local variable because there's no need to make this available to the view.

We then pass that product we found into @cart.line_items.build. This causes a new line item relationship to be built between the @cart object and the product. You can build the relationship from either end, and Rails takes care of establishing the connections on both sides.

We save the resulting line item into an instance variable named @line_item.

The remainder of this method takes care of handling errors, which we'll cover in more detail in *Iteration E2: Handling Errors*, on page 138 (as well as handling JSON requests, which we don't need per se, but that were added by the Rails generator). But for now, we want to modify only one more thing: once the line item is created, we want to redirect users to the cart instead of back to the line item. Since the line item object knows how to find the cart object, all we need to do is add .cart to the method call.

Confident that the code works as intended, we try the Add to Cart buttons in our browser.

And the following screenshot shows what we see.

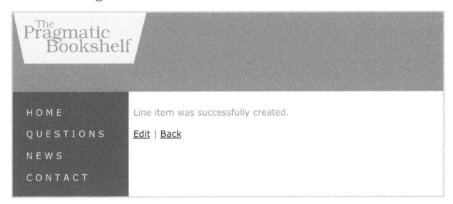

This is a bit underwhelming. We have scaffolding for the cart, but when we created it we didn't provide any attributes, so the view doesn't have anything to show. For now, let's write a trivial template (we'll make it look nicer in a minute). Create or replace the file views/carts/show.html.erb like so:

```
rails51/depot_f/app/views/carts/show.html.erb
<% if notice %>
  <aside id="notice"><%= notice %></aside>
<% end %>

<h2>Your Pragmatic Cart</h2>
<ul>
  <% @cart.line_items.each do |item| %>
    <li><%= item.product.title %></li>
  <% end %>
</ul>
```

We also need to improve the visual appeal of the notice. When a user adds an item to their cart, the notice will say something like "Item successfully added to cart". Rails' default scaffolding styles will show that text in green, but it looks out of place. Let's put it in a green box with a bold font. Add this following to app/assets/application.scss:

rails51/depot_f/app/assets/stylesheets/application.scss
```
.notice, #notice {
  background: #ffb;
  border-radius: 0.5em;
  border: solid 0.177em #882;
  color: #882;
  font-weight: bold;
  margin-bottom: 1em;
  padding: 1em 1.414em;
  text-align: center;
}
```

So, with everything plumbed together, let's go back and click the Add to Cart button again and see our view displayed, as in the next screenshot.

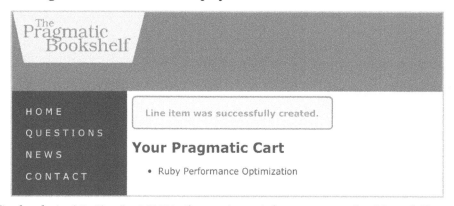

Go back to http://localhost:3000/, the main catalog page, and add a different product to the cart. You'll see the original two entries plus our new item in your cart. It looks like we have sessions working.

We changed the function of our controller, so we know that we need to update the corresponding functional test.

For starters, we only need to pass a product ID on the call to post. Next, we have to deal with the fact that we're no longer redirecting to the line items page. We're instead redirecting to the cart, where the cart ID is internal state data residing a cookie. Because this is an integration test, instead of focusing on how the code is implemented, we should focus on what users see after following the redirect: a page with a heading identifying that they're looking at a cart, with a list item corresponding to the product they added.

We do this by updating test/controllers/line_items_controller_test.rb:

```
rails51/depot_g/test/controllers/line_items_controller_test.rb
  test "should create line_item" do
    assert_difference('LineItem.count') do
➤      post line_items_url, params: { product_id: products(:ruby).id }
    end

➤    follow_redirect!
➤
➤    assert_select 'h2', 'Your Pragmatic Cart'
➤    assert_select 'li', 'Programming Ruby 1.9'
  end
```

We now rerun this set of tests:

```
depot> bin/rails test test/controllers/line_items_controller_test.rb
```

It's time to show our customer, so we call her over and proudly display our handsome new cart. Somewhat to our dismay, she makes that *tsk-tsk* sound that customers make just before telling you that you clearly don't get something.

Real shopping carts, she explains, don't show separate lines for two of the same product. Instead, they show the product line once with a quantity of 2. It looks like we're lined up for our next iteration.

What We Just Did

It's been a busy, productive day so far. We added a shopping cart to our store, and along the way we dipped our toes into some neat Rails features:

• We created a Cart object in one request and successfully located the same cart in subsequent requests by using a session object.

• We added a private method and placed it in a concern, making it accessible to all of our controllers.

• We created relationships between carts and line items and relationships between line items and products, and we were able to navigate using these relationships.

• We added a button that causes a product to be posted to a cart, causing a new line item to be created.

Playtime

Here's some stuff to try on your own:

- Add a new variable to the session to record how many times the user has accessed the store controller's index action. Note that the first time this page is accessed, your count won't be in the session. You can test for this with code like this:

```
if session[:counter].nil?
   ...
```

If the session variable isn't there, you need to initialize it. Then you'll be able to increment it.

- Pass this counter to your template, and display it at the top of the catalog page. Hint: the pluralize helper (definition on page 398) might be useful for forming the message you display.

- Reset the counter to zero whenever the user adds something to the cart.

- Change the template to display the counter only if the count is greater than five.

In this chapter, you'll see:
- Modifying the schema and existing data
- Error diagnosis and handling
- The flash
- Logging

## CHAPTER 10

Task E: A Smarter Cart

Although we have rudimentary cart functionality implemented, we have much to do. To start with, we need to recognize when customers add multiples of the same item to the cart. Once that's done, we'll also have to make sure that the cart can handle error cases and communicate problems encountered along the way to the customer or system administrator, as appropriate.

Iteration E1: Creating a Smarter Cart

Associating a count with each product in our cart is going to require us to modify the line_items table. We've used migrations before; for example, we used a migration in *Applying the Migration*, on page 74 to update the schema of the database. While that was as part of creating the initial scaffolding for a model, the basic approach is the same:

```
depot> bin/rails generate migration add_quantity_to_line_items quantity:integer
```

Rails can tell from the name of the migration that you're adding columns to the line_items table and can pick up the names and data types for each column from the last argument. The two patterns that Rails matches on are AddXXXToTABLE and RemoveXXXFromTABLE, where the value of XXX is ignored; what matters is the list of column names and types that appear after the migration name.

The only thing Rails can't tell is what a reasonable default is for this column. In many cases, a null value would do, but let's make it the value 1 for existing carts by modifying the migration before we apply it:

```
rails51/depot_g/db/migrate/20170425000004_add_quantity_to_line_items.rb
class AddQuantityToLineItems < ActiveRecord::Migration[5.1]
  def change
➤    add_column :line_items, :quantity, :integer, default: 1
  end
end
```

Once it's complete, we run the migration:

```
depot> bin/rails db:migrate
```

Now we need a smart add_product() method in our Cart, one that checks if our list of items already includes the product we're adding; if it does, it bumps the quantity, and if it doesn't, it builds a new LineItem:

rails51/depot_g/app/models/cart.rb

```
def add_product(product)
  current_item = line_items.find_by(product_id: product.id)
  if current_item
    current_item.quantity += 1
  else
    current_item = line_items.build(product_id: product.id)
  end
  current_item
end
```

The find_by() method is a streamlined version of the where() method. Instead of returning an array of results, it returns either an existing LineItem or nil.

We also need to modify the line item controller to use this method:

rails51/depot_g/app/controllers/line_items_controller.rb

```
  def create
    product = Product.find(params[:product_id])
➤   @line_item = @cart.add_product(product)

    respond_to do |format|
      if @line_item.save
        format.html { redirect_to @line_item.cart,
          notice: 'Line item was successfully created.' }
        format.json { render :show,
          status: :created, location: @line_item }
      else
        format.html { render :new }
        format.json { render json: @line_item.errors,
          status: :unprocessable_entity }
      end
    end
  end
```

We make one last quick change to the show view to use this new information:

rails51/depot_g/app/views/carts/show.html.erb

```erb
<% if notice %>
  <aside id="notice"><%= notice %></aside>
<% end %>

<h2>Your Pragmatic Cart</h2>
<ul>
  <% @cart.line_items.each do |item| %>
    <li><%= item.quantity %> &times; <%= item.product.title %></li>
  <% end %>
</ul>
```

Now that all the pieces are in place, we can go back to the store page and click the Add to Cart button for a product that's already in the cart. What we're likely to see is a mixture of individual products listed separately and a single product listed with a quantity of two. This is because we added a quantity of one to existing columns instead of collapsing multiple rows when possible. What we need to do next is migrate the data.

We start by creating a migration:

```
depot> bin/rails generate migration combine_items_in_cart
```

This time, Rails can't infer what we're trying to do, so we can't rely on the generated change() method. What we need to do instead is to replace this method with separate up() and down() methods. First, here's the up() method:

rails51/depot_g/db/migrate/20170425000005_combine_items_in_cart.rb

```ruby
def up
  # replace multiple items for a single product in a cart with a
  # single item
  Cart.all.each do |cart|
    # count the number of each product in the cart
    sums = cart.line_items.group(:product_id).sum(:quantity)

    sums.each do |product_id, quantity|
      if quantity > 1
        # remove individual items
        cart.line_items.where(product_id: product_id).delete_all

        # replace with a single item
        item = cart.line_items.build(product_id: product_id)
        item.quantity = quantity
        item.save!
      end
    end
  end
end
```

This is easily the most extensive code you've seen so far. Let's look at it in small pieces:

- We start by iterating over each cart.

- For each cart, we get a sum of the quantity fields for each of the line items associated with this cart, grouped by product_id. The resulting sums will be a list of ordered pairs of product_ids and quantity.

- We iterate over these sums, extracting the product_id and quantity from each.

- In cases where the quantity is greater than one, we delete all of the individual line items associated with this cart and this product and replace them with a single line item with the correct quantity.

Note how easily and elegantly Rails enables you to express this algorithm.

With this code in place, we apply this migration like any other migration:

```
depot> bin/rails db:migrate
```

We can see the results by looking at the cart, shown in the following screenshot.

Although we have reason to be pleased with ourselves, we're not done yet. An important principle of migrations is that each step needs to be reversible, so we implement a down() too. This method finds line items with a quantity of greater than one; adds new line items for this cart and product, each with a quantity of one; and, finally, deletes the line item:

rails51/depot_g/db/migrate/20170425000005_combine_items_in_cart.rb

```ruby
def down
  # split items with quantity>1 into multiple items
  LineItem.where("quantity>1").each do |line_item|
    # add individual items
    line_item.quantity.times do
      LineItem.create(
        cart_id: line_item.cart_id,
        product_id: line_item.product_id,
        quantity: 1
      )
    end

    # remove original item
    line_item.destroy
  end
end
```

Now, we can just as easily roll back our migration with a single command:

depot> **bin/rails db:rollback**

Rails provides a Rake task to allow you to check the status of your migrations:

depot> **bin/rails db:migrate:status**
```
database: /home/rubys/work/depot/db/development.sqlite3

  Status   Migration ID     Migration Name
--------------------------------------------------
    up      20160407000001   Create products
    up      20160407000002   Create carts
    up      20160407000003   Create line items
    up      20160407000004   Add quantity to line items
   down     20160407000005   Combine items in cart
```

Now, we can modify and reapply the migration or even delete it entirely. To inspect the results of the rollback, we have to move the migration file out of the way so Rails doesn't think it should apply it. You can do that via mv, for example. If you do that, the cart should look like the following screenshot:

Once we move the migration file back and reapply the migration (with the bin/rails db:migrate command), we have a cart that maintains a count for each of the products it holds, and we have a view that displays that count.

Since we changed the output the application produces, we need to update the tests to match. Note that what the user sees isn't the string × but the Unicode character ×. If you can't find a way to enter that character using your keyboard and operating system combination, you can use the escape sequence \u00D7[1] instead (also note the use of double quotes, as this is needed in Ruby to enter the escape sequence):

rails51/depot_h/test/controllers/line_items_controller_test.rb
```ruby
test "should create line_item" do
  assert_difference('LineItem.count') do
    post line_items_url, params: { product_id: products(:ruby).id }
  end

  follow_redirect!

  assert_select 'h2', 'Your Pragmatic Cart'
  assert_select 'li', "1 \u00D7 Programming Ruby 1.9"
end
```

Happy that we have something presentable, we call our customer over and show her the result of our morning's work. She's pleased—she can see the site starting to come together. However, she's also troubled, having just read an article in the trade press on the way ecommerce sites are being attacked and compromised daily. She read that one kind of attack involves feeding requests with bad parameters into web applications, hoping to expose bugs and security flaws. She noticed that the link to the cart looks like carts/nnn, where nnn is our internal cart ID. Feeling malicious, she manually types this request into a browser, giving it a cart ID of wibble. She's not impressed when our application displays the page shown in the screenshot on page 139.

This seems fairly unprofessional. So, our next iteration will be spent making the application more resilient.

Iteration E2: Handling Errors

It's apparent from the page shown in the screenshot on page 139 that our application raised an exception at line 67 of the carts controller. Your line number might be different, as we have some book-related formatting stuff in our source files. If you go to that line, you'll find the following code:

```ruby
@cart = Cart.find(params[:id])
```

---

1. http://www.fileformat.info/info/unicode/char/00d7/index.htm

If the cart can't be found, Active Record raises a RecordNotFound exception, which we clearly need to handle. The question arises—how?

We could silently ignore it. From a security standpoint, this is probably the best move, because it gives no information to a potential attacker. However, it also means that if we ever have a bug in our code that generates bad cart IDs, our application will appear to the outside world to be unresponsive—no one will know that an error occurred.

Instead, we'll take two actions when an exception is raised. First, we'll log the fact to an internal log file using the Rails logger facility.[2] Second, we'll redisplay the catalog page along with a short message (something along the lines of "Invalid cart") to the user, who can then continue to use our site.

Rails has a convenient way of dealing with errors and error reporting. It defines a structure called a *flash*. A flash is a bucket (actually closer to a Hash) in which you can store stuff as you process a request. The contents of the flash are available to the next request in this session before being deleted automatically. Typically, the flash is used to collect error messages. For example, when our

---

2.   http://guides.rubyonrails.org/debugging_rails_applications.html#the-logger

show() method detects that it was passed an invalid cart ID, it can store that error message in the flash area and redirect to the index() action to redisplay the catalog. The view for the index action can extract the error and display it at the top of the catalog page. The flash information is accessible within the views via the flash accessor method.

Why can't we store the error in any old instance variable? Remember that after a redirect is sent by our application to the browser, the browser sends a new request back to our application. By the time we receive that request, our application has moved on; all the instance variables from previous requests are long gone. The flash data is stored in the session to make it available between requests.

Armed with this background about flash data, we can create an invalid_cart() method to report on the problem:

```
rails51/depot_h/app/controllers/carts_controller.rb
class CartsController < ApplicationController
  before_action :set_cart, only: [:show, :edit, :update, :destroy]
➤ rescue_from ActiveRecord::RecordNotFound, with: :invalid_cart
  # GET /carts
  # ...
  private
  # ...

➤   def invalid_cart
➤     logger.error "Attempt to access invalid cart #{params[:id]}"
➤     redirect_to store_index_url, notice: 'Invalid cart'
➤   end
end
```

The rescue_from clause intercepts the exception raised by Cart.find(). In the handler, we do the following:

• Use the Rails logger to record the error. Every controller has a logger attribute. Here we use it to record a message at the error logging level.

• Redirect to the catalog display by using the redirect_to() method. The :notice parameter specifies a message to be stored in the flash as a notice. Why redirect rather than display the catalog here? If we redirect, the user's browser will end up displaying the store URL, rather than http://.../cart/wibble. We expose less of the application this way. We also prevent the user from retriggering the error by clicking the Reload button.

With this code in place, we can rerun our customer's problematic query by entering the following URL:

```
http://localhost:3000/carts/wibble
```

We don't see a bunch of errors in the browser now. Instead, the catalog page is displayed with the error message shown in the following screenshot.

If we look at the end of the log file (development.log in the log directory), we see our message:

```
Started GET "/carts/wibble" for 127.0.0.1 at 2016-01-29 09:37:39 -0500
Processing by CartsController#show as HTML
  Parameters: {"id"=>"wibble"}
  ^[[1m^[[35mCart Load (0.1ms)^[[0m  SELECT "carts".* FROM "carts" WHERE
"carts"."id" = ? LIMIT 1  [["id", "wibble"]]
Attempt to access invalid cart wibble
Redirected to http://localhost:3000/
Completed 302 Found in 3ms (ActiveRecord: 0.4ms)
```

On Unix machines, we'd probably use a command such as tail or less to view this file. On Windows, you can use your favorite editor. It's often a good idea to keep a window open to show new lines as they're added to this file. In Unix, you'd use tail -f. You can download a tail command for Windows[3] or get a GUI-based tool.[4] Finally, some OS X users use Console.app to track log files. Just say open development.log at the command line.

---

3. http://gnuwin32.sourceforge.net/packages/coreutils.htm
4. http://tailforwin32.sourceforge.net/

This being the Internet, we can't worry only about our published web forms; we have to worry about every possible interface, because malicious crackers can get underneath the HTML we provide and attempt to provide additional parameters. Invalid carts aren't our biggest problem here; we also want to prevent access to *other people's carts*.

As always, your controllers are your first line of defense. Let's go ahead and remove cart_id from the list of parameters that are permitted:

rails51/depot_h/app/controllers/line_items_controller.rb

```
    # Never trust parameters from the scary internet, only allow the white
    # list through.
    def line_item_params
➤     params.require(:line_item).permit(:product_id)
    end
```

We can see this in action by rerunning our controller tests:

```
bin/rails test:controllers
```

No tests fail, but a peek into our log/test.log reveals a thwarted attempt to breach security:

```
LineItemsControllerTest: test_should_update_line_item
-------------------------------------------------------
   (0.0ms)  begin transaction
  LineItem Load (0.1ms)  SELECT "line_items".* FROM
"line_items" WHERE "line_items"."id" = ? LIMIT 1  [["id", 980190962]]
Processing by LineItemsController#update as HTML
  Parameters: {"line_item"=>{"product_id"=>nil}, "id"=>"980190962"}
  LineItem Load (0.1ms)  SELECT "line_items".* FROM
"line_items" WHERE "line_items"."id" = ? LIMIT 1  [["id", "980190962"]]
➤ Unpermitted parameter: cart_id
   (0.0ms)  SAVEPOINT active_record_1
   (0.1ms)  RELEASE SAVEPOINT active_record_1
Redirected to http://test.host/line_items/980190962
Completed 302 Found in 2ms (ActiveRecord: 0.2ms)
   (0.0ms)  rollback transaction
```

Let's clean up that test case to make the problem go away:

rails51/depot_h/test/controllers/line_items_controller_test.rb

```
  test "should update line_item" do
➤   patch line_item_url(@line_item),
➤     params: { line_item: { product_id: @line_item.product_id } }
    assert_redirected_to line_item_url(@line_item)
  end
```

At this point, we clear the test logs and rerun the tests:

```
bin/rails log:clear LOGS=test
bin/rails test:controllers
```

A final scan of the logs identifies no further problems.

It makes good sense to review log files periodically. They hold a lot of useful information.

Sensing the end of an iteration, we call our customer over and show her that the error is now properly handled. She's delighted and continues to play with the application. She notices a minor problem on our new cart display: there's no way to empty items out of a cart. This minor change will be our next iteration. We should make it before heading home.

Iteration E3: Finishing the Cart

We know by now that to implement the empty-cart function, we have to add a link to the cart and modify the destroy() method in the carts controller to clean up the session.

David says:
Battle of the Routes:
product_path vs. product_url

It can seem hard in the beginning to know when to use product_path and when to use product_url when you want to link or redirect to a given route. In reality, it's simple.

When you use product_url, you'll get the full enchilada with protocol and domain name, like http://example.com/products/1. That's the thing to use when you're doing redirect_to, because the HTTP spec requires a fully qualified URL when doing 302 Redirect and friends. You also need the full URL if you're redirecting from one domain to another, like product_url(domain: "example2.com", product: product).

The rest of the time, you can happily use product_path. This will generate only the /products/1 part, and that's all you need when doing links or pointing forms, like link_to "My lovely product", product_path(product).

The confusing part is that oftentimes the two are interchangeable because of lenient browsers. You can do a redirect_to with a product_path and it'll probably work, but it won't be valid according to spec. And you can link_to a product_url, but then you're littering up your HTML with needless characters, which is a bad idea too.

Start with the template and use the button_to() method to add a button:

rails51/depot_h/app/views/carts/show.html.erb

```erb
<% if notice %>
  <aside id="notice"><%= notice %></aside>
<% end %>

<h2>Your Pragmatic Cart</h2>
<ul>
  <% @cart.line_items.each do |item| %>
    <li><%= item.quantity %> &times; <%= item.product.title %></li>
  <% end %>
</ul>

<%= button_to 'Empty cart', @cart, method: :delete,
    data: { confirm: 'Are you sure?' } %>
```

In the controller, let's modify the destroy() method to ensure that the user is deleting his or her own cart (think about it!) and to remove the cart from the session before redirecting to the index page with a notification message:

rails51/depot_h/app/controllers/carts_controller.rb

```ruby
  def destroy
    @cart.destroy if @cart.id == session[:cart_id]
    session[:cart_id] = nil
    respond_to do |format|
      format.html { redirect_to store_index_url,
        notice: 'Your cart is currently empty' }
      format.json { head :no_content }
    end
  end
```

And we update the corresponding test in test/controllers/carts_controller_test.rb:

rails51/depot_i/test/controllers/carts_controller_test.rb

```ruby
  test "should destroy cart" do
    post line_items_url, params: { product_id: products(:ruby).id }
    @cart = Cart.find(session[:cart_id])

    assert_difference('Cart.count', -1) do
      delete cart_url(@cart)
    end

    assert_redirected_to store_index_url
  end
```

Now when we view our cart and click the "Empty cart" button, we are taken back to the catalog page and see the message shown in the screenshot on page 145.

We can remove the flash message that's autogenerated when a line item is added:

```
rails51/depot_i/app/controllers/line_items_controller.rb
  def create
    product = Product.find(params[:product_id])
    @line_item = @cart.add_product(product)

    respond_to do |format|
      if @line_item.save
        format.html { redirect_to @line_item.cart }
        format.json { render :show,
          status: :created, location: @line_item }
      else
        format.html { render :new }
        format.json { render json: @line_item.errors,
          status: :unprocessable_entity }
      end
    end
  end
end
```

Finally, we get around to tidying up the cart display. The <li>-based approach makes it hard to style. A table-based layout would be easier. Replace app/views/carts/show.html.erb with the following:

```
rails51/depot_i/app/views/carts/show.html.erb
<article>
  <% if notice %>
    <aside id="notice"><%= notice %></aside>
  <% end %>

  <h2>Your Cart</h2>
  <table>
    <% @cart.line_items.each do |line_item| %>
      <tr>
        <td class="quantity"><%= line_item.quantity %></td>
        <td><%= line_item.product.title %></td>
        <td class="price"><%= number_to_currency(line_item.total_price) %></td>
      </tr>
    <% end %>
    <tfoot>
      <tr>
        <th colspan="2">Total:</th>
        <td class="price"><%= number_to_currency(@cart.total_price) %></td>
      </tr>
    </tfoot>
  </table>
  <%= button_to 'Empty cart', @cart,
                method: :delete,
                data: { confirm: 'Are you sure?' } %>

</article>
```

To make this work, we need to add a method to both the LineItem and Cart models that returns the total price for the individual line item and entire cart, respectively. Here is the line item, which involves only simple multiplication:

```
rails51/depot_i/app/models/line_item.rb
def total_price
  product.price * quantity
end
```

We implement the Cart method using the nifty Array::sum() method to sum the prices of each item in the collection:

```
rails51/depot_i/app/models/cart.rb
def total_price
  line_items.to_a.sum { |item| item.total_price }
end
```

With this in place, we'll style the cart to look a bit nicer. This all gets inserted into app/assets/stylesheet/carts.css.

rails51/depot_i/app/assets/stylesheets/carts.scss

```scss
// Place all the styles related to the Carts controller here.
// They will automatically be included in application.css.
// You can use Sass (SCSS) here: http://sass-lang.com/

.carts {
  table {
    border-collapse: collapse;
  }
  td {
    padding: 0.5em;
  }
  td.quantity {
    white-space: nowrap;
  }
  td.quantity::after {
    content: " ×";
  }
  td.price {
    font-weight: bold;
    text-align: right;
  }
  tfoot {
    th, td.price {
      font-weight: bold;
      padding-top: 1em;
    }
    th {
      text-align: right;
    }
    td.price {
      border-top: solid thin;
    }
  }
  input[type="submit"] {
    background-color: #881;
    border-radius: 0.354em;
    border: solid thin #441;
    color: white;
    font-size: 1em;
    padding: 0.354em 1em;
  }
  input[type="submit"]:hover {
    background-color: #992;
  }
}
```

The following screenshot shows a nicer-looking cart.

Finally, we update our test cases to match the current output:

```
rails51/depot_i/test/controllers/line_items_controller_test.rb
  test "should create line_item" do
    assert_difference('LineItem.count') do
      post line_items_url, params: { product_id: products(:ruby).id }
    end

    follow_redirect!

➤   assert_select 'h2', 'Your Cart'
➤   assert_select 'td', "Programming Ruby 1.9"
  end
```

What We Just Did

Our shopping cart is now something the client is happy with. Along the way, we covered the following:

- Adding a column to an existing table, with a default value
- Migrating existing data into the new table format
- Providing a flash notice of an error that was detected
- Using the logger to log events
- Removing a parameter from the permitted list
- Deleting a record
- Adjusting the way a table is rendered, using CSS

But, just as we think we've wrapped up this functionality, our customer wanders over with a copy of *Information Technology and Golf Weekly*. Apparently, it has an article about the Ajax style of browser interface, where stuff gets updated on the fly. Hmmm...let's look at that tomorrow.

Playtime

Here's some stuff to try on your own:

- Create a migration that copies the product price into the line item, and change the add_product() method in the Cart model to capture the price whenever a new line item is created.

- Write unit tests that add both unique products and duplicate products to a cart. Assert how many products should be in the cart in each instance. Note that you'll need to modify the fixture to refer to products and carts by name—for example, product: ruby.

- Check products and line items for other places where a user-friendly error message would be in order.

- Add the ability to delete individual line items from the cart. This will require buttons on each line, and such buttons will need to be linked to the destroy() action in the LineItemsController.

- We prevented accessing other user's carts in the LineItemsController, but you can still see other carts by navigating directly to a URL like http://localhost/carts/3. See if you can prevent accessing any cart other than than one currently stored in the session.

CHAPTER 11

Task F: Add a Dash of Ajax

Our customer wants us to add Ajax support to the store. But what *is* Ajax?

Back in the old days (up until 2005 or so), browsers were treated as dumb devices. When you wrote a browser-based application, you'd send stuff to the browser and then forget about that session. At some point, the user would fill in some form fields or click a hyperlink, and your application would get woken up by an incoming request. It would render a complete page back to the user, and the whole tedious process would start afresh. That's exactly how our Depot application behaves so far.

But it turns out that browsers aren't really that dumb. (Who knew?) They can run code. All modern browsers can run JavaScript. And it turns out that the JavaScript in the browser can interact behind the scenes with the application on the server, updating the stuff the user sees as a result. Jesse James Garrett named this style of interaction *Ajax* (which once stood for Asynchronous Java-Script and XML but now just means "making browsers suck less").

Browsers can do so much more with JavaScript than interact with the server, and we'll learn about that in *Iteration H1: Adding Fields Dynamically to a Form*, on page 195, but we can do a lot for our users by simply adding a bit of Ajax to some of the user interactions in our application. And we can do it with surprisingly little code.

So, let's Ajaxify our shopping cart. Rather than having a separate shopping cart page, let's put the current cart display into the catalog's sidebar. Then we'll use Ajax to update the cart in the sidebar without redisplaying the whole page.

Whenever you work with Ajax, it's good to start with the non-Ajax version of the application and then gradually introduce Ajax features. That's what we'll do here. For starters, let's move the cart from its own page and put it in the sidebar.

Iteration F1: Moving the Cart

Currently, our cart is rendered by the show action in the CartController and the corresponding .html.erb template. We'd like to move that rendering into the sidebar. This means it'll no longer be in its own page. Instead, we'll render it in the layout that displays the overall catalog. You can do that using *partial templates*.

Partial Templates

Programming languages let you define *methods*. A method is a chunk of code with a name: invoke the method by the name, and the corresponding chunk of code gets run. And, of course, you can pass parameters to a method, which lets you write a piece of code that can be used in many different circumstances.

Think of Rails partial templates (*partials* for short) like a method for views. A partial is simply a chunk of a view in its own separate file. You can invoke (aka *render*) a partial from another template or from a controller, and the partial will render itself and return the results of that rendering. As with methods, you can pass parameters to a partial, so the same partial can render different results.

We'll use partials twice in this iteration. First let's look at the cart display:

```
rails51/depot_i/app/views/carts/show.html.erb
<article>
  <% if notice %>
    <aside id="notice"><%= notice %></aside>
  <% end %>

  <h2>Your Cart</h2>
  <table>
    <% @cart.line_items.each do |line_item| %>
      <tr>
        <td class="quantity"><%= line_item.quantity %></td>
        <td><%= line_item.product.title %></td>
        <td class="price"><%= number_to_currency(line_item.total_price) %></td>
      </tr>
    <% end %>
    <tfoot>
      <tr>
        <th colspan="2">Total:</th>
        <td class="price"><%= number_to_currency(@cart.total_price) %></td>
      </tr>
    </tfoot>
  </table>
  <%= button_to 'Empty cart', @cart,
              method: :delete,
              data: { confirm: 'Are you sure?' } %>

</article>
```

It creates a list of table rows, one for each item in the cart. Whenever you find yourself iterating like this, you should stop and ask yourself, is this too much logic in a template? It turns out we can abstract away the loop by using partials (and, as you'll see, this also sets the stage for some Ajax later). To do this, make use of the fact that you can pass a collection to the method that renders partial templates, and that method will automatically invoke the partial once for each item in the collection. Let's rewrite our cart view to use this feature:

rails51/depot_j/app/views/carts/show.html.erb

```
<article>
  <% if notice %>
    <aside id="notice"><%= notice %></aside>
  <% end %>

  <h2>Your Cart</h2>
  <table>
➤   <%= render(@cart.line_items) %>
    <tfoot>
      <tr>
        <th colspan="2">Total:</th>
        <td class="price"><%= number_to_currency(@cart.total_price) %></td>
      </tr>
    </tfoot>
  </table>
  <%= button_to 'Empty cart', @cart,
                method: :delete,
                data: { confirm: 'Are you sure?' } %>
</article>
```

That's a lot simpler. The render() method will iterate over any collection that's passed to it. The partial template is simply another template file (by default in the same directory as the object being rendered and with the name of the table as the name). However, to keep the names of partials distinct from regular templates, Rails automatically prepends an underscore to the partial name when looking for the file. That means we need to name our partial _line_item.html.erb and place it in the app/views/line_items directory:

rails51/depot_j/app/views/line_items/_line_item.html.erb

```
<tr>
  <td class="quantity"><%= line_item.quantity %></td>
  <td><%= line_item.product.title %></td>
  <td class="price"><%= number_to_currency(line_item.total_price) %></td>
</tr>
```

Something subtle is going on here. Inside the partial template, we refer to the current object by using the variable name that matches the name of the template. In this case, the partial is named line_item, so inside the partial we expect to have a variable called line_item.

So now we've tidied up the cart display, but that hasn't moved it into the sidebar. To do that, let's revisit our layout. If we had a partial template that could display the cart, we could embed a call like this within the sidebar:

```
render("cart")
```

But how would the partial know where to find the cart object? One way is for it to make an assumption. In the layout, we have access to the @cart instance variable that was set by the controller. Turns out that this is also available inside partials called from the layout. But this is like calling a method and passing it a value in a global variable. It works, but it's ugly coding, and it increases coupling (which in turn makes your programs hard to maintain).

Now that we have a partial for a line item, let's do the same for the cart. First we'll create the _cart.html.erb template. This is basically our carts/show.html.erb template but using cart instead of @cart (Note that it's OK for a partial to invoke other partials).

```
rails51/depot_j/app/views/carts/_cart.html.erb
<article>
  <% if notice %>
    <aside id="notice"><%= notice %></aside>
  <% end %>

  <h2>Your Cart</h2>
  <table>
➤    <%= render(cart.line_items) %>
    <tfoot>
      <tr>
        <th colspan="2">Total:</th>
➤        <td class="price"><%= number_to_currency(cart.total_price) %></td>
      </tr>
    </tfoot>
  </table>
➤  <%= button_to 'Empty cart', cart,
                method: :delete,
                data: { confirm: 'Are you sure?' } %>

</article>
```

As the Rails mantra goes, don't repeat yourself (DRY). But we've just done that. At the moment, the two files are in sync, so there may not seem to be much of a problem—but having one set of logic for the Ajax calls and another set of logic to handle the case where JavaScript is disabled invites problems.

Let's avoid all of that and replace the original template with code that causes the partial to be rendered:

rails51/depot_k/app/views/carts/show.html.erb
```erb
➤ <%= render @cart %>
```

Now change the application layout to include this new partial in the sidebar:

rails51/depot_k/app/views/layouts/application.html.erb
```erb
<!DOCTYPE html>
<html>
  <head>
    <title>Pragprog Books Online Store</title>
    <%= csrf_meta_tags %>

    <%= stylesheet_link_tag 'application', media: 'all',
                            'data-turbolinks-track': 'reload' %>
    <%= javascript_include_tag 'application',
                               'data-turbolinks-track': 'reload' %>
  </head>

  <body>
    <header class="main">
      <%= image_tag 'logo.svg', alt: 'The Pragmatic Bookshelf' %>
      <h1><%= @page_title %></h1>
    </header>
    <section class="content">
      <nav class="side_nav">
➤        <div id="cart" class="carts">
➤          <%= render @cart %>
➤        </div>
        <ul>
          <li><a href="/">Home</a></li>
          <li><a href="/questions">Questions</a></li>
          <li><a href="/news">News</a></li>
          <li><a href="/contact">Contact</a></li>
        </ul>
      </nav>
                        <main class='<%= controller.controller_name %>'>
        <%= yield %>
      </main>
    </section>
  </body>
</html>
```

Note that we've given the <article> element that wraps the cart the CSS class carts. This will allow it to pick up the styling we added in *Iteration E3: Finishing the Cart*, on page 143.

Next. we have to make a small change to the store controller. We're invoking the layout while looking at the store's index action, and that action doesn't currently set @cart. That's a quick change:

rails51/depot_k/app/controllers/store_controller.rb

```
class StoreController < ApplicationController
➤   include CurrentCart
➤   before_action :set_cart
    def index
      @products = Product.order(:title)
    end
end
```

The data for the cart is common no matter where it's placed in the output, but there's no requirement that the presentation be identical independently of where this content is placed. In fact, black lettering on a green background is hard to read, so let's provide additional rules for this table when it appears in the sidebar:

rails51/depot_k/app/assets/stylesheets/application.scss

```
#cart {
  article {
    h2 {
      margin-top: 0;
    }
    background: white;
    border-radius: 0.5em;
    margin: 1em;
    padding: 1.414em;
    @media (min-width: 30em) {
      margin: 0; // desktop doesn't need this margin
    }
  }
}
```

If you display the catalog after adding something to your cart, you should see something like the screenshot on page 157.

Let's just wait for the Webby Award nomination.

Changing the Flow

Now that we're displaying the cart in the sidebar, we can change the way that the Add to Cart button works. Rather than display a separate cart page, all it has to do is refresh the main index page.

The change is straightforward. At the end of the create action, we redirect the browser back to the index:

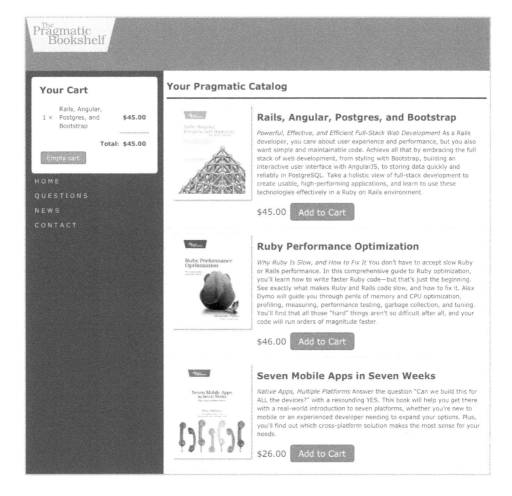

rails51/depot_k/app/controllers/line_items_controller.rb

```ruby
def create
  product = Product.find(params[:product_id])
  @line_item = @cart.add_product(product)

  respond_to do |format|
    if @line_item.save
      format.html { redirect_to store_index_url }
      format.json { render :show,
        status: :created, location: @line_item }
    else
      format.html { render :new }
      format.json { render json: @line_item.errors,
        status: :unprocessable_entity }
    end
  end
end
```

At this point, we rerun our tests and see a number of failures:

```
$ bin/rails test
Run options: --seed 57801

# Running:

...E

Error:
ProductsControllerTest#test_should_show_product:
ActionView::Template::Error: 'nil' is not an ActiveModel-compatible
object. It must implement :to_partial_path.
app/views/layouts/application.html.erb:21:in
`_app_views_layouts_application_html_erb`
```

If we try to display the products index by visiting http://localhost:3000/products in the browser, we see the error shown in the following screenshot.

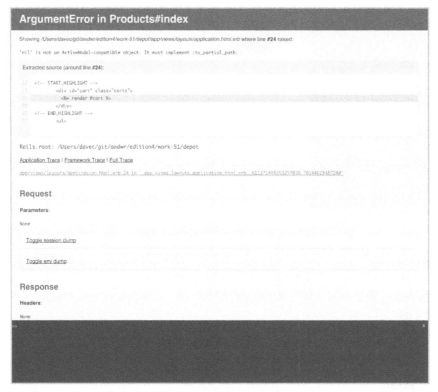

This information is helpful. The message identifies the template file that was being processed at the point where the error occurs (app/views/layouts/application.html.erb), the line number where the error occurred, and an excerpt from the template of lines around the error. From this, we see that the expression being evaluated at the point of error is @cart.line_items, and the message produced is 'nil' is not an ActiveModel-compatible object.

So, @cart is apparently nil when we display an index of our products. That makes sense, because it's set only in the store controller. We can even verify this using the web console provided at the bottom of the web page. Now that we know what the problem is, the fix is to avoid displaying the cart at all unless the value is set:

```
rails51/depot_l/app/views/layouts/application.html.erb
<nav class="side_nav">
  <% if @cart %>

  <div id="cart" class="carts">
    <%= render @cart %>
  </div>
  <% end %>

  <ul>
    <li><a href="/">Home</a></li>
    <li><a href="/questions">Questions</a></li>
    <li><a href="/news">News</a></li>
    <li><a href="/contact">Contact</a></li>
  </ul>
</nav>
```

With this change in place, our tests now pass once again. Imagine what could have happened. A change in one part of an application made to support a new requirement breaks a function implemented in another part of the application. If you are not careful, this can happen in a small application like Depot. Even if you are careful, this will happen in a large application.

Keeping tests up-to-date is an important part of maintaining your application. Rails makes this as easy as possible to do. Agile programmers make testing an integral part of their development efforts. Many even go so far as to write their tests first, before the first line of code is written.

So, now we have a store with a cart in the sidebar. When we click to add an item to the cart, the page is redisplayed with an updated cart. However, if our catalog is large, that redisplay might take a while. It uses bandwidth, and it uses server resources. Fortunately, we can use Ajax to make this better.

Iteration F2: Creating an Ajax-Based Cart

Ajax lets us write code that runs in the browser and interacts with our server-based application. In our case, we'd like to make the Add to Cart buttons invoke the server create action on the LineItems controller in the background. The server can then send down just the HTML for the cart, and we can replace the cart in the sidebar with the server's updates.

Now normally we'd do this by writing JavaScript that runs in the browser and by writing server-side code that communicates with this JavaScript (possibly using a technology such as JavaScript Object Notation [JSON]). The good news is that, with Rails, all this is hidden from us. We can use Ruby to do everything we need to do (and with a whole lot of support from some Rails helper methods).

The trick when adding Ajax to an application is to take small steps. So let's start with the most basic one. Let's change the catalog page to send an Ajax request to our server application and have the application respond with the HTML fragment containing the updated cart.

On the index page, we're using button_to() to create the link to the create action. We want to change this to send an Ajax request instead. To do this, we add a remote: true parameter to the call:

```
rails51/depot_l/app/views/store/index.html.erb
<% if notice %>
  <aside id="notice"><%= notice %></aside>
<% end %>

<h1>Your Pragmatic Catalog</h1>

<ul class="catalog">
  <% cache @products do %>
    <% @products.each do |product| %>
      <% cache product do %>
        <li>
          <%= image_tag(product.image_url) %>
          <h2><%= product.title %></h2>
          <p>
            <%= sanitize(product.description) %>
          </p>
          <div class="price">
            <%= number_to_currency(product.price) %>
            <%= button_to 'Add to Cart', line_items_path(product_id: product),
                remote: true %>
          </div>
        </li>
      <% end %>
    <% end %>
  <% end %>
</ul>
```

So far, we've arranged for the browser to send an Ajax request to our application. The next step is to have the application return a response. The plan is to create the updated HTML fragment that represents the cart and to have the browser stick that HTML into the browser's internal representation of the structure and content of the document being displayed—namely, the

Document Object Model (DOM). By manipulating the DOM, we cause the display to change in front of the user's eyes.

The first change is to stop the create action from redirecting to the index display if the request is for JavaScript. We do this by adding a call to respond_to() telling it that we want to respond with a format of .js:

```
rails51/depot_l/app/controllers/line_items_controller.rb
  def create
    product = Product.find(params[:product_id])
    @line_item = @cart.add_product(product)

    respond_to do |format|
      if @line_item.save
        format.html { redirect_to store_index_url }
        format.js
        format.json { render :show,
          status: :created, location: @line_item }
      else
        format.html { render :new }
        format.json { render json: @line_item.errors,
          status: :unprocessable_entity }
      end
    end
  end
```

This syntax may seem surprising at first, but it's just a method call. The other method calls on format()—like html()—pass an optional block (blocks are described in *Blocks and Iterators*, on page 54). The code you just added doesn't pass a block, which tells Rails to find a JavaScript template to render the response in app/views/line_items called create.js.erb or create.js.coffee. We'll cover the respond_to() method in greater detail in *Selecting a Data Representation*, on page 362.

Both filenames are treated as a template, executed in Ruby, and sent to the browser as JavaScript for execution. Using .js.erb means you want to write a JavaScript template, and .js.coffee means you want to write a CoffeeScript template.

We'll use CoffeeScript,[1] which is a cleaner, more Ruby-like language that Rails compiles down to JavaScript. We'll learn a bit more about it later in the chapter, but it's most common to write client-side code in CoffeeScript, which Rails made the default language in 3.1. Given all this, our template will be in app/views/line_items/create.js.coffee.

```
rails51/depot_l/app/views/line_items/create.js.coffee
cart = document.getElementById("cart")
cart.innerHTML = "<%= j render(@cart) %>"
```

---

1. http://coffeescript.org

This template tells the browser to replace the content of the element whose id is cart with that HTML. Let's analyze how it manages to do that.

The first line of code locates the element that has an id of cart using the built-in JavaScript function getElementById() available on the document global variable.[2,3]

The next line of code renders the HTML into the cart element. This is where we see that this file is a template and not just pure CoffeeScript. This content is formed by a call to the render() method on the @cart object. The output of this method is processed by an escape_javascript() helper method, using a convenient alias named j(), that converts this Ruby string into a format acceptable as input to JavaScript. This is assigned to the cart element's innerHTML property,[4] which inserts the rendered HTML into the page.

Note that this script is executed in the browser. The only parts executed on the server are the portions within the <%= and %> delimiters. The screenshot on page 163 shows this somewhat circuitous flow.

Does it work? Well, it's hard to show in a book, but it sure does. Make sure you reload the index page to get the remote version of the form. Then click one of the Add to Cart buttons. You should see the cart in the sidebar update. And you *shouldn't* see your browser show any indication of reloading the page. You've just created an Ajax application.

Troubleshooting

Although Rails makes Ajax straightforward, it can't make it foolproof. And because you're dealing with the loose integration of a number of technologies, it can be hard to work out why your Ajax doesn't work. That's one of the reasons you should always add Ajax functionality one step at a time.

Here are a few hints if your Depot application didn't show any Ajax interactions:

- Does your browser have any special incantation to force it to reload everything on a page? Sometimes browsers hold local cached versions of page assets, and this can mess up testing. Now would be a good time to do a full reload.

- Did you have any errors reported? Look in development.log in the logs directory. Also look in the Rails server window, because some errors are reported there.

---

2. https://developer.mozilla.org/en-US/docs/Web/API/Document/getElementById
3. https://developer.mozilla.org/en-US/docs/Web/API/Document
4. https://developer.mozilla.org/en-US/docs/Web/API/Element/innerHTML

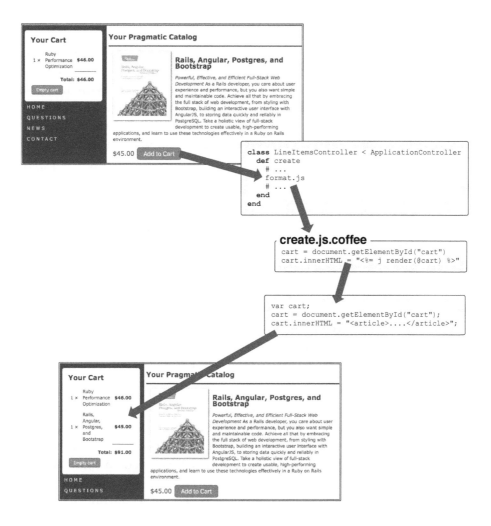

- Still looking at the log file, do you see incoming requests to the create action? If not, it means your browser isn't making Ajax requests. Perhaps your browser has JavaScript execution disabled?

- Some readers have reported that they had to stop and start their application to get the Ajax-based cart to work.

- If you're using Internet Explorer, it may be running in what Microsoft calls "quirks mode," which is backward-compatible with old Internet Explorer releases but is also broken. Internet Explorer switches into "standards mode," which works better with the Ajax stuff, if the first line of the downloaded page is an appropriate DOCTYPE header. Our layouts use this:

```
<!DOCTYPE html>
```

The Customer Is Never Satisfied

We're feeling pretty pleased with ourselves. We changed a handful of lines of code, and our boring old Web 1.0 application now sports Web 2.0 Ajax speed stripes. We breathlessly call the client over to come look. Without saying anything, we proudly click Add to Cart and look at her, eager for the praise we know will come. Instead, she looks surprised. "You called me over to show me a bug?" she asks. "You click that button, and nothing happens."

We patiently explain that, in fact, a lot happened. Just look at the cart in the sidebar. See? When we add something, the quantity changes from 4 to 5.

"Oh," she says, "I didn't notice that." And, if she didn't notice the page update, it's likely that our users won't either. It's time for some user interface hacking.

Iteration F3: Highlighting Changes

A common way to highlight changes made to a page via Ajax is the (now) infamous Yellow Fade Technique.[5] It highlights an element in a browser: by default it flashes the background yellow and then gradually fades it back to white. The user clicks the Add to Cart button, and the count updates to two as the line flares brighter. It then fades back to the background color over a short period of time.

You can implement this with CSS animations.[6] In CSS animations, a class uses the animation attribute to reference a particular animation. The animation itself is defined as a series of keyframes that describe the style of an element at various points in the animation. The animation is executed by the browser when the page loads or when the class is applied to an element. This sounds complicated, but for our case we only need to define the starting and ending states of the element.

Let's see the CSS first. We'll place it inside app/assets/stylesheets/line_items.scss, which was created by the Rails generator you ran back in *Iteration D2: Connecting Products to Carts*, on page 122.

```
rails51/depot_m/app/assets/stylesheets/line_items.scss
// Place all the styles related to the LineItems controller here.
// They will automatically be included in application.css.
// You can use Sass (SCSS) here: http://sass-lang.com/

@keyframes line-item-highlight {
  0% {
```

---

5. https://signalvnoise.com/archives/000558.php
6. https://developer.mozilla.org/en-US/docs/Web/CSS/CSS_Animations/Using_CSS_animations

```
➤       background: #8f8;
➤     }
➤     100% {
➤       background: none;
➤     }
➤   }
➤
➤   .line-item-highlight {
➤     animation: line-item-highlight 1s;
➤   }
```

The @keyframes directive defines an animation, in this case named line-item-highlight. Inside that declaration, we specify what the state of the DOM element should be at various points in the animation. At the start of the animation (0%), the element should have a background color of bright green, which is the highlight color. At the end of the animation (100%), it should have no background color.

Next we define a CSS class named line-item-highlight that uses the animation attribute. It accepts the name of the animation (which we just defined) and an animation time, which we've set at one second (note that you don't have to name the CSS class the same as the animation, but it can help keep it all straight if you do).

The last step is to use this class on the recently added item. To do that, our ERB template needs to know which item is the most recently added item. Set that inside LineItemsController:

```
rails51/depot_m/app/controllers/line_items_controller.rb
  def create
    product = Product.find(params[:product_id])
    @line_item = @cart.add_product(product)

    respond_to do |format|
      if @line_item.save
        format.html { redirect_to store_index_url }
➤       format.js   { @current_item = @line_item }
        format.json { render :show,
          status: :created, location: @line_item }
      else
        format.html { render :new }
        format.json { render json: @line_item.errors,
          status: :unprocessable_entity }
      end
    end
  end
```

In the _line_item.html.erb partial, we then check to see if the item we're rendering is the one that just changed. If so, we give it the animation class we just defined:

rails51/depot_m/app/views/line_items/_line_item.html.erb

```erb
➤ <% if line_item == @current_item %>
➤ <tr class="line-item-highlight">
➤ <% else %>
➤ <tr>
➤ <% end %>
    <td class="quantity"><%= line_item.quantity %></td>
    <td><%= line_item.product.title %></td>
    <td class="price"><%= number_to_currency(line_item.total_price) %></td>
  </tr>
```

As a result of these two minor changes, the <tr> element of the most recently changed item in the cart will be tagged with class="line-item-highlight". When the browser receives this rendered HTML and inserts it into the DOM, the browser will see that the most recently added line item has the class line-item-highlight, which will trigger the animation. No JavaScript needed!

With that change in place, click any Add to Cart button, and you'll see that the changed item in the cart glows a light green before fading back to merge with the background.

We're not done yet. We haven't tested any of our Ajax additions, such as what happens when we click the Add to Cart button. Rails provides the help we need to do that, too.

We already have a should create line_item test, so let's add another one called should create line_item via ajax:

rails51/depot_m/test/controllers/line_items_controller_test.rb

```ruby
test "should create line_item via ajax" do
  assert_difference('LineItem.count') do
    post line_items_url, params: { product_id: products(:ruby).id },
      xhr: true
  end

  assert_response :success
  assert_match /<tr class=\\"line-item-highlight/, @response.body
end
```

This test differs in the name of the test, in the manner of invocation from the create line item test (xhr :post vs. simply post, where xhr stands for the XMLHttpRequest mouthful)—and in the expected results. Instead of a redirect, we expect a successful response containing a call to replace the HTML for the cart...sort of.

If you insert a call to puts @response.body and rerun your test, you can see how Rails renders the response. It's JavaScript that contains your code inside a function that gets invoked. In short, this is how we can ask the browser to run JavaScript for us safely, but we need to assert something about the contents of the JavaScript. The simplest way to do that is to look in the response for <tr class="line-item-highlight">. Parsing the JavaScript and introspecting the rendered string is a bit tricky, so this simple assertion will do for now. In *Iteration H2: Testing Our JavaScript Functionality*, on page 214, we'll learn a better way to test JavaScript-enabled features.

Iteration F4: Hiding an Empty Cart with a Custom Helper

The customer has one last request. Right now, even carts with nothing in them are displayed in the sidebar. Can we arrange for the cart to appear only when it has some content? But of course!

In fact, we have a number of options. The simplest is probably to include the HTML for the cart only if the cart has something in it. We could do this totally within the _cart partial:

```erb
<% unless cart.line_items.empty? %>
<h2>Your Cart</h2>
<table>
  <%= render(cart.line_items) %>

  <tr class="total_line">
    <td colspan="2">Total</td>
    <td class="total_cell"><%= number_to_currency(cart.total_price) %></td>
  </tr>
</table>

<%= button_to 'Empty cart', cart, method: :delete,
    confirm: 'Are you sure?' %>
<% end %>
```

Although this works, the code is a bit odd. Our application layout is rendering a cart partial, which then turns around and avoids rendering anything if the cart is empty. It would be cleaner if the application layout had the logic for rendering the cart only when needed, while the cart partial continues to just render itself when asked. While we could do this with a similar unless statement inside the application layout, let's create a more generic means of doing this using a *helper method*.

A helper method is a function available to your views to handle generic view-related logic or code. In *Iteration C3: Using a Helper to Format the Price*, on page 112, we used the built-in helper number_to_currency(), but you can create your own helpers, too. In fact, it's a good practice to abstract any complex processing into a custom helper method.

If you look in the app directory, you'll find eight subdirectories:

```
depot> ls -p app
assets/          controllers/    jobs/        models/
channels/        helpers/        mailers/     views/
```

Not surprisingly, our helper methods go in the helpers directory. If you look in that directory, you'll find it already contains some files:

```
depot> ls -p app/helpers
application_helper.rb  line_items_helper.rb  store_helper.rb
carts_helper.rb        products_helper.rb
```

The Rails generators automatically created a helper file for each of our controllers (products and store). The rails command itself (the one that created the application initially) created the application_helper.rb file. If you like, you can organize your methods into controller-specific helpers, but since this method will be used in the application layout, let's put it in the application helper.

Let's write a helper method called render_if(). It takes a condition and an object to render. If the condition is true, it uses the built-in render() method on the object, like so:

```
rails51/depot_n/app/views/layouts/application.html.erb
<nav class="side_nav">

  <div id="cart" class="carts">

    <%= render_if @cart && @cart.line_items.any?, @cart %>
  </div>

  <ul>
    <li><a href="/">Home</a></li>
    <li><a href="/questions">Questions</a></li>
    <li><a href="/news">News</a></li>
    <li><a href="/contact">Contact</a></li>
  </ul>
</nav>
```

Since this helper is not specific to any particular controller, we'll add it to application_helper.rb in the app/helpers directory:

```
rails51/depot_n/app/helpers/application_helper.rb
module ApplicationHelper
  def render_if(condition, record)
    if condition
      render record
    end
  end
end
```

This code uses an if to check the condition, calling render() if it holds.

One other thing we need to deal with is the flash message. If you add an item to your cart, then clear your cart, and then add an item, you'll still see the "Your cart is empty" message, even though your cart has an item in it. By using Ajax to insert the cart into the page, we only redrew part of the screen, so the flash message stays around. If you reload the page, the message goes away, but we can hide it using CoffeeScript.

Since the code in app/views/line_items/create.js.coffee is executed when an item is added, you can add code there to also hide the flash message. It's rendered in a <p> tag with the ID notice. Using getElementById(), you can locate that element and, if it's there, set its style's display property to "none", which is a programmatic way of setting the display CSS property.

```
rails51/depot_n/app/views/line_items/create.js.coffee
cart = document.getElementById("cart")
cart.innerHTML = "<%= j render(@cart) %>"
➤ notice = document.getElementById("notice")
➤ if notice
➤   notice.style.display = "none"
```

This shows a bit more of CoffeeScript. Note that the if statement doesn't need parens around the test, doesn't need braces, and doesn't even need an ending tag. The indentation alone lets CoffeeScript know what's inside the if block.

Now that we've added all this Ajax goodness, go ahead and empty your cart and add an item.

So far we've focused on being more responsive to changes initiated by the user viewing the page. But what about changes made by others? It turns out that that's not as complex as it sounds, thanks to a powerful feature of Rails: Action Cable.

Iteration F5: Broadcasting Updates with Action Cable

Up until now, our users' web browsers have requested information from our Rails app, either by going directly to a URL or by clicking a link or button. It's also possible to send information from our Rails app to our users' browsers without a direct request. The technology that enables this is called *Web Sockets*.[7] Prior to Rails 5, setting this up was fairly involved, but Rails 5 introduced *Action Cable*, which simplifies pushing data to all connected browsers.

We can use Action Cable and Web Sockets to broadcast price updates to the users browsing the catalog. To see why we'd want to, bring up the Depot

---

7. https://www.w3.org/TR/websockets/

application in two browser windows or tabs. In the first window, display the catalog. Then, in the second window, update the price of an item. Return to the first window and add that item to the cart. At this point, the cart shows the updated price, but the catalog shows the original price, as illustrated in the following screenshot.

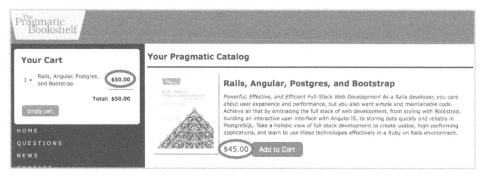

We discuss this with our customer. She agrees to honor the price at the time the item was placed in the cart, but she wants the catalog being displayed to be up-to-date. At this point, we've reached the limits of what Ajax can do for us. So far, the server has only responded to requests and has no way to initiate an update.

In 2011, the Internet Engineering Task Force (IETF) published a Standards Track document describing a two-way WebSocket protocol.[8] Action Cable provides both a client-side JavaScript framework and a server-side Ruby framework that together seamlessly integrate the WebSocket protocol into the rest of your Rails application. This enables features like real-time updates to be easily added to your Rails application in a manner that performs well and is scalable.

Making use of Action Cable is a three-step process: create a channel, broadcast some data, and receive the data. And by now, it should be no surprise that Rails has a generator that does most of the work (for two out of the three steps, anyway):

```
depot> bin/rails generate channel products
     create  app/channels/products_channel.rb
  identical  app/assets/javascripts/cable.js
     create  app/assets/javascripts/channels/products.coffee
```

The way to create a channel is by updating the file created in the app/channels/ directory:

---

8. https://tools.ietf.org/html/rfc6455

```
rails51/depot_o/app/channels/products_channel.rb
class ProductsChannel < ApplicationCable::Channel
  def subscribed
➤    stream_from "products"
  end

  def unsubscribed
    # Any cleanup needed when channel is unsubscribed
  end
end
```

What's important here is the name of the class (ProductsChannel) and the name
of the stream (products). It's possible for a channel to support multiple streams
(for example, a chat application can have multiple rooms), but we only need
one stream for now.

Channels can have security implications, so by default Rails only allows
access from the localhost when running in development mode. If you're doing
development with multiple machines, you must disable this check. Do this
by adding the following line to config/environments/development.rb:

```
config.action_cable.disable_request_forgery_protection = true
```

We'll be sending only data over this channel, and not processing commands,
so this is safe to do.

Next, we're going to broadcast the entire catalog every time an update is made.
We could instead choose to send only portions of the catalog, or any other
data that we might want, but we already have a view for the catalog, so we
might as well use it:

```
rails51/depot_o/app/controllers/products_controller.rb
  def update
    respond_to do |format|
      if @product.update(product_params)
        format.html { redirect_to @product,
          notice: 'Product was successfully updated.' }
        format.json { render :show, status: :ok, location: @product }
➤
➤        @products = Product.all
➤        ActionCable.server.broadcast 'products',
➤          html: render_to_string('store/index', layout: false)
      else
        format.html { render :edit }
        format.json { render json: @product.errors,
          status: :unprocessable_entity }
      end
    end
  end
```

We're using the existing store/index view, which requires a list of products to have been set into the @products instance variable. We call render_to_string() to render the view as a string, passing layout: false, because we want only this view and not the entire page. Broadcast messages typically consist of Ruby hashes, which are converted to JSON to go across the wire and end up as JavaScript objects. In this case, we use html as the hash key.

The final step is to receive the data on the client. This involves subscribing to the channel and defining what'll be done when data is received.

Since this happens in the browser, you'll need to write some more CoffeeScript. Fortunately, Rails generated an outline of what you need to do in app/assets/javascripts/channels/products.coffee. It generated a class with three methods: connected(), disconnected(), and received(). It's received() that we care about, because that's called with the data that gets sent down the channel.

That data has an html attribute that contains the updated HTML. You can then use getElementsByTagName() to locate all the main elements on the page. Since our application only has one of these, we can safely grab the first one using [0] and replace its HTML with the received HTML, like so:

```
rails51/depot_o/app/assets/javascripts/channels/products.coffee
App.products = App.cable.subscriptions.create "ProductsChannel",
  connected: ->
    # Called when the subscription is ready for use on the server

  disconnected: ->
    # Called when the subscription has been terminated by the server

  received: (data) ->
    document.getElementsByTagName("main")[0].innerHTML = data.html
```

The other two methods, connected() and disconnected(), are called when the browser connects and disconnects to the channel, and generally you can leave them empty.

This shows even more of the benefits of CoffeeScript. If you go to the Coffee-Script site,[9] click "Try CoffeeScript," and paste this code, you can see the equivalent in JavaScript. It's a bit longer and more verbose. Of course, the other benefit is that Rails generated most of this code for you, and you only had to add one line. A good place to find out more on this subject is *CoffeeScript: Accelerated JavaScript Development [Bur15]*.

---

9. http://coffeescript.org

To start the Action Cable process (and to pick up the configuration change if that was done), we need to restart the server. The first time you visit the Depot page you'll see additional messages on the server window:

```
Started GET "/cable" for ::1 at 2016-03-13 11:02:42 -0400
Started GET "/cable/" [WebSocket] for ::1 at 2016-03-13 11:02:42 -0400
Successfully upgraded to WebSocket (REQUEST_METHOD: GET,
HTTP_CONNECTION: keep-alive, Upgrade, HTTP_UPGRADE: websocket)
ProductsChannel is transmitting the subscription confirmation
ProductsChannel is streaming from products
```

Again, update the price of a book in one browser window and watch the catalog update instantly in any other browser window that shows the Depot store.

What We Just Did

In this iteration, we added Ajax support to our cart:

- We moved the shopping cart into the sidebar. We then arranged for the create action to redisplay the catalog page.

- We used remote: true to invoke the LineItemsController.create() action using Ajax.

- We then used an ERB template to create CoffeeScript that'll execute on the client.

- We wrote a helper method that renders the cart only if it has anything in it.

- We used Action Cable and CoffeeScript to update the catalog display whenever a product changes.

- We wrote a test that verifies not only the creation of a line item but also the content of the response that's returned from such a request.

The key point to take away is the incremental style of Ajax development. Start with a conventional application and then add Ajax features, one by one. Ajax can be hard to debug; by adding it slowly to an application, you make it easier to track down what changed if your application stops working. And, as you saw, starting with a conventional application makes it easier to support both Ajax and non-Ajax behavior in the same codebase.

Finally, here are a couple of hints. First, if you plan to do a lot of Ajax development, you'll probably need to get familiar with your browser's JavaScript debugging facilities and with its DOM inspectors, such as Firefox's Firebug, Internet Explorer's Developer Tools, Google Chrome's Developer Tools, Safari's Web Inspector, or Opera's Dragonfly. And, second, the NoScript plugin for Firefox makes checking JavaScript/no JavaScript a one-click breeze. Others find it useful to run two different browsers when they're developing—with

JavaScript enabled in one and disabled in the other. Then, as new features are added, poking at it with both browsers will ensure that your application works regardless of the state of JavaScript.

Playtime

Here's some stuff to try on your own:

- The cart is currently hidden when the user empties it by redrawing the entire catalog. Can you change the application to remove it using an Ajax request, so the page doesn't reload?

- Add a button next to each item in the cart. When clicked, it should invoke an action to decrement the quantity of the item, deleting it from the cart when the quantity reaches zero. Get it working without using Ajax first and then add the Ajax goodness.

- Make images clickable. In response to a click, add the associated product to the cart.

- When a product changes, highlight the product that changed in response to receiving a broadcast message.

In this chapter, you'll see:
- Linking tables with foreign keys
- Using belongs_to, has_many, and :through
- Creating forms based on models (form_with)
- Linking forms, models, and views
- Generating a feed using atom_helper on model objects

CHAPTER 12

Task G: Check Out!

Let's take stock. So far, we've put together a basic product administration system, we've implemented a catalog, and we have a pretty spiffy-looking shopping cart. So, now we need to let the buyer actually purchase the contents of that cart. Let's implement the checkout function.

We're not going to go overboard here. For now, all we'll do is capture the customer's contact information and payment details. Using these, we'll construct an order in the database. Along the way, we'll be looking a bit more at models, validation, and form handling.

Iteration G1: Capturing an Order

An order is a set of line items, along with details of the purchase transaction. Our cart already contains line_items, so all we need to do is add an order_id column to the line_items table and create an orders table based on the Initial guess at application data diagram on page 69, combined with a brief chat with our customer.

First we create the order model and update the line_items table:

```
depot> bin/rails generate scaffold Order name address:text email \
          pay_type:integer
depot> bin/rails generate migration add_order_to_line_item order:references
```

Note that we didn't specify any data type for two of the four columns. This is because the data type defaults to string. This is yet another small way in which Rails makes things easier for you in the most common case without making things any more cumbersome when you need to specify a data type.

Note that we defined pay_type as an integer. While this is an efficient way to store data that can only store discrete values, storing data in this way requires keeping track of which values are used for which payment type. Rails can do

this for you through the use of enum declarations placed in the model class.
Add this code to app/models/order.rb:

```
rails51/depot_o/app/models/order.rb
class Order < ApplicationRecord
  enum pay_type: {
    "Check"          => 0,
    "Credit card"    => 1,
    "Purchase order" => 2
  }
end
```

Now that we've created the migrations, we can apply them:

```
depot> bin/rails db:migrate
==  CreateOrders: migrating ========================================
-- create_table(:orders)
    -> 0.0014s
==  CreateOrders: migrated (0.0015s) ===============================

==  AddOrderIdToLineItem: migrating ================================
-- add_column(:line_items, :order_id, :integer)
    -> 0.0008s
==  AddOrderIdToLineItem: migrated (0.0009s) =======================
```

Because the database didn't have entries for these two new migrations in the
schema_migrations table, the db:migrate task applied both migrations to the
database. We could, of course, have applied them separately by running the
migration task after creating the individual migrations.

> **Joe asks:**
> # Where's the Credit-Card Processing?
>
> In the real world, we'd probably want our application to handle the commercial side
> of checkout. We might even want to integrate credit-card processing. However, inte-
> grating with back-end payment-processing systems requires a fair amount of paper-
> work and jumping through hoops. And this would distract from looking at Rails, so
> we're going to punt on this particular detail for the moment.

Creating the Order Capture Form

Now that we have our tables and our models as we need them, we can start
the checkout process. First, we need to add a Checkout button to the shopping
cart. Because it'll create a new order, we'll link it back to a new action in our
order controller:

rails51/depot_o/app/views/carts/_cart.html.erb

```erb
<article>
  <% if notice %>
    <aside id="notice"><%= notice %></aside>
  <% end %>

  <h2>Your Cart</h2>
  <table>

    <%= render(cart.line_items) %>
    <tfoot>
      <tr>
        <th colspan="2">Total:</th>
        <td class="price"><%= number_to_currency(cart.total_price) %></td>
      </tr>
    </tfoot>
  </table>
➤ <div class="actions">
  <%= button_to 'Empty cart', cart,
               method: :delete,
               data: { confirm: 'Are you sure?' } %>

➤ <%= button_to 'Checkout', new_order_path,
➤             method: :get,
➤             class: "checkout"%>
➤ </div>
</article>
```

The first thing we want to do is check to make sure that there's something in the cart. This requires us to have access to the cart. Planning ahead, we'll also need this when we create an order:

rails51/depot_o/app/controllers/orders_controller.rb

```ruby
class OrdersController < ApplicationController
➤  include CurrentCart
➤  before_action :set_cart, only: [:new, :create]
➤  before_action :ensure_cart_isnt_empty, only: :new
   before_action :set_order, only: [:show, :edit, :update, :destroy]

   # GET /orders
   #...
➤
➤  private
➤    def ensure_cart_isnt_empty
➤      if @cart.line_items.empty?
➤        redirect_to store_index_url, notice: 'Your cart is empty'
➤      end
➤    end
   end
```

If nothing is in the cart, we redirect the user back to the storefront, provide a notice of what we did, and return immediately. This prevents people from navigating directly to the checkout option and creating empty orders. Note that we tucked this handling of an exception case into a before_action method. This enables the main line processing logic to remain clean.

And we add a test for requires item in cart and modify the existing test for should get new to ensure that the cart contains an item:

rails51/depot_o/test/controllers/orders_controller_test.rb
```ruby
➤     test "requires item in cart" do
➤       get new_order_url
➤       assert_redirected_to store_index_path
➤       assert_equal flash[:notice], 'Your cart is empty'
➤     end

      test "should get new" do
➤       post line_items_url, params: { product_id: products(:ruby).id }

        get new_order_url
        assert_response :success
      end
```

Now we want the new action to present users with a form, prompting them to enter the information in the orders table: the user's name, address, email address, and payment type. This means we'll need to display a Rails template containing a form. The input fields on this form will have to link to the corresponding attributes in a Rails model object, so we need to create an empty model object in the new action to give these fields something to work with.

As always with HTML forms, the trick is populating any initial values into the form fields and then extracting those values out into our application when the user clicks the submit button.

In the controller, the @order instance variable is set to reference a new Order model object. This is done because the view populates the form from the data in this object. As it stands, that's not particularly interesting. Because it's a new model object, all the fields will be empty. However, consider the general case. Maybe we want to edit an existing order. Or maybe the user has tried to enter an order but the data has failed validation. In these cases, we want any existing data in the model shown to the user when the form is displayed. Passing in the empty model object at this stage makes all these cases consistent. The view can always assume it has a model object available. Then, when the user clicks the submit button, we'd like the new data from the form to be extracted into a model object back in the controller.

Fortunately, Rails makes this relatively painless. It provides us with a bunch of *form helper* methods. These helpers interact with the controller and with the models to implement an integrated solution for form handling. Before we start on our final form, let's look at a small example:

```
<%= form_with(model: @order, local: true) do |form| %>
  <p>
    <%= form.label :name, "Name:" %>
    <%= form.text_field :name, size: 40 %>
  </p>
<% end %>
```

This code does two powerful things for us. First, the form_with() helper on the first line sets up an HTML form that knows about Rails routes and models. The first argument, module: @order tells the helper which instance variable to use when naming fields and sending the form data back to the controller (the second argument tells Rails *not* to post this form via Ajax, which became the default in Rails 5.1).

The second powerful feature of the code is how it creates the form fields themselves. You can see that form_with() sets up a Ruby block environment (that ends on the last line of the listing with the end keyword). Within this block, you can put normal template stuff (such as the <p> tag). But you can also use the block's parameter (form in this case) to reference a form context. We use this context to add a text field with a label by calling text_field() and label(), respectively. Because the text field is constructed in the context of form_with, it's automatically associated with the data in the @order object. This association means that submitting the form will set the right names and values in the data available to the controller, but it will also pre-populate the form fields with any values already existing on the model.

All these relationships can be confusing. It's important to remember that Rails needs to know both the *names* and the *values* to use for the fields associated with a model. The combination of form_with and the various field-level helpers (such as text_field) gives it this information. You can see this process in the figure on page 180.

Now we can update the template for the form that captures a customer's details for checkout. It's invoked from the new action in the order controller, so the template is called new.html.erb, found in the app/views/orders directory:

```
rails51/depot_o/app/views/orders/new.html.erb
<section class="depot_form">
  <h1>Please Enter Your Details</h1>
  <%= render 'form', order: @order %>
</section>
```

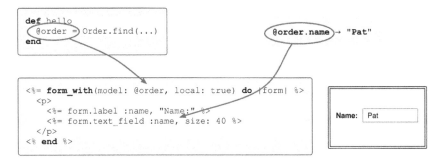

This template makes use of a partial named _form:

```
rails51/depot_o/app/views/orders/_form.html.erb
<%= form_with(model: order, local: true) do |form| %>
  <% if order.errors.any? %>
    <div id="error_explanation">
      <h2><%= pluralize(order.errors.count, "error") %>
      prohibited this order from being saved:</h2>

      <ul>
      <% order.errors.full_messages.each do |message| %>
        <li><%= message %></li>
      <% end %>
      </ul>
    </div>
  <% end %>

  <div class="field">
    <%= form.label :name %>
➤   <%= form.text_field :name, id: :order_name, size: 40 %>
  </div>

  <div class="field">
    <%= form.label :address %>
➤   <%= form.text_area :address, id: :order_address, rows: 3, cols: 40 %>
  </div>

  <div class="field">
    <%= form.label :email %>
➤   <%= form.email_field :email, id: :order_email, size: 40 %>
  </div>

  <div class="field">
    <%= form.label :pay_type %>
➤   <%= form.select :pay_type, Order.pay_types.keys, id: :order_pay_type,
➤                   prompt: 'Select a payment method' %>
  </div>

  <div class="actions">
➤   <%= form.submit 'Place Order' %>
  </div>
<% end %>
```

Rails has form helpers for all the different HTML-level form elements. In the previous code, we use text_field, email_field, and text_area helpers to capture the customer's name, email, and address. We'll cover form helpers in more depth in *Generating Forms*, on page 387.

The only tricky thing in there is the code associated with the selection list. We use the keys defined for the pay_type enum for the list of available payment options. We also pass the :prompt parameter, which adds a dummy selection containing the prompt text.

Let's also add some CSS to make the form work with our existing design. While we're doing this, we'll also add some styling for the error states that Rails renders (which we'll learn about in a moment). You can add all of this at the end of app/assets/stylesheets/application.scss:

```
rails51/depot_o/app/assets/stylesheets/application.scss
.depot_form {
  padding: 0 1em;
  h1 {
    font-size: 1.99em;
    line-height: 1.41em;
    margin-bottom: 0.5em;
    padding: 0;
  }
  .field, .actions {
    margin-bottom: 0.5em;
    padding: 0;
  }
  .actions {
    text-align: right;
    padding: 1em 0;
  }
  input, textarea, select, option {
    border: solid thin #888;
    box-sizing: border-box;
    font-size: 1em;
    padding: 0.5em;
    width: 100%;
  }
  label {
    padding: 0.5em 0;
  }
  input[type="submit"] {
    background-color: #bfb;
    border-radius: 0.354em;
    border: solid thin #888;
    color: black;
    font-size: 1.41em;
    font-weight: bold;
```

```
    padding: 0.354em 1em;
  }
  input[type="submit"]:hover {
    background-color: #9d9;
  }
  // Also, clean up the error styling
  #error_explanation {
    background-color: white;
    border-radius: 1em;
    border: solid thin red;
    margin-bottom: 0.5em;
    padding: 0.5em;
    width: 100%;
    h2 {
      background: none;
      color: red;
      font-size: 1.41em;
      line-height: 1.41em;
      padding: 1em;
    }
    ul {
      margin-top: 0;
      li {
        color: red;
        font-size: 1em;
      }
    }
  }
  .field_with_errors {
    background: none;
    color: red;
    width: 100%;
    label {
      font-weight: bold;
    }
    label::before {
      content: "! ";
    }
    input,textarea {
      background: pink;
    }
  }
}
```

We're ready to play with our form. Add some stuff to your cart, then click the Checkout button. You should see something like the screenshot on page 183.

Looking good! Before we move on, let's finish the new action by adding some validation. We'll change the Order model to verify that the customer enters data for all the input fields. We'll also validate that the payment type is one of the accepted values:

rails51/depot_o/app/models/order.rb
```
class Order < ApplicationRecord
  # ...
➤   validates :name, :address, :email, presence: true
➤   validates :pay_type, inclusion: pay_types.keys
end
```

Some folks might be wondering why we bother to validate the payment type, given that its value comes from a drop-down list that contains only valid values. We do it because an application can't assume that it's being fed values from the forms it creates. Nothing is stopping a malicious user from submitting form data directly to the application, bypassing our form. If the user sets an unknown payment type, that user might conceivably get our products for free.

Note that we already loop over the @order.errors at the top of the page. This'll report validation failures.

Since we modified validation rules, we need to modify our test fixture to match:

rails51/depot_o/test/fixtures/orders.yml
```
# Read about fixtures at
# http://api.rubyonrails.org/classes/ActiveRecord/FixtureSet.html

one:
➤   name: Dave Thomas
    address: MyText
➤   email: dave@example.org
➤   pay_type: Check
```

```
two:
  name: MyString
  address: MyText
  email: MyString
  pay_type: 1
```

Furthermore, for an order to be created, a line item needs to be in the cart, so we need to modify the line items test fixture too:

```
rails51/depot_o/test/fixtures/line_items.yml
# Read about fixtures at
# http://api.rubyonrails.org/classes/ActiveRecord/FixtureSet.html

one:
  product: two
  cart: one

two:
➤ product: ruby
➤ order: one
```

Note that if you didn't choose to do the optional exercises in *Playtime*, on page 149, you need to modify all of the references to products and carts at this time.

Feel free to make other changes, but only the first is currently used in the functional tests. For these tests to pass, we'll need to implement the model.

Capturing the Order Details

Let's implement the create() action in the controller. This method has to do the following:

1. Capture the values from the form to populate a new Order model object.

2. Add the line items from our cart to that order.

3. Validate and save the order. If this fails, display the appropriate messages, and let the user correct any problems.

4. Once the order is successfully saved, delete the cart, redisplay the catalog page, and display a message confirming that the order has been placed.

We define the relationships themselves, first from the line item to the order:

```
rails51/depot_o/app/models/line_item.rb
class LineItem < ApplicationRecord
➤   belongs_to :order, optional: true
➤   belongs_to :product, optional: true
    belongs_to :cart
```

```
  def total_price
    product.price * quantity
  end
end
```

And then we define the relationship from the order to the line item, once again indicating that all line items that belong to an order are to be destroyed whenever the order is destroyed:

rails51/depot_o/app/models/order.rb
```
class Order < ApplicationRecord
➤   has_many :line_items, dependent: :destroy
    # ...
end
```

The method ends up looking something like this:

rails51/depot_o/app/controllers/orders_controller.rb
```
def create
  @order = Order.new(order_params)
➤   @order.add_line_items_from_cart(@cart)

  respond_to do |format|
    if @order.save
➤       Cart.destroy(session[:cart_id])
➤       session[:cart_id] = nil
➤       format.html { redirect_to store_index_url, notice:
➤         'Thank you for your order.' }
        format.json { render :show, status: :created,
          location: @order }
      else
        format.html { render :new }
        format.json { render json: @order.errors,
          status: :unprocessable_entity }
      end
    end
end
```

We start by creating a new Order object and initialize it from the form data. The next line adds into this order the items that are already stored in the cart; we'll write the method to do that in a minute.

Next, we tell the order object to save itself (and its children, the line items) to the database. Along the way, the order object will perform validation (but we'll get to that in a minute).

If the save succeeds, we do two things. First, we ready ourselves for this customer's next order by deleting the cart from the session. Then, we redisplay

> ### Joe asks:
> ## Aren't You Creating Duplicate Orders?
>
> Joe is concerned to see our controller creating Order model objects in two actions: new and create. He's wondering why this doesn't lead to duplicate orders in the database.
>
> The answer is that the new action creates an Order object *in memory* simply to give the template code something to work with. Once the response is sent to the browser, that particular object gets abandoned, and it'll eventually be reaped by Ruby's garbage collector. It never gets close to the database.
>
> The create action also creates an Order object, populating it from the form fields. This object *does* get saved in the database. So, model objects perform two roles: they map data into and out of the database, but they're also regular objects that hold business data. They affect the database only when you tell them to, typically by calling save().

the catalog, using the redirect_to() method to display a cheerful message. If, instead, the save fails, we redisplay the checkout form with the current cart.

In the create action, we assumed that the order object contains the add_line_items_from_cart() method, so let's implement that method now:

rails51/depot_p/app/models/order.rb
```
class Order < ApplicationRecord
  # ...
  def add_line_items_from_cart(cart)
    cart.line_items.each do |item|
      item.cart_id = nil
      line_items << item
    end
  end
end
```

For each item that we transfer from the cart to the order, we need to do two things. First we set the cart_id to nil to prevent the item from going poof when we destroy the cart.

Then we add the item itself to the line_items collection for the order. Notice that we didn't have to do anything special with the various foreign-key fields, such as setting the order_id column in the line item rows to reference the newly created order row. Rails does that knitting for us using the has_many() and belongs_to() declarations we added to the Order and LineItem models. Appending each new line item to the line_items collection hands the responsibility for key management over to Rails. We also need to modify the test to reflect the new redirect:

rails51/depot_p/test/controllers/orders_controller_test.rb

```
test "should create order" do
  assert_difference('Order.count') do
    post orders_url, params: { order: { address: @order.address,
      email: @order.email, name: @order.name,
      pay_type: @order.pay_type } }
  end

➤ assert_redirected_to store_index_url
end
```

So, as a first test of all of this, click the Place Order button on the checkout page without filling in any of the form fields. You should see the checkout page redisplayed along with error messages complaining about the empty fields, as shown in the following screenshot.

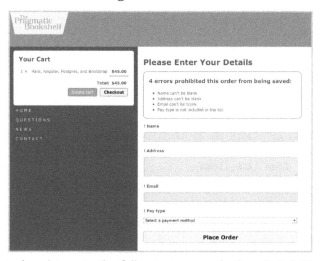

If we fill in data (as shown in the following screenshot) and click Place Order, we should be taken back to the catalog, as shown in the screenshot on page 188.

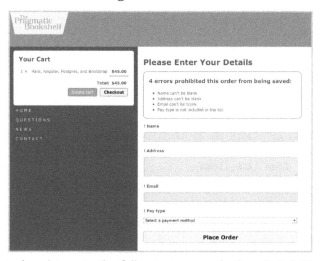

But did it work? Let's look in the database, using the Rails command dbconsole, which tells Rails to open an interactive shell to whatever database we have configured.

```
depot> bin/rails dbconsole
SQLite version 3.8.2
Enter ".help" for instructions
sqlite> .mode line
sqlite> select * from orders;
             id = 1
           name = Dave Thomas
        address = 123 Main St
          email = customer@example.com
       pay_type = 0
     created_at = 2016-05-29 02:31:04.964785
     updated_at = 2016-05-29 02:31:04.964785
sqlite> select * from line_items;
             id = 10
     product_id = 2
        cart_id =
     created_at = 2016-05-29 02:30:26.188914
     updated_at = 2016-05-29 02:31:04.966057
       quantity = 1
          price = 45
       order_id = 1
sqlite> .quit
```

Although what you see will differ on details such as version numbers and dates (and price will be present only if you completed the exercises defined in *Playtime*, on page 149), you should see a single order and one or more line items that match your selections.

Now that users can check out and purchase products, the customer needs a way to view these orders. Going into the database directly is not acceptable. We also don't have time to build a full-fledged admin user interface right now, so we'll take advantage of the various Atom feed readers that exist and have our app export all the orders as an Atom feed, so the customer can quickly see what's been purchased.

Iteration G2: Atom Feeds

By using a standard feed format, such as Atom, you can immediately take advantage of a wide variety of preexisting clients. Because Rails already knows about IDs, dates, and links, it can free you from having to worry about these pesky details and let you focus on producing a human-readable summary. We start by adding a new action to the products controller:

rails51/depot_p/app/controllers/products_controller.rb

```ruby
def who_bought
  @product = Product.find(params[:id])
  @latest_order = @product.orders.order(:updated_at).last
  if stale?(@latest_order)
    respond_to do |format|
      format.atom
    end
  end
end
```

Joe asks:
Why Atom?

A number of different feed formats exit—most notably RSS 1.0, RSS 2.0, and Atom, standardized in 2000, 2002, and 2005, respectively. These three are all widely supported. To aid with the transition, a number of sites provide multiple feeds for the same site, but this is no longer necessary, increases user confusion, and generally isn't recommended.

The Ruby language provides a low-level library that can produce any of these formats as well as a number of other less common versions of RSS. For best results, stick with one of the three main versions.

The Rails framework is all about picking reasonable defaults, and it has chosen Atom as the default for feed formats. It's specified as an Internet standards–track protocol for the Internet community by the IETF, and Rails provides a higher-level helper named atom_feed that takes care of a number of details based on knowledge of Rails naming conventions for things like IDs and dates.

In addition to fetching the product, we check to see if the request is *stale*. Remember in *Iteration C5: Caching of Partial Results*, on page 116 when we cached partial results of responses because the catalog display was expected to be a high-traffic area? Well, feeds are like that, but with a different usage pattern. Instead of a large number of different clients all requesting the same page, we have a small number of clients repeatedly requesting the same page.

You might be familiar with the idea of browser caches; the same concept holds true for feed aggregators.

The way this works is that the responses contain a bit of metadata that identifies when the content was last modified and a hashed value called an *ETag*. If a subsequent request provides this data back, this gives the server the opportunity to respond with an empty response body and an indication that the data hasn't been modified.

As is usual with Rails, you don't need to worry about the mechanics. You just need to identify the source of the content, and Rails does the rest. In this case, we use the last order. Inside the if statement, we process the request normally.

By adding format.atom, we cause Rails to look for a template named who_bought.atom.builder. Such a template can use the generic XML functionality that Builder provides as well as use the knowledge of the Atom feed format that the atom_feed helper provides:

```
rails51/depot_p/app/views/products/who_bought.atom.builder
atom_feed do |feed|
  feed.title "Who bought #{@product.title}"

  feed.updated @latest_order.try(:updated_at)

  @product.orders.each do |order|
    feed.entry(order) do |entry|
      entry.title "Order #{order.id}"
      entry.summary type: 'xhtml' do |xhtml|
        xhtml.p "Shipped to #{order.address}"

        xhtml.table do
          xhtml.tr do
            xhtml.th 'Product'
            xhtml.th 'Quantity'
            xhtml.th 'Total Price'
          end
          order.line_items.each do |item|
            xhtml.tr do
              xhtml.td item.product.title
              xhtml.td item.quantity
              xhtml.td number_to_currency item.total_price
            end
          end
          xhtml.tr do
            xhtml.th 'total', colspan: 2
            xhtml.th number_to_currency \
              order.line_items.map(&:total_price).sum
          end
        end
```

```
        xhtml.p "Paid by #{order.pay_type}"
      end
      entry.author do |author|
        author.name order.name
        author.email order.email
      end
    end
  end
end
```

At the overall feed level, we need to provide only two pieces of information: the title and the date of the latest update. If no orders exist, the updated_at value is null, and Rails supplies the current time instead.

Then we iterate over each order associated with this product by calling @product.orders. Products and orders have no direct relationship to each other, though there is an indirect one via line items. A product's orders would be the orders associated with any of the product's line items. We could implement that ourselves by creating an orders() method, but Rails provides a way to do this for us, since this indirect relationship is a common pattern. The has_many() method we used to tell Rails that a product has many line items takes an optional argument named through: that tells Rails to traverse the indirect relationship. In our case, we'll tell Rails that a product has many orders *through* its existing line items relationship:

rails51/depot_p/app/models/product.rb
```
class Product < ApplicationRecord
  has_many :line_items
➤ has_many :orders, through: :line_items
  #...
end
```

For each order, we provide a title, a summary, and an author. The summary can be full XHTML, and we use this to produce a table of product titles, quantity ordered, and total prices. We follow this table with a paragraph containing the pay_type.

To make this work, we need to define a route. This action will respond to HTTP GET requests and will operate on a member of the collection (in other words, on an individual product) as opposed to the entire collection (which in this case would mean all products):

rails51/depot_p/config/routes.rb
```
Rails.application.routes.draw do
  resources :orders
  resources :line_items
  resources :carts
  root 'store#index', as: 'store_index'
```

```
➤    resources :products do
➤      get :who_bought, on: :member
➤    end

     # For details on the DSL available within this file, see
     # http://guides.rubyonrails.org/routing.html
   end
```

We can try it for ourselves:

```
depot> curl --silent http://localhost:3000/products/3/who_bought.atom
<?xml version="1.0" encoding="UTF-8"?>
<feed xml:lang="en-US" xmlns="http://www.w3.org/2005/Atom">
  <id>tag:localhost,2005:/products/3/who_bought</id>
  <link type="text/html" href="http://localhost:3000" rel="alternate"/>
  <link type="application/atom+xml"
        href="http://localhost:3000/info/who_bought/3.atom" rel="self"/>
  <title>Who bought Programming Ruby 1.9</title>
  <updated>2016-01-29T02:31:04Z</updated>
  <entry>
    <id>tag:localhost,2005:Order/1</id>
    <published>2016-01-29T02:31:04Z</published>
    <updated>2016-01-29T02:31:04Z</updated>
    <link rel="alternate" type="text/html" href="http://localhost:3000/orders/1"/>
    <title>Order 1</title>
    <summary type="xhtml">
      <div xmlns="http://www.w3.org/1999/xhtml">
        <p>Shipped to 123 Main St</p>

        <table>
          ...
        </table>
        <p>Paid by check</p>
      </div>
    </summary>
    <author>
      <name>Dave Thomas</name>
      <email>customer@pragprog.com</email>
    </author>
  </entry>
</feed>
```

Looks good. Now we can subscribe to this in our favorite feed reader.

Best of all, the customer likes it. We've implemented product maintenance, a basic catalog, and a shopping cart, and now we have a simple ordering system. Obviously, we'll also have to write some kind of fulfillment application, but that can wait for a new iteration. (And that iteration is one that we'll skip in this book; it doesn't have much new to say about Rails.)

What We Just Did

In a fairly short amount of time, we did the following:

- We created a form to capture details for the order and linked it to a new order model.

- We added validation and used helper methods to display errors to the user.

- We provided a feed so the administrator can monitor incoming orders.

Playtime

Here's some stuff to try on your own:

- Get HTML- and JSON-formatted views working for who_bought requests. Experiment with including the order information in the JSON view by rendering @product.to_json(include: :orders). Do the same thing for XML using ActiveModel::Serializers::Xml.[1]

- What happens if you click the Checkout button in the sidebar while the checkout screen is already displayed? Can you find a way to disable the button in this circumstance?

- The list of possible payment types is currently stored as a constant in the Order class. Can you move this list into a database table? Can you still make validation work for the field?

---

1. https://github.com/rails/activemodel-serializers-xml#readme

In this chapter, you'll see:
- Using Webpacker to manage app-like Javascript
- Setting up a development environment that includes Webpack
- Using React to build a dynamic web form
- Using Capybara and ChromeDriver to test JavaScript-powered features

CHAPTER 13

Task H: Entering Additional Payment Details

Our customer is enthusiastic about our progress, but after playing with the new checkout feature for a few minutes, she has a question: how does a user enter payment details? It's a great question, since there isn't a way to do that. Making that possible is somewhat tricky, because each payment method requires different details. If users want to pay with a credit card, they need to enter a card number and expiration date. If they want to pay with a check, we'll need a routing number and an account number. And for purchase orders, we need the purchase order number.

Although we could put all five fields on the screen at once, the customer immediately balks at the poor user experience that would result. Can we show the appropriate fields, depending on what payment type is chosen? Changing elements of a user interface dynamically is certainly possible with some JavaScript, but it's quite a bit more complex than the JavaScript we've used thus far. Rails calls JavaScript like this *app-like JavaScript*, and it includes a tool named Webpacker that will help us manage it. Webpacker will handle a lot of complex setup for us so that we can focus most of our efforts on giving our customer—and our users—a great experience checking out. (Refer back to Chapter 1, *Installing Rails*, on page 3, for installation instructions for the tools used in this chapter.)

Iteration H1: Adding Fields Dynamically to a Form

We need a dynamic form that changes what fields are shown based on what pay type the user has selected. While we could cobble something together with jQuery, it would be a bit cleaner if we could use a more modern

JavaScript library like React.[1] This will also form a solid base from which we can easily add additional features later.

Using JavaScript libraries or frameworks can often be difficult, as the configuration burden they bear is far greater than what we've seen with Rails. To help us manage this complexity, Rails includes *Webpacker*, which provides configuration for *Webpack*.[2] Webpack is a tool to manage the JavaScript files that we write. Note the similar names. Webpack*er* is a gem that's part of Rails and sets up Webpack inside our Rails app.

Managing JavaScript is surprisingly complex. By using Webpack we can easily put our JavaScript into several different files, bring in third-party libraries (like React), and use more advanced features of JavaScript not supported by a browser (such as the ability to define classes). Webpack then compiles all of our JavaScript, along with the third-party libraries we are using, into a *pack*. Because this isn't merely sprinkling small bits of JavaScript in our view, Rails refers to this as *app-like* JavaScript.

While we could use Webpack directly with Rails, configuring Webpack is extremely difficult. It's highly customizable and not very opinionated, meaning developers must make many decisions just to get something working. Webpacker essentially *is* the decisions made by the Rails team and bundled up into a gem. Almost everything Webpacker does is to provide a working configuration for Webpack and React so that we can focus on writing JavaScript instead of configuring tools. But Webpack is the tool that manages our JavaScript day-to-day.

React is a JavaScript view library designed to quickly create dynamic user interfaces. We'll use it to create a dynamic payment method details form, and Webpacker will ensure that the configuration and setup for all this is as simple as possible. That said, there's a bit of setup we need to do.

First, we'll configure Webpacker and install React. After that, we'll replace our existing payment-type drop-down with a React-rendered version, which will demonstrate how all the moving parts fit together. With that in place, we'll enhance our React-powered payment type selector to show the dynamic form elements we want.

---

1.   https://facebook.github.io/react/
2.   https://webpack.js.org

Configuring Webpacker and Installing React

Webpacker is a separate gem that you must install in addition to Rails. Add it to your Gemfile like so:

```
gem 'webpacker', '~> 3.0'
```

Install this with bundle install.

Next, set up Webpack by running bin/rails webpacker:install.

```
$ bin/rails webpacker:install
Creating javascript app source directory
    create  app/javascript
    create  app/javascript/packs/application.js
Copying binstubs
     exist  bin
    create  bin/webpack-dev-server
    create  bin/webpack
  identical  bin/yarn
Copying webpack core config and loaders
    create  config/webpack
    create  config/webpack/configuration.js
    create  config/webpack/development.js
    create  config/webpack/development.server.js
    create  config/webpack/development.server.yml
    create  config/webpack/paths.yml
    create  config/webpack/production.js
    create  config/webpack/shared.js
    create  config/webpack/test.js
    create  config/webpack/loaders
    create  config/webpack/loaders/assets.js
    create  config/webpack/loaders/babel.js
    create  config/webpack/loaders/coffee.js
    create  config/webpack/loaders/erb.js
    create  config/webpack/loaders/sass.js
    create  .postcssrc.yml
    append  .gitignore
Installing all JavaScript dependencies
       run  ./bin/yarn add webpack webpack-merge js-yaml…
yarn add v0.20.3
[1/4] Resolving packages...
[2/4] Fetching packages...
[3/4] Linking dependencies...
[4/4] Building fresh packages...

«lots of output»

Done in 24.95s.
Installing dev server for live reloading
       run  ./bin/yarn add --dev webpack-dev-server from "."
yarn add v0.20.3
```

```
[1/4] Resolving packages...
[2/4] Fetching packages...
[3/4] Linking dependencies...
[4/4] Building fresh packages...
success Saved lockfile.
success Saved 82 new dependencies.

«lots more output»

Done in 5.11s.
Webpacker successfully installed
```

As you can see from the output, this created several configuration files in config/webpack and installed various JavaScript libraries. The libraries that were installed are listed in package.json. package.json is the JavaScript equivalent to our Gemfile—it lists all the necessary JavaScript libraries for our app to run. The equivalent of Bundler is *Yarn*.

Just like bundle install downloads all the gems our app needs, yarn install downloads all the JavaScript libraries we need. As a convenience, the webpacker:install task ran yarn install for us.

Webpacker can also install and configure some common JavaScript frameworks such as Angular, Vue, or React. We chose React because it's the simplest overall and is the best fit for solving our problem. To have Webpacker set it all up for us, run the task webpacker:install:react:

```
$ bin/rails webpacker:install:react
Copying react loader to …config/webpack/loaders
      create  config/webpack/loaders/react.js
Copying .babelrc to app root directory
      create  .babelrc
Copying react example entry file to …app/javascript/packs
      create  app/javascript/packs/hello_react.jsx
Installing all react dependencies
      run   ./bin/yarn add react react-dom babel-preset-react from "."
yarn add v0.20.3
[1/4] Resolving packages...
[2/4] Fetching packages...
[3/4] Linking dependencies...
warning "react-dom@15.4.2" has unmet peer dependency "react@^15.4.2".
[4/4] Building fresh packages...
success Saved lockfile.
success Saved 26 new dependencies.

«lots of output»
Done in 7.17s.
Webpacker now supports react.js
```

If you've ever tried to set up Webpack and a JavaScript framework like React before, you'll appreciate how much work Webpacker has just done for us. If you've never had the privilege, trust me, this saves a ton of time and aggravation.

Webpacker also created a rudimentary React component in app/javascript/packs/hello_react.jsx. Don't worry about what that means for now. We're going to use this generated code to validate the installation and set up our development environment. This generated code will append the string "Hello React!" to the end of our page, but it's not activated by default. Let's find out why, configure it to be included in our views, and set up our development environment to work smoothly with Webpacker.

Updating Our Development Environment for Webpack

Webpacker includes a helper method called javascript_pack_tag() that takes as an argument the name of the file in app/javascript/packs whose JavaScript should be included on the page.

The reason Rails doesn't simply include all JavaScript all the time is that you might not want that to happen for performance reasons. Although our payment details code won't be terribly complex, it'll still be a chunk of code our users will have to download. Since it won't be needed anywhere else in our app, we can make the user experience faster and better by only downloading the code when it's needed.

Webpacker allows us to have any number of these separately managed *packs*. We can include any that we like, wherever we like. To see how this works, let's add a call to javascript_pack_tag() to our app/views/orders/new.html.erb page to bring in the sample React component that Webpacker created for us.

```
rails51/depot_pa/app/views/orders/new.html.erb
<section class="depot_form">
  <h1>Please Enter Your Details</h1>
  <%= render 'form', order: @order %>
</section>
```
➤ `<%= javascript_pack_tag("hello_react") %>`

If you add some items to your cart and navigate to the checkout page, you should see the string "Hello React!" at the bottom of the page, as shown in the screenshot on page 200.

This validates that all the internals of Webpack are working with the app (which is always a good practice before writing code so we can be sure what might be the cause if something's wrong). Now we can start building our feature. We need to replace the existing drop-down with one powered by React and our Webpacker-managed JavaScript. Doing *that* requires a slight diversion to learn about React.

Learning Just Enough React

We've validated our Webpack setup, but we still don't have the full picture of what is going on. What is a .jsx file, and what is the odd syntax inside app/javascript/packs/hello_react.jsx? We can answer these questions by talking about what React is and why we're using it.

As mentioned above, React is a view library for JavaScript. Like the .erb files we've been using, React dynamically renders HTML. Unlike ERB, React does this in the browser, and it is optimized to do it fast. Because the selected pay type will only affect a small part of our page, it will be a much better user experience to have React rerender that part of our page than to have the server rerender the entire thing.

React is more than just a library with some handy functions we can call. It's actually a mini-framework that includes extensions to JavaScript to make our work easier—once we understand how to use those extensions. When we do, our job of creating a dynamic payment details form will result in easy-to-understand code that's also easy to manage, thanks to Webpacker.

The core concept in React is *components*. A component is a view, backed by some sort of state. When the state changes, the view rerenders. The view can behave differently depending on the current state inside the component. For us, we'll track the currently selected pay type as our state and have our view render different input tags based on that.

We could certainly accomplish all of this using React's JavaScript API. The resulting code would be verbose, hard to follow, and hard to maintain. We mentioned React's extensions to JavaScript, and that extension is JSX.[3] JSX allows you to intermix JavaScript code and HTML-like markup in one file. The result might look a bit odd at first, but it's quite convenient for implementing components.

React provides a compiler from JSX to JavaScript, and Webpack can use that compiler as part of its build process. Let's learn what JSX is actually like and what it can do by replacing our existing pay type drop-down with a React component that behaves the same way.

Creating a React-Powered Drop-Down

To get a sense of how to work with React and Webpack, we'll replace the existing pay type drop-down that's being rendered by Rails with one that's rendered by React. Doing this requires three steps:

1. Create a new pack called pay_type that'll be the root of our implementation.

2. Create the PayTypeSelector component that we'll use to replace the existing pay type selector drop-down.

3. Bring the component into our checkout view using javascript_pack_tag() and a piece of markup that React can hook into in order to render the component.

This won't change how our application behaves, but it will allow us to see all the moving parts and understand what they do.

Creating a New Pack

As we mentioned, packs go in app/javascript/packs, so we'll create our new pack in app/javascript/packs/pay_type.jsx. This code is *not* a React component, but just a few lines of code to bootstrap our React component and get it onto our page.

The most straightforward way to do that is to locate an element in the DOM and use the React function React.render() to render our component into that element. Let's see the code, and then we'll go through and explain what's happening, line by line.

---

3. https://facebook.github.io/react/docs/introducing-jsx.html

```
rails51/depot_pb/app/javascript/packs/pay_type.jsx
① import React           from 'react'
② import ReactDOM        from 'react-dom'
③ import PayTypeSelector from 'PayTypeSelector'

④ document.addEventListener('turbolinks:load', function() {
⑤   var element = document.getElementById("pay-type-component");
⑥   ReactDOM.render(<PayTypeSelector />, element);
});
```

If you have not done much JavaScript, or have not kept up with recent advances in the language, much of this file will look alien. Let's break it down line by line.

❶ This is how we get access to the main React library. import is like require() in Ruby: it allows us to access code located in other files. Although it's formally part of the JavaScript standard, browsers don't support it. Webpack provides an implementation for us when it compiles our code. When it processes this line, it'll try to find a file named react.js in one of the paths it's configured to search (we'll learn more about this in a bit).

❷ This brings in the ReactDOM object, which has the render() function we need to bootstrap our React component.

❸ Here, we're importing PayTypeSelector, which is the component we'll make next. When we actually build this component, we'll explain how Webpack knows where to find the code. The most important thing about this line for now is the name PayTypeSelector, which we'll reference later in the file.

❹ This uses the standard function addEventListener() available on document to ensure that the code we're about to execute only runs after the entire DOM has loaded.[4] Note that we aren't using the more standard DOMContent-Loaded event.

Due to how Turbolinks works, that event isn't fired every time our page is reloaded. Turbolinks manages the page-loading events for us and instead fires the turbolinks:load event. If you were to use DOMContentLoaded, then navigate away from the page, and then use the back button, the page would not properly set up React and nothing would work. Using turbolinks:load ensures that React is set up every time the page is rendered.

❺ This line is also vanilla JavaScript and is locating an element with the ID pay-type-component. We'll create that element in our Rails view later.

---

4. https://developer.mozilla.org/en-US/docs/Web/API/EventTarget/addEventListener

❻ *This* is the weirdest line in this file. It doesn't even look like JavaScript! ReactDOM.render()'s job is to replace element with the React component PayType-Selector. In a JSX file, the way to do that is via this odd HTML-like value <PayTypeSelector />. We'll see a more involved example of JSX when we build PayTypeSelector, but part of what happens when Webpack compiles a JSX file is to interpret this strange-looking syntax and produce JavaScript that works in our browser. It works because we used PayTypeSelector in the import line above.

That is a lot of new information for just six lines of code. While it looks a bit weird, it makes some sense, and you'll get used to it as you work with React more. Now, let's define PayTypeSelector.

Creating the **PayTypeSelector** Component

We talked about what import does, and now we need to know more about how it does it. When Webpack is compiling our files into a bundle our browser can understand, it's configured with certain paths it will use to locate files we ask to import. The first path is node_modules. This is where Yarn downloaded all of our third-party JavaScript libraries, including React.

If you look inside node_modules, you'll see many, many directories, but react and react-dom are among them. *Our* code doesn't go in node_modules but instead goes in app/javascript. Webpacker has configured Webpack to also look there for files to import.

Webpack isn't just looking for files like app/javascript/PayTypeSelector.jsx. Rails and Webpack both want us to organize our JavaScript into multiple files, so when we ask to import 'PayTypeSelector', Webpack will load the file app/javascript/PayType-Selector/index.jsx.

This might seem odd, but it's consistent with how third-party JavaScript is bundled, and it also allows us to organize files needed by PayTypeSelector into one location—app/javascript/PayTypeSelector. We'll do this later when we build our payment details component in full.

For now, we'll create the file app/javascript/PayTypeSelector/index.jsx. This file will contain a React component that renders the exact same HTML for the pay type drop-down as our current Rails view.

A React component doesn't need much in order to work. It must be a class that extends React.Component and must have a render() method that returns markup for the component's view.

Of course, regular JavaScript that runs in our browser doesn't have classes or methods. However, the latest version of the JavaScript specification *does* support creating classes with methods,[5] just like we do in Ruby. Webpack will gladly translate this code into vanilla JavaScript our browser can execute.

The syntax for this is demonstrated in app/javascript/PayTypeSelector/index.jsx, which you should create like so:

```
rails51/depot_pb/app/javascript/PayTypeSelector/index.jsx
import React from 'react'

class PayTypeSelector extends React.Component {
  render() {
    return (
      <div className="field">
        <label htmlFor="order_pay_type">Pay type</label>
        <select id="pay_type" name="order[pay_type]">
          <option value="">Select a payment method</option>
          <option value="Check">Check</option>
          <option value="Credit card">Credit card</option>
          <option value="Purchase order">Purchase order</option>
        </select>
      </div>
    );
  }
}
export default PayTypeSelector
```

Inside render() we can see a more involved use of the markup-like syntax that JSX allows. It might look like HTML, but it's not. It's usually referred to as "JSX" and it has some subtle deviations from HTML.

First, it must be well-formed XML, meaning that each tag must either have a closing tag (for example foo), or be self-closing (for example <input/>). HTML does not require this, notably for input elements.

Second, JSX cannot use JavaScript keywords for attributes. You'll notice we're using className and htmlFor. In normal HTML, we'd use class and for, but these are reserved words in JavaScript. React's documentation has more details on the differences between this markup and HTML.[6]

Also note that we've judiciously chosen the name value for select in exactly the same way a Rails form helper would. This allows our controller to find the values, even though they are coming from a React-rendered component and not a Rails-rendered view.

---

5.   http://www.ecma-international.org/ecma-262/6.0/#sec-class-definitions

6.   https://facebook.github.io/react/docs/dom-elements.html

The last line of the file contains something new: export. This is the other side of import. In Ruby, a file that is required via require() is simply executed. Any classes it creates are inserted into the global namespace. In JavaScript, you must explicitly state what you are exporting from your file.

Although you could export several different classes or functions from a file, in our case, we just need to export one—PayTypeSelector. The syntax to do that is export default «class».

Now that we've implemented our component and created the glue code in our pack to hook it up, we need to modify our Rails views to use it.

Bringing the PayTypeSelector Component into the Rails View

Inside app/views/orders/new.html.erb we added javascript_pack_tag("hello_react") in order to validate that Webpacker had installed and configured React and that our development environment was working. Let's replace that and bring in the pay_type pack we just created.

```
rails51/depot_pb/app/views/orders/new.html.erb
<section class="depot_form">
  <h1>Please Enter Your Details</h1>
  <%= render 'form', order: @order %>
</section>
```

➤ `<%= javascript_pack_tag("pay_type") %>`

The last thing to do is remove the Rails-rendered pay type drop-down and add in a piece of markup with the ID pay-type-component so that the code inside our pack file can tell React to render there.

```
rails51/depot_pb/app/views/orders/_form.html.erb
  <div class="field">
    <%= form.label :email %>
    <%= form.email_field :email, id: :order_email, size: 40 %>
  </div>
```

➤ `  <div id='pay-type-component'></div>`

```
  <div class="actions">
    <%= form.submit 'Place Order' %>
  </div>
<% end %>
```

The type of element doesn't matter, since React will replace it, but a div is semantically appropriate.

With our new pay type component in place, you should be able to reload the checkout page and see the pay type drop-down exactly as it was. You should also be able to select a pay type, check out, and see the correct data make it into the database.

We are now ready to build the dynamic form we talked about with the customer. React components render their views based on the state inside a component. This means we need to capture the selected pay type as the component's state and render different form fields based on that state.

Dynamically Replacing Components Based on User Actions

To detect events in plain JavaScript, we'd add the onchange attribute to our select element, setting its value to JavaScript code we'd like to execute. This is exactly how it works in React as well, except that we use the attribute onChange (note that capitalized "C"):

```
import React from 'react'

class PayTypeSelector extends React.Component {
  render() {
    return (
      <div className="field">
        <label htmlFor="order_pay_type">Pay type</label>
        <select onChange={this.onPayTypeSelected} name="order[pay_type]">
          <option value="">Select a payment method</option>
          <option value="Check">Check</option>
          <option value="Credit card">Credit card</option>
          <option value="Purchase order">Purchase order</option>
        </select>
      </div>
    );
  }
}
```

Note that we aren't quoting the value to onChange but instead using curly braces. This is another feature of JSX and is part of making the view dynamic. Curly braces allow us to interpolate JavaScript, much like how #{...} does in Ruby or <%= ... %> does in ERB. React knows to put quotes in the right places when the HTML is rendered.

We can now define the method onPayTypeSelected() like so:

```
import React from 'react'

class PayTypeSelector extends React.Component {
➤  onPayTypeSelected(event) {
➤    console.log(event.target.value);
➤  }
```

This implementation demonstrates how we can access the user's selection. The event passed in is a *synthetic event,*[7] which has a property target that is a DOMEventTarget, which itself has a property value that has the value of the selected payment type.

If you reload the page in your browser, open the JavaScript console, and select different payment types, you should see messages in the console. The following screenshot shows this after selecting each pay type one at a time.

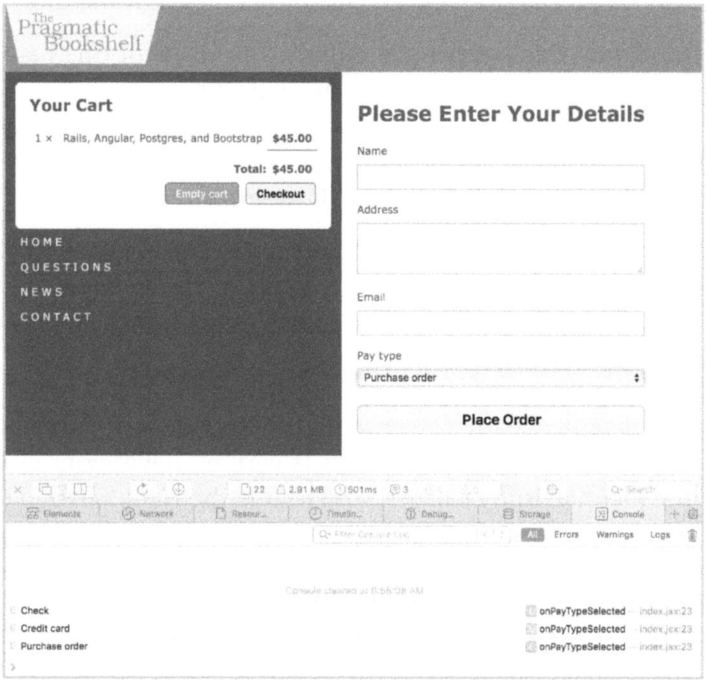

What do we do with this new method? If you recall, a React component is a view and state; and when state changes, the view is rerendered by calling the component's render() method. We want the view to be rerendered when the user changes payment types, so we need to get the currently selected payment type into the component's state.

We can do this via the method setState() provided by our superclass, React.Component:

```
rails51/depot_pc/app/javascript/PayTypeSelector/index.jsx
onPayTypeSelected(event) {
  this.setState({ selectedPayType: event.target.value });
}
```

_____

7.   https://facebook.github.io/react/docs/events.html

Surprisingly this doesn't work, because this is undefined. It's tempting to view this in JavaScript the same way you would self in Ruby, because it often refers to the current instance of the class, just as in Ruby. But "often" isn't "always."

Under the covers, JavaScript classes and methods are just functions. When you call a function in JavaScript, it's possible to control what the value of this is inside that function. When we call a method on an object created from a class, that method is really a function whose value for this is set to the object...except when that method is called from an event handler.

To understand why this happens is outside the scope of this book, but the short explanation is that because we are passing a function to our event handler, when the event fires, the object that function is a part of—which we would very much like to be available as this—is not remembered by JavaScript (this is a complex concept in JavaScript[8]).

To ensure that this is remembered and thus set to the object, we call bind() on the method itself and pass this when this is set to the instance of our class. bind() returns a new function where this is always set how we'd expect.

```
this.onPayTypeSelected = this.onPayTypeSelected.bind(this);
```

The only trick is to make sure we execute this code before the event handler fires and at a time when the value of this is correct. JavaScript classes have constructors, just like Ruby classes, and that is the right location to execute this code. We haven't declared a constructor yet; and as it turns out, React component constructors accept an argument called props that we must pass up to the superclass. We should also initialize our state. This means our constructor will look like so:

```
rails51/depot_pc/app/javascript/PayTypeSelector/index.jsx
class PayTypeSelector extends React.Component {
➤   constructor(props) {
➤     super(props);
➤     this.onPayTypeSelected = this.onPayTypeSelected.bind(this);
➤     this.state = { selectedPayType: null };
➤   }
```

Inside render(), we can examine the value of state by accessing this.state.selected-PayType, which will be the string from our select control.

We now want to render a custom component based on the value of this.state.selectedPayType. We can't easily put control logic inside the JSX, but we can insert a dynamic component by declaring a variable that starts with an

---

8.   https://www.smashingmagazine.com/2014/01/understanding-javascript-function-prototype-bind/

uppercase letter. This is another feature of JSX we can use. Our code will
look something like this:

```
let PayTypeCustomComponent = «to be determined»
return (
  <div>
    <div className="field">
      <label htmlFor="order_pay_type">Pay type</label>
      <select id="pay_type" onChange={this.onPayTypeSelected}
        name="order[pay_type]">
        <option value="">Select a payment method</option>
        <option value="Check">Check</option>
        <option value="Credit card">Credit card</option>
        <option value="Purchase order">Purchase order</option>
      </select>
    </div>
    <PayTypeCustomComponent />
  </div>
);
```

This means we need to make the components we'll use for each pay type,
along with a blank component for when no pay type is selected. We'll import
those into PayTypeSelector and, based on the value of state, assign them to a
local variable named PayTypeCustomComponent.

First, let's set up our imports for the files we'll create in a moment:

rails51/depot_pc/app/javascript/PayTypeSelector/index.jsx
```
import React from 'react'

➤ import NoPayType            from './NoPayType';
➤ import CreditCardPayType    from './CreditCardPayType';
➤ import CheckPayType         from './CheckPayType';
➤ import PurchaseOrderPayType from './PurchaseOrderPayType';
```

Note that each file we're importing is preceded by a dot and a slash (./). This
tells Webpack to locate the file in the same directory as the file being processed. Since the file being processed is app/javascript/PayTypeSelector/index.jsx,
Webpack will look in app/javascript/PayTypeSelector. Hopefully, you can see the
logic of Rails's convention around using a directory with index.jsx in it. It means
that app/javascript/PayTypeSelector will have all the files needed for that component.

Next, we'll enhance render() with the necessary logic to choose the right component based on the value of this.state.selectedPayType:

rails51/depot_pc/app/javascript/PayTypeSelector/index.jsx
```
render() {
➤   let PayTypeCustomComponent = NoPayType;
➤   if (this.state.selectedPayType == "Credit card") {
➤     PayTypeCustomComponent = CreditCardPayType;
```

```
➤    } else if (this.state.selectedPayType == "Check") {
➤      PayTypeCustomComponent = CheckPayType;
➤    } else if (this.state.selectedPayType == "Purchase order") {
➤      PayTypeCustomComponent = PurchaseOrderPayType;
➤    }
     return (
➤      <div>
➤        <div className="field">
➤          <label htmlFor="order_pay_type">Pay type</label>
➤          <select id="pay_type" onChange={this.onPayTypeSelected}
➤            name="order[pay_type]">
➤            <option value="">Select a payment method</option>
➤            <option value="Check">Check</option>
➤            <option value="Credit card">Credit card</option>
➤            <option value="Purchase order">Purchase order</option>
➤          </select>
➤        </div>
➤        <PayTypeCustomComponent />
➤      </div>
     );
   }
```

Note the change in the markup. In addition to adding <PayTypeCustomComponent />,
we've wrapped the entire thing in a div. React components must have a single,
top-level element; and due to the way our CSS works, each line of our form
must be inside a div with the CSS class field.

Now let's see our components. The first is the simplest, NoPayType:

rails51/depot_pc/app/javascript/PayTypeSelector/NoPayType.jsx
```
import React from 'react'

class NoPayType extends React.Component {
  render() {
    return (<div></div>);
  }
}
export default NoPayType
```

Even though this does nothing, it gives us a clear space to put UI later if we
wanted to (for example, a message prompting the user to select a pay type).
Next is CheckPayType:

rails51/depot_pc/app/javascript/PayTypeSelector/CheckPayType.jsx
```
import React from 'react'

class CheckPayType extends React.Component {
  render() {
    return (
      <div>
        <div className="field">
```

```
          <label htmlFor="order_routing_number">Routing #</label>
          <input type="password"
                 name="order[routing_number]"
                 id="order_routing_number" />
        </div>
        <div className="field">
          <label htmlFor="order_account_number">Account #</label>
          <input type="text"
                 name="order[account_number]"
                 id="order_account_number" />
        </div>
      </div>
    );
  }
}
export default CheckPayType
```

Note that we're self-closing the input elements. This isn't required in HTML but *is* in JSX. The CreditCardPayType is similar:

rails51/depot_pc/app/javascript/PayTypeSelector/CreditCardPayType.jsx
```
import React from 'react'

class CreditCardPayType extends React.Component {
  render() {
    return (
      <div>
        <div className="field">
          <label htmlFor="order_credit_card_number">CC #</label>
          <input type="password"
                 name="order[credit_card_number]"
                 id="order_credit_card_number" />
        </div>
        <div className="field">
          <label htmlFor="order_expiration_date">Expiry</label>
          <input type="text"
                 name="order[expiration_date]"
                 id="order_expiration_date"
                 size="9"
                 placeholder="e.g. 03/19" />
        </div>
      </div>
    );
  }
}
export default CreditCardPayType
```

And finally, the PurchaseOrderPayType:

```
rails51/depot_pc/app/javascript/PayTypeSelector/PurchaseOrderPayType.jsx
import React from 'react'

class PurchaseOrderPayType extends React.Component {
  render() {
    return (
      <div>
        <div className="field">
          <label htmlFor="order_po_number">PO #</label>
          <input type="password"
                 name="order[po_number]"
                 id="order_po_number" />
        </div>
      </div>
    );
  }
}
export default PurchaseOrderPayType
```

Note that we've judiciously chosen the fields' name values to match Rails conventions. When our React components use a name like "order[credit_card_number]", we'll be able to access that field's value in Ruby using params[:order][:credit_card_number], as we'll see later.

If you reload the page and select different payment types, you'll see that the form dynamically switches to the right fields for the payment type! See the screenshots on page 213.

For completeness, let's access these values in the controller. We could add the new parameters to order_params(), but let's make it a bit more explicit by creating a method called pay_type_params() that returns only the params relevant to the chosen pay type:

```
rails51/depot_pc/app/controllers/orders_controller.rb
def pay_type_params
  if order_params[:pay_type] == "Credit Card"
    params.require(:order).permit(:credit_card_number, :expiration_date)
  elsif order_params[:pay_type] == "Check"
    params.require(:order).permit(:routing_number, :account_number)
  elsif order_params[:pay_type] == "Purchase Order"
    params.require(:order).permit(:po_number)
  else
    {}
  end
end
```

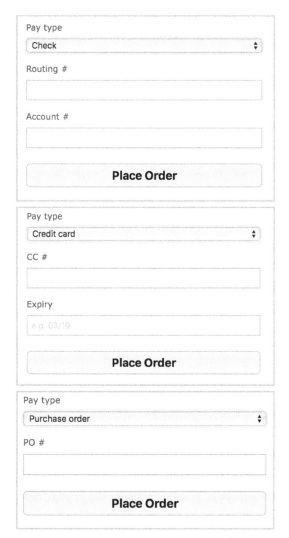

We can use these params to submit the payment details to the customer's back-end payment processing system, which we'll do in *Iteration I2: Connecting to a Slow Payment Processor with Active Job*, on page 225.

Wrapping Up Webpack and React

This was quite a journey, and it might've felt complex. In a sense, this is expected, because we tried to do something more complex than we have previously done. Webpacker exists exactly to help us with complex interactions like the one we implemented. And if you think a lot of setup was needed to get there, know that without Webpacker it would have been far more difficult and would have required making many more decisions.

> ## Do Not Store or Log Credit Card Numbers
>
> I know we aren't actually doing a payments integration, and you should read *Take My Money [Rap17]* if you want to do it for real. If you decide to do a real integration on your own, you should be very careful to never store credit card numbers in your database, as this creates all sorts of problems for you and your customers.
>
> More subtly, you should make sure Rails doesn't log these parameters by adding :credit_card_number to config.filter_parameters in config/application.rb:
>
> rails51/depot_pc/config/application.rb
> ```
> config.filter_parameters += [ :credit_card_number ]
> ```

Webpacker is a great demonstration of the best of Rails. It removes uninteresting decisions, such as where files should go, and provides a basic mechanism that just works so we can spend our time on our problem, not on configuration. Even if you didn't know React before reading this, you now know enough to build some fairly complex features. It's just a matter of putting code in the right place.

One thing that we can no longer do is completely test our application. Because we now depend on JavaScript for a piece of functionality, we can't really test that functionality without executing our application in a web browser. Until Rails 5.1, developers had to configure add-on libraries to be able to do this. As of Rails 5.1, this is baked into the framework and ready for you to use.

Iteration H2: Testing Our JavaScript Functionality

Now that we have application-level functionality in JavaScript code, we are going to need to have tests in place to ensure that the function not only works as intended but continues to work as we make changes to the application.

Testing this functionality involves a lot of steps: visiting the store, selecting an item, adding that item to the card, clicking checkout, filling in a few fields, and selecting a payment type. And from a testing perspective, we are going to need both a Rails server and a browser.

To accomplish this, Rails makes use of a version of the popular Google Chrome web browser named ChromeDriver,[9] which has been augmented to include programming interfaces to enable automation, and Capybara,[10] which is a tool that drives this automation.

---

9. https://sites.google.com/a/chromium.org/chromedriver/
10. https://github.com/teamcapybara/capybara#readme

Tests that pull together a complete and integrated version of the software are called *system tests*, and that is exactly what we will be doing: we will be testing a full end-to-end scenario with a web browser, web server, our application, and a database.

We start by describing the actions and checks we want performed as a system test:

```
rails51/depot_q/test/system/orders_test.rb
require "application_system_test_case"

class OrdersTest < ApplicationSystemTestCase
  test "check routing number" do
    visit store_index_url

    first('.catalog li').click_on 'Add to Cart'

    click_on 'Checkout'

    fill_in 'order_name', with: 'Dave Thomas'
    fill_in 'order_address', with: '123 Main Street'
    fill_in 'order_email', with: 'dave@example.com'

    assert_no_selector "#order_routing_number"

    select 'Check', from: 'pay_type'

    assert_selector "#order_routing_number"
  end
end
```

As you can see, this is pretty straightforward; all it involves is a number of discrete steps: visit() a URL, find the first() li inside the .catalog, click_on() two buttons in a given order, fill_in() three fields, assert that a given HTML element is *not* present, select() a pay type, and finally ensure that the HTML element is now present.

Capybara makes all of this possible using a compact, readable API that requires very little code. For additional information and more methods, we suggest that you familiarize yourself with the domain-specific language (DSL) that Capybara provides.[11]

Now let's run the test we just wrote:

```
$ bin/rails test:system
Run options: --seed 26203

# Running:
```

---

11. https://github.com/teamcapybara/capybara#the-dsl

```
Puma starting in single mode...
* Version 3.9.1 (ruby 2.4.1-p111), codename: Private Caller
* Min threads: 0, max threads: 1
* Environment: test
* Listening on tcp://0.0.0.0:59360
Use Ctrl-C to stop
.

Finished in 3.846935s, 0.2599 runs/s, 0.5199 assertions/s.

1 runs, 2 assertions, 0 failures, 0 errors, 0 skips
```

When you run this, you will note a number of things. First a web server is started on your behalf, and then a browser is launched and the actions you requested are performed. Once the test is complete, both are stopped and the results of the test are reported back to you. All this based on your instructions as to what actions and tests are to be performed, and expressed clearly and succinctly as a system test.

Note that system tests tend to take a bit longer to execute than model or controller tests and as such are not run as a part of bin/rails test.

What We Just Did

- We replaced a static form_select field with a dynamic list of form fields that change instantly based on user selection.

- We used Webpacker to gather up and deliver all of the necessary Java-Script dependencies just in time to the browser to make the dynamic changes happen.

- We used Capybara and ChromeDriver to system-test this functionality.

Playtime

Here's some stuff to try on your own:

- Check is not the only payment type, and routing number is not the only field that is dynamically inserted or deleted based on the payment type. Extend the system test to include other choices and other fields.

- Add a test to verify that the Add to Cart and Empty Cart buttons reveal and hide the cart, respectively.

- Add a test of the highlight feature you added in *Iteration F3: Highlighting Changes*, on page 164.

In this chapter, you'll see:
- Sending email
- Running background code with Active Job
- System testing background jobs and email

## CHAPTER 14

Task I: Processing Emails and Payments Efficiently

At this point, we have a website that responds to requests and provides feeds that allow sales of individual titles to be checked periodically. The customer is happier but still not satisfied. The first bit of feedback is that users aren't getting confirmation emails of their purchases. The second is around payment processing. The customer has arranged for us to integrate with a payment processor that can handle all forms of payment we want to support, but the processor's API is very slow. The customer wants to know if that will slow down the site.

Sending email is a common need for any web application, and Rails has you covered via Action Mailer,[1] which you'll learn in this chapter. Dealing with the slow payment-processing API requires learning about the library Action Mailer is built on, Active Job.[2] Active Job allows you to run code in a background process so that the user doesn't have to wait for it to complete. Sending email is slow, which is why Action Mailer uses Active Job to offload the work. This is a common technique you'll use often when developing web applications. Let's take it one step at a time and learn how to send email.

Iteration I1: Sending Confirmation Emails

Sending email in Rails has three basic parts: configuring how email is to be sent, determining when to send the email, and specifying what you want to say. We'll cover each of these three in turn.

---

1. http://guides.rubyonrails.org/action_mailer_basics.html
2. http://guides.rubyonrails.org/active_job_basics.html

Configuring Email

Email configuration is part of a Rails application's environment and involves a Depot::Application.configure block. If you want to use the same configuration for development, testing, and production, add the configuration to environment.rb in the config directory; otherwise, add different configurations to the appropriate files in the config/environments directory.

Inside the block, you need to have one or more statements. You first have to decide how you want mail delivered:

```
config.action_mailer.delivery_method = :smtp
```

Alternatives to :smtp include :sendmail and :test.

The :smtp and :sendmail options are used when you want Action Mailer to attempt to deliver email. You'll clearly want to use one of these methods in production.

The :test setting is great for unit and functional testing, which we'll make use of in *Testing Email*, on page 224. Email won't be delivered; instead, it'll be appended to an array (accessible via the ActionMailer::Base.deliveries attribute). This is the default delivery method in the test environment. Interestingly, though, the default in development mode is :smtp. If you want Rails to deliver email during the development of your application, this is good. If you'd rather disable email delivery in development mode, edit the development.rb file in the config/environments directory and add the following lines:

```
Depot::Application.configure do
  config.action_mailer.delivery_method = :test
end
```

The :sendmail setting delegates mail delivery to your local system's sendmail program, which is assumed to be in /usr/sbin. This delivery mechanism isn't particularly portable, because sendmail isn't always installed in this directory for every operating system. It also relies on your local sendmail supporting the -i and -t command options.

You achieve more portability by leaving this option at its default value of :smtp. If you do so, you'll need also to specify some additional configuration to tell Action Mailer where to find an SMTP server to handle your outgoing email. This can be the machine running your web application, or it can be a separate box (perhaps at your ISP if you're running Rails in a noncorporate environment). Your system administrator will be able to give you the settings for these parameters. You may also be able to determine them from your own mail client's configuration.

The following are typical settings for Gmail: adapt them as you need.

```
Depot::Application.configure do
  config.action_mailer.delivery_method = :smtp

  config.action_mailer.smtp_settings = {
    address:          "smtp.gmail.com",
    port:             587,
    domain:           "domain.of.sender.net",
    authentication:   "plain",
    user_name:        "dave",
    password:         "secret",
    enable_starttls_auto: true
  }
end
```

As with all configuration changes, you'll need to restart your application if you make changes to any of the environment files.

Sending Email

Now that we have everything configured, let's write some code to send emails.

By now you shouldn't be surprised that Rails has a generator script to create *mailers*. In Rails, a mailer is a class that's stored in the app/mailers directory. It contains one or more methods, with each method corresponding to an email template. To create the body of the email, these methods in turn use views (in the same way that controller actions use views to create HTML and XML). So, let's create a mailer for our store application. We'll use it to send two different types of email: one when an order is placed and a second when the order ships. The rails generate mailer command takes the name of the mailer class, along with the names of the email action methods:

```
depot> bin/rails generate mailer Order received shipped
     create  app/mailers/order.rb
     create  app/mailers/order_mailer.rb
     invoke  erb
     create    app/views/order_mailer
  identical    app/views/layouts/mailer.text.erb
  identical    app/views/layouts/mailer.html.erb
     create    app/views/order_mailer/received.text.erb
     create    app/views/order_mailer/received.html.erb
     create    app/views/order_mailer/shipped.text.erb
     create    app/views/order_mailer/shipped.html.erb
     invoke  test_unit
     create    test/mailers/order_mailer_test.rb
     create    test/mailers/previews/order_mailer_preview.rb
```

Notice that we create an OrderMailer class in app/mailers and two template files, one for each email type, in app/views/order. (We also create a test file; we'll look into this in *Testing Email*, on page 224.)

Each method in the mailer class is responsible for setting up the environment for sending an email. Let's look at an example before going into detail. Here's the code that was generated for our OrderMailer class, with one default changed:

rails51/depot_q/app/mailers/order_mailer.rb

```
class OrderMailer < ApplicationMailer
  default from: 'Sam Ruby <depot@example.com>'

  # Subject can be set in your I18n file at config/locales/en.yml
  # with the following lookup:
  #
  #   en.order_mailer.received.subject
  #
  def received
    @greeting = "Hi"

    mail to: "to@example.org"
  end

  # Subject can be set in your I18n file at config/locales/en.yml
  # with the following lookup:
  #
  #   en.order_mailer.shipped.subject
  #
  def shipped
    @greeting = "Hi"

    mail to: "to@example.org"
  end
end
```

If you're thinking to yourself that this looks like a controller, that's because it does. It includes one method per action. Instead of a call to render(), there's a call to mail(). This method accepts a number of parameters including :to (as shown), :cc, :from, and :subject, each of which does pretty much what you'd expect it to do. Values that are common to all mail() calls in the mailer can be set as defaults by simply calling default, as is done for :from at the top of this class. Feel free to tailor this to your needs.

The comments in this class also indicate that subject lines are already enabled for translation, a subject we'll cover in Chapter 16, *Task K: Internationalization*, on page 253. For now, we'll simply use the :subject parameter.

As with controllers, templates contain the text to be sent, and controllers and mailers can provide values to be inserted into those templates via instance variables.

Email Templates

The generate script created two email templates in app/views/order_mailer, one for each action in the OrderMailer class. These are regular .erb files. We'll use them to create plain-text emails (you'll see later how to create HTML email). As with the templates we use to create our application's web pages, the files contain a combination of static text and dynamic content. We can customize the template in received.text.erb; this is the email that's sent to confirm an order:

```
rails51/depot_q/app/views/order_mailer/received.text.erb
Dear <%= @order.name %>

Thank you for your recent order from The Pragmatic Store.

You ordered the following items:

<%= render @order.line_items -%>

We'll send you a separate e-mail when your order ships.
```

The partial template that renders a line item formats a single line with the item quantity and the title. Because we're in a template, all the regular helper methods, such as truncate(), are available:

```
rails51/depot_q/app/views/line_items/_line_item.text.erb
<%= sprintf("%2d x %s",
            line_item.quantity,
            truncate(line_item.product.title, length: 50)) %>
```

We now have to go back and fill in the received() method in the OrderMailer class:

```
rails51/depot_qa/app/mailers/order_mailer.rb
def received(order)
  @order = order

  mail to: order.email, subject: 'Pragmatic Store Order Confirmation'
end
```

What we did here is add order as an argument to the method-received call, add code to copy the parameter passed into an instance variable, and update the call to mail() specifying where to send the email and what subject line to use.

Generating Emails

Now that we have our template set up and our mailer method defined, we can use them in our regular controllers to create and/or send emails. Note that just calling the method we defined isn't enough; we also need to tell Rails to actually send the email. The reason this doesn't happen automatically is that Rails can't be 100% sure if you want to deliver the email right this moment, while the user waits, or later, in a background job.

Generally, you don't want the user to have to wait for emails to get sent, because this can take a while. Instead, we'll send it in a background job (which we'll learn more about later in the chapter) by calling deliver_later() (to send the email right now, you'd use deliver_now().[3])

rails51/depot_qa/app/controllers/orders_controller.rb
```ruby
def create
  @order = Order.new(order_params)
  @order.add_line_items_from_cart(@cart)

  respond_to do |format|
    if @order.save
      Cart.destroy(session[:cart_id])
      session[:cart_id] = nil
      OrderMailer.received(@order).deliver_later
      format.html { redirect_to store_index_url, notice:
        'Thank you for your order.' }
      format.json { render :show, status: :created,
        location: @order }
    else
      format.html { render :new }
      format.json { render json: @order.errors,
        status: :unprocessable_entity }
    end
  end
end
```

And we need to update shipped() as we did for received():

rails51/depot_qa/app/mailers/order_mailer.rb
```ruby
def shipped(order)
  @order = order

  mail to: order.email, subject: 'Pragmatic Store Order Shipped'
end
```

Now, we have enough of the basics in place that you can place an order and have a plain email sent to yourself, assuming you didn't disable the sending of email in development mode. Let's spice up the email with a bit of formatting.

Delivering Multiple Content Types

Some people prefer to receive email in plain-text format, while others like the look of an HTML email. Rails supports this directly, allowing you to send email messages that contain alternative content formats, allowing users (or their email clients) to decide which they'd prefer to view.

---

3. http://api.rubyonrails.org/classes/ActionMailer/MessageDelivery.html#method-i-deliver_now

> ```
> \|/      Joe asks:
> ᴥ       Can I Also Receive Email?
> ```
>
> Action Mailer also supports writing Rails applications that handle incoming email. Unfortunately, you need to find a way to retrieve appropriate emails from your server environment and inject them into the application; this requires a bit more work.
>
> The easy part is handling an email within your application. In your Action Mailer class, write an instance method called receive() that takes a single parameter. This parameter will be a Mail::Message object corresponding to the incoming email. You can extract fields, the body text, and/or attachments and use them in your application.
>
> All the normal techniques for intercepting incoming email end up running a command, passing that command the content of the email as standard input. If we make the Rails runner script the command that's invoked whenever an email arrives, we can arrange to pass that email into our application's email-handling code. For example, using procmail-based interception, we could write a rule that looks something like the example that follows. Using the arcane syntax of procmail, this rule copies any incoming email whose subject line contains *Bug Report* through our runner script:
>
> ```
> RUBY=/opt/local/bin/ruby
> TICKET_APP_DIR=/Users/dave/Work/depot
> HANDLER='IncomingTicketHandler.receive(STDIN.read)'
>
> :0 c
> * ^Subject:.*Bug Report.*
> | cd $TICKET_APP_DIR && $RUBY bin/rails runner $HANDLER
> ```
>
> The receive() class method is available to all Action Mailer classes. It takes the email text, parses it into a Mail object, creates a new instance of the receiver's class, and passes the Mail object to the receive() instance method in that class.

In the preceding section, we created a plain-text email. The view file for our received action was called received.text.erb. This is the standard Rails naming convention. We can also create HTML-formatted emails.

Let's try this with the order-shipped notification. We don't need to modify any code—we simply need to create a new template:

```
rails51/depot_qa/app/views/order_mailer/shipped.html.erb
<h3>Pragmatic Order Shipped</h3>
<p>
  This is just to let you know that we've shipped your recent order:
</p>

<table>
  <tr><th colspan="2">Qty</th><th>Description</th></tr>
<%= render @order.line_items -%>
</table>
```

We don't need to modify the partial, because the existing one will do just fine:

rails51/depot_qa/app/views/line_items/_line_item.html.erb
```erb
<% if line_item == @current_item %>
<tr class="line-item-highlight">
<% else %>
<tr>
<% end %>
  <td class="quantity"><%= line_item.quantity %></td>
  <td><%= line_item.product.title %></td>
  <td class="price"><%= number_to_currency(line_item.total_price) %></td>
</tr>
```

But for email templates, Rails provides a bit more naming magic. If you create multiple templates with the same name but with different content types embedded in their filenames, Rails will send all of them in one email, arranging the content so that the email client can distinguish each.

This means you'll want to either update or delete the plain-text template that Rails provided for the shipped notifier.

Testing Email

When we used the generate script to create our order mailer, it automatically constructed a corresponding order_test.rb file in the application's test/mailers directory. It's pretty straightforward; it simply calls each action and verifies selected portions of the email produced. Because we've tailored the email, let's update the test case to match:

rails51/depot_qa/test/mailers/order_mailer_test.rb
```ruby
require 'test_helper'

class OrderMailerTest < ActionMailer::TestCase
  test "received" do
    mail = OrderMailer.received(orders(:one))
    assert_equal "Pragmatic Store Order Confirmation", mail.subject
    assert_equal ["dave@example.org"], mail.to
    assert_equal ["depot@example.com"], mail.from
    assert_match /1 x Programming Ruby 1.9/, mail.body.encoded
  end

  test "shipped" do
    mail = OrderMailer.shipped(orders(:one))
    assert_equal "Pragmatic Store Order Shipped", mail.subject
    assert_equal ["dave@example.org"], mail.to
    assert_equal ["depot@example.com"], mail.from
    assert_match /<td[^>]*>1<\/td>\s*<td>Programming Ruby 1.9<\/td>/,
      mail.body.encoded
  end

end
```

The test method instructs the mail class to create (but not to send) an email, and we use assertions to verify that the dynamic content is what we expect. Note the use of assert_match() to validate just part of the body content. Your results may differ depending on how you tailored the default :from line in your OrderMailer.

Now that we've implemented our mailer and tested it, let's move on to that pesky slow payment processor. To deal with that, we'll put our API calls into a job that can be run in the background so the user doesn't have to wait.

Iteration 12: Connecting to a Slow Payment Processor with Active Job

The code inside the controllers is relatively fast and returns a response to the user quickly. This means we can reliably give users feedback by checking and validating their orders and the users won't have to wait too long for a response.

The more we add to the controller, the slower it will become. Slow controllers create several problems. First, the user must wait a long time for a response, even though the processing that's going on might not be relevant to the user experience. In the previous section, we set up sending email. The user certainly needs to get that email but doesn't need to wait for Rails to format and send it just to show a confirmation in the browser.

The second problem caused by slow code is *timeouts*. A timeout is when Rails, a web server, or a browser decides that a request has taken too long and terminates it. This is jarring to the user *and* to the code, because it means the code is interrupted at a potentially odd time. What if we've recorded the order but haven't sent the email? The customer won't get a notification.

In the common case of sending email, Rails handles sending it in the background. We used deliver_later() to trigger sending an email, and Rails executes that code in the background. This means that users don't have to wait for email to be sent before we render a response. This is a great hidden benefit to Rails' integrated approach to building a web app.

Rails achieves this using *Active Job*, which is a generic framework for running code in the background. We'll use this framework to connect to the slow payment processor.

To make this change, you'll implement the integration with the payment processor as a method inside Order, then have the controller use Active Job to execute that method in a background job. Because the end result will be somewhat complex, you'll write a system test to ensure everything is working together.

Moving Logic Into the Model

It's way outside the scope of this book to integrate with an actual payment processor, so we've cooked up a fake one named Pago, along with an implementation, which we'll see in a bit. First, this is the API it provides and a sketch of how you can use it:

```
payment_result = Pago.make_payment(
  order_id: order.id,
  payment_method: :check,
  payment_details: { routing: xxx, account: yyy }
)
```

The fake implementation does some basic validations of the parameters, prints out the payment details it received, pauses for a few seconds, and returns a structure that responds to succeeded?().

```
rails51/depot_qb/lib/pago.rb
require 'ostruct'
class Pago
  def self.make_payment(order_id:,
                        payment_method:,
                        payment_details:)

    case payment_method
    when :check
      Rails.logger.info "Processing check: " +
        payment_details.fetch(:routing).to_s + "/" +
        payment_details.fetch(:account).to_s
    when :credit_card
      Rails.logger.info "Processing credit_card: " +
        payment_details.fetch(:cc_num).to_s + "/" +
        payment_details.fetch(:expiration_month).to_s + "/" +
        payment_details.fetch(:expiration_year).to_s
    when :po
      Rails.logger.info "Processing purchase order: " +
        payment_details.fetch(:po_num).to_s
    else
      raise "Unknown payment_method #{payment_method}"
    end
    sleep 3 unless Rails.env.test?
    Rails.logger.info "Done Processing Payment"
    OpenStruct.new(succeeded?: true)
  end
end
```

If you aren't familiar with OpenStruct, it's part of Ruby's standard library and provides a quick-and-dirty way to make an object that responds to the methods given to its constructor.[4] In this case, we can call succeeded?() on the return value from make_payment(). OpenStruct is handy for creating realistic objects from prototype or faked-out code like Pago.

With the payment API in hand, you need logic to adapt the payment details that you added in Chapter 13, *Task H: Entering Additional*, on page 195, to Pago's API. You'll also move the call to OrderMailer into this method, because you don't want to send the email if there was a problem collecting payment.

In a Rails app, when a bit of logic becomes more complex than a line or two of code, you want to move that out of the controller and into a model. You'll create a new method in Order called charge!() that will handle all this logic.

The method will be somewhat long and has to do three things. First, it must adapt pay_type_params (which you created in *Dynamically Replacing Components Based on User Actions*, on page 206, but didn't use) to the parameters that Pago requires. Second, it should make the call to Pago to collect payment. Finally, it must check to see if the payment succeeded and, if so, send the confirmation email. Here's what the method looks like:

```ruby
rails51/depot_qb/app/models/order.rb
require 'active_model/serializers/xml'
➤ require 'pago'

class Order < ApplicationRecord
  include ActiveModel::Serializers::Xml
  enum pay_type: {
    "Check"          => 0,
    "Credit card"    => 1,
    "Purchase order" => 2
  }
  has_many :line_items, dependent: :destroy
  # ...
  validates :name, :address, :email, presence: true
  validates :pay_type, inclusion: pay_types.keys
  def add_line_items_from_cart(cart)
    cart.line_items.each do |item|
      item.cart_id = nil
      line_items << item
    end
  end
➤ def charge!(pay_type_params)
➤   payment_details = {}
➤   payment_method = nil
```

---

4. https://ruby-doc.org/stdlib-2.4.1/libdoc/ostruct/rdoc/OpenStruct.html

```
    case pay_type
    when "Check"
      payment_method = :check
      payment_details[:routing] = pay_type_params[:routing_number]
      payment_details[:account] = pay_type_params[:account_number]
    when "Credit card"
      payment_method = :credit_card
      month,year = pay_type_params[:expiration_date].split(//)
      payment_details[:cc_num] = pay_type_params[:credit_card_number]
      payment_details[:expiration_month] = month
      payment_details[:expiration_year] = year
    when "Purchase order"
      payment_method = :po
      payment_details[:po_num] = pay_type_params[:po_number]
    end

    payment_result = Pago.make_payment(
      order_id: id,
      payment_method: payment_method,
      payment_details: payment_details
    )

    if payment_result.succeeded?
      OrderMailer.received(self).deliver_later
    else
      raise payment_result.error
    end
  end
end
```

If you weren't concerned with how slow Pago's API is, you'd change the code in the create() method of OrdersController to call charge!():

```
if @order.save
  Cart.destroy(session[:cart_id])
  session[:cart_id] = nil
➤ @order.charge!(pay_type_params) # do not do this
  format.html { redirect_to store_index_url, notice:
    'Thank you for your order.' }
```

Since you already know the call to Pago will be slow, you want it to happen in a background job, so that users can see the confirmation message in their browser immediately without having to wait for the charge to actually happen. To do this, you must create an Active Job class, implement that class to call charge!(), and then add code to the controller to execute this job. The flow looks like the figure on page 229.

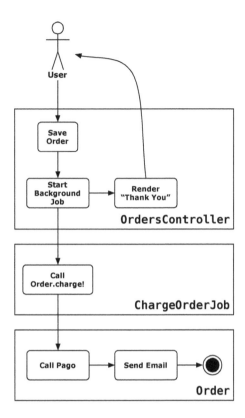

Creating an Active Job Class

Rails provides a generator to create a shell of a job class for us. Create the job using it like so:

```
> bin/rails generate job charge_order
    invoke  test_unit
    create    test/jobs/charge_order_job_test.rb
    create  app/jobs/charge_order_job.rb
```

The argument charge_order tells Rails that the job's class name should be ChargeOrderJob.

You've implemented the logic in the charge!() method of Order, so what goes in the newly created ChargeOrderJob? The purpose of job classes like ChargeOrderJob is to act as a glue between the controller—which wants to run some logic later—and the actual logic in the models.

Here's the code that implements this:

rails51/depot_qb/app/jobs/charge_order_job.rb

```
class ChargeOrderJob < ApplicationJob
  queue_as :default

➤  def perform(order,pay_type_params)
➤
➤    order.charge!(pay_type_params)
  end
end
```

Next, you need to fire this job in the background from the controller.

Queuing a Background Job

Because background jobs run in parallel to the code in the controller, the code you write to initiate the background job isn't the same as calling a method. When you call a method, you expect that method's code to be executed while you wait. Background jobs are different. They often go to a queue, where they wait to be executed outside the controller. Thus, when we talk about executing code in a background job, we often use the phrase "queue the job."

To queue a job using Active Job, use the method perform_later() on the job class and pass it the arguments you want to be given to the perform() method you implemented above. Here's where to do that in the controller (note that this replaces the call to OrderMailer, since that's now part of the charge!() method):

rails51/depot_qb/app/controllers/orders_controller.rb

```
  def create
    @order = Order.new(order_params)
    @order.add_line_items_from_cart(@cart)

    respond_to do |format|
      if @order.save
        Cart.destroy(session[:cart_id])
        session[:cart_id] = nil
➤       ChargeOrderJob.perform_later(@order,pay_type_params.to_h)
        format.html { redirect_to store_index_url, notice:
          'Thank you for your order.' }
        format.json { render :show, status: :created,
          location: @order }
      else
        format.html { render :new }
        format.json { render json: @order.errors,
          status: :unprocessable_entity }
      end
    end
  end
```

With this in place, you can now add an item to the cart, check out, and see everything working just as we did before, with the addition of seeing the calls to Pago. If you look at the Rails log when you check out, you should see some logging like so (formatted to fit the page):

```
[ActiveJob] Enqueued ChargeOrderJob (Job ID: 79da671e-865c-4d51-a1ff-400208c6dbd1)
    to Async(default) with arguments:
      #<GlobalID:0x007fa294a43ce0 @uri=#<URI::GID gid://depot/Order/9>>,
      {"routing_number"=>"23412341234", "account_number"=>"345356345"}
[ActiveJob] [ChargeOrderJob] [79da671e-865c-4d51-a1ff-400208c6dbd1]
    Performing ChargeOrderJob (Job ID: 79da671e-865c-4d51-a1ff-400208c6dbd1) from
    Async(default) with arguments:
    #<GlobalID:0x007fa294a01570 @uri=#<URI::GID gid://depot/Order/9>>,
    {"routing_number"=>"23412341234", "account_number"=>"345356345"}
[ActiveJob] [ChargeOrderJob] [79da671e-865c-4d51-a1ff-400208c6dbd1]
    Processing check: 23412341234/345356345
```

This shows the guts of how Active Job works and is useful for debugging if things aren't working right.

Speaking of debugging and possible failures, this interaction really should have a test.

System Testing the Checkout Flow

In *Iteration H2: Testing Our JavaScript Functionality*, on page 214, you wrote a system test that uses a real browser to simulate user interaction. In order to test the entire flow of checking out, communicating with the payment processor, and sending an email, you'll expand that test.

To test the full, end-to-end workflow, including execution of Active Jobs, you want to do the following:

1. Add a book to the cart.

2. Fill in the checkout form completely (including selecting a pay type).

3. Submit the order.

4. Process all background jobs.

5. Check that the order was created properly.

6. Check that email was sent.

You should already be familiar with how to write most parts of this test. Processing background jobs and checking mail, however, are new. Rails provides helpers for us, so the test will be short and readable when you're done. One of those helpers is available by mixing in the ActiveJob::TestHelper module:

rails51/depot_qb/test/system/orders_test.rb
```
class OrdersTest < ApplicationSystemTestCase
➤   include ActiveJob::TestHelper
```

This provides the method perform_enqueued_jobs(), which you'll see in a moment.

The current test just makes assertions about how the pay type selector changes the DOM. Since you now need to submit the form and assert that an order was created, you need to clear out any orders in the test database that might be hanging around from previous test runs.

rails51/depot_qb/test/system/orders_test.rb
```
test "check routing number" do
➤   LineItem.delete_all
➤   Order.delete_all

    visit store_index_url
```

Next, you'll need to fill in the pay type details. Since the test currently selects the Check pay type, you can use fill_in() to provide a routing number and an account number:

rails51/depot_qb/test/system/orders_test.rb
```
    assert_selector "#order_routing_number"

➤   fill_in "Routing #", with: "123456"
➤   fill_in "Account #", with: "987654"
```

Next, you need to submit the form. Capybara provides the method click_button() that will do that; however it's important to consider what will happen with the background jobs. In a system test, Rails won't process the background jobs automatically. This allows you to have the chance to inspect them and make assertions about them.

Since this test is about the user's experience end-to-end, you don't need to look at the jobs that have been queued—instead we need to make sure they are executed. It's sufficient to assert the *results* of those jobs having been executed. To that end, the method perform_enqueued_jobs() will perform any jobs that get enqueued inside the block of code given to it:

rails51/depot_qb/test/system/orders_test.rb
```
➤   perform_enqueued_jobs do
➤     click_button "Place Order"
➤   end
```

When the "Place Order" button is pressed, the controller executes its code, including queuing a ChargeOrderJob. Because that was initiated inside the block given to perform_enqueued_jobs(), Rails will process any and all jobs that get queued.

Joe asks:

How Are Background Jobs Run in Development or Production?

When running the application locally, the background jobs are executed and emails are sent by Rails. By default, Rails uses an in-memory queue to manage the jobs. This is fine for development, but it could be a problem in production. If your app were to crash before all background jobs were processed or before emails were sent, those jobs would be lost and unrecoverable.

In production, you'd need to use a different *back end*, as detailed in the Active Job Rails Guide.[a] Sidekiq is a popular open-source back end that works great.[b] Setting it up is a bit tricky, since you must have access to a Redis database to store the waiting jobs.[c] If you are using Postgres for your Active Records, Queue Classic is another option for a back end that doesn't require Redis—it uses your existing Postgres database.[d]

---

a.   http://guides.rubyonrails.org/active_job_basics.html#job-execution
b.   http://sidekiq.org/
c.   https://redis.io/
d.   https://github.com/QueueClassic/queue_classic/tree/3-1-stable

Next, check that an order was created in the way you expect by locating the created order and asserting that the values provided in the checkout form were properly saved.

```
rails51/depot_qb/test/system/orders_test.rb
    orders = Order.all
    assert_equal 1, orders.size

    order = orders.first

    assert_equal "Dave Thomas",       order.name
    assert_equal "123 Main Street",   order.address
    assert_equal "dave@example.com", order.email
    assert_equal "Check",             order.pay_type
    assert_equal 1, order.line_items.size
```

Lastly, you need to check that the mail was sent. In the test environment, Rails doesn't actually deliver mail but instead saves it in an array available via ActionMailer::Base.deliveries(). The objects in there respond to various methods that allow you to examine the email:

```
rails51/depot_qb/test/system/orders_test.rb
➤    mail = ActionMailer::Base.deliveries.last
➤    assert_equal ["dave@example.com"],                mail.to
➤    assert_equal 'Sam Ruby <depot@example.com>',      mail[:from].value
➤    assert_equal "Pragmatic Store Order Confirmation", mail.subject
    end
end
```

Note that if you had not used perform_enqueued_jobs() around the call to click_button "Place Order", the test would fail. This is because ChargeOrderJob would not have executed, and therefore it would not have created and sent the email.

If you run this test via bin/rails test test/system/orders_test.rb, it should pass. You've now tested a complex workflow using the browser, background jobs, and email.

What We Just Did

Without much code and with just a few templates, we've managed to pull off the following:

- We configured our development, test, and production environments for our Rails application to enable the sending of outbound emails.

- We created and tailored a mailer that can send confirmation emails in both plain-text and HTML formats to people who order our products.

- We used Active Job to execute slow-running code in the background, so the user doesn't have to wait.

- We enhanced a system test to cover the entire end-to-end workflow, including verifying that the background job executed and the email was sent.

Playtime

Here's some stuff to try on your own:

- Add a ship_date column to the orders table, and send a notification when this value is updated by the OrdersController.

- Update the application to send an email to the system administrator— namely, yourself—when an application failure occurs, such as the one we handled in *Iteration E2: Handling Errors*, on page 138.

- Modify Pago to sometimes return a failure (OpenStruct.new(succeeded?: false)), and handle that by sending a different email with the details of the failure.

- Add system tests for all of the above.

In this chapter, you'll see:
  • Adding secure passwords to models
  • Using more validations
  • Adding authentication to a session
  • Using rails console
  • Using database transactions
  • Writing an Active Record hook

CHAPTER 15

Task J: Logging In

We have a happy customer: in a short time, we've jointly put together a basic shopping cart that she can start showing to her users. She'd like to see just one more change. Right now, anyone can access the administrative functions. She'd like us to add a basic user administration system that would force you to log in to get into the administration parts of the site.

Chatting with our customer, it seems as if we don't need a particularly sophisticated security system for our application. We just need to recognize a number of people based on usernames and passwords. Once recognized, these folks can use all of the administration functions.

Iteration J1: Adding Users

Let's start by creating a model and database table to hold our administrators' usernames and passwords. Rather than store passwords in plain text, we'll store a digest hash value of the password. By doing so, we ensure that even if our database is compromised, the hash won't reveal the original password, so it can't be used to log in as this user using the forms:

```
depot> bin/rails generate scaffold User name:string password:digest
```

We declare the password as a digest type, which is another one of the nice extra touches that Rails provides. Now run the migration as usual:

```
depot> bin/rails db:migrate
```

Next we have to flesh out the user model:

rails51/depot_r/app/models/user.rb
```
class User < ApplicationRecord
  validates :name, presence: true, uniqueness: true
  has_secure_password
end
```

We check that the name is present and unique (that is, no two users can have the same name in the database).

Then there's the mysterious has_secure_password().

You know those forms that prompt you to enter a password and then make you reenter it in a separate field so they can validate that you typed what you thought you typed? That's exactly what has_secure_password() does for you: it tells Rails to validate that the two passwords match. This line was added for you because you specified password:digest when you generated your scaffold.

The next step is to uncomment the bcrypt-ruby gem in your Gemfile:

```
rails51/depot_r/Gemfile
# Use ActiveModel has_secure_password
➤ gem 'bcrypt', '~> 3.1.7'
```

Next, you need to install the gem:

```
depot> bundle install
```

Finally, you need to restart your server.

With this code in place, we have the ability to present both a password and a password confirmation field in a form, as well as the ability to authenticate a user, given a name and a password.

Administering Our Users

In addition to the model and table we set up, we already have some scaffolding generated to administer the model. Let's go through it and make some tweaks as necessary.

We start with the controller. It defines the standard methods: index(), show(), new(), edit(), create(), update(), and delete(). By default, Rails omits the unintelligible password hash from the view. This means that in the case of users, there isn't much to show(), except a name. So, let's avoid the redirect to showing the user after a create operation. Instead, let's redirect to the user's index and add the username to the flash notice:

```
rails51/depot_r/app/controllers/users_controller.rb
  def create
    @user = User.new(user_params)

    respond_to do |format|
      if @user.save
➤       format.html { redirect_to users_url,
➤         notice: "User #{@user.name} was successfully created." }
        format.json { render :show, status: :created, location: @user }
      else
```

```
          format.html { render :new }
          format.json { render json: @user.errors,
            status: :unprocessable_entity }
      end
    end
  end
```

Let's do the same for an update operation:

```
def update
  respond_to do |format|
    if @user.update(user_params)
➤     format.html { redirect_to users_url,
➤       notice: "User #{@user.name} was successfully updated." }
      format.json { render :show, status: :ok, location: @user }
    else
      format.html { render :edit }
      format.json { render json: @user.errors,
        status: :unprocessable_entity }
    end
  end
end
```

While we are here, let's also order the users returned in the index by name:

```
def index
➤   @users = User.order(:name)
end
```

Now that the controller changes are done, let's attend to the view. We need to update the form used both to create a new user and to update an existing user. Note this form is already set up to show the password and password confirmation fields. To improve the appearance of the page, we add <legend> and <fieldset> tags. Next we tweak the labels and the size of the fields. Finally, we wrap the output in a <div> tag with a class we previously defined in our stylesheet:

rails51/depot_r/app/views/users/_form.html.erb
```
➤ <div class="depot_form">
➤
  <%= form_with(model: user, local: true) do |form| %>
    <% if user.errors.any? %>
      <div id="error_explanation">
        <h2><%= pluralize(user.errors.count, "error") %>
          prohibited this user from being saved:</h2>

        <ul>
        <% user.errors.full_messages.each do |message| %>
          <li><%= message %></li>
        <% end %>
        </ul>
      </div>
```

```
      <% end %>
➤     <h2>Enter User Details</h2>
➤
      <div class="field">
➤       <%= form.label :name, 'Name:' %>
➤       <%= form.text_field :name, id: :user_name, size: 40 %>
      </div>

      <div class="field">
➤       <%= form.label :password, 'Password:' %>
➤       <%= form.password_field :password, id: :user_password, size: 40 %>
      </div>

      <div class="field">
➤       <%= form.label :password_confirmation, 'Confirm:' %>

➤       <%= form.password_field :password_confirmation,
➤                               id: :user_password_confirmation,
➤                               size: 40 %>

      </div>

      <div class="actions">
        <%= form.submit %>
      </div>
    <% end %>
➤
➤ </div>
```

Let's try it. Navigate to http://localhost:3000/users/new. For a stunning example of page design, see the following screenshot.

After Create User is clicked, the index is redisplayed with a cheery flash notice. If we look in our database, you'll see that we've stored the user details:

```
depot> sqlite3 -line db/development.sqlite3 "select * from users"
            id = 1
          name = dave
password_digest = $2a$10$lki6/oAcOW4AWg4A0e0T8uxtri2Zx5g9taBXrd4mDSDVl3rQRWRNi
    created_at = 2016-01-29 14:40:06.230622
    updated_at = 2016-01-29 14:40:06.230622
```

As we've done before, we need to update our tests to reflect the validation and redirection changes we've made. First we update the test for the create() method:

rails51/depot_r/test/controllers/users_controller_test.rb
```
  test "should create user" do
    assert_difference('User.count') do
➤     post users_url, params: { user: { name: 'sam',
➤     password: 'secret', password_confirmation: 'secret' } }
    end

➤   assert_redirected_to users_url
  end
```

Because the redirect on the update() method changed too, the update test also needs to change:

```
  test "should update user" do
    patch user_url(@user), params: { user: { name: @user.name,
      password: 'secret', password_confirmation: 'secret' } }
➤   assert_redirected_to users_url
  end
```

We need to update the test fixtures to ensure there are no duplicate names:

rails51/depot_r/test/fixtures/users.yml
```
# Read about fixtures at
# http://api.rubyonrails.org/classes/ActiveRecord/FixtureSet.html

one:
➤   name: dave
    password_digest: <%= BCrypt::Password.create('secret') %>

two:
➤   name: susannah
    password_digest: <%= BCrypt::Password.create('secret') %>
```

Note the use of dynamically computed values in the fixture, specifically for the value of password_digest. This code was also inserted by the scaffolding command and uses the same function that Rails uses to compute the password.[1]

At this point, we can administer our users; we need to first authenticate users and then restrict administrative functions so they'll be accessible only by administrators.

Iteration J2: Authenticating Users

What does it mean to add login support for administrators of our store?

---

1. https://github.com/rails/rails/blob/5-1-stable/activemodel/lib/active_model/secure_password.rb

- We need to provide a form that allows them to enter a username and password.

- Once they're logged in, we need to record that fact somehow for the rest of the session (or until they log out).

- We need to restrict access to the administrative parts of the application, allowing only people who are logged in to administer the store.

We could put all of the logic into a single controller, but it makes more sense to split it into two: a session controller to support logging in and out and a controller to welcome administrators:

```
depot> bin/rails generate controller Sessions new create destroy
depot> bin/rails generate controller Admin index
```

The SessionsController#create action will need to record something in session to say that an administrator is logged in. Let's have it store the ID of that person's User object using the key :user_id. The login code looks like this:

rails51/depot_r/app/controllers/sessions_controller.rb
```
  def create
➤    user = User.find_by(name: params[:name])
➤    if user.try(:authenticate, params[:password])
➤      session[:user_id] = user.id
➤      redirect_to admin_url
➤    else
➤      redirect_to login_url, alert: "Invalid user/password combination"
➤    end
  end
```

This code makes use of the Rails try() method, which checks to see if a variable has a value of nil before trying to call the method. If you're using Ruby 2.3, you can use the version of this that's built into the language instead:

```
if user&.authenticate(params[:password])
```

We're also doing something else new here: using a form that isn't directly associated with a model object. To see how that works, let's look at the template for the sessions#new action:

rails51/depot_r/app/views/sessions/new.html.erb
```
<section class="depot_form">
  <% if flash[:alert] %>
    <aside class="notice"><%= flash[:alert] %></aside>
  <% end %>

  <%= form_tag do %>
    <h2>Please Log In</h2>
```

```
    <div class="field">
      <%= label_tag :name, 'Name:' %>
      <%= text_field_tag :name, params[:name] %>
    </div>
    <div class="field">
      <%= label_tag :password, 'Password:' %>
      <%= password_field_tag :password, params[:password] %>
    </div>
    <div class="actions">
      <%= submit_tag "Login" %>
    </div>
  <% end %>
</section>
```

This form is different from ones you saw earlier. Rather than using form_with, it uses form_tag, which simply builds a regular HTML <form>. Inside that form, it uses text_field_tag and password_field_tag, two helpers that create HTML <input> tags. Each helper takes two parameters. The first is the name to give to the field, and the second is the value with which to populate the field. This style of form allows us to associate values in the params structure directly with form fields—no model object is required. In our case, we choose to use the params object directly in the form. An alternative would be to have the controller set instance variables.

We also make use of the label_tag helpers to create HTML <label> tags. This helper also accepts two parameters. The first contains the name of the field, and the second contains the label to be displayed.

See the figure on page 242. Note how the value of the form field is communicated between the controller and the view via the params hash: the view gets the value to display in the field from params[:name], and when the user submits the form, the new field value is made available to the controller the same way.

If the user successfully logs in, we store the ID of the user record in the session data. We'll use the presence of that value in the session as a flag to indicate that an administrative user is logged in.

As you might expect, the controller actions for logging out are much shorter:

rails51/depot_r/app/controllers/sessions_controller.rb
```
  def destroy
➤   session[:user_id] = nil
➤   redirect_to store_index_url, notice: "Logged out"
  end
```

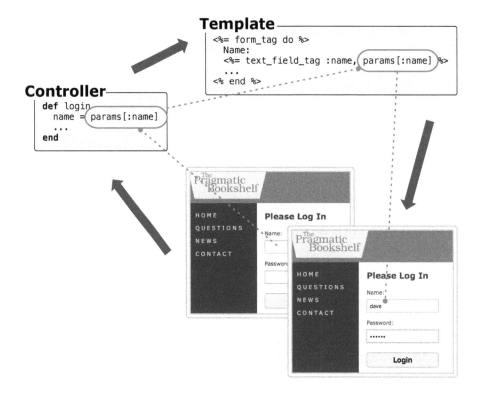

Finally, it's about time to add the index page—the first screen that administrators see when they log in. Let's make it useful. We'll have it display the total number of orders in our store. Create the template in the index.html.erb file in the app/views/admin directory. (This template uses the pluralize() helper, which in this case generates the order or orders string, depending on the cardinality of its first parameter.)

rails51/depot_r/app/views/admin/index.html.erb
```
<h1>Welcome</h1>

<p>
  It's <%= Time.now %>.
  We have <%= pluralize(@total_orders, "order") %>.
</p>
```

The index() action sets up the count:

rails51/depot_r/app/controllers/admin_controller.rb
```
class AdminController < ApplicationController
  def index
    @total_orders = Order.count
  end
end
```

We have one more task to do before we can use this. Whereas previously we relied on the scaffolding generator to create our model and routes for us, this time we simply generated a controller because there's no database-backed model for this controller. Unfortunately, without the scaffolding conventions to guide it, Rails has no way of knowing which actions are to respond to GET requests, which are to respond to POST requests, and so on, for this controller. We need to provide this information by editing our config/routes.rb file:

```
rails51/depot_r/config/routes.rb
Rails.application.routes.draw do
➤   get 'admin' => 'admin#index'

➤   controller :sessions do
➤     get  'login' => :new
➤     post 'login' => :create
➤     delete 'logout' => :destroy
➤   end

    resources :users
    resources :orders
    resources :line_items
    resources :carts
    root 'store#index', as: 'store_index'

    resources :products do
      get :who_bought, on: :member
    end

    # For details on the DSL available within this file, see
    # http://guides.rubyonrails.org/routing.html
end
```

We've touched this before, when we added a root statement in *Iteration C1: Creating the Catalog Listing*, on page 103. What the generate command will add to this file are fairly generic get statements for each of the actions specified. You can (and should) delete the routes provided for sessions/new, sessions/create, and sessions/destroy.

In the case of admin, we'll shorten the URL that the user has to enter (by removing the /index part) and map it to the full action. In the case of session actions, we'll completely change the URL (replacing things like session/create with simply login) as well as tailor the HTTP action that we'll match. Note that login is mapped to both the new and create actions, the difference being whether the request was an HTTP GET or HTTP POST.

We also make use of a shortcut: wrapping the session route declarations in a block and passing it to a controller() class method. This saves us a bit of typing as well as makes the routes easier to read. We'll describe all you can do in this file in *Dispatching Requests to Controllers*, on page 354.

With these routes in place, we can experience the joy of logging in as an administrator. See the following screenshot.

We need to replace the functional tests in the session controller to match what was implemented. First, change the admin controller test to get the admin URL:

rails51/depot_r/test/controllers/admin_controller_test.rb
```ruby
require 'test_helper'

class AdminControllerTest < ActionDispatch::IntegrationTest
  test "should get index" do
    get admin_url
    assert_response :success
  end

end
```

Then we implement several tests for both successful and failed login attempts:

rails51/depot_r/test/controllers/sessions_controller_test.rb
```ruby
require 'test_helper'

class SessionsControllerTest < ActionDispatch::IntegrationTest
  test "should prompt for login" do
    get login_url
    assert_response :success
  end

  test "should login" do
    dave = users(:one)
    post login_url, params: { name: dave.name, password: 'secret' }
    assert_redirected_to admin_url
    assert_equal dave.id, session[:user_id]
  end

  test "should fail login" do
    dave = users(:one)
    post login_url, params: { name: dave.name, password: 'wrong' }
    assert_redirected_to login_url
  end

  test "should logout" do
    delete logout_url
    assert_redirected_to store_index_url
  end

end
```

We show our customer where we are, but she points out that we still haven't controlled access to the administrative pages (which was, after all, the point of this exercise).

Iteration J3: Limiting Access

We want to prevent people without an administrative login from accessing our site's admin pages. It turns out that we can do it with very little code using the Rails *callback* facility.

Rails callbacks allow you to intercept calls to action methods, adding your own processing before they're invoked, after they return, or both. In our case, we'll use a *before action* callback to intercept all calls to the actions in our admin controller. The interceptor can check session[:user_id]. If it's set and if it corresponds to a user in the database, the application knows an administrator is logged in, and the call can proceed. If it's not set, the interceptor can issue a redirect, in this case to our login page.

Where should we put this method? It could sit directly in the admin controller, but—for reasons that'll become apparent shortly—let's put it instead in Applicationcontroller, the parent class of all our controllers. This is in the application_controller.rb file in the app/controllers directory. Note too that we chose to restrict access to this method. This prevents it from ever being exposed to end users as an action:

```
rails51/depot_r/app/controllers/application_controller.rb
class ApplicationController < ActionController::Base
  before_action :authorize

    # ...

  protected

    def authorize
      unless User.find_by(id: session[:user_id])
        redirect_to login_url, notice: "Please log in"
      end
    end
end
```

The before_action() line causes the authorize() method to be invoked before every action in our application.

This is going too far. We've just limited access to the store itself to administrators. That's not good.

We could go back and change things so that we mark only those methods that specifically need authorization. Such an approach, called *blacklisting*, is prone to errors of omission. A much better approach is to *whitelist*—list methods or controllers for which authorization is *not* required. We do this by inserting a skip_before_action() call within the StoreController:

```
rails51/depot_r/app/controllers/store_controller.rb
class StoreController < ApplicationController
  skip_before_action :authorize
```

And we do it again for the SessionsController class:

```
rails51/depot_r/app/controllers/sessions_controller.rb
class SessionsController < ApplicationController
  skip_before_action :authorize
```

We're not done yet; we need to allow people to create, update, and delete carts:

```
rails51/depot_r/app/controllers/carts_controller.rb
class CartsController < ApplicationController
  skip_before_action :authorize, only: [:create, :update, :destroy]
```

And we allow them to create line items:

```
rails51/depot_r/app/controllers/line_items_controller.rb
class LineItemsController < ApplicationController
  skip_before_action :authorize, only: :create
```

We also allow them to create orders (which includes access to the new form):

```
rails51/depot_r/app/controllers/orders_controller.rb
class OrdersController < ApplicationController
  skip_before_action :authorize, only: [:new, :create]
```

With the authorization logic in place, we can now navigate to http://localhost:3000/products. The callback method intercepts us on the way to the product listing and shows us the login screen instead.

Unfortunately, this change pretty much invalidates most of our functional tests, because most operations will now redirect to the login screen instead of doing the function desired. Fortunately, we can address this globally by creating a setup() method in the test_helper. While we're there, we also define some helper methods to login_as() and logout() a user:

```
rails51/depot_r/test/test_helper.rb
class ActionDispatch::IntegrationTest
  def login_as(user)
    post login_url, params: { name: user.name, password: 'secret' }
  end

  def logout
    delete logout_url
  end
```

```
    def setup
      login_as users(:one)
    end
end
```

Note that the setup() method will call login_as() only if session is defined. This prevents the login from being executed in tests that don't involve a controller.

We show our customer and are rewarded with a big smile and a request: could we add a sidebar and put links to the user and product administration stuff in it? And while we're there, could we add the ability to list and delete administrative users? You betcha!

Iteration J4: Adding a Sidebar, More Administration

Let's start with adding links to various administration functions to the sidebar in the layout and have them show up only if a :user_id is in the session:

rails51/depot_r/app/views/layouts/application.html.erb
```erb
<html>
  <head>
    <title>Pragprog Books Online Store</title>
    <%= csrf_meta_tags %>

    <%= stylesheet_link_tag 'application', media: 'all',
                            'data-turbolinks-track': 'reload' %>
    <%= javascript_include_tag 'application',
                               'data-turbolinks-track': 'reload' %>
  </head>

  <body>
    <header class="main">
      <%= image_tag 'logo.svg', alt: 'The Pragmatic Bookshelf' %>
      <h1><%= @page_title %></h1>
    </header>
    <section class="content">
      <nav class="side_nav">

        <div id="cart" class="carts">

          <%= render_if @cart && @cart.line_items.any?, @cart %>
        </div>

        <ul>
          <li><a href="/">Home</a></li>
          <li><a href="/questions">Questions</a></li>
          <li><a href="/news">News</a></li>
          <li><a href="/contact">Contact</a></li>
        </ul>

➤       <% if session[:user_id] %>
➤         <nav class="logged_in_nav">
```

```
➤      <ul>
➤        <li><%= link_to 'Orders',   orders_path   %></li>
➤        <li><%= link_to 'Products', products_path %></li>
➤        <li><%= link_to 'Users',    users_path    %></li>
➤        <li><%= button_to 'Logout', logout_path, method: :delete   %></li>
➤      </ul>
➤    </nav>
➤  <% end %>
    </nav>
    <main class='<%= controller.controller_name %>'>
      <%= yield %>
    </main>
  </section>
  </body>
</html>
```

We should also add some light styling. Let's add this to the end of
app/assets/stylesheets/application.scss:

```
rails51/depot_r/app/assets/stylesheets/application.scss
nav.logged_in_nav {
  border-top: solid thin #bfb;
  padding: 0.354em 0;
  margin-top: 0.354em;
  input[type="submit"] {
    // Make the logout button look like a
    // link, so it matches the nav style
    background: none;
    border: none;
    color: #bfb;
    font-size: 1em;
    letter-spacing: 0.354em;
    margin: 0;
    padding: 0;
    text-transform: uppercase;
  }
  input[type="submit"]:hover {
    color: white;
  }
}
```

Now it's all starting to come together. We can log in, and by clicking a link in
the sidebar, we can see a list of users. Let's see if we can break something.

Would the Last Admin to Leave…

We bring up the user list screen that looks something like the screenshot on
page 249; then we click the Destroy link next to *dave* to delete that user. Sure
enough, our user is removed. But to our surprise, we're then presented with
the login screen instead. We just deleted the only administrative user from

the system. When the next request came in, the authentication failed, so the application refused to let us in. We have to log in again before using any administrative functions.

But now we have an embarrassing problem: there are no administrative users in the database, so we can't log in.

Fortunately, we can quickly add a user to the database from the command line. If you invoke the rails console command, Rails invokes Ruby's irb utility, but it does so in the context of your Rails application. That means you can interact with your application's code by typing Ruby statements and looking at the values they return.

We can use this to invoke our user model directly, having it add a user into the database for us:

```
depot> bin/rails console
Loading development environment.
>> User.create(name: 'dave', password: 'secret', password_confirmation: 'secret')
=> #<User:0x2933060 @attributes={...} ... >
>> User.count
=> 1
```

The >> sequences are prompts. After the first, we call the User class to create a new user, and after the second, we call it again to show that we do indeed have a single user in our database. After each command we enter, rails console displays the value returned by the code (in the first case, it's the model object, and in the second case, it's the count).

Panic over. We can now log back in to the application. But how can we stop this from happening again? We have several ways. For example, we could write code that prevents you from deleting your own user. That doesn't quite work: in theory, A could delete B at just the same time that B deletes A. Let's try a different approach. We'll delete the user inside a database transaction. Transactions provide an all-or-nothing proposition, stating that each work unit performed in a database must either complete in its entirety or none of them will have any effect whatsoever. If no users are left after we've deleted the user, we'll roll the transaction back, restoring the user we just deleted.

To do this, we'll use an Active Record hook method. We've already seen one of these: the validate hook is called by Active Record to validate an object's state. It turns out that Active Record defines sixteen or so hook methods, each called at a particular point in an object's life cycle. We'll use the after_destroy() hook, which is called after the SQL delete is executed. If a method by this name is publicly visible, it'll conveniently be called in the same transaction as the delete—so if it raises an exception, the transaction will be rolled back. The hook method looks like this:

```
rails51/depot_t/app/models/user.rb
after_destroy :ensure_an_admin_remains

class Error < StandardError
end

private
  def ensure_an_admin_remains
    if User.count.zero?
      raise Error.new "Can't delete last user"
    end
  end
```

The key concept is the use of an exception to indicate an error when the user is deleted. This exception serves two purposes. First, because it's raised inside a transaction, it causes an automatic rollback. By raising the exception if the users table is empty after the deletion, we undo the delete and restore that last user.

Second, the exception signals the error back to the controller, where we use a rescue_from block to handle it and report the error to the user in the notice. If you want only to abort the transaction but not otherwise signal an exception, raise an ActiveRecord::Rollback exception instead, because this is the only exception that won't be passed on by ActiveRecord::Base.transaction:

```
rails51/depot_t/app/controllers/users_controller.rb
def destroy
  @user.destroy
  respond_to do |format|
    format.html { redirect_to users_url,
      notice: '"User #{@user.name} deleted"' }
    format.json { head :no_content }
  end
end

rescue_from 'User::Error' do |exception|
  redirect_to users_url, notice: exception.message
end
```

This code still has a potential timing issue: it's still possible for two administrators each to delete the last two users if their timing is right. Fixing this would require more database wizardry than we have space for here.

In fact, the login system described in this chapter is rudimentary. Most applications these days use a plugin to do this.

A number of plugins are available that provide ready-made solutions that not only are more comprehensive than the authentication logic shown here but generally require less code and effort on your part to use. Devise[2] is a common and popular gem that does this.

What We Just Did

By the end of this iteration, we've done the following:

- We used has_secure_password to store an encrypted version of the password into the database.

- We controlled access to the administration functions using before action callbacks to invoke an authorize() method.

- We used rails console to interact directly with a model (and dig us out of a hole after we deleted the last user).

- We used a transaction to help prevent deletion of the last user.

Playtime

Here's some stuff to try on your own:

- Modify the user update function to require and validate the current password before allowing a user's password to be changed.

- When the system is freshly installed on a new machine, no administrators are defined in the database, and hence no administrator can log on. But, if no administrator can log on, then no one can create an administrative user.

  Change the code so that if no administrator is defined in the database, any username works to log on (allowing you to quickly create a real administrator).

- Experiment with rails console. Try creating products, orders, and line items. Watch for the return value when you save a model object—when validation fails, you'll see false returned. Find out why by examining the errors:

---

2. https://github.com/plataformatec/devise

```
>> prd = Product.new
=> #<Product id: nil, title: nil, description: nil, image_url:
nil, created_at: nil, updated_at: nil, price:
#<BigDecimal:246aa1c,'0.0',4(8)>>
>> prd.save
=> false
>> prd.errors.full_messages
=> ["Image url must be a URL for a GIF, JPG, or PNG image",
    "Image url can't be blank", "Price should be at least 0.01",
    "Title can't be blank", "Description can't be blank"]
```

• Look up the authenticate_or_request_with_http_basic() method and utilize it in your
:authorize callback if the request.format is *not* Mime[:HTML]. Test that it works
by accessing an Atom feed:

```
curl --silent --user dave:secret \
  http://localhost:3000/products/2/who_bought.atom
```

• We've gotten our tests working by performing a login, but we haven't yet
written tests that verify that access to sensitive data requires login. Write
at least one test that verifies this by calling logout() and then attempting
to fetch or update some data that requires authentication.

In this chapter, you'll see:
- Localizing templates
- Database design considerations for I18n

## CHAPTER 16

Task K: Internationalization

Now we have a basic cart working, and our customer starts to inquire about languages other than English, noting that her company has a big push on for expansion in emerging markets. Unless we can present something in a language that visitors to our customer's website will understand, our customer will be leaving money on the table. We can't have that.

The first problem is that none of us are professional translators. The customer reassures us that this isn't something we need to concern ourselves with because that part of the effort will be outsourced. All we need to worry about is *enabling* translation. Furthermore, we don't have to worry about the administration pages yet, because all the administrators speak English. What we have to focus on is the store.

That's a relief—but still a tall order. We'll need to define a way to enable the user to select a language, we'll have to provide the translations themselves, and we'll have to change the views to use these translations. But we're up to the task, and—armed with a bit of remembered high-school Spanish—we set off to work.

Joe asks:

If We Stick to One Language, Do We Need to Read This Chapter?

The short answer is no. In fact, many Rails applications are for a small or homogeneous group and never need translating. That being said, pretty much everybody who does find that they need translation agrees that it's best if this is done early. So, unless you're sure that translation won't ever be needed, it's our recommendation that you at least understand what would be involved so that you can make informed decisions.

Iteration K1: Selecting the Locale

We start by creating a new configuration file that encapsulates our knowledge of what locales are available and which one is to be used as the default:

```
rails51/depot_t/config/initializers/i18n.rb
#encoding: utf-8
I18n.default_locale = :en

LANGUAGES = [
  ['English',                'en'],
  ["Espa&ntilde;ol".html_safe, 'es']
]
```

This code is doing two things.

The first thing it does is use the I18n module to set the default locale. I18n is a funny name, but it sure beats typing out *internationalization* all the time. Internationalization, after all, starts with an *i*, ends with an *n*, and has eighteen letters in between.

Then the code defines a list of associations between display names and locale names. Unfortunately, all we have available at the moment is a U.S. keyboard, and Español has a character that can't be directly entered via our keyboard. Different operating systems have different ways of dealing with this, and often the easiest way is to copy and paste the correct text from a website. If you do this, make sure your editor is configured for UTF-8. Meanwhile, we've opted to use the HTML equivalent of the *n con tilde* character in Spanish. If we didn't do anything else, the markup itself would be shown. But by calling html_safe, we inform Rails that the string is safe to be interpreted as containing HTML.

For Rails to pick up this configuration change, the server needs to be restarted.

Since each page that's translated will have an en and an es version (for now—more will be added later), it makes sense to include this in the URL. Let's plan to put the locale up front, make it optional, and have it default to the current locale, which in turn will default to English. To implement this cunning plan, let's start by modifying config/routes.rb:

rails51/depot_t/config/routes.rb

```ruby
Rails.application.routes.draw do
  get 'admin' => 'admin#index'
  controller :sessions do
    get  'login' => :new
    post 'login' => :create
    delete 'logout' => :destroy
  end

  resources :users
  resources :products do
    get :who_bought, on: :member
  end
➤ scope '(:locale)' do
    resources :orders
    resources :line_items
    resources :carts
    root 'store#index', as: 'store_index', via: :all
➤ end
end
```

We've nested our resources and root declarations inside a scope declaration for :locale. Furthermore, :locale is in parentheses, which is the way to say that it's optional. Note that we didn't choose to put the administrative and session functions inside this scope, because it's not our intent to translate them at this time.

What this means is that http://localhost:3000/ will use the default locale (namely, English) and therefore be routed exactly the same as http://localhost:3000/en. http://localhost:3000/es will route to the same controller and action, but we'll want this to cause the locale to be set differently.

At this point, we've made a lot of changes to config.routes, and with the nesting and all the optional parts to the path, the gestalt might be hard to visualize. Never fear: when running a server in development mode, Rails provides a visual aid. All you need to do is navigate to http://localhost:3000/rails/info/routes, and you'll see a list of all your routes. You can even filter the list, as shown in the screenshot on page 256, to quickly find the route you're interested in. More information on the fields shown in this table can be found in the description of rails routes on page 356.

Routes

Routes match in priority from top to bottom

Helper	HTTP Verb	Path	Controller#Action
Path / Url		locale ⊗	
		Paths Matching (locale):	
store_index_path		/(.:locale)(.:format)	store#index
		Paths Containing (locale):	
orders_path	GET	(/:locale)/orders(.:format)	orders#index
	POST	(/:locale)/orders(.:format)	orders#create
new_order_path	GET	(/:locale)/orders/new(.:format)	orders#new
edit_order_path	GET	(/:locale)/orders/:id/edit(.:format)	orders#edit
order_path	GET	(/:locale)/orders/:id(.:format)	orders#show
	PATCH	(/:locale)/orders/:id(.:format)	orders#update
	PUT	(/:locale)/orders/:id(.:format)	orders#update
	DELETE	(/:locale)/orders/:id(.:format)	orders#destroy
line_items_path	GET	(/:locale)/line_items(.:format)	line_items#index
	POST	(/:locale)/line_items(.:format)	line_items#create

With the routing in place, we're ready to extract the locale from the parameters
and make it available to the application. To do this, we need to create a
before_action callback. The logical place to do this is in the common base class
for all of our controllers, which is ApplicationController:

```ruby
rails51/depot_t/app/controllers/application_controller.rb
class ApplicationController < ActionController::Base
  before_action :set_i18n_locale_from_params
  # ...
  protected
    def set_i18n_locale_from_params
      if params[:locale]
        if I18n.available_locales.map(&:to_s).include?(params[:locale])
          I18n.locale = params[:locale]
        else
          flash.now[:notice] =
            "#{params[:locale]} translation not available"
          logger.error flash.now[:notice]
        end
      end
    end
end
```

This set_i18n_locale_from_params does pretty much what it says: it sets the locale from the params, but only if there's a locale in the params; otherwise, it leaves the current locale alone. Care is taken to provide a message for both the user and the administrator when a failure occurs.

With this in place, we can see the results in the following screenshot of navigating to http://localhost:3000/en.

At this point, the English version of the page is available both at the root of the website and at pages that start with /en. If you try another language code, say "es" (or Spanish), you can see that an error message appears saying no translations are available. The screenshot on page 258 shows what this might look like when navigating to http://localhost:3000/es:

Iteration K2: Translating the Storefront

Now it's time to begin providing the translated text. Let's start with the layout, because it's pretty visible. We replace any text that needs to be translated with calls to I18n.translate. Not only is this method conveniently aliased as I18n.t, but a helper named t is provided.

The parameter to the translate function is a unique dot-qualified name. We can choose any name we like, but if we use the t helper function provided, names that start with a dot will first be expanded using the name of the template. So, let's do that:

rails51/depot_t/app/views/layouts/application.html.erb

```erb
<nav class="side_nav">

  <div id="cart" class="carts">

    <%= render_if @cart && @cart.line_items.any?, @cart %>
  </div>

  <ul>
    <li><a href="/"><%= t('.home') %></a></li>
    <li><a href="/questions"><%= t('.questions') %></a></li>
    <li><a href="/news"><%= t('.news') %></a></li>
    <li><a href="/contact"><%= t('.contact') %></a></li>
  </ul>

  <% if session[:user_id] %>
    <nav class="logged_in_nav">
      <ul>
        <li><%= link_to 'Orders',   orders_path   %></li>
        <li><%= link_to 'Products', products_path %></li>
        <li><%= link_to 'Users',    users_path    %></li>
        <li><%= button_to 'Logout', logout_path, method: :delete   %></li>
      </ul>
    </nav>
  <% end %>
</nav>
```

Since this view is named layouts/application.html.erb, the English mappings will expand to en.layouts.application. Here's the corresponding locale file:

rails51/depot_t/config/locales/en.yml

```
en:

  layouts:
    application:
      title:         "The Pragmatic Bookshelf"
      home:          "Home"
      questions:     "Questions"
      news:          "News"
      contact:       "Contact"
```

Here it is in Spanish:

rails51/depot_t/config/locales/es.yml

```
es:

  layouts:
    application:
      title:         "Biblioteca de Pragmatic"
      home:          "Inicio"
      questions:     "Preguntas"
      news:          "Noticias"
      contact:       "Contacto"
```

The format is YAML, the same as the one used to configure the databases. YAML consists of indented names and values, where the indentation in this case matches the structure that we created in our names.

To get Rails to recognize new YAML files, the server needs to be restarted.

Navigating to http://localhost:3000/es now will show some translated text, as shown in the screenshot on page 260.

Next to be updated is the main title as well as the Add to Cart button. Both can be found in the store index template:

rails51/depot_s/app/views/store/index.html.erb

```
<% if notice %>
  <aside id="notice"><%= notice %></aside>
<% end %>

➤ <h1><%= t('.title_html') %></h1>

<ul class="catalog">
  <% cache @products do %>
    <% @products.each do |product| %>
      <% cache product do %>
        <li>
          <%= image_tag(product.image_url) %>
          <h2><%= product.title %></h2>
```

```
      <p>
        <%= sanitize(product.description) %>
      </p>
      <div class="price">
        <%= number_to_currency(product.price) %>
        <%= button_to t('.add_html'), line_items_path(product_id: product),
            remote: true %>
      </div>
    </li>
  <% end %>
  <% end %>
<% end %>
</ul>
```

And here's the corresponding updates to the locales files, first in English:

rails51/depot_t/config/locales/en.yml
```
en:

  store:
    index:
      title_html:  "Your Pragmatic Catalog"
      add_html:    "Add to Cart"
```

And then in Spanish:

rails51/depot_t/config/locales/es.yml
```
es:

  store:
    index:
      title_html:  "Su Cat&aacute;logo de Pragmatic"
      add_html:     "A&ntilde;adir al Carrito"
```

Note that since title_html and add_html end in the characters _html, we're free to use HTML entity names for characters that don't appear on our keyboard. If we didn't name the translation key this way, what you'd end up seeing on the page is the markup. This is yet another convention that Rails has adopted to make your coding life easier. Rails will also treat names that contain html as a component (in other words, the string .html.) as HTML key names.

By refreshing the page in the browser window, we see the results shown in the following screenshot.

Feeling confident, we move on to the cart partial, replacing text that needs translation as well as adding the locale to the new_order_path:

rails51/depot_t/app/views/carts/_cart.html.erb
```erb
<article>
  <% if notice %>
    <aside id="notice"><%= notice %></aside>
  <% end %>
```

```
➤    <h2><%= t('.title') %></h2>
     <table>

       <%= render(cart.line_items) %>
       <tfoot>
         <tr>
           <th colspan="2">Total:</td>
           <td class="price"><%= number_to_currency(cart.total_price) %></td>
         </tr>
       </tfoot>
     </table>

     <div class="actions">
➤      <%= button_to t('.empty'), cart,
                 method: :delete,
                 data: { confirm: 'Are you sure?' } %>

➤      <%= button_to t('.checkout'), new_order_path(locale: I18n.locale),
                 method: :get,
                 class: "checkout"%>
     </div>
   </article>
```

And again, here are the translations:

```
rails51/depot_t/config/locales/en.yml
en:

  carts:
    cart:
      title:       "Your Cart"
      empty:       "Empty cart"
      checkout:    "Checkout"
```

```
rails51/depot_t/config/locales/es.yml
es:

  carts:
    cart:
      title:       "Carrito de la Compra"
      empty:       "Vaciar Carrito"
      checkout:    "Comprar"
```

Refreshing the page, we see the cart title and buttons have been translated, as shown in the screenshot on page 263.

We need to be careful here. The logic to render the cart is rendered in two places: first in the storefront and second in response to pushing the Añadir al Carrito (Add to Cart) button via Ajax. Sure enough, when we click that button, we see the cart rendered in English. To fix this, we need to pass the locale on the remote call:

rails51/depot_t/app/views/store/index.html.erb

```erb
<div class="price">
    <%= number_to_currency(product.price) %>
    <%= button_to t('.add_html'),
    line_items_path(product_id: product, locale: I18n.locale),
        remote: true %>
</div>
```

We now notice our next problem. Languages are not the only thing that varies from locale to locale; currencies do too. And the customary way that numbers are presented varies too.

So first we check with our customer and we verify that we're not worrying about exchange rates at the moment (whew!), because that'll be taken care of by the credit card and/or wire companies, but we do need to display the string USD or $US after the value when we're showing the result in Spanish.

Another variation is the way that numbers themselves are displayed. Decimal values are delimited by a comma, and separators for the thousands place are indicated by a dot.

Currency is a lot more complicated than it first appears, and there are a lot of decisions to be made. Fortunately, Rails knows to look in your translations file for this information; all we need to do is supply it. Here it is for en:

rails51/depot_t/config/locales/en.yml

```yaml
en:

  number:
    currency:
      format:
        unit:      "$"
        precision: 2
        separator: "."
        delimiter: ","
        format:    "%u%n"
```

Here it is for es:

rails51/depot_t/config/locales/es.yml

```
es:

  number:
    currency:
      format:
        unit:       "$US"
        precision: 2
        separator: ","
        delimiter: "."
        format:     "%n %u"
```

We've specified the unit, precision, separator, and delimiter for number.currency.format. That much is pretty self-explanatory. The format is a bit more involved: %n is a placeholder for the number;   is a nonbreaking space character, preventing this value from being split across multiple lines; and %u is a placeholder for the unit. See the following screenshot for the result.

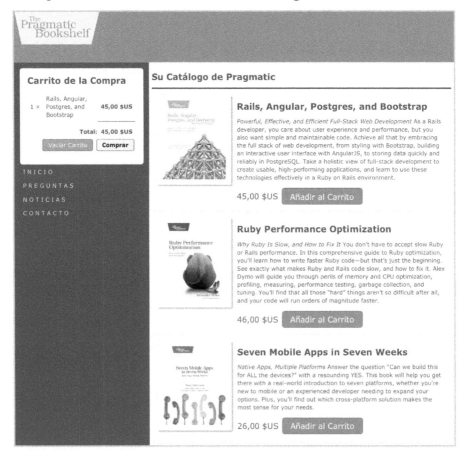

Iteration K3: Translating Checkout

Now we're entering the home stretch. The new order page is next:

```
rails51/depot_t/app/views/orders/new.html.erb
<section class="depot_form">
  <h1><%= t('.legend') %></h1>
  <%= render 'form', order: @order %>
</section>

<%= javascript_pack_tag("pay_type") %>
```

Here's the form that's used by this page:

```
rails51/depot_t/app/views/orders/_form.html.erb
<%= form_with(model: order, local: true) do |form| %>
  <% if order.errors.any? %>
    <div id="error_explanation">
      <h2><%= pluralize(order.errors.count, "error") %>
      prohibited this order from being saved:</h2>

      <ul>
      <% order.errors.full_messages.each do |message| %>
        <li><%= message %></li>
      <% end %>
      </ul>
    </div>
  <% end %>

  <div class="field">
    <%= form.label :name, t('.name') %>
    <%= form.text_field :name, id: :order_name, size: 40 %>
  </div>

  <div class="field">
    <%= form.label :address, t('.address_html') %>
    <%= form.text_area :address, id: :order_address, rows: 3, cols: 40 %>
  </div>

  <div class="field">
    <%= form.label :email, t('.email') %>
    <%= form.email_field :email, id: :order_email, size: 40 %>
  </div>

  <div id='pay-type-component'></div>

  <div class="actions">
    <%= form.submit t('.submit') %>
  </div>
<% end %>
```

That covers the form elements that Rails is rendering, but what about the React-rendered payment details we added in *Iteration H1: Adding Fields Dynamically to a Form*, on page 195? If you recall, we had to create the HTML form elements inside React components, mimicking what Rails form helpers would do.

Since React is rendering our payment details components—not Rails—we need to make our translations available to React, meaning they must be available in JavaScript. The i18n-js library will do just that.[1]

This library will make a copy of our translations as a JavaScript object and provide an object called I18n that allows us to access them. Our React components will use that to provide localized strings for the dynamic form we created earlier.

First, we'll add it to our Gemfile.

rails51/depot_t/Gemfile
```
gem 'i18n-js'
```

Install it with bundle install. Getting i18n-js to work requires a bit of configuration, so let's do that before we start using it in our React components.

First, we'll configure i18n-js to convert our translations. This is done by a *middleware* that the gem provides.[2] A middleware is a way to add behavior to all requests served by a Rails app by manipulating an internal data structure. In the case of i18n-js, its middleware makes sure that the JavaScript copy of our translations is in sync with those in config/locales.

We can set this up by adding a line of code to config/application.rb:

rails51/depot_t/config/application.rb
```
config.middleware.use I18n::JS::Middleware
```

This requires restarting our server, so if you are currently running it, go ahead and restart it now.

Next, we need to tell Rails to serve up the translations that i18n-js provides. We also need to make the I18n object available. We can do that by adding two require directives to app/assets/javascripts/application.js. These directives tell Rails to include the referenced JavaScript libraries when serving up pages. Since the JavaScript files that come with i18n-js are inside a gem, we have to do this explicitly.

rails51/depot_t/app/assets/javascripts/application.js
```
//= require i18n
//= require i18n/translations
```

---

1. https://github.com/fnando/i18n-js
2. http://guides.rubyonrails.org/rails_on_rack.html#configuring-middleware-stack

The last bit of configuration we need for i18n-js is to tell it what the currently chosen locale is. We can do that by rendering a dynamic script tag in our application layout in app/views/layouts/application.html.erb.

```
rails51/depot_t/app/views/layouts/application.html.erb
<%= javascript_include_tag 'application',
                           'data-turbolinks-track': 'reload' %>
➤ <script type="text/javascript">
➤   I18n.defaultLocale = "<%= I18n.default_locale %>";
➤   I18n.locale        = "<%= I18n.locale %>";
➤ </script>
```

Note that we want this tag to appear *after* the call to javascript_include_tag() so that I18n will have been defined.

With this in place, we need to add calls to I18n.t() inside the JSX of our React components. This is straightforward to do using the curly brace syntax we've seen before. Let's start with the main component in app/javascript/PayTypeSelector/index.jsx. Here's the entire render() method, fully localized.

```
rails51/depot_t/app/javascript/PayTypeSelector/index.jsx
render() {
  let PayTypeCustomComponent = NoPayType;
  if (this.state.selectedPayType == "Credit card") {
    PayTypeCustomComponent = CreditCardPayType;
  } else if (this.state.selectedPayType == "Check") {
    PayTypeCustomComponent = CheckPayType;
  } else if (this.state.selectedPayType == "Purchase order") {
    PayTypeCustomComponent = PurchaseOrderPayType;
  }
  return (
    <div>
      <div className="field">
        <label htmlFor="order_pay_type">
          {I18n.t("orders.form.pay_type")}
        </label>

        <select id="pay_type" onChange={this.onPayTypeSelected}
          name="order[pay_type]">
          <option value="">
            {I18n.t("orders.form.pay_prompt_html")}
          </option>

          <option value="Check">
            {I18n.t("orders.form.pay_types.check")}
          </option>

          <option value="Credit card">
            {I18n.t("orders.form.pay_types.credit_card")}
          </option>
```

```
        <option value="Purchase order">
          {I18n.t("orders.form.pay_types.purchase_order")}
        </option>
      </select>
    </div>
    <PayTypeCustomComponent />
  </div>
);
}
```

Although I18n.t() is similar to Rails's t(), note the subtle difference in the argument to the method. In our Rails view, we can simply use t(".pay_type") which, as we learned in *Iteration K2: Translating the Storefront*, on page 257, allows Rails to figure out from the template name where the strings are in the locale YAML files. We can't take advantage of this with i18n-js, so we must specify the complete path to the translation in the YAML file.

Next, let's do this to the three components that make up our payment details view. First up is app/javascript/PayTypeSelector/CheckPayType.jsx:

rails51/depot_t/app/javascript/PayTypeSelector/CheckPayType.jsx
```jsx
import React from 'react'

class CheckPayType extends React.Component {
  render() {
    return (
      <div>
        <div className="field">
          <label htmlFor="order_routing_number">
            {I18n.t("orders.form.check_pay_type.routing_number")}
          </label>

          <input type="password"
                 name="order[routing_number]"
                 id="order_routing_number" />
        </div>
        <div className="field">
          <label htmlFor="order_account_number">
            {I18n.t("orders.form.check_pay_type.account_number")}
          </label>

          <input type="text"
                 name="order[account_number]"
                 id="order_account_number" />
        </div>
      </div>
    );
  }
}
export default CheckPayType
```

Now, CreditCardPayType.jsx:

rails51/depot_t/app/javascript/PayTypeSelector/CreditCardPayType.jsx

```
import React from 'react'

class CreditCardPayType extends React.Component {
  render() {
    return (
      <div>
        <div className="field">
          <label htmlFor="order_credit_card_number">
            {I18n.t("orders.form.credit_card_pay_type.cc_number")}
          </label>

          <input type="password"
                 name="order[credit_card_number]"
                 id="order_credit_card_number" />
        </div>
        <div className="field">
          <label htmlFor="order_expiration_date">
            {I18n.t("orders.form.credit_card_pay_type.expiration_date")}
          </label>

          <input type="text"
                 name="order[expiration_date]"
                 id="order_expiration_date"
                 size="9"
                 placeholder="e.g. 03/19" />
        </div>
      </div>
    );
  }
}
export default CreditCardPayType
```

And finally PurchaseOrderPayType.jsx:

rails51/depot_t/app/javascript/PayTypeSelector/PurchaseOrderPayType.jsx

```
import React from 'react'

class PurchaseOrderPayType extends React.Component {
  render() {
    return (
      <div>
        <div className="field">
          <label htmlFor="order_po_number">
            {I18n.t("orders.form.purchase_order_pay_type.po_number")}
          </label>
```

```
            <input type="password"
                    name="order[po_number]"
                    id="order_po_number" />
        </div>
      </div>
    );
  }
}
export default PurchaseOrderPayType
```

With those done, here are the corresponding locale definitions:

rails51/depot_t/config/locales/en.yml

```
en:

  orders:
    new:
      legend:          "Please Enter Your Details"
      form:
        name:            "Name"
        address_html:  "Address"
        email:           "E-mail"
        pay_type:        "Pay with"
        pay_prompt_html: "Select a payment method"
        submit:          "Place Order"
        pay_types:
          check:             "Check"
          credit_card:       "Credit Card"
          purchase_order:    "Purchase Order"
        check_pay_type:
          routing_number:  "Routing #"
          account_number:  "Account #"
        credit_card_pay_type:
          cc_number:  "CC #"
          expiration_date:  "Expiry"
        purchase_order_pay_type:
          po_number:  "PO #"
```

rails51/depot_t/config/locales/es.yml

```
es:

  orders:
    new:
      legend:          "Por favor, introduzca sus datos"
      form:
        name:            "Nombre"
        address_html:  "Direcci&oacute;n"
        email:           "E-mail"
        pay_type:        "Forma de pago"
        pay_prompt_html: "Seleccione un método de pago"
        submit:          "Realizar Pedido"
        pay_types:
```

```
    check:              "Cheque"
    credit_card:        "Tarjeta de Crédito"
    purchase_order:     "Orden de Compra"
  check_pay_type:
    routing_number: "# de Enrutamiento"
    account_number: "# de Cuenta"
  credit_card_pay_type:
    cc_number: "Número"
    expiration_date: "Expiración"
  purchase_order_pay_type:
    po_number: "Número"
```

See the following screenshot for the completed form.

All looks good until we click the Realizar Pedido button prematurely and see the results shown in the screenshot on page 272. The error messages that Active Record produces can also be translated; what we need to do is supply the translations:

rails51/depot_t/config/locales/es.yml
```
es:

  activerecord:
    errors:
      messages:
        inclusion: "no está included en la lista"
        blank:     "no puede quedar en blanco"
  errors:
    template:
      body:      "Hay problemas con los siguientes campos:"
      header:
        one:     "1 error ha impedido que este %{model} se guarde"
        other:   "%{count} errores han impedido que este %{model} se guarde"
```

Although you can create these with many trips to Google Translate, the Rails i18n gem's GitHub repo contains a lot of translations for common strings in many languages.[3]

Note that messages with counts typically have two forms: errors.template.header.one is the message that's produced when there's one error, and errors.template.header.other is produced otherwise. This gives the translators the opportunity to provide the correct pluralization of nouns and to match verbs with the nouns.

Since we once again made use of HTML entities, we want these error messages to be displayed as is (or in Rails parlance, *raw*). We also need to translate the error messages. So again we modify the form:

```
rails51/depot_u/app/views/orders/_form.html.erb
<%= form_with(model: order, local: true) do |form| %>
  <% if order.errors.any? %>
    <div id="error_explanation">
      <h2><%=raw t('errors.template.header', count: @order.errors.count,
        model: t('activerecord.models.order')) %>.</h2>
      <p><%= t('errors.template.body') %></p>

      <ul>
      <% order.errors.full_messages.each do |message| %>
```

---

3.   https://github.com/svenfuchs/rails-i18n/tree/master/rails/locale

```
    <li><%=raw message %></li>
  <% end %>
  </ul>
 </div>
<% end %>
<!-- ... -->
```

Note that we're passing the count and model name (which is, itself, enabled for translation) on the translate call for the error template header. With these changes in place, we try again and see improvement, as shown in the following screenshot.

That's better, but the names of the model and the attributes bleed through the interface. This is OK in English, because the names we picked work for English. We need to provide translations for each model. This, too, goes into the YAML file:

```
rails51/depot_u/config/locales/es.yml
es:

  activerecord:
    models:
      order:        "pedido"
    attributes:
      order:
        address:    "Direcci&oacute;n"
        name:       "Nombre"
        email:      "E-mail"
        pay_type:   "Forma de pago"
```

Note that there's no need to provide English equivalents for this, because those messages are built into Rails.

We're pleased to see the model and attribute names translated in the following screenshot; we fill out the form, we submit the order, and we get a "Thank you for your order" message.

We need to update the flash messages and add the locale to the store_index_url:

```
rails51/depot_u/app/controllers/orders_controller.rb
  def create
    @order = Order.new(order_params)
    @order.add_line_items_from_cart(@cart)

    respond_to do |format|
      if @order.save
        Cart.destroy(session[:cart_id])
        session[:cart_id] = nil
        ChargeOrderJob.perform_later(@order,pay_type_params.to_h)
        format.html { redirect_to store_index_url(locale: I18n.locale),
          notice: I18n.t('.thanks') }
        format.json { render :show, status: :created,
          location: @order }
      else
        format.html { render :new }
        format.json { render json: @order.errors,
          status: :unprocessable_entity }
      end
    end
  end
```

Next, we adjust the test to match:

rails51/depot_u/test/controllers/orders_controller_test.rb

```
test "should create order" do
  assert_difference('Order.count') do
    post orders_url, params: { order: { address: @order.address,
      email: @order.email, name: @order.name,
      pay_type: @order.pay_type } }
  end

  assert_redirected_to store_index_url(locale: 'en')
end
```

Finally, we provide the translations:

rails51/depot_u/config/locales/en.yml

```
en:

  thanks:            "Thank you for your order"
```

rails51/depot_u/config/locales/es.yml

```
es:

  thanks:            "Gracias por su pedido"
```

See the cheery message in the next screenshot.

Iteration K4: Adding a Locale Switcher

We've completed the task, but we need to advertise its availability more. We spy some unused area in the top-right side of the layout, so we add a form immediately before the image_tag:

```
rails51/depot_u/app/views/layouts/application.html.erb
    <header class="main">
➤     <aside>
➤       <%= form_tag store_index_path, class: 'locale' do %>
➤         <%= select_tag 'set_locale',
➤           options_for_select(LANGUAGES, I18n.locale.to_s),
➤           onchange: 'this.form.submit()' %>
➤         <%= submit_tag 'submit', id: "submit_locale_change" %>
➤       <% end %>
➤     </aside>
      <%= image_tag 'logo.svg', alt: 'The Pragmatic Bookshelf' %>
      <h1><%= @page_title %></h1>
    </header>
```

The form_tag specifies the path to the store as the page to be redisplayed when the form is submitted. A class attribute lets us associate the form with some CSS.

The select_tag is used to define the input field for this form—namely, locale. It's an options list based on the LANGUAGES array we set up in the configuration file, with the default being the current locale (also made available via the I18n module). We also set up an onchange event handler, which submits this form whenever the value changes. This works only if JavaScript is enabled, but it's handy.

This means we don't need to show the Submit button if JavaScript is enabled. The simplest way to do that is to write some CoffeeScript to hide it. If Java-Script is disabled, the CoffeeScript won't execute, and the button remains to allow those users to submit the form. We make this happen by adding an id to the submit_tag() so we can locate the button and set its style.display to "none", which is the programmatic way of setting the CSS display property to none. We'll add this code into a new file called app/assets/javascripts/locale_switcher.coffee, which is automatically brought in by Rails and executed on the page:

```
rails51/depot_u/app/assets/javascripts/locale_switcher.coffee
document.addEventListener 'turbolinks:load', ->
  document.getElementById('submit_locale_change').style.display='none'
```

Then we add a submit_tag for the cases when JavaScript isn't available. To handle the case in which JavaScript is available and the Submit button is unnecessary, we add a tiny bit of JavaScript that hides each of the input tags in the locale form, even though we know that there's only one.

Next, we modify the store controller to redirect to the store path for a given locale if the :set_locale form is used:

rails51/depot_u/app/controllers/store_controller.rb
```
  def index
➤   if params[:set_locale]
➤     redirect_to store_index_url(locale: params[:set_locale])
➤   else
      @products = Product.order(:title)
➤   end
  end
```

Finally, we add a bit of CSS:

rails51/depot_u/app/assets/stylesheets/application.scss
```
.locale {
  float: right;
  margin: 1em;
}
```

For the actual selector, see the following screenshot. We can now switch back and forth between languages with a single mouse click.

At this point, we can place orders in two languages, and our thoughts turn to deployment. But because it's been a busy day, it's time to put down our tools and relax. We'll start on deployment in the morning.

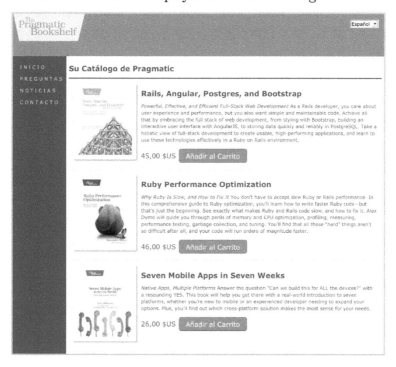

What We Just Did

By the end of this iteration, we've done the following:

- We set the default locale for our application and provided means for the user to select an alternative locale.

- We created translation files for text fields, currency amounts, errors, and model names.

- We altered layouts and views to call out to the I18n module by way of the t() helper to translate textual portions of the interface.

Playtime

Here's some stuff to try on your own:

- Add a locale column to the products database, and adjust the index view to select only the products that match the locale. Adjust the products view so that you can view, enter, and alter this new column. Enter a few products in each locale, and test the resulting application.

- Determine the current exchange rate between U.S. dollars and euros, and localize the currency display to display euros when ES_es is selected.

- Translate the Order::PAYMENT_TYPES shown in the drop-down. You'll need to keep the option value (which is sent to the server) the same. Change only what's displayed.

In this chapter, you'll see:
- Running our application in a production web server
- Configuring the database for MySQL
- Using Bundler and Git for version control
- Deploying our application using Capistrano or Heroku

## CHAPTER 17

Task L: Deployment and Production

Deployment is supposed to mark a happy point in the lifetime of our application. It's when we take the code that we've so carefully crafted and upload it to a server so that other people can use it. It's when the beer, champagne, and hors d'oeuvres are supposed to flow. Shortly thereafter, our application will be written about in *Wired* magazine, and we'll be overnight names in the geek community.

The reality, however, is that it often takes quite a bit of up-front planning to pull off a smooth and repeatable deployment of your application.

By the time we're through with this chapter, our setup will look like the following figure.

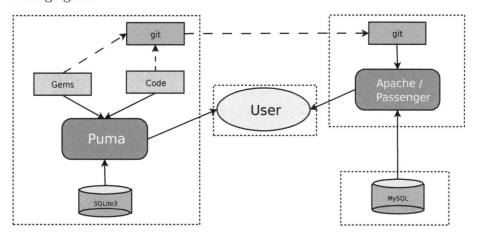

At the moment, we've been doing all of our work on one machine, though user interaction with our web server *could* be done on a separate machine. In the figure, the user's machine is in the center, and the Puma web server is on the left. This server makes use of SQLite 3, various gems you have installed, and your application code. Your code may or may not have also been placed in Git by this point; either way, it will be by the end of the chapter, as will be the gems you're using.

This Git repository will be replicated on the production server, which again could be another machine but need not be. This server will be running a combination of Apache httpd and Phusion Passenger. This code will access a MySQL database on what may be yet a *fourth* machine.

That's a lot of moving parts! To help us keep track of them all, we'll be using Bundler to manage our dependencies, and Capistrano as the tool to update the deployment server(s) remotely, safely, and repeatably from the comfort of our development machine.

Instead of doing it all at once, we'll do it in three iterations. Iteration L1 will get the Depot application up and running with Apache, MySQL, and Passenger —a truly production-quality web server environment.

Joe asks:
Can We Deploy to Microsoft Windows?

Although we can deploy applications to Windows environments, the overwhelming amount of Rails tools and shared knowledge assumes a Unix-based operating system such as Linux or Mac OS X. One such tool, Phusion Passenger, is highly recommended by the Ruby on Rails development team and covered in this chapter.

The techniques described in this chapter can be used by those deploying to Linux or Mac OS X.

We'll leave Git, Bundler, and Capistrano to a second iteration. These tools will enable us to separate our development activities from our deployment environment. This means that by the time we're done, we'll be deploying twice; but that's only this first time and only to ensure that each part is working independently. It also allows us to focus on a smaller set of variables at any one time, which will simplify the process of untangling any problems that we might encounter.

In a third iteration, we'll cover various administrative and cleanup tasks. Let's get started!

Iteration L1: Deploying with Phusion Passenger and MySQL

So far, as we've been developing a Rails application on our local machine, we've been using Puma when we run our server. For the most part, the server used doesn't matter; the rails server command sorts out the most appropriate way to get our application running in development mode on port 3000, based on the contents of our Gemfile. However, a deployed Rails application works a bit differently. We can't just fire up a single Rails server process and let it do all the work. Well, we *could*, but it's far from ideal.

The web is an extremely concurrent environment. Production web servers such as Apache, nginx, and Lighttpd can work on several requests—even tens or hundreds of requests—at the same time. A single-process, Ruby-based web server can't possibly keep up, and luckily it doesn't have to. Instead, the way we deploy a Rails application into production is to use a front-end server, such as Apache, to handle requests from the client. Then, we use the HTTP proxying of Passenger to send requests that should be handled by Rails to one of any number of back-end application processes.

Configuring a Second Machine

If you have a second machine you can use, that's great. If not, you can use a virtual machine. Plenty of free software that you can use for this purpose is available, such as VirtualBox[1] and Ubuntu.[2] If you go with Ubuntu, we recommend 16.04 LTS.

Configure this machine using the instructions in Chapter 1, *Installing Rails*, on page 3. If you like, you can skip the step of installing Rails and instead install Bundler:

```
$ gem install bundler
```

Next, copy your entire directory containing the Depot application from your first machine to your second machine. On the second machine, change into that directory and use Bundler to install all of your application's dependencies:

```
$ bundle install
```

Verify that your installation is working using any combination of the following commands:

---

1. https://www.virtualbox.org/
2. http://www.ubuntu.com/download/desktop

```
$ rails about
$ rails test
$ rails server
```

At this point, you should be able to launch a browser on either machine and see your application. Once you're satisfied that your application is running correctly, stop the server.

These steps of copying directories and starting and stopping servers aren't generally something you want your application developers to be doing, and by the time we're done with this chapter this will all be automated. But for now, knowing what the steps are and that the intermediate results are correct has established the base upon which we can build our deployment.

Installing Passenger

The next step is to ensure that the Apache web server is installed and running on our second machine. Linux users should have already installed Apache in *Installing on Linux*, on page 14. For Mac OS X users, it's already installed with the operating system, but you'll need to enable it. For Mac OS X releases prior to 10.8, you can accomplish this by going into System Preferences > Sharing and enabling Web Sharing. Starting with Mac OS X 10.8, this needs to be done via the Terminal application:

```
$ sudo apachectl start
$ sudo launchctl load -w /System/Library/LaunchDaemons/org.apache.httpd.plist
```

The next step is to install Passenger:

```
$ gem install passenger --version 5.1.3
$ passenger-install-apache2-module
```

If the necessary dependencies aren't met, the latter command will tell you what you need to do. If this happens, follow the provided instructions, and try the Passenger install command again. For example, on a Ubuntu 16.04 (Xenial Xerus), you'll find that you need to install libcurl4-openssl-dev, apache2-prefork-dev, libapr1-dev, and libaprutil1-dev. Mac OS X users may need to run xcode-select --install to (re)install the command-line tools.

Once the dependencies are satisfied, this command causes a number of sources to be compiled and the configuration files to be updated. During the process, it'll ask you to update your Apache configuration. The first request will be to enable your freshly built module, which involves adding lines such as the following to your Apache configuration. (Note: Passenger will tell you the exact lines to copy and paste into this file, so use those, not these. Also, we've had to elide parts of the path specification in the LoadModule line to make it fit the page. Be sure to use the path specification that Passenger provided for you.)

```
PassengerDefaultRuby /usr/bin/passenger_free_ruby
LoadModule passenger_module /var/.../passenger-5.1.2/.../mod_passenger.so
PassengerRoot /var/lib/gems/2.4.1/gems/passenger-5.1.2
PassengerDefaultRuby /usr/bin/ruby2.3
```

To find out where your Apache configuration file is, try issuing the following command:

```
$ apachectl -V | grep HTTPD_ROOT
$ apachectl -V | grep SERVER_CONFIG_FILE
```

On some systems, the command name is apache2ctl; on others, it's httpd. Experiment until you find the correct command.

Instead of modifying this file directly, most modern systems have conventions that allow you to maintain your extensions separately. On Mac OS X, for example, you may see the following line at the end of your httpd.conf file:

```
Include /private/etc/apache2/other/*.conf
```

If you see this line in your httpd.conf, you can put the lines that Passenger provided into a passenger.conf file in that directory. On Ubuntu you can put these lines into /etc/apache2/conf.d/passenger.

Deploying Our Application Locally

The next step is to deploy our application. Whereas the previous step needs to be done only once per server, this step is actually once per application. In your Apache configuration file, substitute your host's name, your application's directory path, and a secret key in the following:

```
<VirtualHost *:80>
   ServerName depot.yourhost.com
   DocumentRoot /home/rubys/deploy/depot/public/
   SetEnv SECRET_KEY_BASE "0123456789abcdef"
   <Directory /home/rubys/deploy/depot/public>
      AllowOverride all
      Options -MultiViews
      Require all granted
   </Directory>
</VirtualHost>
```

bin/rails secret can be used to generate a suitable key to be used as the secret. This key is used to encrypt cookies that are sent to the client. Note that this secret is placed directly on the server and isn't checked into the source-control system, because otherwise it wouldn't be very secret!

Note that the DocumentRoot is set to the public directory in our Rails application and that we mark the public directory as readable.

Again, your Apache installation may have conventions for the best place to put these instructions. On Mac OS X, check your httpd.conf for the following (possibly commented-out) line:

```
#Include /private/etc/apache2/extra/httpd-vhosts.conf
```

If this line is present, consider uncommenting the line and replacing the dummy-host.example.com with your host.

On Ubuntu, the convention is to place these lines in a file in the /etc/apache2/sites-available directory and then to separately enable the site. For example, if you named the file depot, the site can be enabled using the following command:

```
sudo a2ensite depot
```

If you have multiple applications, repeat this VirtualHost block once per application, adjusting the ServerName and DocumentRoot in each block. You'll also need to verify that the following line is present in the configuration files already:

```
NameVirtualHost *:80
```

If this line isn't present, add it before a line that contains the text Listen 80.

The final step is to restart our Apache web server:

```
$ sudo apachectl restart
```

You now need to configure your client so that it maps the host name you chose to the correct machine. This is done in a file named /etc/hosts. On Windows machines, this file can be found in C:\windows\system32\drivers\etc\. To edit this file, you will need to open the file as an administrator.

A typical /etc/hosts line will look like the following:

```
127.0.0.1 depot.yourhost.com
```

That's it! You can now access our application using the host (or virtual host) you specified. Unless you used a port number other than 80, you no longer need to specify a port number on the URL.

You need to be aware of a few things:

- If when restarting your server you see a message that The address or port is invalid, this means the NameVirtualHost line is already present, perhaps in another configuration file in the same directory. If so, remove the line you added, because this directive needs to be present only once.

- If we want to run in an environment other than production, we can include a RailsEnv directive in each VirtualHost in our Apache configuration:

```
RailsEnv development
```

- We can restart our application without restarting Apache at any time by updating or creating a file named restart.txt in the tmp directory of our application:

```
$ touch tmp/restart.txt
```

- The output of the passenger-install-apache2-module command will tell us where we can find additional documentation.

Using MySQL for the Database

The SQLite website[3] is refreshingly honest when it comes to describing what this database is good at and what it's not good at. In particular, SQLite isn't recommended for high-volume, high-concurrency websites with large datasets. And, of course, we want our website to be such a website.

Plenty of alternatives to SQLite, both free and commercial, are available. We'll go with MySQL. It's available via your native packaging tool in Linux, and an installer is provided for OS X on the MySQL website.[4]

Download the Mac OS X version that matches your operating system release. If you don't want to sign up, look for the "No thanks, just take me to the downloads!" link at the bottom of the page.

In addition to installing the MySQL database, you'll also need to add the mysql gem to the Gemfile:

```
rails51/depot_u/Gemfile
group :production do
  gem 'mysql2', '~> 0.4.0'
end
```

By putting this gem in the production group, we prevent it from being loaded when running in development or test. If you like, you can put the sqlite3 gem into (separate) development and test groups.

Install the gem using bundle install. You may need to locate and install the MySQL database development files for your operating system first. On Ubuntu, for example, you need to install libmysqlclient-dev.

---

3. http://www.sqlite.org/whentouse.html
4. http://dev.mysql.com/downloads/mysql/

You can use the mysql command-line client to create your database. Or, if you're more comfortable with tools such as phpmyadmin or CocoaMySQL, go for it:

```
depot> mysql -u root
mysql> CREATE DATABASE depot_production DEFAULT CHARACTER SET utf8;
mysql> GRANT ALL PRIVILEGES ON depot_production.*
    ->   TO 'username'@'localhost' IDENTIFIED BY 'password';
mysql> EXIT;
```

If you picked a different database name, remember it, because you'll need to adjust the configuration file to match the name you picked. Let's look at that configuration file now.

The config/database.yml file contains information on database connections. It has three sections—one each for the development, test, and production databases. The current production section contains the following:

```
production:
  adapter: sqlite3
  database: db/production.sqlite3
  pool: 5
  timeout: 5000
```

Replace that section with the following, changing the username, password, and database fields as necessary:

```
production:
  adapter: mysql2
  encoding: utf8
  reconnect: false
  database: depot_production
  pool: 5
  username: username
  password: password
  host: localhost
```

Loading the Database

Next, we apply our migrations:

```
depot> bin/rails db:setup RAILS_ENV="production"
```

One of two things will happen. If all is set up correctly, you'll see output like the following:

```
-- create_table("carts", {:force=>:cascade})
   -> 0.0299s
-- create_table("line_items", {:force=>:cascade})
   -> 0.0152s
-- create_table("orders", {:force=>:cascade})
   -> 0.0130s
```

```
-- create_table("products", {:force=>:cascade})
   -> 0.0134s
-- create_table("users", {:force=>:cascade})
   -> 0.0137s
-- initialize_schema_migrations_table()
   -> 0.0160s
```

If instead you see an error of some sort, don't panic! It's probably a small configuration issue. Here are some things to try:

- Check the name you gave for the database in the production: section of database.yml. It should be the same as the name of the database you created (using mysqladmin or some other database administration tool).

- Check that the username and password in database.yml match what you used when you created the database on page 286.

- Check that your database server is running.

- Check that you can connect to it from the command line. If you're using MySQL, run the following command:

```
depot> mysql depot_production
mysql>
```

- If you can connect from the command line, can you create a dummy table? (This tests that the database user has sufficient access rights to the database.)

```
mysql> create table dummy(i int);
mysql> drop table dummy;
```

- If you can create tables from the command line but bin/rails db:migrate fails, double-check the database.yml file. If the file includes socket: directives, try commenting them out by putting a hash character (#) in front of each.

- If you see an error saying No such file or directory... and the filename in the error is mysql.sock, your Ruby MySQL libraries can't find your MySQL database. This might happen if you installed the libraries before you installed the database or if you installed the libraries using a binary distribution and that distribution made the wrong assumption about the location of the MySQL socket file. To fix this, the best idea is to reinstall your Ruby MySQL libraries. If this isn't an option, double-check that the socket: line in your database.yml file contains the correct path to the MySQL socket on your system.

- If you get the error Mysql not loaded, it means you're running an old version of the Ruby MySQL library. Rails needs at least version 2.5.

- Some readers also report getting the error message Client does not support authentication protocol requested by server; consider upgrading MySQL client. To resolve this incompatibility between the installed version of MySQL and the libraries used to access it, follow the instructions at http://dev.mysql.com/doc/mysql/en/old-client.html and issue a MySQL command such as:

```
set password for 'some_user'@'some_host'= OLD_PASSWORD('newpwd');
```

- If you're using MySQL under Cygwin on Windows, you may have problems if you specify a host of localhost. Try using 127.0.0.1 instead.

- Finally, you might have problems in the format of the database.yml file. The YAML library that reads this file is strangely sensitive to tab characters. If your file contains tab characters, you'll have problems. (And you thought you'd chosen Ruby over Python because you didn't like Python's significant whitespace, eh?)

Rerun the bin/rails db:setup command as many times as necessary to correct any configuration issues you may have.

If all this sounds scary, don't worry. In reality, database connections work like a charm most of the time. And once you have Rails talking to the database, you don't have to worry about it again.

At this point, you're up and running. Nothing looks any different when you're running as a single user. The differences become apparent only when you have a large number of concurrent users or a large database.

The next step is to split our development from our production machine.

Iteration L2: Deploying Remotely with Capistrano

If you're a large shop, having a pool of dedicated servers that you administer so that you can ensure that they're running the same version of the necessary software is the way to go. For more modest needs, a shared server will do, but you'll have to take additional care to deal with the fact that the versions of software installed might not always match the version that you have installed on your development machine.

Don't worry, we'll talk you through it.

Prepping Your Deployment Server

Although putting our software under version control is a really, really good idea during development, not putting our software under version control when it comes to deployment is downright foolhardy—enough so that the software that we've selected to manage our deployment, Capistrano, all but requires it.

Plenty of software configuration management (SCM) systems are available. Subversion, for example, is a particularly good one. But if you haven't yet chosen one, go with Git, which is easy to set up and doesn't require a separate server process. The examples that follow will be based on Git, but if you picked a different SCM system, don't worry. Capistrano doesn't much care which one you pick, as long as you pick one that it supports (which includes Git, Subversion, and Mercurial).

The first step is to create an empty repository on a machine accessible by your deployment servers. In fact, if you have only one deployment server, there's no reason why it can't do double duty as your Git server. So, log onto that server, and issue the following commands:

```
$ mkdir -p ~/git/depot.git
$ cd ~/git/depot.git
$ git --bare init
```

The next thing to be aware of is that even if the SCM server and our web server are the same physical machine, Capistrano will be accessing our SCM software as if it were remote. We can make this smoother by generating a public key (if you don't already have one) and then using it to give ourselves permission to access our own server:

```
$ test -e ~/.ssh/id_dsa.pub || ssh-keygen -t dsa
$ cat ~/.ssh/id_dsa.pub >> ~/.ssh/authorized_keys
```

Test this by sshing into your own server. Among other things, this will ensure that your known_hosts file is updated.

While we're here, we have one last thing to attend to. Capistrano will insert a directory named current between our application directory name and the Rails subdirectories, including the public subdirectory. This means you'll have to adjust the DocumentRoot and Directory lines in your httpd.conf if you control your own server or in a control panel for your shared host:

```
DocumentRoot /home/rubys/deploy/depot/current/public/
<Directory /home/rubys/deploy/depot/current/public>
```

Restart your Apache server. You'll see a warning that the depot/current/public directory doesn't exist. That's fine, because we'll be creating it shortly.

Finally, ensure that the changes you made to your Gemfile and config/database.yml are copied from the Depot application on your second machine to the Depot application on your first machine.

That's it for the server! From here on out, you'll be doing everything from your development machine.

Getting an Application Under Control

The first thing we're going to do now is update our Gemfile to indicate that we're using Capistrano. The capistrano-rails gem is already in the Gemfile, but commented out, so uncomment it and add capistrano-rvm, capistrano-bundler, and capistrano-passenger:

rails51/depot_u/Gemfile
```
# Use Capistrano for deployment
➤ gem 'capistrano-rails', group: :development
➤ gem 'capistrano-rvm', group: :development
➤ gem 'capistrano-bundler', group: :development
➤ gem 'capistrano-passenger', group: :development
```

We can now install Capistrano using bundle install. We used this command in Iteration J1 on page 236 to install the bcrypt-ruby gem.

If you haven't put your application under configuration control, do so now:

```
$ cd your_application_directory
$ git init
$ git add .
$ git commit -m "initial commit"
```

This next step is optional but might be a good idea if either you don't have full control of the deployment server or you have many deployment servers to manage. We're going to use a second feature of Bundler—namely, the package command. What it does is put the version of the software that you're dependent on into the repository:

```
$ bundle package
$ git add Gemfile.lock vendor/cache
$ git commit -m "bundle gems"
```

From here, push all your code out to the server:

```
$ git remote add origin ssh://user@host/~/git/depot.git
$ git push origin master
```

Be sure to substitute user and host with the name of your user and host on the remote machine.

With these few steps, you've gained control over what's being deployed. You control *what* is being committed to your local repository. You control *when* this is being pushed out to your server. Next up, you'll control putting this code into production.

Deploying the Application Remotely

We previously deployed the application locally on a server. Now we're going to do a second deployment, this time remotely.

The prep work is done. Our code is now on the SCM server where it can be accessed by the app server. Again, it matters not whether these two servers are the same; what's important here are the *roles* that are being performed.

To add the necessary files to the project for Capistrano to do its magic, execute the following command:

```
$ cap install STAGES=production
mkdir -p config/deploy
mkdir -p lib/capistrano/tasks
create config/deploy.rb
create config/deploy/production.rb
create Capfile
Capified
```

From the output, we can see that Capistrano set up three files. The last, Capfile, is Capistrano's analog to a Rakefile. You need to uncomment a few lines; after you do this, you won't need to touch this file further:

```
rails51/depot_u/Capfile
# Load DSL and set up stages
require "capistrano/setup"

# Include default deployment tasks
require "capistrano/deploy"

# Load the SCM plugin appropriate to your project:
#
# require "capistrano/scm/hg"
# install_plugin Capistrano::SCM::Hg
# or
# require "capistrano/scm/svn"
# install_plugin Capistrano::SCM::Svn
# or
require "capistrano/scm/git"
install_plugin Capistrano::SCM::Git

# Include tasks from other gems included in your Gemfile
#
# For documentation on these, see for example:
#
#   https://github.com/capistrano/rvm
#   https://github.com/capistrano/rbenv
#   https://github.com/capistrano/chruby
#   https://github.com/capistrano/bundler
#   https://github.com/capistrano/rails
#   https://github.com/capistrano/passenger
```

```
       #
  ➤    require "capistrano/rvm"
       # require "capistrano/rbenv"
       # require "capistrano/chruby"
  ➤    require "capistrano/bundler"
  ➤    require "capistrano/rails/assets"
  ➤    require "capistrano/rails/migrations"
  ➤    require "capistrano/passenger"

       # Load custom tasks from `lib/capistrano/tasks` if you have any defined
       Dir.glob("lib/capistrano/tasks/*.rake").each { |r| import r }
```

Uncomment at most one of rvm, rbenv, or chruby, and then uncomment the rest, as we will be using Bundler, assets, migrations, and Passenger.

The first file—namely, config/deploy.rb—contains the configuration needed to deploy our application. Capistrano will provide us with a minimal version of this file, but the following is a somewhat more complete version that you can download and use as a starting point:

```
rails51/depot_u/config/deploy.rb
# be sure to change these values
user = 'davec'
domain = 'depot.pragprog.com'

# adjust if you are using RVM, remove if you are not
set :rvm_type, :system
set :rvm_ruby_string, 'ruby-2.4.1/'

# file paths
set :application, 'depot'
set :repo_url, "#{user}@#{domain}:git/#{fetch(:application)}.git"
set :deploy_to, "/home/#{user}/deploy/#{fetch(:application)}"

# distribute your applications across servers (the instructions below put them
# all on the same server, defined above as 'domain', adjust as necessary)
role :app, domain
role :web, domain
role :db, domain

# you might need to set this if you aren't seeing password prompts
# or are seeing errors like 'no tty present and no askpass program specified'
#
# set :pty true

# As Capistrano executes in a non-interactive mode and therefore doesn't cause
# any of your shell profile scripts to be run, the following might be needed
# if (for example) you have locally installed gems or applications.  Note:
# this needs to contain the full values for the variables set, not simply
# the deltas.
#
# set :default_environment, {
#   'PATH' => '<your paths>:/usr/local/bin:/usr/bin:/bin',
```

```
#    'GEM_PATH' => '<your paths>:/usr/lib/ruby/gems/1.8'
# }
#
# See https://rvm.io/deployment/capistrano#environment for more info.
```

We'll need to edit several properties to match our application. We certainly need to change the user, domain, and :application. The :repo_url matches where we put our Git file earlier. The :deploy_to may need to be tweaked to match where we told Apache it could find the public directory for the application. We've also included a few lines to show how to instruct Capistrano to make use of RVM.[5]

If RVM was not installed as root on your deployment machine, change the set :rvm_type line to specify :user instead of :system. Adjust the :rvm_ruby_string to match the version of the Ruby interpreter that you have installed and want to use. If you're not using RVM at all, remove these lines.

You may also need to configure paths for the default environment if some of the needed software is in a non-standard location on your machine. At this point, we should be off to the races.

Wash, Rinse, Repeat

Once we've gotten this far, our server is ready to have versions of our application deployed to it any time we want. All we need to do is check our changes into the repository and then deploy. At this point, we have three Capistrano files that haven't been checked in. Although they aren't needed by the app server, we can still use them to test the deployment process:

```
$ git add .
$ git commit -m "add cap files"
$ git push
$ cap production deploy
```

The first three commands update the SCM server. Once you become more familiar with Git, you may want to have finer control over when and which files are added, you may want to incrementally commit multiple changes before deployment, and so on. It's only the final command that will update our app, web, and database servers. If for some reason we need to step back in time and go back to a previous version of our application, we can use this:

```
$ cap production deploy:rollback
```

We now have a fully deployed application and can deploy as needed to update the code running on the server. Each time we deploy our application, a new

---

5.   https://rvm.io/integration/capistrano/

version of it is checked out onto the server, some symlinks are updated, and the Passenger processes are restarted.

Iteration L3: Checking Up on a Deployed Application

Once we have our application deployed, we'll no doubt need to check up from time to time on how it's running. We can do this in two primary ways. The first is to monitor the various log files output by both our front-end web server and the Apache server running our application. The second is to connect to our application using rails console.

Looking at Log Files

To get a quick look at what's happening in our application, we can use the tail command to examine log files as requests are made against our application. The most interesting data will usually be in the log files from the application itself. Even if Apache is running multiple applications, the logged output for each application is placed in the production.log file for that application.

Assuming that our application is deployed into the location we showed earlier, here's how we look at our running log file:

```
# On your server
$ cd /home/rubys/deploy/depot/current
$ tail -f log/production.log
```

Sometimes, we need lower-level information—what's going on with the data in our application? When this is the case, it's time to break out the most useful live server debugging tool.

Using Console to Look at a Live Application

We've already created a large amount of functionality in our application's model classes. Of course, we created these to be used by our application's controllers. But we can also interact with them directly. The gateway to this world is the rails console script. We can launch it on our server with this:

```
# On your server
$ cd /home/rubys/deploy/depot/current/
$ rails console production
Loading production environment.
irb(main):001:0> p = Product.find_by(title: "CoffeeScript")
=> #<Product:0x24797b4 @attributes={. . .}
irb(main):002:0> p.price = 29.00
=> 29.0
irb(main):003:0> p.save
=> true
```

Once we have a console session open, we can poke and prod all the various methods on our models. We can create, inspect, and delete records. In a way, it's like having a root console to your application.

Once we put an application into production, we need to take care of a few chores to keep the application running smoothly. These chores aren't automatically taken care of for us, but luckily we can automate them.

Dealing with Log Files

As an application runs, it constantly adds data to its log file. Eventually, the log files can grow extremely large. To overcome this, most logging solutions can *roll over* log files to create a progressive set of log files of increasing age. This breaks up our log files into manageable chunks that can be archived or even deleted after a certain amount of time has passed.

The Logger class supports rollover. We need to specify how many (or how often) log files we want and the size of each, using a line like one of the following in the file config/environments/production.rb:

```
config.logger = Logger.new(config.paths['log'].first, 'daily')
```

Or perhaps this:

```
require 'active_support/core_ext/numeric/bytes'
config.logger = Logger.new(config.paths['log'].first, 10, 10.megabytes)
```

Note that in this case an explicit require of active_support is needed, because this statement is processed early in the initialization of your application —before the Active Support libraries have been included. In fact, one of the configuration options that Rails provides is to not include Active Support libraries at all:

```
config.active_support.bare = true
```

Alternatively, we can direct our logs to the system logs for our machine:

```
config.logger = SyslogLogger.new
```

Find more options at http://guides.rubyonrails.org/configuring.html.

Iteration L4: Deploying with Fewer Steps on Heroku

If you are willing to give up some measure of control, a *platform as a service* can make deploying much easier. Heroku is a popular service that will deploy and manage your Rails application without requiring almost any of the steps above.

With Heroku, you do a bit of up-front configuration, then use Git to push your app's repository to them. That git push triggers Heroku to deploy your app. Heroku connects your app to a database (Postgres in this case) and handles managing logs, running background workers, and everything else you'd need.

It comes at a price. For free, your app will sleep after inactivity and has a limited pool of requests it can serve per day. To have your app up and running all the time, you have to use a paid plan. *But,* you don't have to manage or run any servers or create any scripts for deployment. Let's see what Heroku is like, which requires creating an app in Heroku, setting up our app to use Postgres, and deploying.

Setting Up the Initial App

The official Heroku docs for working with Rails should supersede what we're about to do,[6] but the basic steps for getting a Rails app in Heroku have not changed significantly in many years.

First, you'll need to sign up at https://heroku.com for an account. Once you've done that, install the Heroku Toolbelt, which is a command-line application that allows you to interact with Heroku. The installation method depends on your operating system.

For Mac OS, use Homebrew:

```
> brew install heroku
```

For recent versions of Heroku, or if you're using Window's Bash subsystem, use Snap:

```
> sudo snap install heroku
```

For Windows without the Bash subsystem, you'll need to download an installer linked from the Toolbelt's install page.[7] This page also covers other versions of Linux.

With the Toolbelt installed, you should log in on the command line using the account you just created:

```
> heroku login
Enter your Heroku credentials:
Email: «your email»
Password: «your password»
```

---

6.   https://devcenter.heroku.com/articles/getting-started-with-rails5
7.   https://devcenter.heroku.com/articles/heroku-cli

Next, create your app in Heroku. Heroku will automatically create a unique name and URL for your app when you create it. For getting started, this is the most straightforward thing to do, but you can customize the names and URLs later.

```
> heroku create
Creating app... done, free-flying-61534
http://free-flying-61534.herokuapp.com/ |
    https://git.heroku.com/free-flying-61534.git
```

Once you deploy your app, it will be available at http://free-flying-61534.herokuapp.com. The heroku command you ran also created a *git remote* that lives inside Heroku. This is a remote Git repository that you can push code to, just like pushing code to GitHub or Gitlab. This git remote is how we'll trigger a deployment, which we'll see in a moment.

Next you need to configure your application to use Postgres for its database in production, since that is what Heroku supports.

Using Postgres in Production

Rails will use Postgres if you add the pg gem to your Gemfile. For now, do this in the production group (and remove any reference to MySQL if you added that previously):

```
group :production do
  gem 'pg'
end
```

To install this gem, you will need Postgres installed locally. Postgres's download page has instructions, which are different depending on your operating system.[8]

Once you've done this, run bundle install to install the pg gem.

To configure Rails to access Postgres in production, you should remove the entire production: section from config/database.yml. Heroku will set an environment variable named DATABASE_URL with the information needed to connect to the Postgres instance running in Heroku. Rails and Active Record are already configured to use this environment variable.

Commit the changes you made to your app using Git:

```
> git add .
> git commit -m 'configure Heroku deployments'
```

Now we're ready to deploy.

---

8.   https://www.postgresql.org/download/

Deploying to Heroku

As mentioned above, triggering a deploy is a matter of pushing your code to Heroku's git remote using Git:

```
> git push heroku master
remote: Compressing source files... done.
remote: Building source:
remote:
remote: -----> Ruby app detected
remote: -----> Compiling Ruby/Rails

«A lot more output»

remote: Verifying deploy... done.
To https://git.heroku.com/free-flying-61534.git
 * [new branch]      master -> master
```

Your app won't work yet because the database hasn't been set up. Heroku allows you to run Rake tasks remotely using the Toolbelt, so the first thing you should do when the deploy completes is to migrate the database:

```
> heroku run bin/rails db:migrate
```

You can also use heroku run to run any task, including seeding the database:

```
> heroku run bin/rails db:seed
```

At this point, your app is deployed and should be working on Heroku. You can do this without remembering the weird name Heroku assigned via this command:

```
> heroku open
```

You can also view the Rails log:

```
> heroku logs --tail
```

«Rails log»

And you can interact with the production application via the Rails console like so:

```
> heroku run rails c
irb(main):001:0>
```

Heroku uses a file named Procfile to know what processes you want to run when you deploy your app. Although Heroku can often guess correctly, based on the source code of your app, it's a good practice to be explicit. A Procfile is a text file that describes a process per line. The process is defined as a key followed by a colon followed by the command-line invocation you want to run.

In Heroku, the web key is required for running web servers, which means our Procfile should look like so:

```
web:     bin/rails server
```

Commit these changes to Git:

```
> git add Procfile
> git commit -m 'configure production Procfile'
```

Now deploy the changes:

```
> git push heroku master
```

Look at how streamlined that deploy was! We've talked about how agile it is to use Rails—this is a pretty agile deployment mechanism.

Moving On to Launch and Beyond

Once we've set up our initial deployment, we're ready to finish the development of our application and launch it into production. We'll likely set up additional deployment servers, and the lessons we learn from our first deployment will tell us a lot about how we should structure later deployments. For example, we'll likely find that Rails is one of the slower components of our system: more of the request time will be spent in Rails than in waiting on the database or filesystem. This indicates that the way to scale up is to add machines to split up the Rails load.

However, we might find that the bulk of the time a request takes is in the database. If this is the case, we'll want to look at how to optimize our database activity. Maybe we'll want to change how we access data. Or maybe we'll need to custom-craft some SQL to replace the default Active Record behaviors.

One thing is for sure: every application will require a different set of tweaks over its lifetime. The most important activity is to listen to it over time and discover what needs to be done. Our job isn't done when we launch our application. It's actually just starting.

Although our job is just starting when we first deploy our application to production, we've completed our tour of the Depot application. After we recap what we did in this chapter, let's look back at what we've accomplished in remarkably few lines of code.

What We Just Did

We covered a lot of ground in this chapter. We took our code that ran locally on our development machine for a single user and placed it on a different machine, running a different web server, accessing a different database, and possibly even running a different operating system.

To accomplish this, we used a number of products:

- We installed and configured Phusion Passenger and Apache httpd, a production-quality web server.

- We installed and configured MySQL, a production-quality database server.

- We got our application's dependencies under control using Bundler and Git.

- We installed and configured Capistrano, which enables us to confidently and repeatably deploy our application.

- We also used an alternative hosting service, Heroku, to manage our app in a simpler way.

Playtime

Here's some stuff to try on your own:

- If we have multiple developers collaborating on development, we might feel uncomfortable putting the details of the configuration of our database (potentially including passwords!) into our configuration management system. To address this, copy the completed database.yml into the shared directory and write a task instructing Capistrano to copy this file into your current directory each time you deploy.

- This chapter has focused on stable, tried-and-true, and perhaps somewhat conservative deployment choices, but a lot of innovation is going on in this area. At the moment, Capistrano and Git appear to be virtually uncontested choices. Everything else is up for grabs. Here are some things to play with:

  - Try replacing RVM with rbenv and ruby-build.[9,10]

  - Try replacing both Phusion Passenger and Apache httpd with Unicorn and nginx.[11,12]

Being agile means more than making the right choices. It requires both adaptive planning and rapid and flexible responses to change.

---

9. https://github.com/sstephenson/rbenv/#readme
10. https://github.com/sstephenson/ruby-build#readme
11. http://unicorn.bogomips.org/
12. http://wiki.nginx.org/Main

In this chapter, you'll see:
• Reviewing Rails concepts: model, view, controller, config-
uration, testing, and deployment
• Documenting what we've done

CHAPTER 18

Depot Retrospective

Congratulations! By making it this far, you've obtained a solid understanding of the basics of every Rails application. There's much more to learn, which we'll pick back up again in Part III. For now, relax, and let's recap what you've seen in Part II.

Rails Concepts

In Chapter 3, *The Architecture of Rails Applications*, on page 39 we introduced models, views, and controllers. Now let's see how we applied each of these concepts in the Depot application. Then let's explore how we used configuration, testing, and deployment.

Model

Models are where all of the persistent data retained by your application is managed. In developing the Depot application, we created five models: Cart, LineItem, Order, Product, and User.

By default, all models have id, created_at, and updated_at attributes. To our models, we added attributes of type string (examples: title, name), integer (quantity), text (description, address), and decimal (price), as well as foreign keys (product_id, cart_id). We even created a virtual attribute that's never stored in the database—namely, a password.

We created has_many and belongs_to relationships that we can use to navigate among our model objects, such as from Carts to LineItems to Products.

We employed migrations to update the databases, not only to introduce new schema information but also to modify existing data. We demonstrated that they can be applied in a fully reversible manner.

The models we created were not merely passive receptacles for our data. For starters, they actively validate the data, preventing errors from propagating. We created validations for presence, inclusion, numericality, range, uniqueness, format, and confirmation (and length too, if you completed the exercises). We created custom validations for ensuring that deleted products aren't referenced by any line item. We used an Active Record hook to ensure that an administrator always remains, and used a transaction to roll back incomplete updates on failure.

We also created logic to add a product to a cart, add all line items from a cart to an order, encrypt and authenticate a password, and compute various totals.

Finally, we created a default sort order for products for display purposes.

View

Views control the way our application presents itself to the external world. By default, Rails scaffolding provides edit, index, new, and show, as well as a partial named form that's shared between edit and new. We modified a number of these, as well as created new partials for carts and line items.

In addition to the model-backed resource views, we created entirely new views for admin, sessions, and the store itself.

We updated an overall layout to establish a common look and feel for the entire site. We linked in a stylesheet. We made use of templates to generate JavaScript that takes advantage of Ajax and WebSocket technologies to make our website more interactive.

We made use of a helper to direct when to hide the cart from the main view.

We localized the customer views for display both in English and in Spanish.

Although we focused primarily on HTML views, we also created plain-text views and Atom views. Not all of the views were designed for browsers: we created views for email too, and those views were able to share partials for displaying line items.

Controller

By the time we were done, we created eight controllers: one each for the five models and the three additional ones to support the views for admin, sessions, and the store itself.

These controllers interacted with the models in a number of ways, from finding and fetching data and putting it into instance variables to updating models and saving data entered via forms. When done, we either redirected to another action or rendered a view. We rendered views in HTML, JSON, and Atom.

We limited the set of permitted parameters on the line item controller.

We created callback actions that were run before selected actions to find the cart, set the language, and authorize requests. We placed logic common to a number of controllers into a concern—namely, the CurrentCart module.

We managed sessions, keeping track of the logged-in user (for administrators) and carts (for customers). We kept track of the current locale used for internationalization of our output. We captured errors, logged them, and informed the user via notices.

We employed fragment caching on the storefront and page-level caching on the Atom feeds.

We also sent confirmation emails on receipt of an order.

Configuration

Conventions keep to a minimum the amount of configuration required for a Rails application, but we did do a bit of customization.

We modified our database configuration to use MySQL in production.

We defined routes for our resources, admin and session controllers, and the *root* of our website—namely, our storefront. We defined a who_bought member of our products resource to access Atom feeds that contain this information.

We created an initializer for i18n purposes and updated the locales information for both English (en) and Spanish (es).

We created seed data for our database.

We created a Capistrano script for deployment, including the definition of a few custom tasks.

Testing

We maintained and enhanced tests throughout.

We employed unit tests to validation methods. We also tested increasing the quantity on a given line item.

Rails provided basic tests for all our scaffolded controllers, which we maintained as we made changes. We added tests along the way for things such as Ajax and ensuring that a cart has items before we create an order.

We used fixtures to provide test data to fuel our tests.

We created an integration test to test an end-to-end scenario involving a user adding product to a cart, entering an order, and receiving a confirmation email.

Deployment

We deployed our application to a production-quality web server (Apache httpd) using a production-quality database server (MySQL). Along the way, we installed and configured Phusion Passenger to run our application, Bundler to track dependencies, and Git to configuration manage our code. Capistrano was employed to orchestrate updating the deployed web server in production from our development machine.

We made use of test and production environments to prevent our experimentation during development from affecting production. Our development environment made use of the lightweight SQLite database server and web server, Puma. Our tests were run in a controlled environment with test data provided by fixtures.

Documenting What We've Done

To complete our retrospective, let's see how much code we've written. There's a Rails command for that, too:

```
depot> bin/rails stats
+-----------------------+--------+--------+---------+---------+-----+-------+
| Name                  | Lines  |   LOC  | Classes | Methods | M/C | LOC/M |
+-----------------------+--------+--------+---------+---------+-----+-------+
| Controllers           |   625  |   382  |     9   |    55   |  6  |    4  |
| Helpers               |    26  |    24  |     0   |     1   |  0  |   22  |
| Jobs                  |     2  |     2  |     1   |     0   |  0  |    0  |
| Models                |   137  |    77  |     6   |     7   |  1  |    9  |
| Mailers               |    33  |    15  |     2   |     2   |  1  |    5  |
| Javascripts           |    66  |     7  |     0   |     3   |  0  |    0  |
| Libraries             |    23  |    18  |     0   |     0   |  0  |    0  |
| Tasks                 |    23  |    18  |     0   |     0   |  0  |    0  |
| Controller tests      |   386  |   274  |     8   |    46   |  5  |    3  |
| Helper tests          |     0  |     0  |     0   |     0   |  0  |    0  |
| Model tests           |   130  |    90  |     5   |     9   |  1  |    8  |
| Mailer tests          |    39  |    26  |     2   |     4   |  2  |    4  |
| Integration tests     |   219  |   153  |     2   |    10   |  5  |   13  |
+-----------------------+--------+--------+---------+---------+-----+-------+
| Total                 |  1709  |  1086  |    35   |   137   |  3  |    5  |
+-----------------------+--------+--------+---------+---------+-----+-------+
  Code LOC: 543     Test LOC: 543     Code to Test Ratio: 1:1.0
```

Think about it: you've accomplished a lot and with not all that much code. Furthermore, much of it was generated for you. This is the magic of Rails.

Part III

Rails in Depth

In this chapter, you'll see:
  • The directory structure of a Rails application
  • Naming conventions
  • Adding Rake tasks
  • Configuration

CHAPTER 19

Finding Your Way Around Rails

Having survived our Depot project, you are now prepared to dig deeper into Rails. For the rest of the book, we'll go through Rails topic by topic (which pretty much means module by module). You have seen most of these modules in action before. We will cover not only what each module does but also how to extend or even replace the module and why you might want to do so.

The chapters in Part III cover all the major subsystems of Rails: Active Record, Active Resource, Action Pack (including both Action Controller and Action View), and Active Support. This is followed by an in-depth look at migrations.

Then we are going to delve into the interior of Rails and show how the components are put together, how they start up, and how they can be replaced. Having shown how the parts of Rails can be put together, we'll complete this book with a survey of a number of popular replacement parts, many of which can be used outside of Rails.

We need to set the scene. This chapter covers all the high-level stuff you need to know to understand the rest: directory structures, configuration, and environments.

Where Things Go

Rails assumes a certain runtime directory layout and provides application and scaffold generators, which will create this layout for you. For example, if we generate *my_app* using the command rails new my_app, the top-level directory for our new application appears as shown in the figure on page 308.

```
my_app/
    app/
        | Model, view, and controller files go here.
    bin/
        | Wrapper scripts
    config/
        | Configuration and database connection parameters.
    config.ru - Rack server configuration.
    db/
        | Schema and migration information.
    Gemfile - Gem Dependencies.
    lib/
        | Shared code.
    log/
        | Log files produced by your application.
    public/
        | Web-accessible directory. Your application runs from here.
    Rakefile - Build script.
    README.md - Installation and usage information.
    test/
        | Unit, functional, and integration tests, fixtures, and mocks.
    tmp/
        | Runtime temporary files.
    vendor/
        | Imported code.
```

\|//
ᝍᔍ

Joe asks:

So, Where's Rails?

One of the interesting aspects of Rails is how componentized it is. From a developer's perspective, you spend all your time dealing with high-level modules such as Active Record and Action View. There is a component called Rails, but it sits below the other components, silently orchestrating what they do and making them all work together seamlessly. Without the Rails component, not much would happen. But at the same time, only a small part of this underlying infrastructure is relevant to developers in their day-to-day work. We'll cover the parts that *are* relevant in the rest of this chapter.

Let's start with the text files in the top of the application directory:

- config.ru configures the Rack Webserver Interface, either to create Rails Metal applications or to use Rack Middlewares in your Rails application. These are discussed further in the Rails Guides.[1]

---

1. http://guides.rubyonrails.org/rails_on_rack.html

- Gemfile specifies the dependencies of your Rails application. You have already seen this in use when the bcrypt-ruby gem was added to the Depot application. Application dependencies also include the database, web server, and even scripts used for deployment.

  Technically, this file isn't used by Rails but rather by your application. You can find calls to the Bundler[2] in the config/application.rb and config/boot.rb files.

- Gemfile.lock records the specific versions for each of your Rails application's dependencies. This file is maintained by Bundler and should be checked into your repository.

- Rakefile defines tasks to run tests, create documentation, extract the current structure of your schema, and more. Type rake -T at a prompt for the full list. Type rake -D task to see a more complete description of a specific task.

- README contains general information about the Rails framework.

Let's look at what goes into each directory (although not necessarily in order).

A Place for Our Application

Most of our work takes place in the app directory. The main code for the application lives below the app directory, as shown in the figure on page 310. We'll talk more about the structure of the app directory as we look at the various Rails modules such as Active Record, Action Controller, and Action View in more detail later in the book.

A Place for Our Tests

As we have seen in *Iteration B2: Unit Testing of Models*, on page 91, *Iteration C4: Functional Testing of Controllers*, on page 114, and *Iteration H2: Testing Our JavaScript Functionality*, on page 214, Rails has ample provisions for testing your application, and the test directory is the home for all testing-related activities, including fixtures that define data used by our tests.

A Place for Supporting Libraries

The lib directory holds application code that doesn't fit neatly into a model, view, or controller. For example, you may have written a library that creates PDF receipts that your store's customers can download. These receipts are sent directly from the controller to the browser (using the send_data() method). The code that creates these PDF receipts will sit naturally in the lib directory.

---

2. https://github.com/bundler/bundler

```
app/
  assets/
    images/
      rails.png
    javascripts/
      application.js
      products.js.coffee
    stylesheets/
      application.css
      products.css.scss
      scaffolds.css.scss
  controllers/
    application_controller.rb
    products_controller.rb
    concerns/
      current_cart.rb
  helpers/
    application_helper.rb
    products_helper.rb
  mailers/
    notifier.rb
  models/
    product.rb
  views/
    layouts/
      application.html.erb
    products/
      index.html.erb
      who_bought.atom.builder
    line_items/
      create.js.rjs
      _line_item.html.erb
```

The lib directory is also a good place to put code that's shared among models, views, or controllers. Maybe you need a library that validates a credit card number's checksum, that performs some financial calculation, or that works out the date of Easter. Anything that isn't directly a model, view, or controller should be slotted into lib.

Don't feel that you have to stick a bunch of files directly into the lib directory. Feel free to create subdirectories in which you group related functionality under lib. For example, on the Pragmatic Programmer site, the code that generates receipts, customs documentation for shipping, and other PDF-formatted documentation is in the directory lib/pdf_stuff.

In previous versions of Rails, the files in the lib directory were automatically included in the load path used to resolve require statements. This is now an option that you need to explicitly enable. To do so, place the following in config/application.rb:

```
config.autoload_paths += %W(#{Rails.root}/lib)
```

Once you have files in the lib directory and the lib added to your autoload paths, you can use them in the rest of your application. If the files contain classes or modules and the files are named using the lowercase form of the class or module name, then Rails will load the file automatically. For example, we might have a PDF receipt writer in the file receipt.rb in the directory lib/pdf_stuff. As long as our class is named PdfStuff::Receipt, Rails will be able to find and load it automatically.

For those times where a library cannot meet these automatic loading conditions, you can use Ruby's require mechanism. If the file is in the lib directory, you can require it directly by name. For example, if our Easter calculation library is in the file lib/easter.rb, we can include it in any model, view, or controller using this:

```
require "easter"
```

If the library is in a subdirectory of lib, remember to include that directory's name in the require statement. For example, to include a shipping calculation for airmail, we might add the following line:

```
require "shipping/airmail"
```

A Place for Our Rake Tasks

You'll also find an empty tasks directory under lib. This is where you can write your own Rake tasks, allowing you to add automation to your project. This isn't a book about Rake, so we won't elaborate, but here's a simple example.

Rails provides a Rake task to tell you the latest migration that has been performed. But it may be helpful to see a list of *all* the migrations that have been performed. We'll write a Rake task that prints the versions listed in the schema_migration table. These tasks are Ruby code, but they need to be placed into files with the extension .rake. We'll call ours db_schema_migrations.rake:

rails51/depot_u/lib/tasks/db_schema_migrations.rake
```ruby
namespace :db do
  desc "Prints the migrated versions"
  task :schema_migrations => :environment do
    puts ActiveRecord::Base.connection.select_values(
      'select version from schema_migrations order by version' )
  end
end
```

We can run this from the command line just like any other Rake task:

```
depot> bin/rails db:schema_migrations
(in /Users/rubys/Work/...)
20170425000001
20170425000002
20170425000003
20170425000004
20170425000005
20170425000006
20170425000007
```

Consult the Rake documentation at https://github.com/ruby/rake#readme for more information on writing Rake tasks.

A Place for Our Logs

As Rails runs, it produces a bunch of useful logging information. This is stored (by default) in the log directory. Here you'll find three main log files, called development.log, test.log, and production.log. The logs contain more than just trace lines; they also contain timing statistics, cache information, and expansions of the database statements executed.

Which file is used depends on the environment in which your application is running (and we'll have more to say about environments when we talk about the config directory in *A Place for Configuration*, on page 314).

A Place for Static Web Pages

The public directory is the external face of your application. The web server takes this directory as the base of the application. In here you place *static* (in other words, unchanging) files, generally related to the running of the server.

A Place for Script Wrappers

If you find it helpful to write scripts that are launched from the command line and perform various maintenance tasks for your application, the bin directory is the place to put wrappers that call those scripts. You can use bundle binstubs to populate this directory.

This directory also holds the Rails script. This is the script that is run when you run the rails command from the command line. The first argument you pass to that script determines the function Rails will perform:

console
> Allows you to interact with your Rails application methods.

dbconsole
> Allows you to directly interact with your database via the command line.

destroy
> Removes autogenerated files created by generate.

generate
> A code generator. Out of the box, it will create controllers, mailers, models, scaffolds, and web services. Run generate with no arguments for usage information on a particular generator; here's an example:

```
bin/rails generate migration
```

new
> Generates Rails application code.

runner
> Executes a method in your application outside the context of the Web. This is the noninteractive equivalent of rails console. You could use this to invoke cache expiry methods from a cron job or handle incoming email.

server
> Runs your Rails application in a self-contained web server, using the web server listed in your Gemfile, or WEBrick if none is listed. We've been using Puma in our Depot application during development.

A Place for Temporary Files

It probably isn't a surprise that Rails keeps its temporary files tucked in the tmp directory. You'll find subdirectories for cache contents, sessions, and sockets in here. Generally these files are cleaned up automatically by Rails, but occasionally if things go wrong, you might need to look in here and delete old files.

A Place for Third-Party Code

The vendor directory is where third-party code lives. You can install Rails and all of its dependencies into the vendor directory, as we saw in *Getting an Application Under Control*, on page 290.

If you want to go back to using the system-wide version of gems, you can delete the vendor/cache directory.

A Place for Configuration

The config directory contains files that configure Rails. In the process of developing Depot, we configured a few routes, configured the database, created an initializer, modified some locales, and defined deployment instructions. The rest of the configuration was done via Rails conventions.

Before running your application, Rails loads and executes config/environment.rb and config/application.rb. The standard environment set up automatically by these files includes the following directories (relative to your application's base directory) in your application's load path:

- The app/controllers directory and its subdirectories
- The app/models directory
- The vendor directory and the lib contained in each plugin subdirectory
- The directories app, app/helpers, app/mailers, and app/*/concerns

Each of these directories is added to the load path only if it exists.

In addition, Rails will load a per-environment configuration file. This file lives in the environments directory and is where you place configuration options that vary depending on the environment.

This is done because Rails recognizes that your needs, as a developer, are very different when writing code, testing code, and running that code in production. When writing code, you want lots of logging, convenient reloading of changed source files, in-your-face notification of errors, and so on. In testing, you want a system that exists in isolation so you can have repeatable results. In production, your system should be tuned for performance, and users should be kept away from errors.

The switch that dictates the runtime environment is external to your application. This means that no application code needs to be changed as you move from development through testing to production. In Chapter 17, *Task L: Deployment and Production*, on page 279, we specified the environment on the rake command using a RAILS_ENV parameter and to Phusion Passenger using a RailsEnv line in our Apache configuration file. When starting a server with the bin/rails server command, we use the -e option:

```
depot> bin/rails server -e development
depot> bin/rails server -e test
depot> bin/rails server -e production
```

If you have special requirements, such as if you favor having a *staging* environment, you can create your own environments. You'll need to add a new section to the database configuration file and a new file to the config/environments directory.

What you put into these configuration files is entirely up to you. You can find a list of configuration parameters you can set in the Configuring Rails Applications guide.[3]

Naming Conventions

Newcomers to Rails are sometimes puzzled by the way it automatically handles the naming of things. They're surprised that they call a model class Person and Rails somehow knows to go looking for a database table called people. In this section, you'll learn how this implicit naming works.

The rules here are the default conventions used by Rails. You can override all of these conventions using configuration options.

Mixed Case, Underscores, and Plurals

We often name variables and classes using short phrases. In Ruby, the convention is to have variable names where the letters are all lowercase and words are separated by underscores. Classes and modules are named differently: there are no underscores, and each word in the phrase (including the first) is capitalized. (We'll call this *mixed case*, for fairly obvious reasons.) These conventions lead to variable names such as order_status and class names such as LineItem.

Rails takes this convention and extends it in two ways. First, it assumes that database table names, such as variable names, have lowercase letters and underscores between the words. Rails also assumes that table names are always plural. This leads to table names such as orders and third_parties.

On another axis, Rails assumes that files are named using lowercase with underscores.

Rails uses this knowledge of naming conventions to convert names automatically. For example, your application might contain a model class that handles line items. You'd define the class using the Ruby naming convention, calling it LineItem. From this name, Rails would automatically deduce the following:

---

3.   http://guides.rubyonrails.org/configuring.html

- That the corresponding database table will be called line_items. That's the class name, converted to lowercase, with underscores between the words and pluralized.

- Rails would also know to look for the class definition in a file called line_item.rb (in the app/models directory).

Rails controllers have additional naming conventions. If our application has a store controller, then the following happens:

- Rails assumes the class is called StoreController and that it's in a file named store_controller.rb in the app/controllers directory.

- Rails also looks for a helper module named StoreHelper in the file store_helper.rb located in the app/helpers directory.

- It will look for view templates for this controller in the app/views/store directory.

- It will by default take the output of these views and wrap them in the layout template contained in the file store.html.erb or store.xml.erb in the directory app/views/layouts.

All these conventions are shown in the following tables.

Model Naming

Table	line_items
File	app/models/line_item.rb
Class	LineItem

Controller Naming

URL	http://../store/list
File	app/controllers/store_controller.rb
Class	StoreController
Method	list
Layout	app/views/layouts/store.html.erb

View Naming

URL	http://../store/list
File	app/views/store/list.html.erb (or .builder)
Helper	module StoreHelper
File	app/helpers/store_helper.rb

There's one extra twist. In normal Ruby code you have to use the require keyword to include Ruby source files before you reference the classes and modules in those files. Since Rails knows the relationship between filenames and class names, require isn't normally necessary in a Rails application. The first time you reference a class or module that isn't known, Rails uses the naming conventions to convert the class name to a filename and tries to load that file behind the scenes. The net effect is that you can typically reference (say) the name of a model class, and that model will be automatically loaded into your application.

Grouping Controllers into Modules

So far, all our controllers have lived in the app/controllers directory. It is sometimes convenient to add more structure to this arrangement. For example, our store might end up with a number of controllers performing related but disjoint administration functions. Rather than pollute the top-level namespace, we might choose to group them into a single admin namespace.

 David says:
Why Plurals for Tables?

Because it sounds good in conversation. Really. "Select a Product from products." And "Order has_many :line_items."

The intent is to bridge programming and conversation by creating a domain language that can be shared by both. Having such a language means cutting down on the mental translation that otherwise confuses the discussion of a *product description* with the client when it's really implemented as *merchandise body*. These communications gaps are bound to lead to errors.

Rails sweetens the deal by giving you most of the configuration for free if you follow the standard conventions. Developers are thus rewarded for doing the right thing, so it's less about giving up "your ways" and more about getting productivity for free.

Rails does this using a simple naming convention. If an incoming request has a controller named (say) admin/book, Rails will look for the controller called book_controller in the directory app/controllers/admin. That is, the final part of the controller name will always resolve to a file called *name*_controller.rb, and any leading path information will be used to navigate through subdirectories, starting in the app/controllers directory.

Imagine that our program has two such groups of controllers (say, admin/*xxx* and content/*xxx*) and that both groups define a book controller. There'd be a file called book_controller.rb in both the admin and content subdirectories of app/controllers.

Both of these controller files would define a class named BookController. If Rails took no further steps, these two classes would clash.

To deal with this, Rails assumes that controllers in subdirectories of the directory app/controllers are in Ruby modules named after the subdirectory. Thus, the book controller in the admin subdirectory would be declared like this:

```
class Admin::BookController < ActionController::Base
  # ...
end
```

The book controller in the content subdirectory would be in the Content module:

```
class Content::BookController < ActionController::Base
  # ...
end
```

The two controllers are therefore kept separate inside your application.

The templates for these controllers appear in subdirectories of app/views. Thus, the view template corresponding to this request:

```
http://my.app/admin/book/edit/1234
```

will be in this file:

```
app/views/admin/book/edit.html.erb
```

You'll be pleased to know that the controller generator understands the concept of controllers in modules and lets you create them with commands such as this:

```
myapp> bin/rails generate controller Admin::Book action1 action2 ...
```

What We Just Did

Everything in Rails has a place, and we systematically explored each of those nooks and crannies. In each place, files and the data contained in them follow naming conventions, and we covered that too. Along the way, we filled in a few missing pieces:

- We added a Rake task to print the migrated versions.
- We showed how to configure each of the Rails execution environments.

Next up are the major subsystems of Rails, starting with the largest, Active Record.

In this chapter, you'll see:
- The establish_connection method
- Tables, classes, columns, and attributes
- IDs and relationships
- Create, read, update, and delete operations
- Callbacks and transactions

CHAPTER 20

Active Record

Active Record is the object-relational mapping (ORM) layer supplied with Rails. It is the part of Rails that implements your application's model.

In this chapter, we'll build on the mapping data to rows and columns that we did in Depot. Then we'll look at using Active Record to manage table relationships and in the process cover create, read, update, and delete operations (commonly referred to in the industry as CRUD methods). Finally, we will dig into the Active Record object life cycle (including callbacks and transactions).

Defining Your Data

In Depot, we defined a number of models, including one for an Order. This particular model has a number of attributes, such as an email address of type String. In addition to the attributes that we defined, Rails provided an attribute named id that contains the primary key for the record. Rails also provides several additional attributes, including attributes that track when each row was last updated. Finally, Rails supports relationships between models, such as the relationship between orders and line items.

When you think about it, Rails provides a lot of support for models. Let's examine each in turn.

Organizing Using Tables and Columns

Each subclass of ApplicationRecord, such as our Order class, wraps a separate database table. By default, Active Record assumes that the name of the table associated with a given class is the plural form of the name of that class. If the class name contains multiple capitalized words, the table name is assumed to have underscores between these words.

Classname	Table Name
Order	orders
TaxAgency	tax_agencies
Batch	batches
Diagnosis	diagnoses
LineItem	line_items
Person	people
Datum	data
Quantity	quantities

These rules reflect Rails' philosophy that class names should be singular while the names of tables should be plural.

Although Rails handles most irregular plurals correctly, occasionally you may stumble across one that is not handled correctly. If you encounter such a case, you can add to Rails' understanding of the idiosyncrasies and inconsistencies of the English language by modifying the inflection file provided:

```
rails51/depot_u/config/initializers/inflections.rb
# Be sure to restart your server when you modify this file.

# Add new inflection rules using the following format. Inflections
# are locale specific, and you may define rules for as many different
# locales as you wish. All of these examples are active by default:
# ActiveSupport::Inflector.inflections(:en) do |inflect|
#   inflect.plural /^(ox)$/i, '\1en'
#   inflect.singular /^(ox)en/i, '\1'
#   inflect.irregular 'person', 'people'
#   inflect.uncountable %w( fish sheep )
# end

# These inflection rules are supported but not enabled by default:
# ActiveSupport::Inflector.inflections(:en) do |inflect|
#   inflect.acronym 'RESTful'
# end

ActiveSupport::Inflector.inflections do |inflect|
  inflect.irregular 'tax', 'taxes'
end
```

If you have legacy tables you have to deal with or don't like this behavior, you can control the table name associated with a given model by setting the table_name for a given class:

```
class Sheep < ApplicationRecord
  self.table_name = "sheep"
end
```

David says:
Where Are Our Attributes?

The notion of a database administrator (DBA) as a separate role from programmer has led some developers to see strict boundaries between code and schema. Active Record blurs that distinction, and no other place is that more apparent than in the lack of explicit attribute definitions in the model.

But fear not. Practice has shown that it makes little difference whether we're looking at a database schema, a separate XML mapping file, or inline attributes in the model. The composite view is similar to the separations already happening in the Model-View-Controller pattern—just on a smaller scale.

Once the discomfort of treating the table schema as part of the model definition has dissipated, you'll start to realize the benefits of keeping DRY. When you need to add an attribute to the model, you simply have to create a new migration and reload the application.

Taking the "build" step out of schema evolution makes it just as agile as the rest of the code. It becomes much easier to start with a small schema and extend and change it as needed.

Instances of Active Record classes correspond to rows in a database table. These objects have attributes corresponding to the columns in the table. You probably noticed that our definition of class Order didn't mention any of the columns in the orders table. That's because Active Record determines them dynamically at runtime. Active Record reflects on the schema inside the database to configure the classes that wrap tables.

In the Depot application, our orders table is defined by the following migration:

```
rails51/depot_r/db/migrate/20170425000007_create_orders.rb
class CreateOrders < ActiveRecord::Migration[5.1]
  def change
    create_table :orders do |t|
      t.string :name
      t.text :address
      t.string :email
      t.integer :pay_type

      t.timestamps
    end
  end
end
```

Let's use the handy-dandy bin/rails console command to play with this model. First, we'll ask for a list of column names:

```
depot> bin/rails console
Loading development environment (Rails 5.1.3)
>> Order.column_names
=> ["id", "name", "address", "email", "pay_type", "created_at", "updated_at"]
```

Then we'll ask for the details of the pay_type column:

```
>> Order.columns_hash["pay_type"]
=> #<ActiveRecord::ConnectionAdapters::SQLite3Column:0x00000003618228
  @name="pay_type", @sql_type="varchar(255)", @null=true, @limit=255,
  @precision=nil, @scale=nil, @type=:string, @default=nil,
  @primary=false, @coder=nil>
```

Notice that Active Record has gleaned a fair amount of information about the pay_type column. It knows that it's a string of at most 255 characters, it has no default value, it isn't the primary key, and it may contain a null value. Rails obtained this information by asking the underlying database the first time we tried to use the Order class.

The attributes of an Active Record instance generally correspond to the data in the corresponding row of the database table. For example, our orders table might contain the following data:

```
depot> sqlite3 -line db/development.sqlite3 "select * from orders limit 1"
        id = 1
      name = Dave Thomas
   address = 123 Main St
     email = customer@example.com
  pay_type = Check
created_at = 2016-01-29 14:39:12.375458
updated_at = 2016-01-29 14:39:12.375458
```

If we fetched this row into an Active Record object, that object would have seven attributes. The id attribute would be 1 (a Fixnum), the name attribute would be the string "Dave Thomas", and so on.

We access these attributes using accessor methods. Rails automatically constructs both attribute readers and attribute writers when it reflects on the schema:

```
o = Order.find(1)
puts o.name              #=> "Dave Thomas"
o.name = "Fred Smith"    # set the name
```

Setting the value of an attribute does not change anything in the database— we must save the object for this change to become permanent.

The value returned by the attribute readers is cast by Active Record to an appropriate Ruby type if possible (so, for example, if the database column is a timestamp, a Time object will be returned). If we want to get the raw value of an attribute, we append _before_type_cast to its name, as shown in the following code:

```
product.price_before_type_cast        #=> 34.95, a float
product.updated_at_before_type_cast #=> "2016-02-13 10:13:14"
```

Inside the code of the model, we can use the read_attribute() and write_attribute() private methods. These take the attribute name as a string parameter.

We can see the mapping between SQL types and their Ruby representation in the following table. Decimal and Boolean columns are slightly tricky.

SQL Type	Ruby Class
int, integer	Fixnum
float, double	Float
decimal, numeric	BigDecimal
char, varchar, string	String
interval, date	Date
datetime, time	Time
clob, blob, text	String
boolean	See text

Rails maps columns with Decimals with no decimal places to Fixnum objects; otherwise, it maps them to BigDecimal objects, ensuring that no precision is lost.

In the case of Boolean, a convenience method is provided with a question mark appended to the column name:

```
user = User.find_by(name: "Dave")
if user.superuser?
  grant_privileges
end
```

In addition to the attributes we define, there are a number of attributes that either Rails provides automatically or have special meaning.

Additional Columns Provided by Active Record

A number of column names have special significance to Active Record. Here's a summary:

created_at, created_on, updated_at, updated_on

> These are automatically updated with the timestamp of a row's creation or last update. Make sure the underlying database column is capable of receiving a date, datetime, or string. Rails applications conventionally use the _on suffix for date columns and the _at suffix for columns that include a time.

id

> This is the default name of a table's primary key column (in *Identifying Individual Rows*, on page 324).

xxx_id

> This is the default name of a foreign key reference to a table named with the plural form of xxx.

xxx_count

> This maintains a counter cache for the child table xxx.

Additional plugins, such as acts_as_list,[1] may define additional columns.

Both primary keys and foreign keys play a vital role in database operations and merit additional discussion.

Locating and Traversing Records

In the Depot application, LineItems have direct relationships to three other models: Cart, Order, and Product. Additionally, models can have indirect relationships mediated by resource objects. The relationship between Orders and Products through LineItems is an example of such a relationship.

All of this is made possible through IDs.

Identifying Individual Rows

Active Record classes correspond to tables in a database. Instances of a class correspond to the individual rows in a database table. Calling Order.find(1), for instance, returns an instance of an Order class containing the data in the row with the primary key of 1.

If you're creating a new schema for a Rails application, you'll probably want to go with the flow and let it add the id primary key column to all your tables. However, if you need to work with an existing schema, Active Record gives you a way of overriding the default name of the primary key for a table.

---

1. https://github.com/rails/acts_as_list

For example, we may be working with an existing legacy schema that uses the ISBN as the primary key for the books table.

We specify this in our Active Record model using something like the following:

```
class LegacyBook < ApplicationRecord
  self.primary_key = "isbn"
end
```

Normally, Active Record takes care of creating new primary key values for records that we create and add to the database—they'll be ascending integers (possibly with some gaps in the sequence). However, if we override the primary key column's name, we also take on the responsibility of setting the primary key to a unique value before we save a new row. Perhaps surprisingly, we still set an attribute called id to do this. As far as Active Record is concerned, the primary key attribute is always set using an attribute called id. The primary_key= declaration sets the name of the column to use in the table. In the following code, we use an attribute called id even though the primary key in the database is isbn:

```
book = LegacyBook.new
book.id = "0-12345-6789"
book.title = "My Great American Novel"
book.save
# ...
book = LegacyBook.find("0-12345-6789")
puts book.title     # => "My Great American Novel"
p book.attributes   #=> {"isbn" =>"0-12345-6789",
                    #     "title"=>"My Great American Novel"}
```

Just to make life more confusing, the attributes of the model object have the column names isbn and title—id doesn't appear. When you need to set the primary key, use id. At all other times, use the actual column name.

Model objects also redefine the Ruby id() and hash() methods to reference the model's primary key. This means that model objects with valid IDs may be used as hash keys. It also means that unsaved model objects cannot reliably be used as hash keys (because they won't yet have a valid ID).

One final note: Rails considers two model objects as equal (using ==) if they are instances of the same class and have the same primary key. This means that unsaved model objects may compare as equal even if they have different attribute data. If you find yourself comparing unsaved model objects (which is not a particularly frequent operation), you might need to override the == method.

As we will see, IDs also play an important role in relationships.

Specifying Relationships in Models

Active Record supports three types of relationship between tables: one-to-one, one-to-many, and many-to-many. You indicate these relationships by adding declarations to your models: has_one, has_many, belongs_to, and the wonderfully named has_and_belongs_to_many.

One-to-One Relationships

A one-to-one association (or, more accurately, a one-to-zero-or-one relationship) is implemented using a foreign key in one row in one table to reference at most a single row in another table. A *one-to-one* relationship might exist between orders and invoices: for each order there's at most one invoice.

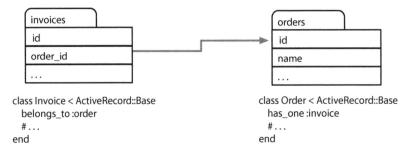

As the example shows, we declare this in Rails by adding a has_one declaration to the Order model and by adding a belongs_to declaration to the Invoice model.

There's an important rule illustrated here: the model for the table that contains the foreign key *always* has the belongs_to declaration.

One-to-Many Relationships

A one-to-many association allows you to represent a collection of objects. For example, an order might have any number of associated line items. In the database, all the line item rows for a particular order contain a foreign key column referring to that order.

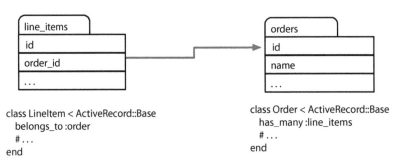

In Active Record, the parent object (the one that logically contains a collection of child objects) uses has_many to declare its relationship to the child table, and the child table uses belongs_to to indicate its parent. In our example, class LineItem belongs_to :order, and the orders table has_many :line_items.

Note that, again, because the line item contains the foreign key, it has the belongs_to declaration.

Many-to-Many Relationships

Finally, we might categorize our products. A product can belong to many categories, and each category may contain multiple products. This is an example of a *many-to-many* relationship. It's as if each side of the relationship contains a collection of items on the other side.

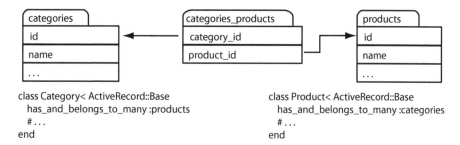

In Rails we can express this by adding the has_and_belongs_to_many declaration to both models.

Many-to-many associations are symmetrical—both of the joined tables declare their association with each other using "habtm."

Rails implements many-to-many associations using an intermediate join table. This contains foreign key pairs linking the two target tables. Active Record assumes that this join table's name is the concatenation of the two target table names in alphabetical order. In our example, we joined the table categories to the table products, so Active Record will look for a join table named categories_products.

We can also define join tables directly. In the Depot application, we defined a LineItems join, which joined Products to either Carts or Orders. Defining it ourselves also gave us a place to store an additional attribute, namely, a quantity.

Now that we have covered data definitions, the next thing you would naturally want to do is access the data contained within the database, so let's do that.

Creating, Reading, Updating, and Deleting (CRUD)

Names such as SQLite and MySQL emphasize that all access to a database is via the Structured Query Language (SQL). In most cases, Rails will take care of this for you, but that is completely up to you. As you will see, you can provide clauses or even entire SQL statements for the database to execute.

If you are familiar with SQL already, as you read this section take note of how Rails provides places for familiar clauses such as select, from, where, group by, and so on. If you are not already familiar with SQL, one of the strengths of Rails is that you can defer knowing more about such things until you actually need to access the database at this level.

In this section, we'll continue to work with the Order model from the Depot application for an example. We will be using Active Record methods to apply the four basic database operations: create, read, update, and delete.

Creating New Rows

Given that Rails represents tables as classes and rows as objects, it follows that we create rows in a table by creating new objects of the appropriate class. We can create new objects representing rows in our orders table by calling Order.new(). We can then fill in the values of the attributes (corresponding to columns in the database). Finally, we call the object's save() method to store the order back into the database. Without this call, the order would exist only in our local memory.

```
rails51/e1/ar/new_examples.rb
an_order = Order.new
an_order.name     = "Dave Thomas"
an_order.email    = "dave@example.com"
an_order.address  = "123 Main St"
an_order.pay_type = "check"
an_order.save
```

Active Record constructors take an optional block. If present, the block is invoked with the newly created order as a parameter. This might be useful if you wanted to create and save an order without creating a new local variable.

```
rails51/e1/ar/new_examples.rb
Order.new do |o|
  o.name     = "Dave Thomas"
  # . . .
  o.save
end
```

Finally, Active Record constructors accept a hash of attribute values as an optional parameter. Each entry in this hash corresponds to the name and value of an attribute to be set. This is useful for doing things like storing values from HTML forms into database rows.

```
rails51/e1/ar/new_examples.rb
an_order = Order.new(
  name:     "Dave Thomas",
  email:    "dave@example.com",
  address:  "123 Main St",
  pay_type: "check")
an_order.save
```

Note that in all of these examples we did not set the id attribute of the new row. Because we used the Active Record default of an integer column for the primary key, Active Record automatically creates a unique value and sets the id attribute as the row is saved. We can subsequently find this value by querying the attribute:

```
rails51/e1/ar/new_examples.rb
an_order = Order.new
an_order.name = "Dave Thomas"
# ...
an_order.save
puts "The ID of this order is #{an_order.id}"
```

The new() constructor creates a new Order object in memory; we have to remember to save it to the database at some point. Active Record has a convenience method, create(), that both instantiates the model object and stores it into the database:

```
rails51/e1/ar/new_examples.rb
an_order = Order.create(
  name:     "Dave Thomas",
  email:    "dave@example.com",
  address:  "123 Main St",
  pay_type: "check")
```

You can pass create() an array of attribute hashes; it'll create multiple rows in the database and return an array of the corresponding model objects:

```
rails51/e1/ar/new_examples.rb
orders = Order.create(
  [ { name:     "Dave Thomas",
      email:    "dave@example.com",
      address:  "123 Main St",
      pay_type: "check"
    },
    { name:     "Andy Hunt",
```

```
    email:    "andy@example.com",
    address:  "456 Gentle Drive",
    pay_type: "po"
  } ] )
```

The *real* reason that new() and create() take a hash of values is that you can construct model objects directly from form parameters:

```
@order = Order.new(order_params)
```

If you think this line looks familiar, it is because you have seen it before. It appears in orders_controller.rb in the Depot application.

Reading Existing Rows

Reading from a database involves first specifying which particular rows of data you are interested in—you'll give Active Record some kind of criteria, and it will return objects containing data from the row(s) matching the criteria.

The most direct way of finding a row in a table is by specifying its primary key. Every model class supports the find() method, which takes one or more primary key values. If given just one primary key, it returns an object containing data for the corresponding row (or throws an ActiveRecord::RecordNotFound exception). If given multiple primary key values, find() returns an array of the corresponding objects. Note that in this case a RecordNotFound exception is raised if *any* of the IDs cannot be found (so if the method returns without raising an error, the length of the resulting array will be equal to the number of IDs passed as parameters).

```
an_order = Order.find(27)    # find the order with id == 27

# Get a list of product ids from a form, then
# find the associated Products
product_list = Product.find(params[:product_ids])
```

Often, though, you need to read in rows based on criteria other than their primary key value. Active Record provides additional methods enabling you to express more complex queries.

SQL and Active Record

To illustrate how Active Record works with SQL, pass a string to the where() method call corresponding to a SQL where clause. For example, to return a list of all orders for Dave with a payment type of "po," we could use this:

```
pos = Order.where("name = 'Dave' and pay_type = 'po'")
```

The result will be an ActiveRecord::Relation object containing all the matching rows, each neatly wrapped in an Order object.

David says:

To Raise or Not to Raise?

When you use a finder driven by primary keys, you're looking for a particular record. You expect it to exist. A call to Person.find(5) is based on our knowledge of the people table. We want the row with an ID of 5. If this call is unsuccessful—if the record with the ID of 5 has been destroyed—we're in an exceptional situation. This mandates the raising of an exception, so Rails raises RecordNotFound.

On the other hand, finders that use criteria to search are looking for a *match*. So, Person.where(name: 'Dave').first is the equivalent of telling the database (as a black box) "Give me the first person row that has the name Dave." This exhibits a distinctly different approach to retrieval; we're not certain up front that we'll get a result. It's entirely possible the result set may be empty. Thus, returning nil in the case of finders that search for one row and an empty array for finders that search for many rows is the natural, nonexceptional response.

That's fine if our condition is predefined, but how do we handle it when the name of the customer is set externally (perhaps coming from a web form)? One way is to substitute the value of that variable into the condition string:

```
# get the name from the form
name = params[:name]
# DON'T DO THIS!!!
pos = Order.where("name = '#{name}' and pay_type = 'po'")
```

As the comment suggests, this really isn't a good idea. Why? It leaves the database wide open to something called a *SQL injection* attack, which the Ruby on Rails Guides[2] describe in more detail. For now, take it as a given that substituting a string from an external source into a SQL statement is effectively the same as publishing your entire database to the whole online world.

Instead, the safe way to generate dynamic SQL is to let Active Record handle it. Doing this allows Active Record to create properly escaped SQL, which is immune from SQL injection attacks. Let's see how this works.

If we pass multiple parameters to a where() call, Rails treats the first parameter as a template for the SQL to generate. Within this SQL, we can embed placeholders, which will be replaced at runtime by the values in the rest of the array.

One way of specifying placeholders is to insert one or more question marks in the SQL. The first question mark is replaced by the second element of the

---

2. http://guides.rubyonrails.org/security.html#sql-injection

array, the next question mark by the third, and so on. For example, we could rewrite the previous query as this:

```
name = params[:name]
pos = Order.where(["name = ? and pay_type = 'po'", name])
```

We can also use named placeholders. We do that by placing placeholders of the form :name into the string and by providing corresponding values in a hash, where the keys correspond to the names in the query:

```
name     = params[:name]
pay_type = params[:pay_type]
pos = Order.where("name = :name and pay_type = :pay_type",
                   pay_type: pay_type, name: name)
```

We can take this a step further. Because params is effectively a hash, we can simply pass it all to the condition. If we have a form that can be used to enter search criteria, we can use the hash of values returned from that form directly:

```
pos = Order.where("name = :name and pay_type = :pay_type",
                   params[:order])
```

We can take this even further. If we pass just a hash as the condition, Rails generates a where clause using the hash keys as column names and the hash values as the values to match. Thus, we could have written the previous code even more succinctly:

```
pos = Order.where(params[:order])
```

Be careful with this latter form of condition: it takes *all* the key-value pairs in the hash you pass in when constructing the condition. An alternative would be to specify which parameters to use explicitly:

```
pos = Order.where(name: params[:name],
                   pay_type: params[:pay_type])
```

Regardless of which form of placeholder you use, Active Record takes great care to quote and escape the values being substituted into the SQL. Use these forms of dynamic SQL, and Active Record will keep you safe from injection attacks.

Using Like Clauses

We might be tempted to use parameterized like clauses in conditions:

```
# Doesn't work
User.where("name like '?%'", params[:name])
```

Rails doesn't parse the SQL inside a condition and so doesn't know that the name is being substituted into a string. As a result, it will go ahead and add extra quotes around the value of the name parameter. The correct way to do this is to construct the full parameter to the like clause and pass that parameter into the condition:

```
# Works
User.where("name like ?", params[:name]+"%")
```

Of course, if we do this, we need to consider that characters such as percent signs, should they happen to appear in the value of the name parameter, will be treated as wildcards.

Subsetting the Records Returned

Now that we know how to specify conditions, let's turn our attention to the various methods supported by ActiveRecord::Relation, starting with first() and all().

As you may have guessed, first() returns the first row in the relation. It returns nil if the relation is empty. Similarly, to_a() returns all the rows as an array. ActiveRecord::Relation also supports many of the methods of Array objects, such as each() and map(). It does so by implicitly calling the all() first.

It's important to understand that the query is not evaluated until one of these methods is used. This enables us to modify the query in a number of ways, namely, by calling additional methods, prior to making this call. Let's look at these methods now.

order

SQL doesn't require rows to be returned in any particular order unless we explicitly add an order by clause to the query. The order() method lets us specify the criteria we'd normally add after the order by keywords. For example, the following query would return all of Dave's orders, sorted first by payment type and then by shipping date (the latter in descending order):

```
orders = Order.where(name: 'Dave').
  order("pay_type, shipped_at DESC")
```

limit

We can limit the number of rows returned by calling the limit() method. Generally when we use the limit method, we'll probably also want to specify the sort order to ensure consistent results. For example, the following returns the first ten matching orders:

```
orders = Order.where(name: 'Dave').
  order("pay_type, shipped_at DESC").
  limit(10)
```

offset

The offset() method goes hand in hand with the limit() method. It allows us to specify the offset of the first row in the result set that will be returned:

```
# The view wants to display orders grouped into pages,
# where each page shows page_size orders at a time.
# This method returns the orders on page page_num (starting
# at zero).
def Order.find_on_page(page_num, page_size)
  order(:id).limit(page_size).offset(page_num*page_size)
end
```

We can use offset in conjunction with limit to step through the results of a query *n* rows at a time.

select

By default, ActiveRecord::Relation fetches all the columns from the underlying database table—it issues a select * from... to the database. Override this with the select() method, which takes a string that will appear in place of the * in the select statement.

This method allows us to limit the values returned in cases where we need only a subset of the data in a table. For example, our table of podcasts might contain information on the title, speaker, and date and might also contain a large BLOB containing the MP3 of the talk. If you just wanted to create a list of talks, it would be inefficient to also load the sound data for each row. The select() method lets us choose which columns to load:

```
list = Talk.select("title, speaker, recorded_on")
```

joins

The joins() method lets us specify a list of additional tables to be joined to the default table. This parameter is inserted into the SQL immediately after the name of the model's table and before any conditions specified by the first parameter. The join syntax is database-specific. The following code returns a list of all line items for the book called *Programming Ruby*:

```
LineItem.select('li.quantity').
  where("pr.title = 'Programming Ruby 1.9'").
  joins("as li inner join products as pr on li.product_id = pr.id")
```

readonly

The readonly() method causes ActiveRecord::Resource to return Active Record objects that cannot be stored back into the database.

If we use the joins() or select() method, objects will automatically be marked readonly.

group

The group() method adds a group by clause to the SQL:

```
summary = LineItem.select("sku, sum(amount) as amount").
                  group("sku")
```

lock

The lock() method takes an optional string as a parameter. If we pass it a string, it should be a SQL fragment in our database's syntax that specifies a kind of lock. With MySQL, for example, a *share mode* lock gives us the latest data in a row and guarantees that no one else can alter that row while we hold the lock. We could write code that debits an account only if there are sufficient funds using something like the following:

```
Account.transaction do
  ac = Account.where(id: id).lock("LOCK IN SHARE MODE").first
  ac.balance -= amount if ac.balance > amount
  ac.save
end
```

If we don't specify a string value or we give lock() a value of true, the database's default exclusive lock is obtained (normally this will be "for update"). We can often eliminate the need for this kind of locking using transactions (discussed starting in *Transactions*, on page 348).

Databases do more than simply find and reliably retrieve data; they also do a bit of data reduction analysis. Rails provides access to these methods too.

Getting Column Statistics

Rails has the ability to perform statistics on the values in a column. For example, given a table of products, we can calculate the following:

```
average = Product.average(:price)  # average product price
max     = Product.maximum(:price)
min     = Product.minimum(:price)
total   = Product.sum(:price)
number  = Product.count
```

These all correspond to aggregate functions in the underlying database, but they work in a database-independent manner.

As before, methods can be combined:

```
Order.where("amount > 20").minimum(:amount)
```

These functions aggregate values. By default, they return a single result, producing, for example, the minimum order amount for orders meeting some condition. However, if you include the group method, the functions instead produce a series of results, one result for each set of records where the grouping expression has the same value. For example, the following calculates the maximum sale amount for each state:

```
result = Order.group(:state).maximum(:amount)
puts result  #=> {"TX"=>12345, "NC"=>3456, ...}
```

This code returns an ordered hash. You index it using the grouping element ("TX", "NC", ... in our example). You can also iterate over the entries in order using each(). The value of each entry is the value of the aggregation function.

The order and limit methods come into their own when using groups.

For example, the following returns the three states with the highest orders, sorted by the order amount:

```
result = Order.group(:state).
              order("max(amount) desc").
              limit(3)
```

This code is no longer database independent—in order to sort on the aggregated column, we had to use the SQLite syntax for the aggregation function (max, in this case).

Scopes

As these chains of method calls grow longer, making the chains themselves available for reuse becomes a concern. Once again, Rails delivers. An Active Record *scope* can be associated with a Proc and therefore may have arguments:

```
class Order < ApplicationRecord
  scope :last_n_days, ->(days) { where('updated < ?' , days) }
end
```

Such a named scope would make finding the worth of last week's orders a snap.

```
orders = Order.last_n_days(7)
```

Simpler scopes may have no parameters at all:

```
class Order < ApplicationRecord
  scope :checks, -> { where(pay_type: :check) }
end
```

Scopes can also be combined. Finding the last week's worth of orders that were paid by check is just as straightforward:

```
orders = Order.checks.last_n_days(7)
```

In addition to making your application code easier to write and easier to read, scopes can make your code more efficient. The previous statement, for example, is implemented as a single SQL query.

ActiveRecord::Relation objects are equivalent to an anonymous scope:

```
in_house = Order.where('email LIKE "%@pragprog.com"')
```

Of course, relations can also be combined:

```
in_house.checks.last_n_days(7)
```

Scopes aren't limited to where conditions; we can do pretty much anything we can do in a method call: limit, order, join, and so on. Just be aware that Rails doesn't know how to handle multiple order or limit clauses, so be sure to use these only once per call chain.

In nearly every case, the methods we have been describing are sufficient. But Rails is not satisfied with only being able to handle nearly every case, so for cases that require a human-crafted query, there is an API for that too.

Writing Our Own SQL

Each of the methods we have been looking at contributes to the construction of a full SQL query string. The method find_by_sql() lets our application take full control. It accepts a single parameter containing a SQL select statement (or an array containing SQL and placeholder values, as for find()) and returns an array of model objects (that is potentially empty) from the result set. The attributes in these models will be set from the columns returned by the query. We'd normally use the select * form to return all columns for a table, but this isn't required:

```
rails51/e1/ar/find_examples.rb
orders = LineItem.find_by_sql("select line_items.* from line_items, orders " +
                              " where order_id = orders.id            " +
                              "   and orders.name = 'Dave Thomas'     ")
```

Only those attributes returned by a query will be available in the resulting model objects. We can determine the attributes available in a model object using the attributes(), attribute_names(), and attribute_present?() methods. The first returns a hash of attribute name-value pairs, the second returns an array of names, and the third returns true if a named attribute is available in this model object:

```
rails51/e1/ar/find_examples.rb
orders = Order.find_by_sql("select name, pay_type from orders")
first = orders[0]
p first.attributes
p first.attribute_names
p first.attribute_present?("address")
```

This code produces the following:

```
{"name"=>"Dave Thomas", "pay_type"=>"check"}
["name", "pay_type"]
false
```

find_by_sql() can also be used to create model objects containing derived column data. If we use the as xxx SQL syntax to give derived columns a name in the result set, this name will be used as the name of the attribute:

```
rails51/e1/ar/find_examples.rb
items = LineItem.find_by_sql("select *,                               " +
                             "  products.price as unit_price,         " +
                             "  quantity*products.price as total_price, " +
                             "  products.title as title               " +
                             "  from line_items, products             " +
                             "  where line_items.product_id = products.id ")
li = items[0]
puts "#{li.title}: #{li.quantity}x#{li.unit_price} => #{li.total_price}"
```

As with conditions, we can also pass an array to find_by_sql(), where the first element is a string containing placeholders. The rest of the array can be either a hash or a list of values to be substituted.

```
Order.find_by_sql(["select * from orders where amount > ?",
                    params[:amount]])
```

In the old days of Rails, people frequently resorted to using find_by_sql(). Since then, all the options added to the basic find() method mean you can avoid resorting to this low-level method.

Reloading Data

In an application where the database is potentially being accessed by multiple processes (or by multiple applications), there's always the possibility that a fetched model object has become stale—someone may have written a more recent copy to the database.

To some extent, this issue is addressed by transactional support (which we describe in *Transactions*, on page 348). However, there'll still be times where you need to refresh a model object manually. Active Record makes this one

David says:
But Isn't SQL Dirty?

Ever since developers first wrapped relational databases with an object-oriented layer, they've debated the question of how deep to run the abstraction. Some object-relational mappers seek to eliminate the use of SQL entirely, hoping for object-oriented purity by forcing all queries through an OO layer.

Active Record does not. It was built on the notion that SQL is neither dirty nor bad, just verbose in the trivial cases. The focus is on removing the need to deal with the verbosity in those trivial cases (writing a ten-attribute insert by hand will leave any programmer tired) but keeping the expressiveness around for the hard queries—the type SQL was created to deal with elegantly.

Therefore, you shouldn't feel guilty when you use find_by_sql() to handle either performance bottlenecks or hard queries. Start out using the object-oriented interface for productivity and pleasure and then dip beneath the surface for a close-to-the-metal experience when you need to do so.

line of code—call its reload() method, and the object's attributes will be refreshed from the database:

```
stock = Market.find_by(ticker: "RUBY")
loop do
  puts "Price = #{stock.price}"
  sleep 60
  stock.reload
end
```

In practice, reload() is rarely used outside the context of unit tests.

Updating Existing Rows

After such a long discussion of finder methods, you'll be pleased to know that there's not much to say about updating records with Active Record.

If you have an Active Record object (perhaps representing a row from our orders table), you can write it to the database by calling its save() method. If this object had previously been read from the database, this save will update the existing row; otherwise, the save will insert a new row.

If an existing row is updated, Active Record will use its primary key column to match it with the in-memory object. The attributes contained in the Active Record object determine the columns that will be updated—a column will be updated in the database only if its value has been changed. In the following example, all the values in the row for order 123 can be updated in the database table:

```
order = Order.find(123)
order.name = "Fred"
order.save
```

However, in the following example, the Active Record object contains just the attributes id, name, and paytype—only these columns can be updated when the object is saved. (Note that you have to include the id column if you intend to save a row fetched using find_by_sql().)

```
orders = Order.find_by_sql("select id, name, pay_type from orders where id=123")
first = orders[0]
first.name = "Wilma"
first.save
```

In addition to the save() method, Active Record lets us change the values of attributes and save a model object in a single call to update():

```
order = Order.find(321)
order.update(name: "Barney", email: "barney@bedrock.com")
```

The update() method is most commonly used in controller actions where it merges data from a form into an existing database row:

```
def save_after_edit
  order = Order.find(params[:id])
  if order.update(order_params)
    redirect_to action: :index
  else
    render action: :edit
  end
end
```

We can combine the functions of reading a row and updating it using the class methods update() and update_all(). The update() method takes an id parameter and a set of attributes. It fetches the corresponding row, updates the given attributes, saves the result to the database, and returns the model object.

```
order = Order.update(12, name: "Barney", email: "barney@bedrock.com")
```

We can pass update() an array of IDs and an array of attribute value hashes, and it will update all the corresponding rows in the database, returning an array of model objects.

Finally, the update_all() class method allows us to specify the set and where clauses of the SQL update statement. For example, the following increases the prices of all products with *Java* in their title by 10 percent:

```
result = Product.update_all("price = 1.1*price", "title like '%Java%'")
```

The return value of update_all() depends on the database adapter; most (but not Oracle) return the number of rows that were changed in the database.

save, save!, create, and create!

It turns out that there are two versions of the save and create methods. The variants differ in the way they report errors.

- save returns true if the record was saved; it returns nil otherwise.

- save! returns true if the save succeeded; it raises an exception otherwise.

- create returns the Active Record object regardless of whether it was successfully saved. You'll need to check the object for validation errors if you want to determine whether the data was written.

- create! returns the Active Record object on success; it raises an exception otherwise.

Let's look at this in a bit more detail.

Plain old save() returns true if the model object is valid and can be saved:

```
if order.save
  # all OK
else
  # validation failed
end
```

It's up to us to check on each call to save() to see that it did what we expected. The reason Active Record is so lenient is that it assumes save() is called in the context of a controller's action method and the view code will be presenting any errors back to the end user. And for many applications, that's the case.

However, if we need to save a model object in a context where we want to make sure to handle all errors programmatically, we should use save!(). This method raises a RecordInvalid exception if the object could not be saved:

```
begin
  order.save!
rescue RecordInvalid => error
  # validation failed
end
```

Deleting Rows

Active Record supports two styles of row deletion. First, it has two class-level methods, delete() and delete_all(), that operate at the database level. The delete() method takes a single ID or an array of IDs and deletes the corresponding row(s) in the underlying table. delete_all() deletes rows matching a given condition (or all rows if no condition is specified). The return values from both calls depend on the adapter but are typically the number of rows affected. An exception is not thrown if the row doesn't exist prior to the call.

```
Order.delete(123)
User.delete([2,3,4,5])
Product.delete_all(["price > ?", @expensive_price])
```

The various destroy methods are the second form of row deletion provided by Active Record. These methods all work via Active Record model objects.

The destroy() instance method deletes from the database the row corresponding to a particular model object. It then freezes the contents of that object, preventing future changes to the attributes.

```
order = Order.find_by(name: "Dave")
order.destroy
# ... order is now frozen
```

There are two class-level destruction methods, destroy() (which takes an ID or an array of IDs) and destroy_all() (which takes a condition). Both methods read the corresponding rows in the database table into model objects and call the instance-level destroy() method of those objects. Neither method returns anything meaningful.

```
Order.destroy_all(["shipped_at < ?", 30.days.ago])
```

Why do we need both the delete and destroy class methods? The delete methods bypass the various Active Record callback and validation functions, while the destroy methods ensure that they are all invoked. In general, it is better to use the destroy methods if you want to ensure that your database is consistent according to the business rules defined in your model classes.

We covered validation in Chapter 7, *Task B: Validation and Unit Testing*, on page 87. We cover callbacks next.

Participating in the Monitoring Process

Active Record controls the life cycle of model objects—it creates them, monitors them as they are modified, saves and updates them, and watches sadly as they are destroyed. Using callbacks, Active Record lets our code participate in this monitoring process. We can write code that gets invoked at any significant event in the life of an object. With these callbacks we can perform complex validation, map column values as they pass in and out of the database, and even prevent certain operations from completing.

Active Record defines sixteen callbacks. Fourteen of these form before/after pairs and bracket some operation on an Active Record object. For example, the before_destroy callback will be invoked just before the destroy() method is called, and after_destroy will be invoked after. The two exceptions are after_find and after_initialize, which have no corresponding before_*xxx* callback. (These two callbacks are different in other ways, too, as we'll see later.)

In the following figure we can see how Rails wraps the sixteen paired callbacks around the basic create, update, and destroy operations on model objects. Perhaps surprisingly, the before and after validation calls are not strictly nested.

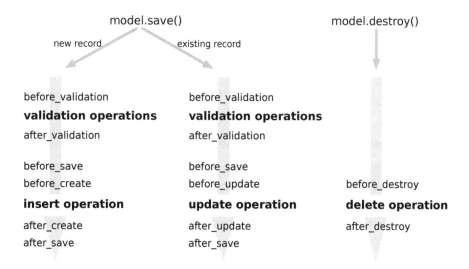

The before_validation and after_validation calls also accept the on: :create or on: :update parameter, which will cause the callback to be called only on the selected operation.

In addition to these sixteen calls, the after_find callback is invoked after any find operation, and after_initialize is invoked after an Active Record model object is created.

To have your code execute during a callback, you need to write a handler and associate it with the appropriate callback.

There are two basic ways of implementing callbacks.

The preferred way to define a callback is to declare handlers. A handler can be either a method or a block. You associate a handler with a particular event using class methods named after the event. To associate a method, declare it as private or protected, and specify its name as a symbol to the handler declaration. To specify a block, simply add it after the declaration. This block receives the model object as a parameter:

```
class Order < ApplicationRecord
  before_validation :normalize_credit_card_number
  after_create do |order|
    logger.info "Order #{order.id} created"
  end
  protected
  def normalize_credit_card_number
    self.cc_number.gsub!(/[-\s]/, '')
  end
end
```

You can specify multiple handlers for the same callback. They will generally be invoked in the order they are specified unless a handler thows :abort, in which case the callback chain is broken early.

Alternately, you can define the callback instance methods using callback objects, inline methods (using a proc), or inline eval methods (using a string). See the online documentation for more details.[3]

Grouping Related Callbacks Together

If you have a group of related callbacks, it may be convenient to group them into a separate handler class. These handlers can be shared between multiple models. A handler class is simply a class that defines callback methods (before_save(), after_create(), and so on). Create the source files for these handler classes in app/models.

In the model object that uses the handler, you create an instance of this handler class and pass that instance to the various callback declarations. A couple of examples will make this clearer.

If our application uses credit cards in multiple places, we might want to share our normalize_credit_card_number() method across multiple models. To do that, we'd extract the method into its own class and name it after the event we want it to handle. This method will receive a single parameter, the model object that generated the callback:

---

3.   http://api.rubyonrails.org/classes/ActiveRecord/Callbacks.html#label-Types+of+callbacks

```
class CreditCardCallbacks

  # Normalize the credit card number
  def before_validation(model)
    model.cc_number.gsub!(/[-\s]/, '')
  end
end
```

Now, in our model classes, we can arrange for this shared callback to be invoked:

```
class Order < ApplicationRecord
  before_validation CreditCardCallbacks.new
  # ...
end

class Subscription < ApplicationRecord
  before_validation CreditCardCallbacks.new
  # ...
end
```

In this example, the handler class assumes that the credit card number is held in a model attribute named cc_number; both Order and Subscription would have an attribute with that name. But we can generalize the idea, making the handler class less dependent on the implementation details of the classes that use it.

For example, we could create a generalized encryption and decryption handler. This could be used to encrypt named fields before they are stored in the database and to decrypt them when the row is read back. You could include it as a callback handler in any model that needed the facility.

The handler needs to encrypt a given set of attributes in a model just before that model's data is written to the database. Because our application needs to deal with the plain-text versions of these attributes, it arranges to decrypt them again after the save is complete. It also needs to decrypt the data when a row is read from the database into a model object. These requirements mean we have to handle the before_save, after_save, and after_find events. Because we need to decrypt the database row both after saving and when we find a new row, we can save code by aliasing the after_find() method to after_save()—the same method will have two names:

rails51/e1/ar/encrypter.rb
```
class Encrypter
  # We're passed a list of attributes that should
  # be stored encrypted in the database
  def initialize(attrs_to_manage)
    @attrs_to_manage = attrs_to_manage
  end
```

```ruby
  # Before saving or updating, encrypt the fields using the NSA and
  # DHS approved Shift Cipher
  def before_save(model)
    @attrs_to_manage.each do |field|
      model[field].tr!("a-z", "b-za")
    end
  end

  # After saving, decrypt them back
  def after_save(model)
    @attrs_to_manage.each do |field|
      model[field].tr!("b-za", "a-z")
    end
  end

  # Do the same after finding an existing record
  alias_method :after_find, :after_save
end
```

This example uses trivial encryption—you might want to beef it up before using this class for real.

We can now arrange for the Encrypter class to be invoked from inside our orders model:

```ruby
require "encrypter"
class Order < ApplicationRecord
  encrypter = Encrypter.new([:name, :email])
  before_save encrypter
  after_save  encrypter
  after_find  encrypter
protected
  def after_find
  end
end
```

We create a new Encrypter object and hook it up to the events before_save, after_save, and after_find. This way, just before an order is saved, the method before_save() in the encrypter will be invoked, and so on.

So, why do we define an empty after_find() method? Remember that we said that for performance reasons after_find and after_initialize are treated specially. One of the consequences of this special treatment is that Active Record won't know to call an after_find handler unless it sees an actual after_find() method in the model class. We have to define an empty placeholder to get after_find processing to take place.

This is all very well, but every model class that wants to use our encryption handler would need to include some eight lines of code, just as we did with our Order class. We can do better than that. We'll define a helper method that does all the work and make that helper available to all Active Record models. To do that, we'll add it to the ApplicationRecord class:

```
rails51/e1/ar/encrypter.rb
class ApplicationRecord < ActiveRecord::Base
  self.abstract_class = true

  def self.encrypt(*attr_names)
    encrypter = Encrypter.new(attr_names)

    before_save encrypter
    after_save  encrypter
    after_find  encrypter

    define_method(:after_find) { }
  end
end
```

Given this, we can now add encryption to any model class's attributes using a single call:

```
class Order < ApplicationRecord
  encrypt(:name, :email)
end
```

A small driver program lets us experiment with this:

```
o = Order.new
o.name = "Dave Thomas"
o.address = "123 The Street"
o.email   = "dave@example.com"
o.save
puts o.name

o = Order.find(o.id)
puts o.name
```

On the console, we see our customer's name (in plain text) in the model object:

```
ar> ruby encrypter.rb
Dave Thomas
Dave Thomas
```

In the database, however, the name and email address are obscured by our industrial-strength encryption:

```
depot> sqlite3 -line db/development.sqlite3 "select * from orders"
     id = 1
user_id =
   name = Dbwf Tipnbt
address = 123 The Street
  email = ebwf@fybnqmf.dpn
```

Callbacks are a fine technique, but they can sometimes result in a model class taking on responsibilities that aren't really related to the nature of the model. For example, in *Participating in the Monitoring Process*, on page 342, we created a callback that generated a log message when an order was created. That functionality isn't really part of the basic Order class—we put it there because that's where the callback executed.

When used in moderation, such an approach doesn't lead to significant problems. If, however, you find yourself repeating code, consider using concerns[4] instead.

Transactions

A database transaction groups a series of changes in such a way that either the database applies all of the changes or it applies none of the changes. The classic example of the need for transactions (and one used in Active Record's own documentation) is transferring money between two bank accounts. The basic logic is straightforward:

```
account1.deposit(100)
account2.withdraw(100)
```

However, we have to be careful. What happens if the deposit succeeds but for some reason the withdrawal fails (perhaps the customer is overdrawn)? We'll have added $100 to the balance in account1 without a corresponding deduction from account2. In effect, we'll have created $100 out of thin air.

Transactions to the rescue. A transaction is something like the Three Musketeers with their motto "All for one and one for all." Within the scope of a transaction, either every SQL statement succeeds or they all have no effect. Putting that another way, if any statement fails, the entire transaction has no effect on the database.

In Active Record we use the transaction() method to execute a block in the context of a particular database transaction. At the end of the block, the transaction is committed, updating the database, *unless* an exception is raised within the block, in which case the database rolls back all of the changes. Because transactions exist in the context of a database connection, we have to invoke them with an Active Record class as a receiver.

---

4. http://37signals.com/svn/posts/3372-put-chubby-models-on-a-diet-with-concerns

Thus, we could write this:

```
Account.transaction do
  account1.deposit(100)
  account2.withdraw(100)
end
```

Let's experiment with transactions. We'll start by creating a new database table. (Make sure your database supports transactions, or this code won't work for you.)

rails51/e1/ar/transactions.rb
```
create_table :accounts, force: true do |t|
  t.string  :number
  t.decimal :balance, precision: 10, scale: 2, default: 0
end
```

Next, we'll define a rudimentary bank account class. This class defines instance methods to deposit money to and withdraw money from the account. It also provides some basic validation—for this particular type of account, the balance can never be negative.

rails51/e1/ar/transactions.rb
```
class Account < ActiveRecord::Base
  validates :balance, numericality: {greater_than_or_equal_to: 0}
  def withdraw(amount)
    adjust_balance_and_save!(-amount)
  end
  def deposit(amount)
    adjust_balance_and_save!(amount)
  end
  private
  def adjust_balance_and_save!(amount)
    self.balance += amount
    save!
  end
end
```

Let's look at the helper method, adjust_balance_and_save!(). The first line simply updates the balance field. The method then calls save! to save the model data. (Remember that save!() raises an exception if the object cannot be saved—we use the exception to signal to the transaction that something has gone wrong.)

So, now let's write the code to transfer money between two accounts. It's pretty straightforward:

rails51/e1/ar/transactions.rb
```ruby
peter = Account.create(balance: 100, number: "12345")
paul  = Account.create(balance: 200, number: "54321")

Account.transaction do
  paul.deposit(10)
  peter.withdraw(10)
end
```

We check the database, and, sure enough, the money got transferred:

```
depot> sqlite3 -line db/development.sqlite3 "select * from accounts"
     id = 1
 number = 12345
balance = 90

     id = 2
 number = 54321
balance = 210
```

Now let's get radical. If we start again but this time try to transfer $350, we'll run Peter into the red, which isn't allowed by the validation rule. Let's try it:

rails51/e1/ar/transactions.rb
```ruby
peter = Account.create(balance: 100, number: "12345")
paul  = Account.create(balance: 200, number: "54321")
```

rails51/e1/ar/transactions.rb
```ruby
Account.transaction do
  paul.deposit(350)
  peter.withdraw(350)
end
```

When we run this, we get an exception reported on the console:

```
.../validations.rb:736:in `save!': Validation failed: Balance is negative
from transactions.rb:46:in `adjust_balance_and_save!'
  :         :         :
from transactions.rb:80
```

Looking in the database, we can see that the data remains unchanged:

```
depot> sqlite3 -line db/development.sqlite3 "select * from accounts"
     id = 1
 number = 12345
balance = 100

     id = 2
 number = 54321
balance = 200
```

However, there's a trap waiting for you here. The transaction protected the database from becoming inconsistent, but what about our model objects? To see what happened to them, we have to arrange to intercept the exception to allow the program to continue running:

```
rails51/e1/ar/transactions.rb
peter = Account.create(balance: 100, number: "12345")
paul  = Account.create(balance: 200, number: "54321")
```

```
rails51/e1/ar/transactions.rb
begin
  Account.transaction do
    paul.deposit(350)
    peter.withdraw(350)
  end
rescue
  puts "Transfer aborted"
end

puts "Paul has #{paul.balance}"
puts "Peter has #{peter.balance}"
```

What we see is a little surprising:

```
Transfer aborted
Paul has 550.0
Peter has -250.0
```

Although the database was left unscathed, our model objects were updated anyway. This is because Active Record wasn't keeping track of the before and after states of the various objects—in fact, it couldn't, because it had no easy way of knowing just which models were involved in the transactions.

Built-in Transactions

When we discussed parent and child tables in *Specifying Relationships in Models*, on page 326, we said that Active Record takes care of saving all the dependent child rows when you save a parent row. This takes multiple SQL statement executions (one for the parent and one each for any changed or new children).

Clearly, this change should be atomic, but until now we haven't been using transactions when saving these interrelated objects. Have we been negligent?

Fortunately, no. Active Record is smart enough to wrap all the updates and inserts related to a particular save() (and also the deletes related to a destroy()) in a transaction; either they all succeed or no data is written permanently to the database. You need explicit transactions only when you manage multiple SQL statements yourself.

While we have covered the basics, transactions are actually very subtle. They exhibit the so-called ACID properties: they're Atomic, they ensure Consistency, they work in Isolation, and their effects are Durable (they are made permanent when the transaction is committed). It's worth finding a good database book and reading up on transactions if you plan to take a database application live.

What We Just Did

We learned the relevant data structures and naming conventions for tables, classes, columns, attributes, IDs, and relationships. We saw how to create, read, update, and delete this data. Finally, we now understand how transactions and callbacks can be used to prevent inconsistent changes.

This, coupled with validation as described in Chapter 7, *Task B: Validation and Unit Testing*, on page 87, covers all the essentials of Active Record that every Rails programmer needs to know. If you have specific needs beyond what is covered here, look to the Rails Guides[5] for more information.

The next major subsystem to cover is Action Pack, which covers both the view and controller portions of Rails.

---

5.   http://guides.rubyonrails.org/

In this chapter, you'll see:
  • Representational State Transfer (REST)
  • Defining how requests are routed to controllers
  • Selecting a data representation
  • Testing routes
  • The controller environment
  • Rendering and redirecting
  • Sessions, flash, and callbacks

CHAPTER 21

Action Dispatch and Action Controller

Action Pack lies at the heart of Rails applications. It consists of three Ruby modules: ActionDispatch, ActionController, and ActionView. Action Dispatch routes requests to controllers. Action Controller converts requests into responses. Action View is used by Action Controller to format those responses.

As a concrete example, in the Depot application, we routed the root of the site (/) to the index() method of the StoreController. At the completion of that method, the template in app/views/store/index.html.erb was rendered. Each of these activities was orchestrated by modules in the Action Pack component.

Working together, these three submodules provide support for processing incoming requests and generating outgoing responses. In this chapter, we'll look at both Action Dispatch and Action Controller. In the next chapter, we will cover Action View.

When we looked at Active Record, we saw it could be used as a freestanding library; we can use Active Record as part of a nonweb Ruby application. Action Pack is different. Although it is possible to use it directly as a framework, you probably won't. Instead, you'll take advantage of the tight integration offered by Rails. Components such as Action Controller, Action View, and Active Record handle the processing of requests, and the Rails environment knits them together into a coherent (and easy-to-use) whole. For that reason, we'll describe Action Controller in the context of Rails. Let's start by looking at how Rails applications handle requests. We'll then dive down into the details of routing and URL handling. We'll continue by looking at how you write code in a controller. Finally, we will cover sessions, flash, and callbacks.

Dispatching Requests to Controllers

At its most basic, a web application accepts an incoming request from a browser, processes it, and sends a response.

The first question that springs to mind is, how does the application know what to do with the incoming request? A shopping cart application will receive requests to display a catalog, add items to a cart, create an order, and so on. How does it route these requests to the appropriate code?

It turns out that Rails provides two ways to define how to route a request: a comprehensive way that you will use when you need to and a convenient way that you will generally use whenever you can.

The comprehensive way lets you define a direct mapping of URLs to actions based on pattern matching, requirements, and conditions. The convenient way lets you define routes based on resources, such as the models that you define. And because the convenient way is built on the comprehensive way, you can freely mix and match the two approaches.

In both cases, Rails encodes information in the request URL and uses a subsystem called *Action Dispatch* to determine what should be done with that request. The actual process is very flexible, but at the end of it Rails has determined the name of the *controller* that handles this particular request, along with a list of any other request parameters. In the process, either one of these additional parameters or the HTTP method itself is used to identify the *action* to be invoked in the target controller.

Rails routes support the mapping between URLs and actions based on the contents of the URL and on the HTTP method used to invoke the request. We've seen how to do this on a URL-by-URL basis using anonymous or named routes. Rails also supports a higher-level way of creating groups of related routes. To understand the motivation for this, we need to take a little diversion into the world of Representational State Transfer.

REST: Representational State Transfer

The ideas behind REST were formalized in Chapter 5 of Roy Fielding's 2000 PhD dissertation.[1] In a REST approach, servers communicate with clients using stateless connections. All the information about the state of the interaction between the two is encoded into the requests and responses between them. Long-term state is kept on the server as a set of identifiable *resources*.

---

1. http://www.ics.uci.edu/~fielding/pubs/dissertation/rest_arch_style.htm

Clients access these resources using a well-defined (and severely constrained) set of resource identifiers (URLs in our context). REST distinguishes the content of resources from the presentation of that content. REST is designed to support highly scalable computing while constraining application architectures to be decoupled by nature.

There's a lot of abstract stuff in this description. What does REST mean in practice?

First, the formalities of a RESTful approach mean that network designers know when and where they can cache responses to requests. This enables load to be pushed out through the network, increasing performance and resilience while reducing latency.

Second, the constraints imposed by REST can lead to easier-to-write (and maintain) applications. RESTful applications don't worry about implementing remotely accessible services. Instead, they provide a regular (and straightforward) interface to a set of resources. Your application implements a way of listing, creating, editing, and deleting each resource, and your clients do the rest.

Let's make this more concrete. In REST, we use a basic set of verbs to operate on a rich set of nouns. If we're using HTTP, the verbs correspond to HTTP methods (GET, PUT, PATCH, POST, and DELETE, typically). The nouns are the resources in our application. We name those resources using URLs.

The Depot application that we produced contained a set of products. There are implicitly two resources here. First, there are the individual products. Each constitutes a resource. There's also a second resource: the collection of products.

To fetch a list of all the products, we could issue an HTTP GET request against this collection, say on the path /products. To fetch the contents of an individual resource, we have to identify it. The Rails way would be to give its primary key value (that is, its ID). Again we'd issue a GET request, this time against the URL /products/1.

To create a new product in our collection, we use an HTTP POST request directed at the /products path, with the post data containing the product to add. Yes, that's the same path we used to get a list of products. If you issue a GET to it, it responds with a list, and if you do a POST to it, it adds a new product to the collection.

Take this a step further. We've already seen you can retrieve the content of a product—you just issue a GET request against the path /products/1. To update that product, you'd issue an HTTP PUT request against the same URL. And, to delete it, you could issue an HTTP DELETE request, using the same URL.

Take this further. Maybe our system also tracks users. Again, we have a set of resources to deal with. REST tells us to use the same set of verbs (GET, POST, PATCH, PUT, and DELETE) against a similar-looking set of URLs (/users, /users/1, and so on).

Now we see some of the power of the constraints imposed by REST. We're already familiar with the way Rails constrains us to structure our applications a certain way. Now the REST philosophy tells us to structure the interface to our applications too. Suddenly our world gets a lot simpler.

Rails has direct support for this type of interface; it adds a kind of macro route facility, called *resources*. Let's take a look at how the config/routes.rb file might have looked back in *Creating a Rails Application*, on page 71:

```
Depot::Application.routes.draw do
  resources :products
end
```

The resources line caused seven new routes to be added to our application. Along the way, it assumed that the application will have a controller named ProductsController, containing seven actions with given names.

You can take a look at the routes that were generated for us. We do this by making use of the handy rails routes command.

```
        Prefix Verb   URI Pattern
                      Controller#Action
      products GET    /products(.:format)
                      {:action=>"index", :controller=>"products"}
               POST   /products(.:format)
                      {:action=>"create", :controller=>"products"}
   new_product GET    /products/new(.:format)
                      {:action=>"new", :controller=>"products"}
  edit_product GET    /products/:id/edit(.:format)
                      {:action=>"edit", :controller=>"products"}
       product GET    /products/:id(.:format)
                      {:action=>"show", :controller=>"products"}
               PATCH  /products/:id(.:format)
                      {:action=>"update", :controller=>"products"}
               DELETE /products/:id(.:format)
                      {:action=>"destroy", :controller=>"products"}
```

All the routes defined are spelled out in a columnar format. The lines will generally wrap on your screen; in fact, they had to be broken into two lines per route to fit on this page. The columns are (optional) route name, HTTP method, route path, and (on a separate line on this page) route requirements.

Fields in parentheses are optional parts of the path. Field names preceded by a colon are for variables into which the matching part of the path is placed for later processing by the controller.

Now let's look at the seven controller actions that these routes reference. Although we created our routes to manage the products in our application, let's broaden this to talk about resources—after all, the same seven methods will be required for all resource-based routes:

index
> Returns a list of the resources.

create
> Creates a new resource from the data in the POST request, adding it to the collection.

new
> Constructs a new resource and passes it to the client. This resource will not have been saved on the server. You can think of the new action as creating an empty form for the client to fill in.

show
> Returns the contents of the resource identified by params[:id].

update
> Updates the contents of the resource identified by params[:id] with the data associated with the request.

edit
> Returns the contents of the resource identified by params[:id] in a form suitable for editing.

destroy
> Destroys the resource identified by params[:id].

You can see that these seven actions contain the four basic CRUD operations (create, read, update, and delete). They also contain an action to list resources and two auxiliary actions that return new and existing resources in a form suitable for editing on the client.

If for some reason you don't need or want all seven actions, you can limit the actions produced using :only or :except options on your resources:

```
resources :comments, except: [:update, :destroy]
```

Several of the routes are named routes enabling you to use helper functions such as products_url and edit_product_url(id:1).

Note that each route is defined with an optional format specifier. We will cover formats in more detail in *Selecting a Data Representation*, on page 362.

Let's take a look at the controller code:

rails51/depot_a/app/controllers/products_controller.rb
```ruby
class ProductsController < ApplicationController
  before_action :set_product, only: [:show, :edit, :update, :destroy]

  # GET /products
  # GET /products.json
  def index
    @products = Product.all
  end

  # GET /products/1
  # GET /products/1.json
  def show
  end

  # GET /products/new
  def new
    @product = Product.new
  end

  # GET /products/1/edit
  def edit
  end

  # POST /products
  # POST /products.json
  def create
    @product = Product.new(product_params)

    respond_to do |format|
      if @product.save
        format.html { redirect_to @product,
          notice: 'Product was successfully created.' }
        format.json { render :show, status: :created,
          location: @product }
      else
        format.html { render :new }
        format.json { render json: @product.errors,
          status: :unprocessable_entity }
      end
    end
  end

  # PATCH/PUT /products/1
  # PATCH/PUT /products/1.json
  def update
```

```
    respond_to do |format|
      if @product.update(product_params)
        format.html { redirect_to @product,
          notice: 'Product was successfully updated.' }
        format.json { render :show, status: :ok, location: @product }
      else
        format.html { render :edit }
        format.json { render json: @product.errors,
          status: :unprocessable_entity }
      end
    end
  end

  # DELETE /products/1
  # DELETE /products/1.json
  def destroy
    @product.destroy
    respond_to do |format|
      format.html { redirect_to products_url,
          notice: 'Product was successfully destroyed.' }
      format.json { head :no_content }
    end
  end

  private
    # Use callbacks to share common setup or constraints between actions.
    def set_product
      @product = Product.find(params[:id])
    end

    # Never trust parameters from the scary internet, only allow the white
    # list through.
    def product_params
      params.require(:product).permit(:title, :description, :image_url, :price)
    end
end
```

Notice how we have one action for each of the RESTful actions. The comment before each shows the format of the URL that invokes it.

Notice also that many of the actions contain a respond_to() block. As we saw in Chapter 11, *Task F: Add a Dash of Ajax*, on page 151, Rails uses this to determine the type of content to send in a response. The scaffold generator automatically creates code that will respond appropriately to requests for HTML or JSON content. We'll play with that in a little while.

The views created by the generator are fairly straightforward. The only tricky thing is the need to use the correct HTTP method to send requests to the server. For example, the view for the index action looks like this:

rails51/depot_a/app/views/products/index.html.erb
```erb
<% if notice %>
  <aside id="notice"><%= notice %></aside>
<% end %>

<h1>Products</h1>

<table>
  <tfoot>
    <tr>
      <td colspan="3">
        <%= link_to 'New product', new_product_path %>
      </td>
    </tr>
  </tfoot>
  <tbody>
    <% @products.each do |product| %>
      <tr class="<%= cycle('list_line_odd', 'list_line_even') %>">
        <td class="image">
          <%= image_tag(product.image_url, class: 'list_image') %>
        </td>
        <td class="description">
          <h1><%= product.title %></h1>
          <p>
            <%= truncate(strip_tags(product.description),
                         length: 80) %>
          </p>
        </td>
        <td class="actions">
          <ul>
            <li><%= link_to 'Show', product %></li>
            <li><%= link_to 'Edit', edit_product_path(product) %></li>
            <li>
              <%= link_to 'Destroy',
                          product,
                          method: :delete,
                          data: { confirm: 'Are you sure?' } %>
            </li>
          </ul>
        </td>
      </tr>
    <% end %>
  </tbody>
</table>
```

The links to the actions that edit a product and add a new product should both use regular GET methods, so a standard link_to works fine. However, the request to destroy a product must issue an HTTP DELETE, so the call includes the method: :delete option to link_to.

Adding Additional Actions

Rails resources provide you with an initial set of actions, but you don't need to stop there. In *Iteration G2: Atom Feeds*, on page 189, we added an interface to allow people to fetch a list of people who bought any given product. To do that with Rails, we use an extension to the resources call:

```
Depot::Application.routes.draw do
  resources :products do
    get :who_bought, on: :member
  end
end
```

That syntax is straightforward. It says "We want to add a new action named who_bought, invoked via an HTTP GET. It applies to each member of the collection of products."

Instead of specifying :member, if we instead specified :collection, then the route would apply to the collection as a whole. This is often used for scoping; for example, you may have collections of products on clearance or products that have been discontinued.

Nested Resources

Often our resources themselves contain additional collections of resources. For example, we may want to allow folks to review our products. Each review would be a resource, and collections of review would be associated with each product resource. Rails provides a convenient and intuitive way of declaring the routes for this type of situation:

```
resources :products do
  resources :reviews
end
```

This defines the top-level set of product routes and additionally creates a set of subroutes for reviews. Because the review resources appear inside the products block, a review resource *must* be qualified by a product resource. This means that the path to a review must always be prefixed by the path to a particular product. To fetch the review with ID 4 for the product with an ID of 99, you'd use a path of /products/99/reviews/4.

The named route for /products/:product_id/reviews/:id is product_review, not simply review. This naming simply reflects the nesting of these resources.

As always, you can see the full set of routes generated by our configuration by using the rails routes command.

Routing Concerns

So far, we have been dealing with a fairly small set of resources. On a larger system there may be types of objects for which a review may be appropriate or to which a who_bought action might reasonably be applied. Instead of repeating these instructions for each resource, consider refactoring your routes using concerns to capture the common behavior.

```
concern :reviewable do
  resources :reviews
end

resources :products, concern: :reviewable
resources :users, concern: :reviewable
```

The preceding definition of the products resource is equivalent to the one in the previous section.

Shallow Route Nesting

At times, nested resources can produce cumbersome URLs. A solution to this is to use shallow route nesting:

```
resources :products, shallow: true do
  resources :reviews
end
```

This will enable the recognition of the following routes:

```
/products/1          => product_path(1)
/products/1/reviews => product_reviews_index_path(1)
/reviews/2           => reviews_path(2)
```

Try the rails routes command to see the full mapping.

Selecting a Data Representation

One of the goals of a REST architecture is to decouple data from its representation. If a human uses the URL path /products to fetch products, they should see nicely formatted HTML. If an application asks for the same URL, it could elect to receive the results in a code-friendly format (YAML, JSON, or XML, perhaps).

We've already seen how Rails can use the HTTP Accept header in a respond_to block in the controller. However, it isn't always easy (and sometimes it's plain impossible) to set the Accept header. To deal with this, Rails allows you to pass the format of response you'd like as part of the URL. As you have seen, Rails accomplishes this by including a field called :format in your route definitions. To do this, set a :format parameter in your routes to the file extension of the MIME type you'd like returned:

```
GET     /products(.:format)
        {:action=>"index", :controller=>"products"}
```

Because a full stop (period) is a separator character in route definitions, :format is treated as just another field. Because we give it a nil default value, it's an optional field.

Having done this, we can use a respond_to() block in our controllers to select our response type depending on the requested format:

```
def show
  respond_to do |format|
    format.html
    format.json { render json: @product.to_json }
  end
end
```

Given this, a request to /store/show/1 or /store/show/1.html will return HTML content, while /store/show/1.xml will return XML, and /store/show/1.json will return JSON. You can also pass the format in as an HTTP request parameter:

```
GET HTTP://pragprog.com/store/show/123?format=xml
```

Although the idea of having a single controller that responds with different content types seems appealing, the reality is tricky. In particular, it turns out that error handling can be tough. Although it's acceptable on error to redirect a user to a form, showing them a nice flash message, you have to adopt a different strategy when you serve XML. Consider your application architecture carefully before deciding to bundle all your processing into single controllers.

Rails makes it straightforward to develop an application that is based on resource-based routing. Many claim it greatly simplifies the coding of their applications. However, it isn't always appropriate. Don't feel compelled to use it if you can't find a way of making it work. And you can always mix and match. Some controllers can be resource based, and others can be based on actions. Some controllers can even be resource based with a few extra actions.

Processing of Requests

In the previous section, we worked out how Action Dispatch routes an incoming request to the appropriate code in your application. Now let's see what happens inside that code.

Action Methods

When a controller object processes a request, it looks for a public instance method with the same name as the incoming action. If it finds one, that method is invoked. If it doesn't find one and the controller implements method_missing(), that method is called, passing in the action name as the first parameter and an empty argument list as the second. If no method can be called, the controller looks for a template named after the current controller and action. If found, this template is rendered directly. If none of these things happens, an AbstractController::ActionNotFound error is generated.

Controller Environment

The controller sets up the environment for actions (and, by extension, for the views that they invoke). Many of these methods provide direct access to information contained in the URL or request:

action_name
>   The name of the action currently being processed.

cookies
>   The cookies associated with the request. Setting values into this object stores cookies on the browser when the response is sent. Rails support for sessions is based on cookies. We discuss sessions in *Rails Sessions*, on page 375.

headers
>   A hash of HTTP headers that will be used in the response. By default, Cache-Control is set to no-cache. You might want to set Content-Type headers for special-purpose applications. Note that you shouldn't set cookie values in the header directly—use the cookie API to do this.

params
>   A hash-like object containing request parameters (along with pseudoparameters generated during routing). It's hash-like because you can index entries using either a symbol or a string—params[:id] and params['id'] return the same value. Idiomatic Rails applications use the symbol form.

request
>   The incoming request object. It includes these attributes:
>
>   • request_method returns the request method, one of :delete, :get, :head, :post, or :put.
>
>   • method returns the same value as request_method except for :head, which it returns as :get because these two are functionally equivalent from an application point of view.
>
>   • delete?, get?, head?, post?, and put? return true or false based on the request method.

- xml_http_request? and xhr? return true if this request was issued by one of the Ajax helpers. Note that this parameter is independent of the method parameter.

- url(), which returns the full URL used for the request.

- protocol(), host(), port(), path(), and query_string(), which return components of the URL used for the request, based on the following pattern: protocol://host:port/path?query_string.

- domain(), which returns the last two components of the domain name of the request.

- host_with_port(), which is a host:port string for the request.

- port_string(), which is a :port string for the request if the port is not the default port (80 for HTTP, 443 for HTTPS).

- ssl?(), which is true if this is an SSL request; in other words, the request was made with the HTTPS protocol.

- remote_ip(), which returns the remote IP address as a string. The string may have more than one address in it if the client is behind a proxy.

- env(), the environment of the request. You can use this to access values set by the browser, such as this:

  ```
  request.env['HTTP_ACCEPT_LANGUAGE']
  ```

- accepts(), which is an array with Mime::Type objects that represent the MIME types in the Accept header.

- format(), which is computed based on the value of the Accept header, with Mime[:HTML] as a fallback.

- content_type(), which is the MIME type for the request. This is useful for put and post requests.

- headers(), which is the complete set of HTTP headers.

- body(), which is the request body as an I/O stream.

- content_length(), which is the number of bytes purported to be in the body.

Rails leverages a gem named Rack to provide much of this functionality. See the documentation of Rack::Request for full details.

response

The response object, filled in during the handling of the request. Normally, this object is managed for you by Rails. As we'll see when we look at callbacks in *Callbacks*, on page 381, we sometimes access the internals for specialized processing.

session

A hash-like object representing the current session data. We describe this in *Rails Sessions*, on page 375.

In addition, a logger is available throughout Action Pack.

Responding to the User

Part of the controller's job is to respond to the user. There are basically four ways of doing this:

• The most common way is to render a template. In terms of the MVC paradigm, the template is the view, taking information provided by the controller and using it to generate a response to the browser.

• The controller can return a string directly to the browser without invoking a view. This is fairly rare but can be used to send error notifications.

• The controller can return nothing to the browser. This is sometimes used when responding to an Ajax request. In all cases, however, the controller returns a set of HTTP headers, because some kind of response is expected.

• The controller can send other data to the client (something other than HTML). This is typically a download of some kind (perhaps a PDF document or a file's contents).

A controller always responds to the user exactly one time per request. This means you should have just one call to a render(), redirect_to(), or send_xxx() method in the processing of any request. (A DoubleRenderError exception is thrown on the second render.)

Because the controller must respond exactly once, it checks to see whether a response has been generated just before it finishes handling a request. If not, the controller looks for a template named after the controller and action and automatically renders it. This is the most common way that rendering takes place. You may have noticed that in most of the actions in our shopping cart tutorial we never explicitly rendered anything. Instead, our action methods set up the context for the view and return. The controller notices that no rendering has taken place and automatically invokes the appropriate template.

You can have multiple templates with the same name but with different extensions (for example, .html.erb, .xml.builder, and .coffee). If you don't specify an extension in a render request, Rails assumes html.erb.

Rendering Templates

A *template* is a file that defines the content of a response for our application. Rails supports three template formats out of the box: *erb*, which is embedded Ruby code (typically with HTML); *builder*, a more programmatic way of constructing XML content; and *RJS*, which generates JavaScript. We'll talk about the contents of these files starting in *Using Templates*, on page 385.

By convention, the template for action *action* of controller *controller* will be in the file app/views/controller/action.type.xxx (where *type* is the file type, such as html, atom, or js; and *xxx* is one of erb, builder, coffee or scss). The app/views part of the name is the default. You can override this for an entire application by setting this:

```
ActionController.prepend_view_path dir_path
```

The render() method is the heart of all rendering in Rails. It takes a hash of options that tell it what to render and how to render it.

It is tempting to write code in our controllers that looks like this:

```
# DO NOT DO THIS
def update
  @user = User.find(params[:id])
  if @user.update(user_params)
    render action: show
  end
  render template: "fix_user_errors"
end
```

It seems somehow natural that the act of calling render (and redirect_to) should somehow terminate the processing of an action. This is not the case. The previous code will generate an error (because render is called twice) in the case where update succeeds.

Let's look at the render options used in the controller here (we'll look separately at rendering in the view starting in *Partial-Page Templates*, on page 406):

render()

> With no overriding parameter, the render() method renders the default template for the current controller and action. The following code will render the template app/views/blog/index.html.erb:
>
> ```
> class BlogController < ApplicationController
>   def index
>     render
>   end
> end
> ```

So will the following (as the default behavior of a controller is to call render() if the action doesn't):

```
class BlogController < ApplicationController
  def index
  end
end
```

And so will this (because the controller will call a template directly if no action method is defined):

```
class BlogController < ApplicationController
end
```

render(text: string)

Sends the given string to the client. No template interpretation or HTML escaping is performed.

```
class HappyController < ApplicationController
  def index
    render(text: "Hello there!")
  end
end
```

render(inline: string, [type: "erb"|"builder"|"coffee"|"scss"], [locals: hash])

Interprets *string* as the source to a template of the given type, rendering the results back to the client. You can use the :locals hash to set the values of local variables in the template.

The following code adds method_missing() to a controller if the application is running in development mode. If the controller is called with an invalid action, this renders an inline template to display the action's name and a formatted version of the request parameters:

```
class SomeController < ApplicationController
  if RAILS_ENV == "development"
    def method_missing(name, *args)
      render(inline: %{
        <h2>Unknown action: #{name}</h2>
        Here are the request parameters:<br/>
        <%= debug(params) %> })
    end
  end
end
```

render(action: action_name)

Renders the template for a given action in this controller. Sometimes folks use the :action form of render() when they should use redirects. See the discussion starting in *Redirects*, on page 372, for why this is a bad idea.

```
def display_cart
  if @cart.empty?
    render(action: :index)
  else
    # ...
  end
end
```

Note that calling render(:action...) does not call the action method; it simply displays the template. If the template needs instance variables, these must be set up by the method that calls the render() method.

Let's repeat this, because this is a mistake that beginners often make: calling render(:action...) does not invoke the action method. It simply renders that action's default template.

render(template: name, [locals: hash])

Renders a template and arranges for the resulting text to be sent back to the client. The :template value must contain both the controller and action parts of the new name, separated by a forward slash. The following code will render the template app/views/blog/short_list:

```
class BlogController < ApplicationController
  def index
    render(template: "blog/short_list")
  end
end
```

render(file: path)

Renders a view that may be entirely outside of your application (perhaps one shared with another Rails application). By default, the file is rendered without using the current layout. This can be overridden with layout: true.

render(partial: name, ...)

Renders a partial template. We talk about partial templates in depth in *Partial-Page Templates*, on page 406.

render(nothing: true)

Returns nothing—sends an empty body to the browser.

render(xml: stuff)

Renders *stuff* as text, forcing the content type to be application/xml.

render(json: stuff, [callback: hash])

Renders *stuff* as JSON, forcing the content type to be application/json. Specifying :callback will cause the result to be wrapped in a call to the named callback function.

render(:update) do |page| ... end

Renders the block as an RJS template, passing in the page object.

```
render(:update) do |page|
  page[:cart].replace_html partial: 'cart', object: @cart
  page[:cart].visual_effect :blind_down if @cart.total_items == 1
end
```

All forms of render() take optional :status, :layout, and :content_type parameters. The :status parameter provides the value used in the status header in the HTTP response. It defaults to "200 OK". Do not use render() with a 3xx status to do redirects; Rails has a redirect() method for this purpose.

The :layout parameter determines whether the result of the rendering will be wrapped by a layout. (We first came across layouts in *Iteration C2: Adding a Page Layout*, on page 107. We'll look at them in depth starting in *Reducing Maintenance with Layouts and Partials*, on page 402.) If the parameter is false, no layout will be applied. If set to nil or true, a layout will be applied only if there is one associated with the current action. If the :layout parameter has a string as a value, it will be taken as the name of the layout to use when rendering. A layout is never applied when the :nothing option is in effect.

The :content_type parameter lets you specify a value that will be passed to the browser in the Content-Type HTTP header.

Sometimes it is useful to be able to capture what would otherwise be sent to the browser in a string. The render_to_string() method takes the same parameters as render() but returns the result of rendering as a string—the rendering is not stored in the response object and so will not be sent to the user unless you take some additional steps.

Calling render_to_string does not count as a real render. You can invoke the real render method later without getting a DoubleRender error.

Sending Files and Other Data

We've looked at rendering templates and sending strings in the controller. The third type of response is to send data (typically, but not necessarily, file contents) to the client.

```
send_data(data, options...)
```

Sends a data stream to the client. Typically the browser will use a combination of the content type and the disposition, both set in the options, to determine what to do with this data.

```
def sales_graph
png_data = Sales.plot_for(Date.today.month)
send_data(png_data, type: "image/png", disposition: "inline")
end
```

The options are:

:disposition (string)

> Suggests to the browser that the file should be displayed inline (option inline) or downloaded and saved (option attachment, the default).

:filename string

> A suggestion to the browser of the default filename to use when saving this data.

:status (string)

> The status code (defaults to "200 OK").

:type (string)

> The content type, defaulting to application/octet-stream.

:url_based_filename boolean

> If true and :filename is not set, this option prevents Rails from providing the basename of the file in the Content-Disposition header. Specifying the basename of the file is necessary in order to make some browsers handle i18n filenames correctly.

A related method is send_file, which sends the contents of a file to the client.

```
send_file(path, options…)
```

Sends the given file to the client. The method sets the Content-Length, Content-Type, Content-Disposition, and Content-Transfer-Encoding headers.

:buffer_size (number)

> The amount sent to the browser in each write if streaming is enabled (:stream is true).

:disposition (string)

> Suggests to the browser that the file should be displayed inline (option inline) or downloaded and saved (option attachment, the default).

:filename (string)

> A suggestion to the browser of the default filename to use when saving the file. If not set, defaults to the filename part of *path*.

:status string

> The status code (defaults to "200 OK").

:stream (true or false)

> If false, the entire file is read into server memory and sent to the client. Otherwise, the file is read and written to the client in :buffer_size chunks.

:type (string)

> The content type, defaulting to application/octet-stream.

You can set additional headers for either send_ method by using the headers attribute in the controller:

```
def send_secret_file
  send_file("/files/secret_list")
  headers["Content-Description"] = "Top secret"
end
```

We show how to upload files starting in *Uploading Files to Rails Applications*, on page 391.

Redirects

An HTTP redirect is sent from a server to a client in response to a request. In effect, it says, "I'm done processing this request, and you should go here to see the results." The redirect response includes a URL that the client should try next along with some status information saying whether this redirection is permanent (status code 301) or temporary (307). Redirects are sometimes used when web pages are reorganized; clients accessing pages in the old locations will get referred to the page's new home. More commonly, Rails applications use redirects to pass the processing of a request off to some other action.

Redirects are handled behind the scenes by web browsers. Normally, the only way you'll know that you've been redirected is a slight delay and the fact that the URL of the page you're viewing will have changed from the one you requested. This last point is important—as far as the browser is concerned, a redirect from a server acts pretty much the same as having an end user enter the new destination URL manually.

Redirects turn out to be important when writing well-behaved web applications. Let's look at a basic blogging application that supports comment posting. After a user has posted a comment, our application should redisplay the article, presumably with the new comment at the end.

It's tempting to code this using logic such as the following:

```
class BlogController
  def display
    @article = Article.find(params[:id])
  end

  def add_comment
    @article = Article.find(params[:id])
    comment  = Comment.new(params[:comment])
    @article.comments << comment
    if @article.save
      flash[:note] = "Thank you for your valuable comment"
    else
      flash[:note] = "We threw your worthless comment away"
    end
    # DON'T DO THIS
    render(action: 'display')
  end
end
```

The intent here was clearly to display the article after a comment has been posted. To do this, the developer ended the add_comment() method with a call to render(action:'display'). This renders the display view, showing the updated article to the end user. But think of this from the browser's point of view. It sends a URL ending in blog/add_comment and gets back an index listing. As far as the browser is concerned, the current URL is still the one that ends in blog/add_comment. This means that if the user hits Refresh or Reload (perhaps to see whether anyone else has posted a comment), the add_comment URL will be sent again to the application. The user intended to refresh the display, but the application sees a request to add another comment. In a blog application, this kind of unintentional double entry is inconvenient. In an online store, it can get expensive.

In these circumstances, the correct way to show the added comment in the index listing is to redirect the browser to the display action. We do this using the Rails redirect_to() method. If the user subsequently hits Refresh, it will simply reinvoke the display action and not add another comment.

```
def add_comment
  @article = Article.find(params[:id])
  comment = Comment.new(params[:comment])
  @article.comments << comment
  if @article.save
    flash[:note] = "Thank you for your valuable comment"
  else
    flash[:note] = "We threw your worthless comment away"
  end
➤ redirect_to(action: 'display')
end
```

Rails has a lightweight yet powerful redirection mechanism. It can redirect to an action in a given controller (passing parameters), to a URL (on or off the current server), or to the previous page. Let's look at these three forms in turn:

redirect_to(action: ..., options...) Sends a temporary redirection to the browser based on the values in the options hash. The target URL is generated using url_for(), so this form of redirect_to() has all the smarts of Rails routing code behind it.

redirect_to(path) Redirects to the given path. If the path does not start with a protocol (such as http://), the protocol and port of the current request will be prepended. This method does not perform any rewriting on the URL, so it should not be used to create paths that are intended to link to actions in the application (unless you generate the path using url_for or a named route URL generator).

```ruby
def save
  order = Order.new(params[:order])
  if order.save
    redirect_to action: "display"
  else
    session[:error_count] ||= 0
    session[:error_count] += 1
    if session[:error_count] < 4
      self.notice = "Please try again"
    else
      # Give up -- user is clearly struggling
      redirect_to("/help/order_entry.html")
    end
  end
end
```

redirect_to(:back) Redirects to the URL given by the HTTP_REFERER header in the current request.

```ruby
def save_details
  unless params[:are_you_sure] == 'Y'
    redirect_to(:back)
  else
    # ...
  end
end
```

By default all redirections are flagged as temporary (they will affect only the current request). When redirecting to a URL, it's possible you might want to make the redirection permanent. In that case, set the status in the response header accordingly:

```ruby
headers["Status"] = "301 Moved Permanently"
redirect_to("http://my.new.home")
```

Because redirect methods send responses to the browser, the same rules apply as for the rendering methods—you can issue only one per request.

So far, we have been looking at requests and responses in isolation. Rails also provides a number of mechanisms that span requests.

Objects and Operations That Span Requests

While the bulk of the state that persists across requests belongs in the database and is accessed via Active Record, some other bits of state have different life spans and need to be managed differently. In the Depot application, while the Cart itself was stored in the database, knowledge of which cart is the current cart was managed by sessions. Flash notices were used to communicate messages such as "Can't delete the last user" to the next request after a redirect. And callbacks were used to extract locale data from the URLs themselves.

In this section, we will explore each of these mechanisms in turn.

Rails Sessions

A Rails session is a hash-like structure that persists across requests. Unlike raw cookies, sessions can hold any objects (as long as those objects can be marshaled), which makes them ideal for holding state information in web applications. For example, in our store application, we used a session to hold the shopping cart object between requests. The Cart object could be used in our application just like any other object. But Rails arranged things such that the cart was saved at the end of handling each request and, more important, that the correct cart for an incoming request was restored when Rails started to handle that request. Using sessions, we can pretend that our application stays around between requests.

And that leads to an interesting question: exactly where does this data stay around between requests? One choice is for the server to send it down to the client as a cookie. This is the default for Rails. It places limitations on the size and increases the bandwidth but means that there is less for the server to manage and clean up. Note that the contents are (by default) encrypted, which means that users can neither see nor tamper with the contents.

The other option is to store the data on the server. It requires more work to set up and is rarely necessary. First, Rails has to keep track of sessions. It does this by creating (by default) a 32-hex character key (which means there are 16^{32} possible combinations). This key is called the *session ID*, and it's effectively random. Rails arranges to store this session ID as a cookie (with the key _session_id) on the user's browser. Because subsequent requests come into the application from this browser, Rails can recover the session ID.

Second, Rails keeps a persistent store of session data on the server, indexed by the session ID. When a request comes in, Rails looks up the data store using the session ID. The data that it finds there is a serialized Ruby object. It deserializes this and stores the result in the controller's session attribute, where the data is available to our application code. The application can add to and modify this data to its heart's content. When it finishes processing each request, Rails writes the session data back into the data store. There it sits until the next request from this browser comes along.

What should you store in a session? You can store anything you want, subject to a few restrictions and caveats:

- There are some restrictions on what kinds of object you can store in a session. The details depend on the storage mechanism you choose (which we'll look at shortly). In the general case, objects in a session must be serializable (using Ruby's Marshal functions). This means, for example, that you cannot store an I/O object in a session.

- If you store any Rails model objects in a session, you'll have to add model declarations for them. This causes Rails to preload the model class so that its definition is available when Ruby comes to deserialize it from the session store. If the use of the session is restricted to just one controller, this declaration can go at the top of that controller.

```
class BlogController < ApplicationController

  model :user_preferences

  # . . .
```

  However, if the session might get read by another controller (which is likely in any application with multiple controllers), you'll probably want to add the declaration to application_controller.rb in app/controllers.

- You probably don't want to store massive objects in session data—put them in the database, and reference them from the session. This is particularly true for cookie-based sessions, where the overall limit is 4KB.

- You probably don't want to store volatile objects in session data. For example, you might want to keep a tally of the number of articles in a blog and store that in the session for performance reasons. But, if you do that, the count won't get updated if some other user adds an article.

It is tempting to store objects representing the currently logged-in user in session data. This might not be wise if your application needs to be able to invalidate users. Even if a user is disabled in the database, their session data will still reflect a valid status.

Store volatile data in the database, and reference it from the session instead.

- You probably don't want to store critical information solely in session data. For example, if your application generates an order confirmation number in one request and stores it in session data so that it can be saved to the database when the next request is handled, you risk losing that number if the user deletes the cookie from their browser. Critical information needs to be in the database.

There's one more caveat, and it's a big one. If you store an object in session data, then the next time you come back to that browser, your application will end up retrieving that object. However, if in the meantime you've updated your application, the object in session data may not agree with the definition of that object's class in your application, and the application will fail while processing the request. There are three options here. One is to store the object in the database using conventional models and keep just the ID of the row in the session. Model objects are far more forgiving of schema changes than the Ruby marshaling library. The second option is to manually delete all the session data stored on your server whenever you change the definition of a class stored in that data.

The third option is slightly more complex. If you add a version number to your session keys and change that number whenever you update the stored data, you'll only ever load data that corresponds with the current version of the application. You can potentially version the classes whose objects are stored in the session and use the appropriate classes depending on the session keys associated with each request. This last idea can be a lot of work, so you'll need to decide whether it's worth the effort.

Because the session store is hash-like, you can save multiple objects in it, each with its own key.

There is no need to also disable sessions for particular actions. Because sessions are lazily loaded, simply don't reference a session in any action in which you don't need a session.

Session Storage

Rails has a number of options when it comes to storing your session data. Each has good and bad points. We'll start by listing the options and then compare them at the end.

The session_store attribute of ActionController::Base determines the session storage mechanism—set this attribute to a class that implements the storage strategy. This class must be defined in the ActiveSupport::Cache::Store module. You use symbols to name the session storage strategy; the symbol is converted into a CamelCase class name.

session_store = :cookie_store
> This is the default session storage mechanism used by Rails, starting with version 2.0. This format represents objects in their marshaled form, which allows any serializable data to be stored in sessions but is limited to 4KB total. This is the option we used in the Depot application.

session_store = :active_record_store
> You can use the activerecord-session_store gem[2] to store your session data in your application's database using ActiveRecordStore.

session_store = :drb_store
> DRb is a protocol that allows Ruby processes to share objects over a network connection. Using the DRbStore database manager, Rails stores session data on a DRb server (which you manage outside the web application). Multiple instances of your application, potentially running on distributed servers, can access the same DRb store. DRb uses Marshal to serialize objects.

session_store = :mem_cache_store
> memcached is a freely available, distributed object caching system maintained by Dormando.[3] memcached is more complex to use than the other alternatives and is probably interesting only if you are already using it for other reasons at your site.

session_store = :memory_store
> This option stores the session data locally in the application's memory. Because no serialization is involved, any object can be stored in an in-memory session. As we'll see in a minute, this generally is not a good idea for Rails applications.

---

2. https://github.com/rails/activerecord-session_store#installation
3. http://memcached.org/

session_store = :file_store

> Session data is stored in flat files. It's pretty much useless for Rails applications, because the contents must be strings. This mechanism supports the additional configuration options :prefix, :suffix, and :tmpdir.

Comparing Session Storage Options

With all these session options to choose from, which should you use in your application? As always, the answer is "It depends."

There are few absolutes when it comes to performance, and everyone's context is different. Your hardware, network latencies, database choices, and possibly even the weather will impact how all the components of session storage interact. Our best advice is to start with the simplest workable solution and then monitor it. If it starts to slow you down, find out why before jumping out of the frying pan.

If you have a high-volume site, keeping the size of the session data small and going with cookie_store is the way to go.

If we rule out memory store as being too simplistic, file store as too restrictive, and memcached as overkill, the server-side choices boil down to CookieStore, Active Record store, and DRb-based storage. Should you need to store more in a session than you can with cookies, we recommend you start with an Active Record solution. If, as your application grows, you find this becoming a bottleneck, you can migrate to a DRb-based solution.

Session Expiry and Cleanup

One problem with all the server-side session storage solutions is that each new session adds something to the session store. This means you'll eventually need to do some housekeeping or you'll run out of server resources.

There's another reason to tidy up sessions. Many applications don't want a session to last forever. Once a user has logged in from a particular browser, the application might want to enforce a rule that the user stays logged in only as long as they are active; when they log out or some fixed time after they last use the application, their session should be terminated.

You can sometimes achieve this effect by expiring the cookie holding the session ID. However, this is open to end-user abuse. Worse, it is hard to synchronize the expiry of a cookie on the browser with the tidying up of the session data on the server.

We therefore suggest you expire sessions by simply removing their server-side session data. Should a browser request subsequently arrive containing a session ID for data that has been deleted, the application will receive no session data; the session will effectively not be there.

Implementing this expiration depends on the storage mechanism being used.

For Active Record–based session storage, use the updated_at columns in the sessions table. You can delete all sessions that have not been modified in the last hour (ignoring daylight saving time changes) by having your sweeper task issue SQL such as this:

```
delete from sessions
 where now() - updated_at > 3600;
```

For DRb-based solutions, expiry takes place within the DRb server process. You'll probably want to record timestamps alongside the entries in the session data hash. You can run a separate thread (or even a separate process) that periodically deletes the entries in this hash.

In all cases, your application can help this process by calling reset_session() to delete sessions when they are no longer needed (for example, when a user logs out).

Flash: Communicating Between Actions

When we use redirect_to() to transfer control to another action, the browser generates a separate request to invoke that action. That request will be handled by our application in a fresh instance of a controller object—instance variables that were set in the original action are not available to the code handling the redirected action. But sometimes we need to communicate between these two instances. We can do this using a facility called the *flash*.

The flash is a temporary scratchpad for values. It is organized like a hash and stored in the session data, so you can store values associated with keys and later retrieve them. It has one special property. By default, values stored into the flash during the processing of a request will be available during the processing of the immediately following request. Once that second request has been processed, those values are removed from the flash.

Probably the most common use of the flash is to pass error and informational strings from one action to the next. The intent here is that the first action notices some condition, creates a message describing that condition, and redirects to a separate action. By storing the message in the flash, the second action is able to access the message text and use it in a view. An example of such usage can be found in Iteration E1 on page 139.

It is sometimes convenient to use the flash as a way of passing messages into a template in the current action. For example, our display() method might want to output a cheery banner if there isn't another, more pressing note. It doesn't need that message to be passed to the next action—it's for use in the current request only. To do this, it could use flash.now, which updates the flash but does not add to the session data.

While flash.now creates a transient flash entry, flash.keep does the opposite, making entries that are currently in the flash stick around for another request cycle. If you pass no parameters to flash.keep, then all the flash contents are preserved.

Flashes can store more than just text messages—you can use them to pass all kinds of information between actions. Obviously, for longer-term information you'd want to use the session (probably in conjunction with your database) to store the data, but the flash is great if you want to pass parameters from one request to the next.

Because the flash data is stored in the session, all the usual rules apply. In particular, every object must be serializable. We strongly recommend passing only basic objects like Strings or Hashes in the flash.

Callbacks

Callbacks enable you to write code in your controllers that wrap the processing performed by actions—you can write a chunk of code once and have it be called before or after any number of actions in your controller (or your controller's subclasses). This turns out to be a powerful facility. Using callbacks, we can implement authentication schemes, logging, response compression, and even response customization.

Rails supports three types of callbacks: before, after, and around. Such callbacks are called just prior to and/or just after the execution of actions. Depending on how you define them, they either run as methods inside the controller or are passed the controller object when they are run. Either way, they get access to details of the request and response objects, along with the other controller attributes.

Before and After Callbacks

As their names suggest, before and after callbacks are invoked before or after an action. Rails maintains two chains of callbacks for each controller. When a controller is about to run an action, it executes all the callbacks on the before chain. It executes the action before running the callbacks on the after chain.

Callbacks can be passive, monitoring activity performed by a controller. They can also take a more active part in request handling. If a before action callback returns false, then processing of the callback chain terminates, and the action is not run. A callback may also render output or redirect requests, in which case the original action never gets invoked.

We saw an example of using callbacks for authorization in the administration part of our store example in *Iteration J3: Limiting Access*, on page 245. We defined an authorization method that redirected to a login screen if the current session didn't have a logged-in user. We then made this method a before action callback for all the actions in the administration controller.

Callback declarations also accept blocks and the names of classes. If a block is specified, it will be called with the current controller as a parameter. If a class is given, its filter() class method will be called with the controller as a parameter.

By default, callbacks apply to all actions in a controller (and any subclasses of that controller). You can modify this with the :only option, which takes one or more actions on which the callback is invoked, and the :except option, which lists actions to be excluded from callback.

The before_action and after_action declarations append to the controller's chain of callbacks. Use the variants prepend_before_action() and prepend_after_action() to put callbacks at the front of the chain.

After callbacks can be used to modify the outbound response, changing the headers and content if required. Some applications use this technique to perform global replacements in the content generated by the controller's templates (for example, by substituting a customer's name for the string <customer/> in the response body). Another use might be compressing the response if the user's browser supports it.

Around callbacks wrap the execution of actions. You can write an around callback in two different styles. In the first, the callback is a single chunk of code. That code is called before the action is executed. If the callback code invokes yield, the action is executed. When the action completes, the callback code continues executing.

Thus, the code before the yield is like a before action callback, and the code after is the after action callback. If the callback code never invokes yield, the action is not run—this is the same as a before action callback return false.

The benefit of around callbacks is that they can retain context across the invocation of the action.

As well as passing around_action the name of a method, you can pass it a block or a filter class.

If you use a block as a callback, it will be passed two parameters: the controller object and a proxy for the action. Use call() on this second parameter to invoke the original action.

A second form allows you to pass an object as a callback. This object should implement a method called filter(). This method will be passed the controller object. It yields to invoke the action.

Like before and after callbacks, around callbacks take :only and :except parameters.

Around callbacks are (by default) added to the callback chain differently: the first around action callback added executes first. Subsequently added around callbacks will be nested within existing around callbacks.

Callback Inheritance

If you subclass a controller containing callbacks, the callbacks will be run on the child objects as well as in the parent. However, callbacks defined in the children will not run in the parent.

If you don't want a particular callback to run in a child controller, you can override the default processing with the skip_before_action and skip_after_action declarations. These accept the :only and :except parameters.

You can use skip_action to skip any action callback (before, after, and around). However, it works only for callbacks that were specified as the (symbol) name of a method.

We made use of skip_before_action in *Iteration J3: Limiting Access*, on page 245.

What We Just Did

We learned how Action Dispatch and Action Controller cooperate to enable our server to respond to requests. The importance of this can't be emphasized enough. In nearly every application, this is the primary place where the creativity of your application is expressed. While Active Record and Action View are hardly passive, our routes and our controllers are where the action is.

We started this chapter by covering the concept of REST, which was the inspiration for the way in which Rails approaches the routing of requests. We saw how this provided seven basic actions as a starting point and how to add more actions. We also saw how to select a data representation (for example, JSON or XML). And we covered how to test routes.

We then covered the environment that Action Controller provides for your actions, as well as the methods it provides for rendering and redirecting. Finally, we covered sessions, flash, and callbacks, each of which is available for use in your application's controllers.

Along the way, we showed how these concepts were used in the Depot application. Now that you have seen each in use and have been exposed to the theory behind each, how you combine and use these concepts is limited only by your own creativity.

In the next chapter, we will cover the remaining component of Action Pack, namely, Action View, which handles the rendering of results.

In this chapter, you'll see:
- Templates
- Forms including fields and uploading files
- Helpers
- Layouts and partials

## CHAPTER 22

Action View

We've seen how the routing component determines which controller to use and how the controller chooses an action. We've also seen how the controller and action between them decide what to render to the user. Normally rendering takes place at the end of the action, and involves a template. That's what this chapter is all about. Action View encapsulates all the functionality needed to render templates, most commonly generating HTML, XML, or JavaScript back to the user. As its name suggests, Action View is the view part of our MVC trilogy.

In this chapter, we will start with templates, for which Rails provides a range of options. We will then cover a number of ways in which users provide input: forms, file uploads, and links. We will complete this chapter by looking at a number of ways to reduce maintenance using helpers, layouts, and partials.

Using Templates

When you write a view, you're writing a template: something that will get expanded to generate the final result. To understand how these templates work, we need to look at three areas:

- Where the templates go
- The environment they run in
- What goes inside them

Where Templates Go

The render() method expects to find templates in the app/views directory of the current application. Within this directory, the convention is to have a separate subdirectory for the views of each controller. Our Depot application, for instance, includes products and store controllers. As a result, our application has templates in app/views/products and app/views/store. Each directory typically contains templates named after the actions in the corresponding controller.

You can also have templates that aren't named after actions. You render such templates from the controller using calls such as these:

```
render(action:   'fake_action_name')
render(template: 'controller/name')
render(file:     'dir/template')
```

The last of these allows you to store templates anywhere on your filesystem. This is useful if you want to share templates across applications.

The Template Environment

Templates contain a mixture of fixed text and code. The code in the template adds dynamic content to the response. That code runs in an environment that gives it access to the information set up by the controller:

- All instance variables of the controller are also available in the template. This is how actions communicate data to the templates.

- The controller object's flash, headers, logger, params, request, response, and session are available as accessor methods in the view. Apart from the flash, view code probably should not use these directly, because the responsibility for handling them should rest with the controller. However, we do find this useful when debugging. For example, the following html.erb template uses the debug() method to display the contents of the session, the details of the parameters, and the current response:

```
<h4>Session</h4>   <%= debug(session) %>
<h4>Params</h4>    <%= debug(params) %>
<h4>Response</h4> <%= debug(response) %>
```

- The current controller object is accessible using the attribute named controller. This allows the template to call any public method in the controller (including the methods in ActionController::Base).

- The path to the base directory of the templates is stored in the attribute base_path.

What Goes in a Template

Out of the box, Rails supports five types of templates:

- ERB templates are a mixture of content and embedded Ruby. They are typically used to generate HTML pages.

- Jbuilder[1] templates generate JSON responses.

---

1. https://github.com/rails/jbuilder

- Builder templates use the Builder library[2] to construct XML responses.

- CoffeeScript or JavaScript templates create JavaScript, which can change both the presentation and the behavior of your content in the browser.

- SCSS templates create CSS stylesheets to control the presentation of your content in the browser.

By far, the one that you will be using the most will be ERB. In fact, you made extensive use of ERB templates in developing the Depot application.

So far in this chapter, we have focused on producing output. In Chapter 21, *Action Dispatch and Action Controller*, on page 353, we focused on processing input. In a well-designed application, these two are not unrelated: the output we produce contains forms, links, and buttons that guide the end user to producing the next set of inputs. As you might expect by now, Rails provides a considerable amount of help in this area too.

Generating Forms

HTML provides a number of elements, attributes, and attribute values that control how input is gathered. You certainly could hand-code your form directly into the template, but there really is no need to do that.

In this section, we will cover a number of *helpers* that Rails provides that assist with this process. In *Using Helpers*, on page 395, we will show you how you can create your own helpers.

HTML provides a number of ways to collect data in forms. A few of the more common means are shown in the following screenshot. Note that the form itself is not representative of any sort of typical use; in general, you will use only a subset of these methods to collect data.

---

2. http://api.rubyonrails.org/classes/ActionView/Base.html

Let's look at the template that was used to produce that form:

rails51/views/app/views/form/input.html.erb

```
Line 1  <%= form_for(:model) do |form| %>
    -     <p>
    -       <%= form.label :input %> <!-- -->
    -       <%= form.text_field :input, :placeholder => 'Enter text here...' %> <!-- -->
    5     </p>
    -
    -     <p>
    -       <%= form.label :address, :style => 'float: left' %>
    -       <%= form.text_area :address, :rows => 3, :cols => 40 %> <!-- -->
    10    </p>
    -
    -     <p>
    -       <%= form.label :color %>:
    -       <%= form.radio_button :color, 'red' %> <!-- -->
    15      <%= form.label :red %>
    -       <%= form.radio_button :color, 'yellow' %>
    -       <%= form.label :yellow %>
    -       <%= form.radio_button :color, 'green' %>
    -       <%= form.label :green %>
    20    </p>
    -
    -     <p>
    -       <%= form.label 'condiment' %>:
    -       <%= form.check_box :ketchup %> <!-- -->
    25      <%= form.label :ketchup %>
    -       <%= form.check_box :mustard %>
    -       <%= form.label :mustard %>
    -       <%= form.check_box :mayonnaise %>
    -       <%= form.label :mayonnaise %>
    30    </p>
    -
    -     <p>
    -       <%= form.label :priority %>:
    -       <%= form.select :priority, (1..10) %> <!-- -->
    35    </p>
    -
    -     <p>
    -       <%= form.label :start %>:
    -       <%= form.date_select :start %> <!-- -->
    40    </p>
    -
    -     <p>
    -       <%= form.label :alarm %>:
    -       <%= form.time_select :alarm %> <!-- -->
    45    </p>
    -   <% end %>
```

In that template, you will see a number of labels, such as the one on line 3. You use labels to associate text with an input field for a specified attribute. The text of the label will default to the attribute name unless you specify it explicitly.

You use the text_field() and text_area() helpers (on lines 4 and 9, respectively) to gather single-line and multiline input fields. You may specify a placeholder, which will be displayed inside the field until the user provides a value. Not every browser supports this function, but those that don't simply will display an empty box. Since this will degrade gracefully, there is no need for you to design to the least common denominator—make use of this feature, because those who can see it will benefit from it immediately.

Placeholders are one of the many small "fit and finish" features provided with HTML5, and once again, Rails is ready even if the browser your users have installed is not. You can use the search_field(), telephone_field(), url_field(), email_field(), number_field(), and range_field() helpers to prompt for a specific type of input. How the browser will make use of this information varies. Some may display the field slightly differently in order to more clearly identify its function. Safari on Mac, for example, will display search fields with rounded corners and will insert a little x for clearing the field once data entry begins. Some may provide added validation. For example, Opera will validate URL fields prior to submission. The iPad will even adjust the virtual onscreen keyboard to provide ready access to characters such as the @ sign when entering an email address.

Although the support for these functions varies by browser, those that don't provide extra support for these functions simply display a plain, unadorned input box. Once again, nothing is gained by waiting. If you have an input field that's expected to contain an email address, don't simply use text_field()—go ahead and start using email_field() now.

Lines 14, 24, and 34 demonstrate three different ways to provide a constrained set of options. Although the display may vary a bit from browser to browser, these approaches are all well supported across all browsers. The select() method is particularly flexible—it can be passed an Enumeration as shown here, an array of pairs of name-value pairs, or a Hash. A number of form options helpers[3] are available to produce such lists from various sources, including the database.

---

3. http://api.rubyonrails.org/classes/ActionView/Helpers/FormOptionsHelper.html

Finally, lines 39 and 44 show prompts for a date and time, respectively. As you might expect by now, Rails provides plenty of options here too.[4]

Not shown in this example are hidden_field() and password_field(). A hidden field is not displayed at all, but the value is passed back to the server. This may be useful as an alternative to storing transient data in sessions, enabling data from one request to be passed onto the next. Password fields are displayed, but the text entered in them is obscured.

This is more than an adequate starter set for most needs. Should you find that you have additional needs, you are quite likely to find a helper or gem is already available for you. A good place to start is with the Rails Guides.[5]

Meanwhile, let's explore how the data forms submit is processed.

Processing Forms

In the figure on page 391 we can see how the various attributes in the model pass through the controller to the view, on to the HTML page, and back again into the model. The model object has attributes such as name, country, and password. The template uses helper methods to construct an HTML form to let the user edit the data in the model. Note how the form fields are named. The country attribute, for example, maps to an HTML input field with the name user[country].

When the user submits the form, the raw POST data is sent back to our application. Rails extracts the fields from the form and constructs the params hash. Simple values (such as the id field, extracted by routing from the form action) are stored directly in the hash. But, if a parameter name has brackets in it, Rails assumes that it is part of more structured data and constructs a hash to hold the values. Inside this hash, the string inside the brackets acts as the key. This process can repeat if a parameter name has multiple sets of brackets in it.

Form Parameters	Params
id=123	{ id: "123" }
user[name]=Dave	{ user: { name: "Dave" }}
user[address][city]=Wien	{ user: { address: { city: "Wien" }}}

In the final part of the integrated whole, model objects can accept new attribute values from hashes, which allows us to say this:

```
user.update(user_params)
```

4.   http://api.rubyonrails.org/classes/ActionView/Helpers/DateHelper.html
5.   http://guides.rubyonrails.org/form_helpers.html

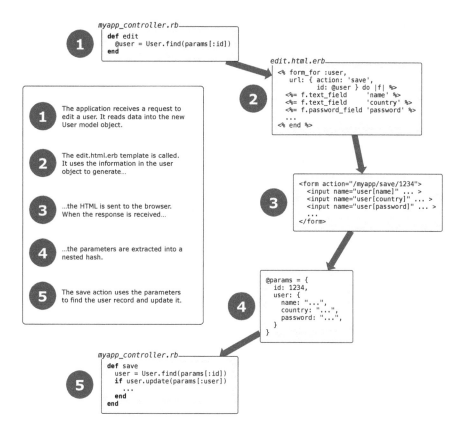

Rails integration goes deeper than this. Looking at the .html.erb file in the preceding figure, we can see that the template uses a set of helper methods to create the form's HTML; these are methods such as form_with() and text_field().

Before moving on, it is worth noting that params may be used for more than text. Entire files can be uploaded. We'll cover that next.

Uploading Files to Rails Applications

Your application may allow users to upload files. For example, a bug-reporting system might let users attach log files and code samples to a problem ticket, or a blogging application could let its users upload a small image to appear next to their articles.

In HTTP, files are uploaded as a *multipart/form-data* POST message. As the name suggests, forms are used to generate this type of message. Within that form, you'll use <input> tags with type="file". When rendered by a browser, this allows the user to select a file by name. When the form is subsequently submitted, the file or files will be sent back along with the rest of the form data.

To illustrate the file upload process, we'll show some code that allows a user to upload an image and display that image alongside a comment. To do this, we first need a pictures table to store the data:

rails51/e1/views/db/migrate/20170425000004_create_pictures.rb
```ruby
class CreatePictures < ActiveRecord::Migration
  def change
    create_table :pictures do |t|
      t.string :comment
      t.string :name
      t.string :content_type
      # If using MySQL, blobs default to 64k, so we have to give
      # an explicit size to extend them
      t.binary :data, :limit => 1.megabyte
    end
  end
end
```

We'll create a somewhat artificial upload controller just to demonstrate the process. The get action is pretty conventional; it simply creates a new picture object and renders a form:

rails51/e1/views/app/controllers/upload_controller.rb
```ruby
class UploadController < ApplicationController
  def get
    @picture = Picture.new
  end
  # . . .
  private
    # Never trust parameters from the scary internet, only allow the white
    # list through.
    def picture_params
      params.require(:picture).permit(:comment, :uploaded_picture)
    end
end
```

The get template contains the form that uploads the picture (along with a comment). Note how we override the encoding type to allow data to be sent back with the response:

rails51/e1/views/app/views/upload/get.html.erb
```erb
<%= form_for(:picture,
             url: {action: 'save'},
             html: {multipart: true}) do |form| %>

    Comment:            <%= form.text_field("comment") %><br/>
    Upload your picture: <%= form.file_field("uploaded_picture") %><br/>

    <%= submit_tag("Upload file") %>
<% end %>
```

The form has one other subtlety. The picture uploads into an attribute called uploaded_picture. However, the database table doesn't contain a column of that name. That means that there must be some magic happening in the model:

rails51/e1/views/app/models/picture.rb
```ruby
class Picture < ActiveRecord::Base

  validates_format_of :content_type,
                      with: /\Aimage/,
                      message: "must be a picture"
  def uploaded_picture=(picture_field)
    self.name         = base_part_of(picture_field.original_filename)
    self.content_type = picture_field.content_type.chomp
    self.data         = picture_field.read
  end

  def base_part_of(file_name)
    File.basename(file_name).gsub(/[^\w._-]/, '')
  end
end
```

We define an accessor called uploaded_picture=() to receive the file uploaded by the form. The object returned by the form is an interesting hybrid. It is file-like, so we can read its contents with the read() method; that's how we get the image data into the data column. It also has the attributes content_type and original_filename, which let us get at the uploaded file's metadata. Accessor methods pick all this apart, resulting in a single object stored as separate attributes in the database.

Note that we also add a validation to check that the content type is of the form image/*xxx*. We don't want someone uploading JavaScript.

The save action in the controller is totally conventional:

rails51/e1/views/app/controllers/upload_controller.rb
```ruby
def save
  @picture = Picture.new(picture_params)
  if @picture.save
    redirect_to(action: 'show', id: @picture.id)
  else
    render(action: :get)
  end
end
```

Now that we have an image in the database, how do we display it? One way is to give it its own URL and link to that URL from an image tag. For example, we could use a URL such as upload/picture/123 to return the image for picture 123. This would use send_data() to return the image to the browser. Note how we set the content type and filename—this lets browsers interpret the data and supplies a default name should the user choose to save the image:

rails51/e1/views/app/controllers/upload_controller.rb
```
def picture
  @picture = Picture.find(params[:id])
  send_data(@picture.data,
            filename: @picture.name,
            type: @picture.content_type,
            disposition: "inline")
end
```

Finally, we can implement the show action, which displays the comment and the image. The action simply loads the picture model object:

rails51/e1/views/app/controllers/upload_controller.rb
```
def show
  @picture = Picture.find(params[:id])
end
```

In the template, the image tag links back to the action that returns the picture content. In the following screenshot, we can see the get and show actions.

rails51/e1/views/app/views/upload/show.html.erb
```
<h3><%= @picture.comment %></h3>

<img src="<%= url_for(:action => 'picture', :id => @picture.id) %>"/>
```

If you'd like an easier way of dealing with uploading and storing images, take a look at thoughtbot's Paperclip[6] or Rick Olson's attachment_fu[7] plugins.

---

6.   https://github.com/thoughtbot/paperclip#readme
7.   https://github.com/technoweenie/attachment_fu

Create a database table that includes a given set of columns (documented on Rick's site), and the plugin will automatically manage storing both the uploaded data and the upload's metadata. Unlike our previous approach, it handles storing the uploads in either your filesystem or a database table.

Forms and uploads are just two examples of helpers that Rails provides. Next we will show you how you can provide your own helpers and introduce you to a number of other helpers that come with Rails.

Using Helpers

Earlier we said that it's OK to put code in templates. Now we're going to modify that statement. It's perfectly acceptable to put *some* code in templates —that's what makes them dynamic. However, it's poor style to put too much code in templates.

There are three main reasons for this. First, the more code you put in the view side of your application, the easier it is to let discipline slip and start adding application-level functionality to the template code. This is definitely poor form; you want to put application stuff in the controller and model layers so that it is available everywhere. This will pay off when you add new ways of viewing the application.

The second reason is that html.erb is basically HTML. When you edit it, you're editing an HTML file. If you have the luxury of having professional designers create your layouts, they'll want to work with HTML. Putting a bunch of Ruby code in there just makes it hard to work with.

The final reason is that code embedded in views is hard to test, whereas code split out into helper modules can be isolated and tested as individual units.

Rails provides a nice compromise in the form of helpers. A *helper* is simply a module containing methods that assist a view. Helper methods are output-centric. They exist to generate HTML (or XML, or JavaScript)—a helper extends the behavior of a template.

Your Own Helpers

By default, each controller gets its own helper module. Additionally, there is an application-wide helper named application_helper.rb. It won't be surprising to learn that Rails makes certain assumptions to help link the helpers into the controller and its views. While all view helpers are available to all controllers, it often is good practice to organize helpers. Helpers that are unique to the views associated with the ProductController tend to be placed in a helper module called ProductHelper in the file product_helper.rb in the app/helpers directory. You don't have to remember all these details—the rails generate controller script creates a stub helper module automatically.

In *Iteration F4: Hiding an Empty Cart with a Custom Helper*, on page 167, we created such a helper method named hidden_div_if(), which enabled us to hide the cart under specified conditions. We can use the same technique to clean up the application layout a bit. Currently we have the following:

```
<h3><%= @page_title || "Pragmatic Store" %></h3>
```

Let's move the code that works out the page title into a helper method. Because we're in the store controller, we edit the store_helper.rb file in app/helpers:

```ruby
module StoreHelper
  def page_title
    @page_title || "Pragmatic Store"
  end
end
```

Now the view code simply calls the helper method:

```
<h3><%= page_title %></h3>
```

(We might want to eliminate even more duplication by moving the rendering of the entire title into a separate partial template, shared by all the controller's views, but we don't talk about partial templates until *Partial-Page Templates*, on page 406.)

Helpers for Formatting and Linking

Rails comes with a bunch of built-in helper methods, available to all views. Here, we'll touch on the highlights, but you'll probably want to look at the Action View RDoc for the specifics—there's a lot of functionality in there.

Aside from the general convenience these helpers provide, many of them also handle internationalization and localization. In Chapter 16, *Task K: Internationalization*, on page 253, we translated much of the application. Many of the helpers we used handled that for us, such as number_to_currency(). It's always a good practice to use Rails helpers where they are appropriate, even if it seems just as easy to hard-code the output you want.

Formatting Helpers

One set of helper methods deals with dates, numbers, and text:

```
<%= distance_of_time_in_words(Time.now, Time.local(2016, 12, 25)) %>
    4 months
```

```
<%= distance_of_time_in_words(Time.now, Time.now + 33, include_seconds: false) %>
    1 minute
```

```
<%= distance_of_time_in_words(Time.now, Time.now + 33, include_seconds: true) %>
    Half a minute
```

```
<%= time_ago_in_words(Time.local(2012, 12, 25)) %>
    7 months
```

```
<%= number_to_currency(123.45) %>
    $123.45
```

```
<%= number_to_currency(234.56, unit: "CAN$", precision: 0) %>
    CAN$235
```

```
<%= number_to_human_size(123_456) %>
    120.6 KB
```

```
<%= number_to_percentage(66.66666) %>
    66.667%
```

```
<%= number_to_percentage(66.66666, precision: 1) %>
    66.7%
```

```
<%= number_to_phone(2125551212) %>
    212-555-1212
```

```
<%= number_to_phone(2125551212, area_code: true, delimiter: " ") %>
    (212) 555 1212
```

```
<%= number_with_delimiter(12345678) %>
    12,345,678
```

```
<%= number_with_delimiter(12345678, delimiter: "_") %>
    12_345_678
```

```
<%= number_with_precision(50.0/3, precision: 2) %>
    16.67
```

The debug() method dumps out its parameter using YAML and escapes the result so it can be displayed in an HTML page. This can help when trying to look at the values in model objects or request parameters:

```
<%= debug(params) %>
```

```
--- !ruby/hash:HashWithIndifferentAccess
name: Dave
language: Ruby
action: objects
controller: test
```

Yet another set of helpers deals with text. There are methods to truncate strings and highlight words in a string:

`<%= simple_format(@trees) %>`

Formats a string, honoring line and paragraph breaks. You could give it the plain text of the Joyce Kilmer poem *Trees*[8], and it would add the HTML to format it as follows.

`<p>` I think that I shall never see `<br />`A poem lovely as a tree.`</p>` `<p>`A tree whose hungry mouth is prest `<br />`Against the sweet earth's flowing breast; `</p>`

`<%= excerpt(@trees, "lovely", 8) %>`

...A poem lovely as a tre...

`<%= highlight(@trees, "tree") %>`

I think that I shall never see A poem lovely as a `<strong class="highlight">`tree`</strong>`. A `<strong class="highlight">`tree`</strong>` whose hungry mouth is prest Against the sweet earth's flowing breast;

`<%= truncate(@trees, length: 20) %>`

I think that I sh...

There's a method to pluralize nouns:

`<%= pluralize(1, "person") %> but <%= pluralize(2, "person") %>`

1 person but 2 people

If you'd like to do what the fancy websites do and automatically hyperlink URLs and email addresses, there are helpers to do that. There's another that strips hyperlinks from text.

Back in Iteration A2 on page 83, we saw how the cycle() helper can be used to return the successive values from a sequence each time it's called, repeating the sequence as necessary. This is often used to create alternating styles for the rows in a table or list. The current_cycle() and reset_cycle() methods are also available.

Finally, if you're writing something like a blog site or you're allowing users to add comments to your store, you could offer them the ability to create their text in Markdown (BlueCloth)[9] or Textile (RedCloth)[10] format. These are formatters that take text written in human-friendly markup and convert it into HTML.

---

8. https://www.poetryfoundation.org/poetrymagazine/poems/12744/trees
9. https://github.com/rtomayko/rdiscount
10. http://redcloth.org/

Linking to Other Pages and Resources

The ActionView::Helpers::AssetTagHelper and ActionView::Helpers::UrlHelper modules contain a number of methods that let you reference resources external to the current template. Of these, the most commonly used is link_to(), which creates a hyperlink to another action in your application:

```
<%= link_to "Add Comment", new_comments_path %>
```

The first parameter to link_to() is the text displayed for the link. The next is a string or hash specifying the link's target.

An optional third parameter provides HTML attributes for the generated link:

```
<%= link_to "Delete", product_path(@product),
    { class: "dangerous", method: 'delete' }
%>
```

This third parameter also supports two additional options that modify the behavior of the link. Each requires JavaScript to be enabled in the browser.

The :method option is a hack—it allows you to make the link look to the application as if the request were created by a POST, PUT, PATCH, or DELETE, rather than the normal GET method. This is done by creating a chunk of JavaScript that submits the request when the link is clicked—if JavaScript is disabled in the browser, a GET will be generated.

The :data parameter allows you to set custom data attributes. The most commonly used one is the :confirm option, which takes a short message. If present, an unobtrusive JavaScript driver will display the message and get the user's confirmation before the link is followed:

```
<%= link_to "Delete", product_path(@product),
                method: :delete,
                data: { confirm: 'Are you sure?' }
%>
```

The button_to() method works the same as link_to() but generates a button in a self-contained form, rather than a straight hyperlink. This is the preferred method of linking to actions that have side effects. However, these buttons live in their own forms, which imposes a couple of restrictions: they cannot appear inline, and they cannot appear inside other forms.

Rails has conditional linking methods that generate hyperlinks if some condition is met or just return the link text otherwise. link_to_if() and link_to_unless() take a condition parameter, followed by the regular parameters to link_to. If the condition is true (for link_to_if) or false (for link_to_unless), a regular link will be created using the remaining parameters. If not, the name will be added as plain text (with no hyperlink).

The link_to_unless_current() helper creates menus in sidebars where the current page name is shown as plain text and the other entries are hyperlinks:

```
<ul>
<% %w{ create list edit save logout }.each do |action| %>
    <li>
      <%= link_to_unless_current(action.capitalize, action: action) %>
    </li>
<% end %>
</ul>
```

The link_to_unless_current() helper may also be passed a block that is evaluated only if the current action is the action given, effectively providing an alternative to the link. There also is a current_page() helper method that simply tests whether the current request URI was generated by the given options.

As with url_for(), link_to() and friends also support absolute URLs:

```
<%= link_to("Help", "http://my.site/help/index.html") %>
```

The image_tag() helper creates <img> tags. Optional :size parameters (of the form *widthxheight*) or separate width and height parameters define the size of the image:

```
<%= image_tag("/assets/dave.png", class: "bevel", size: "80x120") %>
<%= image_tag("/assets/andy.png", class: "bevel",
              width: "80", height: "120") %>
```

If you don't give an :alt option, Rails synthesizes one for you using the image's filename. If the image path doesn't start with a / character, Rails assumes that it lives under the app/assets/images directory.

You can make images into links by combining link_to() and image_tag():

```
<%= link_to(image_tag("delete.png", size: "50x22"),
            product_path(@product),
            data: { confirm: "Are you sure?" },
            method: :delete)
%>
```

The mail_to() helper creates a mailto: hyperlink that, when clicked, normally loads the client's email application. It takes an email address, the name of the link, and a set of HTML options. Within these options, you can also use :bcc, :cc, :body, and :subject to initialize the corresponding email fields. Finally, the magic option encode: "javascript" uses client-side JavaScript to obscure the generated link, making it harder for spiders to harvest email addresses from your site. Unfortunately, it also means your users won't see the email link if they have JavaScript disabled in their browsers.

```
<%= mail_to("support@pragprog.com", "Contact Support",
            subject: "Support question from #{@user.name}",
            encode:  "javascript") %>
```

As a weaker form of obfuscation, you can use the :replace_at and :replace_dot options to replace the at sign and dots in the displayed name with other strings. This is unlikely to fool harvesters.

The AssetTagHelper module also includes helpers that make it easy to link to stylesheets and JavaScript code from your pages and to create autodiscovery Atom feed links. We created links in the layouts for the Depot application using the stylesheet_link_tag() and javascript_link_tag() methods in the head:

```
rails51/depot_r/app/views/layouts/application.html.erb
<html>
  <head>
    <title>Pragprog Books Online Store</title>
    <%= csrf_meta_tags %>

    <%= stylesheet_link_tag 'application', media: 'all',
                            'data-turbolinks-track': 'reload' %>
    <%= javascript_include_tag 'application',
                               'data-turbolinks-track': 'reload' %>
  </head>
```

The javascript_include_tag() method takes a list of JavaScript filenames (assumed to live in assets/javascripts) and creates the HTML to load these into a page.

An RSS or Atom link is a header field that points to a URL in our application. When that URL is accessed, the application should return the appropriate RSS or Atom XML:

```
<html>
  <head>
    <%= auto_discovery_link_tag(:atom, products_url(format: 'atom')) %>
  </head>
  . . .
```

Finally, the JavaScriptHelper module defines a number of helpers for working with JavaScript. These create JavaScript snippets that run in the browser to generate special effects and to have the page dynamically interact with our application.

By default, image and stylesheet assets are assumed to live in the images and stylesheets directories relative to the application's assets directory. If the path given to an asset tag method starts with a forward slash, then the path is assumed to be absolute, and no prefix is applied. Sometimes it makes sense to move this static content onto a separate box or to different locations on the current box. Do this by setting the configuration variable asset_host:

```
config.action_controller.asset_host = "http://media.my.url/assets"
```

Although this list of helpers may seem to be comprehensive, Rails provides many more, new helpers are introduced with each release, and a select few are retired or moved off into a plugin where they can be evolved at a different pace than Rails.

Reducing Maintenance with Layouts and Partials

So far in this chapter we've looked at templates as isolated chunks of code and HTML. But one of the driving ideas behind Rails is honoring the DRY principle and eliminating the need for duplication. The average website, though, has lots of duplication:

- Many pages share the same tops, tails, and sidebars.

- Multiple pages may contain the same snippets of rendered HTML (a blog site, for example, may display an article in multiple places).

- The same functionality may appear in multiple places. Many sites have a standard search component or a polling component that appears in most of the sites' sidebars.

Rails provides both layouts and partials that reduce the need for duplication in these three situations.

Layouts

Rails allows you to render pages that are nested inside other rendered pages. Typically this feature is used to put the content from an action within a standard site-wide page frame (title, footer, and sidebar). In fact, if you've been using the generate script to create scaffold-based applications, then you've been using these layouts all along.

When Rails honors a request to render a template from within a controller, it actually renders two templates. Obviously, it renders the one you ask for (or the default template named after the action if you don't explicitly render anything). But Rails also tries to find and render a layout template (we'll talk about how it finds the layout in a second). If it finds the layout, it inserts the action-specific output into the HTML produced by the layout.

Let's look at a layout template:

```
<html>
  <head>
    <title>Form: <%= controller.action_name %></title>
    <%= stylesheet_link_tag 'scaffold' %>
  </head>
  <body>

    <%= yield :layout %>

  </body>
</html>
```

The layout sets out a standard HTML page, with the head and body sections. It uses the current action name as the page title and includes a CSS file. In the body, there's a call to yield. This is where the magic takes place. When the template for the action was rendered, Rails stored its content, labeling it :layout. Inside the layout template, calling yield retrieves this text. In fact, :layout is the default content returned when rendering, so you can write yield instead of yield :layout. We personally prefer the slightly more explicit version.

If the my_action.html.erb template contained this:

```
<h1><%= @msg %></h1>
```

and the controller set @msg to Hello, World!, then the browser would see the following HTML:

```
<html>
  <head>
    <title>Form: my_action</title>
    <link href="/stylesheets/scaffold.css" media="screen"
          rel="Stylesheet" type="text/css" />
  </head>
  <body>

    <h1>Hello, World!</h1>

  </body>
</html>
```

Locating Layout Files

As you've probably come to expect, Rails does a good job of providing defaults for layout file locations, but you can override the defaults if you need something different.

Layouts are controller-specific. If the current request is being handled by a controller called *store*, Rails will by default look for a layout called store (with the usual .html.erb or .xml.builder extension) in the app/views/layouts directory. If you create a layout called application in the layouts directory, it will be applied to all controllers that don't otherwise have a layout defined for them.

You can override this using the layout declaration inside a controller. The most basic invocation is to pass it the name of a layout as a string. The following declaration will make the template in the file standard.html.erb or standard.xml.builder the layout for all actions in the store controller. The layout file will be looked for in the app/views/layouts directory:

```
class StoreController < ApplicationController

  layout "standard"

  # ...
end
```

You can qualify which actions will have the layout applied to them using the :only and :except qualifiers:

```
class StoreController < ApplicationController

  layout "standard", except: [ :rss, :atom ]

  # ...
end
```

Specifying a layout of nil turns off layouts for a controller.

Sometimes you need to change the appearance of a set of pages at runtime. For example, a blogging site might offer a different-looking side menu if the user is logged in, or a store site might have different-looking pages if the site is down for maintenance. Rails supports this need with dynamic layouts. If the parameter to the layout declaration is a symbol, it's taken to be the name of a controller instance method that returns the name of the layout to be used:

```
class StoreController < ApplicationController
  layout :determine_layout
  # ...
  private

  def determine_layout
    if Store.is_closed?
      "store_down"
    else
      "standard"
    end
  end
end
```

Subclasses of a controller use the parent's layout unless they override it using the layout directive. Finally, individual actions can choose to render using a specific layout (or with no layout at all) by passing render() the :layout option:

```
def rss
  render(layout: false)   # never use a layout
end
def checkout
  render(layout: "layouts/simple")
end
```

Passing Data to Layouts

Layouts have access to all the same data that's available to conventional templates. In addition, any instance variables set in the normal template will be available in the layout (because the regular template is rendered before the layout is invoked). This might be used to parameterize headings or menus in the layout. For example, the layout might contain this:

```
<html>
  <head>
    <title><%= @title %></title>
    <%= stylesheet_link_tag 'scaffold' %>
  </head>
  <body>
    <h1><%= @title %></h1>
    <%= yield :layout %>
  </body>
</html>
```

An individual template could set the title by assigning to the @title variable:

```
<% @title = "My Wonderful Life" %>
<p>
  Dear Diary:
</p>
<p>
  Yesterday I had pizza for dinner. It was nice.
</p>
```

We can take this further. The same mechanism that lets us use yield :layout to embed the rendering of a template into the layout also lets you generate arbitrary content in a template, which can then be embedded into any template.

For example, different templates may need to add their own template-specific items to the standard page sidebar. We'll use the content_for mechanism in those templates to define content and then use yield in the layout to embed this content into the sidebar.

In each regular template, use a content_for to give a name to the content rendered inside a block. This content will be stored inside Rails and will not contribute to the output generated by the template:

```
<h1>Regular Template</h1>

<% content_for(:sidebar) do %>
  <ul>
    <li>this text will be rendered</li>
    <li>and saved for later</li>
    <li>it may contain <%= "dynamic" %> stuff</li>
  </ul>
<% end %>
<p>
  Here's the regular stuff that will appear on
  the page rendered by this template.
</p>
```

Then, in the layout, use yield :sidebar to include this block in the page's sidebar:

```
<!DOCTYPE .... >
<html>
  <body>
    <div class="sidebar">
      <p>
        Regular sidebar stuff
      </p>
      <div class="page-specific-sidebar">
        <%= yield :sidebar %>
      </div>
    </div>
  </body>
</html>
```

This same technique can be used to add page-specific JavaScript functions into the <head> section of a layout, create specialized menu bars, and so on.

Partial-Page Templates

Web applications commonly display information about the same application object or objects on multiple pages. A shopping cart might display an order line item on the shopping cart page and again on the order summary page. A blog application might display the contents of an article on the main index page and again at the top of a page soliciting comments. Typically this would involve copying snippets of code between the different template pages.

Rails, however, eliminates this duplication with the *partial-page templates* (more frequently called *partials*). You can think of a partial as a kind of subroutine. You invoke it one or more times from within another template, potentially passing it objects to render as parameters. When the partial template finishes rendering, it returns control to the calling template.

Internally, a partial template looks like any other template. Externally, there's a slight difference. The name of the file containing the template code must start with an underscore character, differentiating the source of partial templates from their more complete brothers and sisters.

For example, the partial to render a blog entry might be stored in the file _article.html.erb in the normal views directory, app/views/blog:

```
<div class="article">
  <div class="articleheader">
    <h3><%= article.title %></h3>
  </div>
  <div class="articlebody">
    <%= article.body %>
  </div>
</div>
```

Other templates use the render(partial:) method to invoke this:

```
<%= render(partial: "article", object: @an_article) %>
<h3>Add Comment</h3>
. . .
```

The :partial parameter to render() is the name of the template to render (but without the leading underscore). This name must be both a valid filename and a valid Ruby identifier (so a-b and 20042501 are not valid names for partials). The :object parameter identifies an object to be passed into the partial. This object will be available within the template via a local variable with the same name as the template. In this example, the @an_article object will be passed to the template, and the template can access it using the local variable article. That's why we could write things such as article.title in the partial.

You can set additional local variables in the template by passing render() a :locals parameter. This takes a hash where the entries represent the names and values of the local variables to set:

```
render(partial: 'article',
       object:  @an_article,
       locals:  { authorized_by: session[:user_name],
                  from_ip:       request.remote_ip })
```

Partials and Collections

Applications commonly need to display collections of formatted entries. A blog might show a series of articles, each with text, author, date, and so on. A store might display entries in a catalog, where each has an image, a description, and a price.

The :collection parameter to render() works in conjunction with the :partial parameter. The :partial parameter lets us use a partial to define the format of an individual entry, and the :collection parameter applies this template to each member of the collection.

To display a list of article model objects using our previously defined _article.html.erb partial, we could write this:

```
<%= render(partial: "article", collection: @article_list) %>
```

Inside the partial, the local variable article will be set to the current article from the collection—the variable is named after the template. In addition, the variable article_counter will have its value set to the index of the current article in the collection.

The optional :spacer_template parameter lets you specify a template that will be rendered between each of the elements in the collection. For example, a view might contain the following:

```
rails51/e1/views/app/views/partial/_list.html.erb
<%= render(partial:        "animal",
           collection:     %w{ ant bee cat dog elk },
           spacer_template: "spacer")
%>
```

This uses _animal.html.erb to render each animal in the given list, rendering the partial _spacer.html.erb between each. If _animal.html.erb contains this:

```
rails51/e1/views/app/views/partial/_animal.html.erb
<p>The animal is <%= animal %></p>
```

and _spacer.html.erb contains this:

```
rails51/e1/views/app/views/partial/_spacer.html.erb
<hr />
```

your users would see a list of animal names with a line between each.

Shared Templates

If the first option or :partial parameter to a render call is a String with no slashes, Rails assumes that the target template is in the current controller's view directory. However, if the name contains one or more / characters, Rails assumes that the part up to the last slash is a directory name and the rest is the template name. The directory is assumed to be under app/views. This makes it easy to share partials and subtemplates across controllers.

The convention among Rails applications is to store these shared partials in a subdirectory of app/views called shared. Render shared partials using statements such as these:

```
<%= render("shared/header", locals: {title: @article.title}) %>
<%= render(partial: "shared/post", object: @article) %>
. . .
```

In this previous example, the @article object will be assigned to the local variable post within the template.

Partials with Layouts

Partials can be rendered with a layout, and you can apply a layout to a block within any template:

```
<%= render partial: "user", layout: "administrator" %>

<%= render layout: "administrator" do %>
  # ...
<% end %>
```

Partial layouts are to be found directly in the app/views directory associated with the controller, along with the customary underbar prefix, such as app/views/users/_administrator.html.erb.

Partials and Controllers

It isn't just view templates that use partials. Controllers also get in on the act. Partials give controllers the ability to generate fragments from a page using the same partial template as the view. This is particularly important when you are using Ajax support to update just part of a page from the controller—use partials, and you know your formatting for the table row or line item that you're updating will be compatible with that used to generate its brethren initially.

Taken together, partials and layouts provide an effective way to make sure that the user interface portion of your application is maintainable. But being maintainable is only part of the story; doing so in a way that also performs well is also crucial.

What We Just Did

Views are the public face of Rails applications, and we have seen that Rails delivers extensive support for what you need to build robust and maintainable user and application programming interfaces.

We started with templates, of which Rails provides built-in support for four types: ERB, Builder, CoffeeScript, and SCSS. Templates make it easy for us to provide HTML, JSON, XML, CSS, and JavaScript responses to any request. We will discuss adding another option in *Creating HTML Templates with Slim*, on page 433.

We dove into forms, which are the primary means by which users will interact with your application. Along the way, we covered uploading files.

We continued with helpers, which enable us to factor out complex application logic to allow our views to focus on presentation aspects. We explored a number of helpers that Rails provides, ranging from basic formatting to hypertext links, which are the final way in which users interact with HTML pages.

We completed our tour of Action View by covering two related ways of factoring out large chunks of content for reuse. We use layouts to factor out the outermost layers of a view and provide a common look and feel. We use partials to factor out common inner components, such as a single form or table.

That covers how a user with a browser will access our Rails application. Next up: covering how we define and maintain the schema of the database our application will use to store data.

CHAPTER 23

Migrations

Rails encourages an agile, iterative style of development. We don't expect to get everything right the first time. Instead, we write tests and interact with our customers to refine our understanding as we go.

For that to work, we need a supporting set of practices. We write tests to help us design our interfaces and to act as a safety net when we change things, and we use version control to store our application's source files, allowing us to undo mistakes and to monitor what changes day to day.

But there's another area of the application that changes, an area that we can't directly manage using version control. The database schema in a Rails application constantly evolves as we progress through the development: we add a table here, rename a column there, and so on. The database changes in step with the application's code.

With Rails, each of those steps is made possible through the use of a *migration*. You saw this in use throughout the development of the Depot application, starting when we created the first products table in *Generating the Scaffold*, on page 72, and when we performed such tasks as adding a quantity to the line_items table in *Iteration E1: Creating a Smarter Cart*, on page 133. Now it is time to dig deeper into how migrations work and what else you can do with them.

Creating and Running Migrations

A migration is simply a Ruby source file in your application's db/migrate directory. Each migration file's name starts with a number of digits (typically fourteen) and an underscore. Those digits are the key to migrations, because they define the sequence in which the migrations are applied—they are the individual migration's version number.

The version number is the Coordinated Universal Time (UTC) timestamp at the time the migration was created. These numbers contain the four-digit year, followed by two digits each for the month, day, hour, minute, and second, all based on the mean solar time at the Royal Observatory in Greenwich, London. Because migrations tend to be created relatively infrequently and the accuracy is recorded down to the second, the chances of any two people getting the same timestamp is vanishingly small. And the benefit of having timestamps that can be deterministically ordered far outweighs the miniscule risk of this occurring.

Here's what the db/migrate directory of our Depot application looks like:

```
depot> ls db/migrate
20170425000001_create_products.rb
20170425000002_create_carts.rb
20170425000003_create_line_items.rb
20170425000004_add_quantity_to_line_items.rb
20170425000005_combine_items_in_cart.rb
20170425000006_create_orders.rb
20170425000007_add_order_id_to_line_item.rb
20170425000008_create_users.rb
```

Although you could create these migration files by hand, it's easier (and less error prone) to use a generator. As we saw when we created the Depot application, there are actually two generators that create migration files:

- The *model* generator creates a migration to in turn create the table associated with the model (unless you specify the --skip-migration option). As the example that follows shows, creating a model called discount also creates a migration called *yyyyMMddhhmmss*_create_discounts.rb:

```
depot> bin/rails generate model discount
      invoke  active_record
➤     create      db/migrate/20121113133549_create_discounts.rb
      create      app/models/discount.rb
      invoke    test_unit
      create       test/models/discount_test.rb
      create       test/fixtures/discounts.yml
```

- You can also generate a migration on its own.

```
depot> bin/rails generate migration add_price_column
      invoke  active_record
➤     create      db/migrate/20121113133814_add_price_column.rb
```

Later, starting in *Anatomy of a Migration*, we'll see what goes in the migration files. But for now, let's jump ahead a little in the workflow and see how to run migrations.

Running Migrations

Migrations are run using the db:migrate Rake task:

```
depot> bin/rails db:migrate
```

To see what happens next, let's dive down into the internals of Rails.

The migration code maintains a table called schema_migrations inside every Rails database. This table has just one column, called version, and it will have one row per successfully applied migration.

When you run bin/rails db:migrate, the task first looks for the schema_migrations table. If it doesn't yet exist, it will be created.

The migration code then looks at the migration files in db/migrate and skips from consideration any that have a version number (the leading digits in the filename) that is already in the database. It then proceeds to apply the remainder of the migrations, creating a row in the schema_migrations table for each.

If we were to run migrations again at this point, nothing much would happen. Each of the version numbers of the migration files would match with a row in the database, so there would be no migrations to apply.

However, if we subsequently create a new migration file, it will have a version number not in the database. This is true even if the version number was *before* one or more of the already applied migrations. This can happen when multiple users are using a version control system to store the migration files. If we then run migrations, this new migration file—and only this migration file—will be executed. This may mean that migrations are run out of order, so you might want to take care and ensure that these migrations are independent. Or you might want to revert your database to a previous state and then apply the migrations in order.

You can force the database to a specific version by supplying the VERSION= parameter to the rake db:migrate command:

```
depot> bin/rails db:migrate VERSION=20170425000009
```

If the version you give is greater than any of the migrations that have yet to be applied, these migrations will be applied.

If, however, the version number on the command line is less than one or more versions listed in the schema_migrations table, something different happens. In these circumstances, Rails looks for the migration file whose number matches the database version and *undoes* it. It repeats this process until there are no more versions listed in the schema_migrations table that exceed the number you specified on the command line. That is, the migrations are unapplied in reverse order to take the schema back to the version that you specify.

You can also redo one or more migrations:

```
depot> bin/rails db:migrate:redo STEP=3
```

By default, redo will roll back one migration and rerun it. To roll back multiple migrations, pass the STEP= parameter.

Anatomy of a Migration

Migrations are subclasses of the Rails class ActiveRecord::Migration. When necessary, migrations can contain up() and down() methods:

```
class SomeMeaningfulName < ActiveRecord::Migration
  def up
    # ...
  end

  def down
    # ...
  end
end
```

The name of the class, after all uppercase letters are downcased and preceded by an underscore, must match the portion of the filename after the version number. For example, the previous class could be found in a file named 20170425000017_some_meaningful_name.rb. No two migrations can contain classes with the same name.

The up() method is responsible for applying the schema changes for this migration, while the down() method undoes those changes. Let's make this more concrete. Here's a migration that adds an e_mail column to the orders table:

```
class AddEmailToOrders < ActiveRecord::Migration
  def up
    add_column :orders, :e_mail, :string
  end

  def down
    remove_column :orders, :e_mail
  end
end
```

See how the down() method undoes the effect of the up() method? You can also see that there is a bit of duplication here. In many cases, Rails can detect how to automatically undo a given operation. For example, the opposite of add_column() is clearly remove_column(). In such cases, by simply renaming up() to change(), you can eliminate the need for a down():

```
class AddEmailToOrders < ActiveRecord::Migration
  def change
    add_column :orders, :e_mail, :string
  end
end
```

Now isn't that much cleaner?

Column Types

The third parameter to add_column specifies the type of the database column. In the prior example, we specified that the e_mail column has a type of :string. But what does this mean? Databases typically don't have column types of :string.

Remember that Rails tries to make your application independent of the underlying database; you could develop using SQLite 3 and deploy to Postgres if you wanted, for example. But different databases use different names for the types of columns. If you used a SQLite 3 column type in a migration, that migration might not work if applied to a Postgres database. So, Rails migrations insulate you from the underlying database type systems by using logical types. If we're migrating a SQLite 3 database, the :string type will create a column of type varchar(255). On Postgres, the same migration adds a column with the type char varying(255).

The types supported by migrations are :binary, :boolean, :date, :datetime, :decimal, :float, :integer, :string, :text, :time, and :timestamp. The default mappings of these types for the database adapters in Rails are shown in the following tables:

	db2	mysql	openbase	oracle
:binary	blob(32768)	blob	object	blob
:boolean	decimal(1)	tinyint(1)	boolean	number(1)
:date	date	date	date	date
:datetime	timestamp	datetime	datetime	date
:decimal	decimal	decimal	decimal	decimal
:float	float	float	float	number
:integer	int	int(11)	integer	number(38)
:string	varchar(255)	varchar(255)	char(4096)	varchar2(255)
:text	clob(32768)	text	text	clob
:time	time	time	time	date
:timestamp	timestamp	datetime	timestamp	date

	postgresql	sqlite	sqlserver	sybase
:binary	bytea	blob	image	image
:boolean	boolean	boolean	bit	bit
:date	date	date	date	datetime
:datetime	timestamp	datetime	datetime	datetime
:decimal	decimal	decimal	decimal	decimal
:float	float	float	float(8)	float(8)
:integer	integer	integer	int	int
:string	(note 1)	varchar(255)	varchar(255)	varchar(255)
:text	text	text	text	text
:time	time	datetime	time	time
:timestamp	timestamp	datetime	datetime	timestamp

Using these tables, you could work out that a column declared to be :integer in a migration would have the underlying type integer in SQLite 3 and number(38) in Oracle.

There are three options you can use when defining most columns in a migration; decimal columns take an additional two options. Each of these options is given as a key: value pair. The common options are as follows:

null: true or false   If false, the underlying column has a not null constraint added (if the database supports it). Note: this is independent of any presence: true validation, which may be performed at the model layer.

limit: size   This sets a limit on the size of the field. This basically appends the string (*size*) to the database column type definition.

default: value   This sets the default value for the column. As this is performed by the database, you don't see this in a new model object when you initialize it or even when you save it. You have to reload the object from the database to see this value. Note that the default is calculated once, at the point the migration is run, so the following code will set the default column value to the date and time when the migration was run:

```
add_column :orders, :placed_at, :datetime, default: Time.now
```

In addition, decimal columns take the options :precision and :scale. The :precision option specifies the number of significant digits that will be stored, and the :scale option determines where the decimal point will be located in these digits (think of the scale as the number of digits after the decimal point). A decimal number with a precision of 5 and a scale of 0 can store numbers from -99,999 to +99,999. A decimal number with a precision of 5 and a scale of 2 can store the range -999.99 to +999.99.

The :precision and :scale parameters are optional for decimal columns. However, incompatibilities between different databases lead us to strongly recommend that you include the options for each decimal column.

Here are some column definitions using the migration types and options:

```
add_column :orders, :attn, :string, limit: 100
add_column :orders, :order_type, :integer
add_column :orders, :ship_class, :string, null: false, default: 'priority'
add_column :orders, :amount, :decimal, precision: 8, scale: 2
```

Renaming Columns

When we refactor our code, we often change our variable names to make them more meaningful. Rails migrations allow us to do this to database column names, too. For example, a week after we first added it, we might decide that e_mail isn't the best name for the new column. We can create a migration to rename it using the rename_column() method:

```
class RenameEmailColumn < ActiveRecord::Migration
  def change
    rename_column :orders, :e_mail, :customer_email
  end
end
```

As rename_column() is reversible, separate up() and down() methods are not required in order to use it.

Note that the rename doesn't destroy any existing data associated with the column. Also be aware that renaming is not supported by all the adapters.

Changing Columns

change_column() Use the change_column() method to change the type of a column or to alter the options associated with a column. Use it the same way you'd use add_column, but specify the name of an existing column. Let's say that the order type column is currently an integer, but we need to change it to be a string. We want to keep the existing data, so an order type of 123 will become the string "123". Later, we'll use noninteger values such as "new" and "existing".

Changing from an integer column to a string is one line of code:

```
def up
  change_column :orders, :order_type, :string
end
```

However, the opposite transformation is problematic. We might be tempted to write the obvious down() migration:

```
def down
  change_column :orders, :order_type, :integer
end
```

But if our application has taken to storing data like "new" in this column, the down() method will lose it—"new" can't be converted to an integer. If that's acceptable, then the migration is acceptable as it stands. If, however, we want to create a one-way migration—one that cannot be reversed—we'll want to stop the down migration from being applied. In this case, Rails provides a special exception that we can throw:

```
class ChangeOrderTypeToString < ActiveRecord::Migration
  def up
    change_column :orders, :order_type, :string, null: false
  end

  def down
    raise ActiveRecord::IrreversibleMigration
  end
end
```

ActiveRecord::IrreversibleMigration is also the name of the exception that Rails will raise if you attempt to call a method that can't be automatically reversed from within a change() method.

Managing Tables

So far we've been using migrations to manipulate the columns in existing tables. Now let's look at creating and dropping tables:

```
class CreateOrderHistories < ActiveRecord::Migration
  def change
    create_table :order_histories do |t|
      t.integer :order_id, null: false
      t.text :notes

      t.timestamps
    end
  end
end
```

create_table() takes the name of a table (remember, table names are plural) and a block. (It also takes some optional parameters that we'll look at in a minute.) The block is passed a table definition object, which we use to define the columns in the table.

Generally the call to drop_table() is not needed, as create_table() is reversible. drop_table() accepts a single parameter, which is the name of the table to drop.

The calls to the various table definition methods should look familiar—they're similar to the add_column method we used previously except these methods don't take the name of the table as the first parameter, and the name of the method itself is the data type desired. This reduces repetition.

Note that we don't define the id column for our new table. Unless we say otherwise, Rails migrations automatically add a primary key called id to all tables they create. For a deeper discussion of this, see *Primary Keys*, on page 422.

The timestamps method creates both the created_at and updated_at columns, with the correct timestamp data type. Although there is no requirement to add these columns to any particular table, this is yet another example of Rails making it easy for a common convention to be implemented easily and consistently.

Options for Creating Tables

You can pass a hash of options as a second parameter to create_table. If you specify force: true, the migration will drop an existing table of the same name before creating the new one. This is a useful option if you want to create a migration that forces a database into a known state, but there's clearly a potential for data loss.

The temporary: true option creates a temporary table—one that goes away when the application disconnects from the database. This is clearly pointless in the context of a migration, but as we will see later, it does have its uses elsewhere.

The options: "xxxx" parameter lets you specify options to your underlying database. They are added to the end of the CREATE TABLE statement, right after the closing parenthesis. Although this is rarely necessary with SQLite 3, it may at times be useful with other database servers. For example, some versions of MySQL allow you to specify the initial value of the autoincrementing id column. We can pass this in through a migration as follows:

```
create_table :tickets, options: "auto_increment = 10000" do |t|
  t.text :description
  t.timestamps
end
```

Behind the scenes, migrations will generate the following DDL from this table description when configured for MySQL:

```
CREATE TABLE "tickets" (
  "id" int(11) default null auto_increment primary key,
  "description" text,
  "created_at" datetime,
  "updated_at" datetime
) auto_increment = 10000;
```

Be careful when using the :options parameter with MySQL. The Rails MySQL database adapter sets a default option of ENGINE=InnoDB. This overrides any local defaults you have and forces migrations to use the InnoDB storage engine for new tables. Yet, if you override :options, you'll lose this setting; new tables will be created using whatever database engine is configured as the default for your site. You may want to add an explicit ENGINE=InnoDB to the options string to force the standard behavior in this case. You probably want to keep using InnoDB if you're using MySQL, because this engine gives you transaction support. You might need this support in your application, and you'll definitely need it in your tests if you're using the default of transactional test fixtures.

Renaming Tables

If refactoring leads us to rename variables and columns, then it's probably not a surprise that we sometimes find ourselves renaming tables, too. Migrations support the rename_table() method:

```
class RenameOrderHistories < ActiveRecord::Migration
  def change
    rename_table :order_histories, :order_notes
  end
end
```

Rolling back this migration undoes the change by renaming the table back.

Problems with rename_table

There's a subtle problem when we rename tables in migrations.

For example, let's assume that in migration 4 we create the order_histories table and populate it with some data:

```
def up
  create_table :order_histories do |t|
    t.integer :order_id, null: false
    t.text :notes

    t.timestamps
  end

  order = Order.find :first
  OrderHistory.create(order_id: order, notes: "test")
end
```

Later, in migration 7, we rename the table order_histories to order_notes. At this point we'll also have renamed the model OrderHistory to OrderNote.

Now we decide to drop our development database and reapply all migrations. When we do so, the migrations throw an exception in migration 4: our application no longer contains a class called OrderHistory, so the migration fails.

One solution, proposed by Tim Lucas, is to create local, dummy versions of the model classes needed by a migration within the migration. For example, the following version of the fourth migration will work even if the application no longer has an OrderHistory class:

```
class CreateOrderHistories < ActiveRecord::Migration
  class Order < ApplicationRecord::Base; end
  class OrderHistory < ApplicationRecord::Base; end

  def change
    create_table :order_histories do |t|
      t.integer :order_id, null: false
      t.text :notes

      t.timestamps
    end

    order = Order.find :first
    OrderHistory.create(order: order_id, notes: "test")
  end
end
```

This works as long as our model classes do not contain any additional functionality that would have been used in the migration—all we're creating here is a bare-bones version.

Defining Indices

Migrations can (and probably should) define indices for tables. For example, we might notice that once our application has a large number of orders in the database, searching based on the customer's name takes longer than we'd like. It's time to add an index using the appropriately named add_index() method:

```
class AddCustomerNameIndexToOrders < ActiveRecord::Migration
  def change
    add_index :orders, :name
  end
end
```

If we give add_index the optional parameter unique: true, a unique index will be created, forcing values in the indexed column to be unique.

By default the index will be given the name *index_table_on_column*. We can override this using the name: "somename" option. If we use the :name option when adding an index, we'll also need to specify it when removing the index.

We can create a *composite index*—an index on multiple columns—by passing an array of column names to add_index.

Indices are removed using the remove_index() method.

Primary Keys

Rails assumes every table has a numeric primary key (normally called id) and ensures the value of this column is unique for each new row added to a table. We'll rephrase that.

Rails doesn't work too well unless each table has a primary key that Rails can manage. By default, Rails will create numeric primary keys, but you can also use other types such as UUIDs, depending on what your actual database provides. Rails is less fussy about the name of the column. So, for your average Rails application, our strong advice is to go with the flow and let Rails have its id column.

If you decide to be adventurous, you can start by using a different name for the primary key column (but keeping it as an incrementing integer). Do this by specifying a :primary_key option on the create_table call:

```
create_table :tickets, primary_key: :number do |t|
  t.text :description

  t.timestamps
end
```

This adds the number column to the table and sets it up as the primary key:

```
$ sqlite3 db/development.sqlite3 ".schema tickets"
CREATE TABLE tickets ("number" INTEGER PRIMARY KEY AUTOINCREMENT
NOT NULL, "description" text DEFAULT NULL, "created_at" datetime
DEFAULT NULL, "updated_at" datetime DEFAULT NULL);
```

The next step in the adventure might be to create a primary key that isn't an integer. Here's a clue that the Rails developers don't think this is a good idea: migrations don't let you do this (at least not directly).

Tables with No Primary Key

Sometimes we may need to define a table that has no primary key. The most common case in Rails is for *join tables*—tables with just two columns where each column is a foreign key to another table. To create a join table using migrations, we have to tell Rails not to automatically add an id column:

```
create_table :authors_books, id: false do |t|
  t.integer :author_id, null: false
  t.integer :book_id,   null: false
end
```

In this case, you might want to investigate creating one or more indices on this table to speed navigation between books and authors.

Advanced Migrations

Most Rails developers use the basic facilities of migrations to create and maintain their database schemas. However, every now and then it's useful to push migrations just a bit further. This section covers some more advanced migration usage.

Using Native SQL

Migrations give you a database-independent way of maintaining your application's schema. However, if migrations don't contain the methods you need to be able to do what you need to do, you'll need to drop down to database-specific code. Rails provides two ways to do this. One is with options arguments to methods like add_column(). The second is the execute() method.

When you use options or execute(), you might well be tying your migration to a specific database engine, because any SQL you provide in these two locations uses your database's native syntax.

An example of where you might need to use raw SQL is if you are creating a custom data type inside your database. Postgres, for example, allows you to specify *enumerated types*. Enumerated types work just fine with Rails; but to create them in a migration, you have to use SQL and thus execute(). Suppose we wanted to create an enumerated type for the various pay types we supported in our checkout form (which we created in Chapter 12, *Task G: Check Out!*, on page 175):

```
class AddPayTypes < ActiveRecord::Migrations[5.1]
  def up
    execute %{
      CREATE TYPE
        pay_type
      AS ENUM (
        'check',
        'credit card',
        'purchase order'
      )
    }
  end
```

```
  def down
    execute "DROP TYPE pay_type"
  end
end
```

Note that if you need to model your database using execute(), you should consider changing your schema dump format from "ruby" to "SQL," as outlined in the Rails Guide.[1] The schema dump is used during tests to create an empty database with the same schema you are using in production.

Custom Messages and Benchmarks

Although not exactly an advanced migration, something that is useful to do within advanced migrations is to output our own messages and benchmarks. We can do this with the say_with_time() method:

```
def up
  say_with_time "Updating prices..." do
    Person.all.each do |p|
      p.update_attribute :price, p.lookup_master_price
    end
  end
end
```

say_with_time() prints the string passed before the block is executed and prints the benchmark after the block completes.

When Migrations Go Bad

Migrations suffer from one serious problem. The underlying DDL statements that update the database schema are not transactional. This isn't a failing in Rails—most databases just don't support the rolling back of create table, alter table, and other DDL statements.

Let's look at a migration that tries to add two tables to a database:

```
class ExampleMigration < ActiveRecord::Migration
  def change
    create_table :one do ...
    end
    create_table :two do ...
    end
  end
end
```

---

1.   http://guides.rubyonrails.org/active_record_migrations.html#schema-dumping-and-you

In the normal course of events, the up() method adds tables, one and two, and the down() method removes them.

But what happens if there's a problem creating the second table? We'll end up with a database containing table one but not table two. We can fix whatever the problem is in the migration, but now we can't apply it—if we try, it will fail because table one already exists.

We could try to roll the migration back, but that won't work. Because the original migration failed, the schema version in the database wasn't updated, so Rails won't try to roll it back.

At this point, you could mess around and manually change the schema information and drop table one. But it probably isn't worth it. Our recommendation in these circumstances is simply to drop the entire database, re-create it, and apply migrations to bring it back up-to-date. You'll have lost nothing, and you'll know you have a consistent schema.

All this discussion suggests that migrations are dangerous to use on production databases. Should you run them? We really can't say. If you have database administrators in your organization, it'll be their call. If it's up to you, you'll have to weigh the risks. But, if you decide to go for it, you really must back up your database first. Then, you can apply the migrations by going to your application's directory on the machine with the database role on your production servers and executing this command:

```
depot> RAILS_ENV=production bin/rails db:migrate
```

This is one of those times where the legal notice at the start of this book kicks in. We're not liable if this deletes your data.

Schema Manipulation Outside Migrations

All the migration methods described so far in this chapter are also available as methods on Active Record connection objects and so are accessible within the models, views, and controllers of a Rails application.

For example, you might have discovered that a particular long-running report runs a lot faster if the orders table has an index on the city column. However, that index isn't needed during the day-to-day running of the application, and tests have shown that maintaining it slows the application appreciably.

Let's write a method that creates the index, runs a block of code, and then drops the index. This could be a private method in the model or could be implemented in a library:

```
def run_with_index(*columns)
  connection.add_index(:orders, *columns)
  begin
    yield
  ensure
    connection.remove_index(:orders, *columns)
  end
end
```

The statistics-gathering method in the model can use this as follows:

```
def get_city_statistics
  run_with_index(:city) do
    # .. calculate stats
  end
end
```

What We Just Did

While we had been informally using migrations throughout the development of the Depot application and even into deployment, in this chapter we saw how migrations are the basis for a principled and disciplined approach to configuration management of the schema for your database.

You learned how to create, rename, and delete columns and tables; to manage indices and keys; to apply and back out entire sets of changes; and even to mix in your own custom SQL into the mix, all in a completely reproducible manner.

At this point we've covered the externals of Rails. The next few chapters are going to delve deeper. We are going to show you how to take Rails apart and put it back together. The first stop along the way is to show you how to use select Rails classes and methods outside the context of a web server.

In this chapter, you'll see:
 • Replacing Rails' testing framework with RSpec
 • Using Slim for HTML templates instead of ERB
 • Serving CSS with Webpack
 • Post-processing CSS with cssnext

CHAPTER 24

Customizing and Extending Rails

As you've come to learn, Rails provides an answer for almost every question you have about building a modern web application. It provides the basics for handling requests, accessing a database, writing user interfaces, and running tests. It does this by having a tightly integrated design, which is often referred to as Rails being "opinionated software."

This tight coupling comes at a price. If, for example, the way Rails manages CSS doesn't meet the needs of your project, you could be in trouble. Or, if you prefer to write your tests in a different way, Rails doesn't give you a lot of options. Or does it? In past versions of Rails, customizing it was difficult or impossible. In Rails 3, much effort was expended to make Rails more customizable, and by Rails 4, developers had a lot more flexibility to use the tools they prefer or that work the way they want to work. That's what we'll explore in this chapter.

We'll replace three parts of Rails in this chapter. First, we'll see how to use RSpec to write our tests instead of Rails' default testing library. Next, we'll replace ERB for the alternative templating language Slim. Finally, we'll see how to manage CSS using Webpack instead of putting it in app/assets/stylesheets. This chapter will demonstrate another benefit to Rails, which is that you don't have to throw out the parts that work for you to use alternatives that work better. Let's get started.

Testing with RSpec

RSpec is an alternative to MiniTest, which Rails uses. It's different in almost every way, and many developers prefer it. Here's what one of our existing tests might look like, written in RSpec:

```ruby
RSpec.describe Cart do

  let(:cart)     { Cart.create }
  let(:book_one) { products(:ruby) }
  let(:book_two) { products(:two) }

  before do
    cart.add_product(book_one).save!
    cart.add_product(book_two).save!
  end

  it "can have multiple products added" do
    expect(cart.line_items.size).to eq(2)
  end

  it "calculates the total price of all products" do
    expect(cart.total_price).to eq(book_one.price + book_two.price)
  end
end
```

It almost looks like a different programming language! Developers that prefer RSpec like that the test reads like English: "Describe Cart, it can have multiple products added, expect cart.line_items.size to eq 2."

We're going to quickly go through how to write tests in RSpec without too much explanation. There's a *great book for that already [MD17]*, so we'll learn just enough RSpec to see it working with Rails, which demonstrates Rails' configurability. Although many developers that use RSpec set it up from the start of a project, you don't have to. RSpec can be added at any time, and that's what we'll do here.

Add rspec-rails to your Gemfile, putting it in the development and test groups:

```ruby
group :development, :test do
  gem 'rspec-rails'
end
```

After you bundle install, a new generator will set up RSpec for you:

```
> bin/rails generate rspec:install
    create  .rspec
    create  spec
    create  spec/spec_helper.rb
    create  spec/rails_helper.rb
```

Verify the configuration is working by running the new task Rspec installed, spec:

```
> bin/rails spec
No examples found.


Finished in 0.00058 seconds (files took 0.11481 seconds to load)
0 examples, 0 failures
```

Let's reimplement the test for Cart as an RSpec test or *spec*. RSpec includes generators to create starter specs for us, similar to what Rails does with scaffolding. To create a model spec, use the spec:model generator:

```
> bin/rails generate spec:model Cart
      create  spec/models/cart_spec.rb
```

Now, rerun spec and we can see RSpec's generator has created a pending spec:

```
> bin/rails spec
Pending: (Failures listed here are expected and do not affect your suite's status)

  1) Cart add some examples to (or delete) spec/models/cart_spec.rb
     # Not yet implemented
     # ./spec/models/cart_spec.rb:4


Finished in 0.00284 seconds (files took 1.73 seconds to load)
1 example, 0 failures, 1 pending
```

To reimplement the test for Cart as a spec, let's first review the existing test:

```
rails51/depot_u/test/models/cart_test.rb
require 'test_helper'

class CartTest < ActiveSupport::TestCase
  def setup
    @cart     = Cart.create
    @book_one = products(:ruby)
    @book_two = products(:two)
  end

  test "add unique products" do
    @cart.add_product(@book_one).save!
    @cart.add_product(@book_two).save!
    assert_equal 2, @cart.line_items.size
    assert_equal @book_one.price + @book_two.price, @cart.total_price
  end

  test "add duplicate product" do
    @cart.add_product(@book_one).save!
    @cart.add_product(@book_one).save!
    assert_equal 2*@book_one.price, @cart.total_price
    assert_equal 1, @cart.line_items.size
    assert_equal 2, @cart.line_items[0].quantity
  end
end
```

The setup creates a cart and fetches two products from the fixtures. It then tests the add_product() in two ways: by adding two distinct products and by adding the same product twice.

Let's start with the setup. By default, RSpec is configured to look in spec/fixtures for fixtures. This is correct for a project using RSpec from the start, but for us, the fixtures are in test/fixtures. Change this by editing spec/rails_helper.rb:

rails51/depot_xa/spec/rails_helper.rb

```
RSpec.configure do |config|
  # Remove this line if you're not using ActiveRecord or ActiveRecord fixtures
➤ config.fixture_path = "#{::Rails.root}/test/fixtures"
```

Back to the spec, its setup will need to create a Cart to use in our tests as well as fetch two products from fixtures. By default, fixtures aren't available in specs, but you can call fixtures() to make them available. Here's what the setup looks like:

rails51/depot_xa/spec/models/cart_spec.rb

```
require 'rails_helper'

RSpec.describe Cart, type: :model do
➤   fixtures :products
➤   subject(:cart) { Cart.new }
➤
➤   let(:book_one) { products(:ruby) }
➤   let(:book_two) { products(:two) }
```

This definitely doesn't look like our original test! The call to subject() declares the variable cart, which you will use in the tests later. The calls to let() declare other variables that can be used in the tests. The reason for two methods that seemingly do the same thing is an RSpec convention. The object that is the focus of the test is declared with subject(). Ancillary data needed for the test is declared with let().

The tests themselves will also look quite different from their equivalents in a standard Rails test. For one thing, they aren't called tests but rather *examples*. Furthermore, it's customary for each example to make only one assertion. The existing test of adding different products makes two assertions, so in the spec, that means two examples.

Assertions look different in RSpec as well:

```
expect(actual_value).to eq(expected_value)
```

Applying this to the two assertions around adding distinct items, we have two examples (we'll show you where this code goes in a moment):

```
it "has two line items" do
  expect(cart.line_items.size).to eq(2)
end
it "has a total price of the two items' price" do
  expect(cart.total_price).to eq(book_one.price + book_two.price)
end
```

These assertions won't succeed unless items are added to the cart first. That code *could* go inside each example, but RSpec allows you to extract duplicate setup code into a block using before():

```ruby
before do
  cart.add_product(book_one).save!
  cart.add_product(book_two).save!
end
it "has two line items" do
  expect(cart.line_items.size).to eq(2)
end
it "has a total price of the two items' price" do
  expect(cart.total_price).to eq(book_one.price + book_two.price)
end
```

This setup is only relevant to some of the tests of the add_product() method, specifically the tests around adding different items. To test adding the same item twice, you'll need different setups. To make this happen, wrap the above code in a block using context(). context() takes a string that describes the context we're creating and acts as a scope for before() blocks. It's also customary to wrap all examples of the behavior of a method inside a block given to describe(). Given all that, here's what the first half of your spec should look like:

```ruby
rails51/depot_xa/spec/models/cart_spec.rb
describe "#add_product" do
  context "adding unique products" do
    before do
      cart.add_product(book_one).save!
      cart.add_product(book_two).save!
    end

    it "has two line items" do
      expect(cart.line_items.size).to eq(2)
    end
    it "has a total price of the two items' price" do
      expect(cart.total_price).to eq(book_one.price + book_two.price)
    end
  end
end
```

Here is the second half of the spec, which tests the behavior of add_product() when adding the same item twice:

```ruby
rails51/depot_xa/spec/models/cart_spec.rb
context "adding duplicate products" do
  before do
    cart.add_product(book_one).save!
    cart.add_product(book_one).save!
  end
```

```
➤      it "has one line item" do
➤        expect(cart.line_items.size).to eq(1)
➤      end
➤      it "has a line item with a quantity of 2" do
➤        expect(cart.line_items.first.quantity).to eq(2)
➤      end
➤      it "has a total price of twice the product's price" do
➤        expect(cart.total_price).to eq(book_one.price * 2)
➤      end
➤    end
➤  end
```

Running bin/rails spec, it should pass:

```
> bin/rails spec
.....

Finished in 0.11007 seconds (files took 1.72 seconds to load)
5 examples, 0 failures
```

A lot of code in this file isn't executing a test, but all the calls to describe(), context(), and it() aren't for naught. Passing SPEC_OPTS="--format=doc" to the spec task, the test output is formatted like the documentation of the Cart class:

```
> bin/rails spec SPEC_OPTS="--format=doc"
Cart
  #add_product
    adding unique products
      has two line items
      has a total price of the two items' price
    adding duplicate products
      has one line item
      has a line item with a quantity of 2
      has a total price of twice the product's price

Finished in 0.14865 seconds (files took 1.76 seconds to load)
5 examples, 0 failures
```

Also note that rspec-rails changes the Rails generators to create empty spec files in spec/ instead of test files in test/. This means that you use all the generators and scaffolding you are used to in your normal workflow without having to worry about the wrong type of test file being created.

If all of this seems strange to you, you are not alone. It *is* strange, and the reasons RSpec is designed this way, as well as why you might want to use it, are nuanced and beyond the scope of this book. The main point all this proves is that you can replace a major part of Rails with an alternative and still get all the benefits of the rest of Rails. It's also worth noting that RSpec is quite popular, and you are very likely to see it in the wild.

Let's learn more about Rails' configurability by replacing another major piece of Rails—ERB templates.

Creating HTML Templates with Slim

Slim is a templating language that can replace ERB.[1] It is designed to require much less code to achieve the same results, and it does this by using a nested structure instead of HTML tags. Consider this ERB:

```
<h2><%= t('.title') %></h2>
<table>
  <%= render(cart.line_items) %>

  <tr class="total_line">
    <td colspan="2">Total</td>
    <td class="total_cell"><%= number_to_currency(cart.total_price) %></td>
  </tr>

</table>
```

In Slim, this would look like so:

```
h2
  = t('.title')
table
  = render(cart.line_items)

  tr.total_line
    td.colspan=2
      Total
    td.total_cell
      = number_to_currency(cart.total_price)
```

Slim treats each line as an opening HTML tag, and anything indented under that line will be rendered inside that tag. Helper methods and instance variables can be accessed using =, like so:

```
ul
  li = link_to @product.name, product_path(@product)
```

To execute logic, such as looping over a collection, use -, like so:

```
ul
  - @products.each do |product|
    li
      - if product.available?
        = link_to product.name, product_path(product)
      - else
        = "#{product.name} out of stock"
```

---

1. http://slim-lang.com

The code after · is executed as Ruby, but note that no end keyword is needed —Slim inserts that for you.

Slim allows you to specify HTML classes by following a tag with a . and the class name:

```
h1.title This title has the "title" class!
```

And, in a final bit of ultracompactness, if you want to create a div with an HTML class on it, you can omit div entirely. This creates a div with the class login-form that contains two text inputs:

```
.login-form
  input type=text name=username
  input type=password name=password
```

Putting all this together, let's install Slim and reimplement the home page in app/views/store/index.html.erb using it. This will demonstrate how Rails allows us to completely replace its templating engine.

First, install slim-rails by adding it to the Gemfile:

```
gem 'slim-rails'
```

After you bundle install, your Rails app will now render files ending in .slim as a Slim template. We can see this by removing app/views/store/index.html.erb and creating app/views/stores/index.slim like so:

```
rails51/depot_xb/app/views/store/index.slim
- if notice
  aside#notice = notice

h1 = t('.title_html')

ul.catalog
  - cache @products do
    - @products.each do |product|
      - cache product do
        li
          = image_tag(product.image_url)
          h2 = product.title
          p = sanitize(product.description)
          .price
            = number_to_currency(product.price)
            = button_to t('.add_html'),
                line_items_path(product_id: product, locale: I18n.locale),
                remote: true
```

Restart your server if you have it running, and you should see the home page render the same as before.

In addition to being able to render Slim, installing slim-rails changes Rails generators to create Slim files instead of ERB, so all of the scaffolding and other generators you're used to will now produce Slim templates automatically. You can even convert your existing ERB templates to Slim by using the erb2slim command, available by installing the html2slim Ruby gem.[2]

Let's learn one more thing about Rails' configurability by configuring our app to serve CSS from Webpack.

Serving CSS via Webpack

We've been writing CSS in files located in app/assets/stylesheets. Rails will find whatever .css files are there, bundle them all up together, and make the combined CSS available to your views. If you want to use modern CSS tools or techniques, such as CSS modules or Post CSS,[3,4] it's not easy or possible to use them with the CSS that Rails serves up.

The part of Rails that handles CSS is called Sprockets, and while new gems are always being produced to give Sprockets new abilities, the state of the art in CSS is part of the JavaScript ecosystem and available via Webpack. Prior to Rails 5.1, setting up Webpack was extremely difficult. But as we learned in Chapter 13, *Task H: Entering Additional*, on page 195, Rails now includes full support for Webpack, and it turns out that Webpacker has configured Webpack to serve CSS already!

We'll modify the app so that Webpack is serving CSS, and we'll demonstrate the benefit of this by installing cssnext.[5] cssnext allows you to use features of CSS that aren't supported in the browser by post-processing the CSS you write.

Webpacker configured Webpack to look for CSS in app/javascript/packs, which is strange, but since it's the default, let's go with it. Move app/assets/stylesheets/application.scss into app/javascript/packs. Next, create the directory app/javascript/packs/css, and move all the other .scss files from app/assets/javascripts into that directory.

If you open up app/javascript/packs/application.scss, you should see a large comment at the top of the file. At the end of the comment, there are two *directives* that look like this:

```
//= require_tree .
//= require_self
```

2.   https://github.com/slim-template/html2slim
3.   https://github.com/css-modules/css-modules
4.   https://github.com/postcss/postcss
5.   http://cssnext.io/

These directives tell Sprockets to include all the .scss files in the current directory, which allows us to put CSS in several different files. Webpack doesn't support these directives, so we'll need to add some code to application.scss to replicate what they do.

As mentioned way back in *Iteration A2: Making Prettier Listings*, on page 78, our CSS files are actually Sass files, and Sass has the ability to import external files using @import. Unfortunately, we can't @import all files with one line of code, so you'll need to add one @import for each file:

rails51/depot_xc/app/javascript/packs/application.scss
```
➤ @import "css/admin.scss";
➤ @import "css/carts.scss";
➤ @import "css/line_items.scss";
➤ @import "css/orders.scss";
➤ @import "css/products.scss";
➤ @import "css/scaffolds.scss";
➤ @import "css/sessions.scss";
➤ @import "css/store.scss";
➤ @import "css/users.scss";
```

Webpack will now serve up CSS, but the application layout needs to be changed to bring it in. Replace the call to stylesheet_link_tag() with the Webpacker-provided stylesheet_pack_tag().

rails51/depot_xc/app/views/layouts/application.html.erb
```
➤ <%= stylesheet_pack_tag "application" %>
```

Restart your server, and the app should appear the same as it did before.

We can take advantage of this new way of serving CSS by configuring cssnext. cssnext is a plugin to Post CSS, which is a general CSS post-processor. Fortunately for us, Webpacker has already configured it, so we only need to install and configure cssnext.

To install it, use Yarn to add it to the project:

```
> yarn add postcss-cssnext
```

Webpacker created the file .postcssrc.yml to allow configuration of Post CSS. With cssnext installed, all we need to do is add a line to the end of the file indicating we want cssnext to be included when post-processing the CSS:

rails51/depot_xc/.postcssrc.yml
```
plugins:
  postcss-smart-import: {}
  postcss-cssnext: {}
```

To see this in action, let's use the new CSS function gray(),[6] which generates various shades of gray. Few browsers support this, and cssnext will convert any call to gray() into something the browser does support. We'll change the black border at the top of the home page to gray, like so:

rails51/depot_xc/app/javascript/packs/css/store.scss

```
.store {
  max-width: 80em;
  ul.catalog {
    border-top: solid 0.250em gray(50%);
```

Restart your server and reload the page. The border should be gray. To see what happened, open up http://0.0.0.0:8080/packs/application.css in your browser. This will show you the CSS that's actually being served up. If you scroll down to the CSS from store.scss, you should see that it's not the same—the gray() function is gone, replaced by a call to rgb(), which modern browsers *do* support.

Customizing Rails in Other Ways

Customizing the edges of Rails, like you did above with CSS, HTML templates, and tests, tends to be more straightforward and more options are out there for you. Customizing Rails' internals is more difficult. If you want, you can remove Active Record entirely and use libraries like Sequel or ROM,[7,8] but you'd be giving up a lot—Active Record is tightly coupled with many parts of Rails.

Tight coupling is usually viewed as a problem, but it's this coupling that allows you to be so productive using Rails. The more you change your Rails app into a loosely coupled assembly of unrelated libraries, the more work you have to do getting the pieces to talk to each other. Finding the right balance is up to you, your team, or your project.

The Rails ecosystem is also filled with plugins and enhancements to address common needs that aren't quite common enough to be added to Rails itself. For example, Kaminari provides pagination for when you need to let a user browse hundreds or thousands of records.[9] Ransack and Searchkick provide advanced ways of searching your database with Active Record.[10,11] CarrierWave

---

6. http://cssnext.io/features/#gray-function
7. http://sequel.jeremyevans.net/
8. http://rom-rb.org/
9. https://github.com/kaminari/kaminari
10. https://github.com/activerecord-hackery/ransack
11. https://github.com/ankane/searchkick

makes uploading files to your Rails app much more straightforward than hand-rolling it yourself.[12]

And if you want to analyze and improve the code inside your Rails app, RuboCop can check that you are using a consistent style,[13] while Brakeman can check for common security vulnerabilities.[14]

These extras are the tip of the iceberg. The community of extensions and plugins for Rails is yet another benefit to building your next web application with Rails.

Where to Go from Here

Congratulations! We've covered a lot of ground together.

In Part I, you installed Rails, verified the installation using a basic application, got exposed to the architecture of Rails, and got acquainted (or maybe reacquainted) with the Ruby language.

In Part II, you iteratively built an application, built up test cases along the way, and ultimately deployed it using Capistrano. We designed this application to touch on all aspects of Rails that every developer needs to be aware of.

Whereas Parts I and II of this book each served a single purpose, Part III served a dual role.

For some of you, Part III methodically filled in the gaps and covered enough for you to get real work done. For others, these will be the first steps of a much longer journey.

For most of you, the real value is a bit of both. A firm foundation is required in order for you to be able to explore further. And that's why we started this part with a chapter that not only covered the convention and configuration of Rails but also covered the generation of documentation.

Then we proceeded to devote a chapter each to the model, views, and controller, which are the backbone of the Rails architecture. We covered topics ranging from database relationships to the REST architecture to HTML forms and helpers.

We covered migration as an essential maintenance tool for the deployed application's database.

---

12. https://github.com/carrierwaveuploader/carrierwave
13. https://github.com/bbatsov/rubocop
14. https://github.com/presidentbeef/brakeman

Finally, we split Rails apart and explored the concept of gems from a number of perspectives, from making use of individual Rails components separately to making full use of the foundation upon which Rails is built and finally to building and extending the framework to suit your needs.

At this point, you have the necessary context and background to more deeply explore whatever areas suit your fancy or are needed to solve that vexing problem you face. We recommend you start by visiting the Ruby on Rails site and exploring each of the links across the top of that page.[15] Some of this will be quick refreshers of materials presented in this book, but you will also find plenty of links to current information on how report problems, learn more, and keep up-to-date.

Additionally, please continue to contribute to the forums mentioned in the book's introduction.

Pragmatic Bookshelf has more books on Ruby and Rails subjects. There also are plenty of related categories that go beyond Ruby and Rails, such as technical practices; testing, design, and cloud computing; and tools, frameworks, and languages. You can find these and many other categories at http://www.pragprog.com/.

We hope you have enjoyed learning about Ruby on Rails as much as we have enjoyed writing this book!

---

15. http://rubyonrails.org/

Bibliography

[Bur15]   Trevor Burnham. *CoffeeScript*. The Pragmatic Bookshelf, Raleigh, NC, 2015.

[CC16]   Hampton Lintorn Catlin and Michael Lintorn Catlin. *Pragmatic Guide to Sass 3*. The Pragmatic Bookshelf, Raleigh, NC, 2016.

[FH13]   Dave Thomas, with Chad Fowler and Andy Hunt. *Programming Ruby 1.9 & 2.0 (4th edition)*. The Pragmatic Bookshelf, Raleigh, NC, 4th, 2013.

[HT99]   Andrew Hunt and David Thomas. *The Pragmatic Programmer*. The Pragmatic Bookshelf, Raleigh, NC, 1999.

[MD17]   Myron Marston and Ian Dees. *Effective Testing with RSpec 3*. The Pragmatic Bookshelf, Raleigh, NC, 2017.

[Rap17]   Noel Rappin. *Take My Money*. The Pragmatic Bookshelf, Raleigh, NC, 2017.

[Val13]   José Valim. *Crafting Rails 4 Applications*. The Pragmatic Bookshelf, Raleigh, NC, 2013.

Index

Thank you!

How did you enjoy this book? Please let us know. Take a moment and email us at support@pragprog.com with your feedback. Tell us your story and you could win free ebooks. Please use the subject line "Book Feedback."

Ready for your next great Pragmatic Bookshelf book? Come on over to https://pragprog.com and use the coupon code BUYANOTHER2017 to save 30% on your next ebook.

Void where prohibited, restricted, or otherwise unwelcome. Do not use ebooks near water. If rash persists, see a doctor. Doesn't apply to *The Pragmatic Programmer* ebook because it's older than the Pragmatic Bookshelf itself. Side effects may include increased knowledge and skill, increased marketability, and deep satisfaction. Increase dosage regularly.

And thank you for your continued support,

Andy Hunt, Publisher

The Modern Web

Get up to speed on the latest HTML, CSS, JavaScript techniques, and secure your Node applications.

HTML5 and CSS3 (2nd edition)

HTML5 and CSS3 are more than just buzzwords – they're the foundation for today's web applications. This book gets you up to speed on the HTML5 elements and CSS3 features you can use right now in your current projects, with backwards compatible solutions that ensure that you don't leave users of older browsers behind. This new edition covers even more new features, including CSS animations, IndexedDB, and client-side validations.

Brian P. Hogan
(314 pages) ISBN: 9781937785598. $38
https://pragprog.com/book/bhh52e

Secure Your Node.js Web Application

Cyber-criminals have your web applications in their crosshairs. They search for and exploit common security mistakes in your web application to steal user data. Learn how you can secure your Node.js applications, database and web server to avoid these security holes. Discover the primary attack vectors against web applications, and implement security best practices and effective countermeasures. Coding securely will make you a stronger web developer and analyst, and you'll protect your users.

Karl Düüna
(230 pages) ISBN: 9781680500851. $36
https://pragprog.com/book/kdnodesec

Level Up

From data structures to architecture and design, we have what you need.

A Common-Sense Guide to Data Structures and Algorithms

If you last saw algorithms in a university course or at a job interview, you're missing out on what they can do for your code. Learn different sorting and searching techniques, and when to use each. Find out how to use recursion effectively. Discover structures for specialized applications, such as trees and graphs. Use Big O notation to decide which algorithms are best for your production environment. Beginners will learn how to use these techniques from the start, and experienced developers will rediscover approaches they may have forgotten.

Jay Wengrow
(218 pages) ISBN: 9781680502442. $45.95
https://pragprog.com/book/jwdsal

Design It!

Don't engineer by coincidence—design it like you mean it! Grounded by fundamentals and filled with practical design methods, this is the perfect introduction to software architecture for programmers who are ready to grow their design skills. Ask the right stakeholders the right questions, explore design options, share your design decisions, and facilitate collaborative workshops that are fast, effective, and fun. Become a better programmer, leader, and designer. Use your new skills to lead your team in implementing software with the right capabilities—and develop awesome software!

Michael Keeling
(358 pages) ISBN: 9781680502091. $41.95
https://pragprog.com/book/mkdsa

Explore Testing

Explore the uncharted waters of exploratory testing and delve deeper into web testing.

Explore It!

Uncover surprises, risks, and potentially serious bugs with exploratory testing. Rather than designing all tests in advance, explorers design and execute small, rapid experiments, using what they learned from the last little experiment to inform the next. Learn essential skills of a master explorer, including how to analyze software to discover key points of vulnerability, how to design experiments on the fly, how to hone your observation skills, and how to focus your efforts.

Elisabeth Hendrickson
(186 pages) ISBN: 9781937785024. $29
https://pragprog.com/book/ehxta

The Way of the Web Tester

This book is for everyone who needs to test the web. As a tester, you'll automate your tests. As a developer, you'll build more robust solutions. And as a team, you'll gain a vocabulary and a means to coordinate how to write and organize automated tests for the web. Follow the testing pyramid and level up your skills in user interface testing, integration testing, and unit testing. Your new skills will free you up to do other, more important things while letting the computer do the one thing it's really good at: quickly running thousands of repetitive tasks.

Jonathan Rasmusson
(256 pages) ISBN: 9781680501834. $29
https://pragprog.com/book/jrtest

Put the "Fun" in Functional and Dive Deeper into Rails

Elixir puts the "fun" back into functional programming. And by the creator of Elixir: go further into the depths of Rails itself.

Programming Elixir 1.3

Explore functional programming without the academic overtones (tell me about monads just one more time). Create concurrent applications, but get them right without all the locking and consistency headaches. Meet Elixir, a modern, functional, concurrent language built on the rock-solid Erlang VM. Elixir's pragmatic syntax and built-in support for metaprogramming will make you productive and keep you interested for the long haul. Maybe the time is right for the Next Big Thing. Maybe it's Elixir. This book is *the* introduction to Elixir for experienced programmers, completely updated for Elixir 1.3.

Dave Thomas
(362 pages) ISBN: 9781680502008. $38
https://pragprog.com/book/elixir13

Crafting Rails 4 Applications

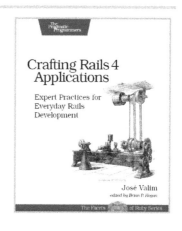

Get ready to see Rails as you've never seen it before. Learn how to extend the framework, change its behavior, and replace whole components to bend it to your will. Eight different test-driven tutorials will help you understand Rails' inner workings and prepare you to tackle complicated projects with solutions that are well-tested, modular, and easy to maintain.

This second edition of the bestselling *Crafting Rails Applications* has been updated to Rails 4 and discusses new topics such as streaming, mountable engines, and thread safety.

José Valim
(208 pages) ISBN: 9781937785550. $36
https://pragprog.com/book/jvrails2

Long Live the Command Line!

Use tmux and Vim for incredible mouse-free productivity.

tmux 2

Your mouse is slowing you down. The time you spend
context switching between your editor and your con-
soles eats away at your productivity. Take control of
your environment with tmux, a terminal multiplexer
that you can tailor to your workflow. With this updated
second edition for tmux 2.3, you'll customize, script,
and leverage tmux's unique abilities to craft a productive terminal environment that lets you keep your fin-
gers on your keyboard's home row.

Brian P. Hogan
(102 pages) ISBN: 9781680502213. $21.95
https://pragprog.com/book/bhtmux2

Practical Vim, Second Edition

Vim is a fast and efficient text editor that will make
you a faster and more efficient developer. It's available
on almost every OS, and if you master the techniques
in this book, you'll never need another text editor. In
more than 120 Vim tips, you'll quickly learn the editor's
core functionality and tackle your trickiest editing and
writing tasks. This beloved bestseller has been revised
and updated to Vim 8 and includes three brand-new
tips and five fully revised tips.

Drew Neil
(354 pages) ISBN: 9781680501278. $29
https://pragprog.com/book/dnvim2

Exercises and Teams

From exercises to make you a better programmer to techniques for creating better teams, we've got you covered.

Exercises for Programmers

When you write software, you need to be at the top of your game. Great programmers practice to keep their skills sharp. Get sharp and stay sharp with more than fifty practice exercises rooted in real-world scenarios. If you're a new programmer, these challenges will help you learn what you need to break into the field, and if you're a seasoned pro, you can use these exercises to learn that hot new language for your next gig.

Brian P. Hogan
(118 pages) ISBN: 9781680501223. $24
https://pragprog.com/book/bhwb

Creating Great Teams

People are happiest and most productive if they can choose what they work on and who they work with. Self-selecting teams give people that choice. Build well-designed and efficient teams to get the most out of your organization, with step-by-step instructions on how to set up teams quickly and efficiently. You'll create a process that works for you, whether you need to form teams from scratch, improve the design of existing teams, or are on the verge of a big team re-shuffle.

Sandy Mamoli and David Mole
(102 pages) ISBN: 9781680501285. $17
https://pragprog.com/book/mmteams

The Pragmatic Bookshelf

The Pragmatic Bookshelf features books written by developers for developers. The titles continue the well-known Pragmatic Programmer style and continue to garner awards and rave reviews. As development gets more and more difficult, the Pragmatic Programmers will be there with more titles and products to help you stay on top of your game.

Visit Us Online

This Book's Home Page
https://pragprog.com/book/rails51
Source code from this book, errata, and other resources. Come give us feedback, too!

Register for Updates
https://pragprog.com/updates
Be notified when updates and new books become available.

Join the Community
https://pragprog.com/community
Read our weblogs, join our online discussions, participate in our mailing list, interact with our wiki, and benefit from the experience of other Pragmatic Programmers.

New and Noteworthy
https://pragprog.com/news
Check out the latest pragmatic developments, new titles and other offerings.

Save on the eBook

Save on the eBook versions of this title. Owning the paper version of this book entitles you to purchase the electronic versions at a terrific discount.

PDFs are great for carrying around on your laptop—they are hyperlinked, have color, and are fully searchable. Most titles are also available for the iPhone and iPod touch, Amazon Kindle, and other popular e-book readers.

Buy now at *https://pragprog.com/coupon*

Contact Us

Online Orders:	*https://pragprog.com/catalog*
Customer Service:	*support@pragprog.com*
International Rights:	*translations@pragprog.com*
Academic Use:	*academic@pragprog.com*
Write for Us:	*http://write-for-us.pragprog.com*
Or Call:	+1 800-699-7764

Lightning Source UK Ltd.
Milton Keynes UK
UKHW030306200219

337593UK00003B/28/P